The Authors Imprint Endowment Fund of the University of California Press Foundation was established to support exceptional scholarship by first-time authors.

The publisher gratefully acknowledges the generous support of the African American Studies Endowment Fund of the University of California Press Foundation.

We Sell Drugs

AMERICAN CROSSROADS

Edited by Earl Lewis, George Lipsitz, George Sánchez, Dana Takagi, Laura Briggs, and Nikhil Pal Singh

We Sell Drugs

The Alchemy of US Empire

Suzanna Reiss

UNIVERSITY OF CALIFORNIA PRESS

University of California Press, one of the most
distinguished university presses in the United States,
enriches lives around the world by advancing scholarship
in the humanities, social sciences, and natural sciences. Its
activities are supported by the UC Press Foundation and
by philanthropic contributions from individuals and
institutions. For more information, visit www.ucpress.edu.

University of California Press
Oakland, California

© 2014 by The Regents of the University of California

Library of Congress Cataloging-in-Publication Data

Reiss, Suzanna.
    We sell drugs : the alchemy of US empire / Suzanna
Reiss.
        pages cm. — (American crossroads ; 39)
    Includes bibliographical references and index.
    ISBN 978-0-520-28077-9 (cloth : alk. paper)—
    ISBN 978-0-520-28078-6 (pbk. : alk. paper)—
    ISBN 978-0-520-95902-6 (ebook)
        1. Drug control—Political aspects—United States—
History. 2. Drug abuse—Political aspects—United
States—History. 3. Pharmaceutical industry—Political
aspects—United States—History. 4. Balance of
power. 5. United States—Politics and government.
I. Title.
    HV5825.R434 2014
    382'.4561510973—dc23

                                        2013047208

Manufactured in the United States of America
23 22 21 20 19 18 17 16 15 14
10 9 8 7 6 5 4 3 2 1

In keeping with a commitment to support
environmentally responsible and sustainable printing
practices, UC Press has printed this book on Natures
Natural, a fiber that contains 30% post-consumer waste
and meets the minimum requirements of ANSI/NISO
Z39.48-1992 (R 1997) (Permanence of Paper).

Cover design: Glynnis Koike
Cover image: iStock

*Dedicated to my brothers, Justin and
Matthew, with love*

Contents

Illustrations

MAP

TABLES

Acronyms

AAAS	American Association for the Advancement of Science
AID	Agency for International Development
AmPharMA	American Pharmaceutical Manufacturers' Association
APRA	Alianza Popular Revolucionaria Americana
ARC	Addiction Research Center
BDC	Bolivian Development Corporation
BEW	Board of Economic Warfare
CND	UN Commission on Narcotics Drugs
DEA	Drug Enforcement Administration
DSB	UN Drug Supervisory Body
ECLA	UN Economic Commission for Latin America
ECOSOC	UN Economic and Social Council
FBN	Federal Bureau of Narcotics
FSA	Federal Security Administration
NIH	National Institutes of Health
ODM	Office of Defense Mobilization
OSRD	Office of Scientific Research and Development
PASB	Pan American Sanitary Bureau
PCOB	UN Permanent Central Opium Board
PRC	People's Republic of China

SPY	Sociedad de Proprietarios de Yungas
UN	United Nations
US	United States
USPHS	United States Public Health Service
USSR	Union of Soviet Socialist Republics
WHO	World Health Organization

Introduction

The United States government has never waged a war on drugs. On the contrary, drugs in general—and so-called "narcotic" drugs such as cocaine in particular—constitute part of a powerful arsenal that the government flexibly deploys to wage war and to demonstrate its capacity to bring health, peace, and economic prosperity. Drugs historically have not been targets but rather tools; the ability to supply, withhold, stockpile, and police drugs, and to influence the public conversation about drugs, has been central to projections of US imperial power since the middle of the twentieth century.

This book explores the relationship between drugs and war from World War II through the early Cold War and, in particular, how policing and profiting from their intersection has propelled the consolidation of US economic and political power on a global scale. It is an historical account of the international geography and regulatory sinews attached to one group of commodities that was foundational to international drug control: coca leaves and the various substances and consumer products derived from them. Throughout the time period of this study—the 1940s through the early 1960s—and still to the present day, those commodities included pharmaceutical-grade cocaine and the beverage Coca-Cola. The story reveals the importance of the pharmaceutical industry and drug control to US national power by examining the implementation of regulatory controls, cultural narratives, and economic hierarchies that accompanied the delineation of legal and illegal participation within the coca commodities marketplace. This history provides an important perspective on the origins of ongoing global and domestic economic hierarchies that influence the access of people and communities to vital medicines. It also illuminates the profound limitations and biases that currently shape national and international drug control policy and debate.

The "war on drugs" has inspired public and political debate for decades. Its origins are commonly attributed to the administration of President Richard Nixon, who in a special message to Congress in 1969 warned the American public that drugs were a "growing menace to the general welfare." By 1971, drug abuse was "public enemy number one" and Nixon called upon the country to "wage an all-out offensive against that deadly enemy."[1] This was not the beginning of the purported war on drugs, but rather the culmination of transformations over the previous three decades that had established the material and symbolic foundations for this assault. This book argues that to understand the modern war on drugs, one must examine an often overlooked but critical period for the emergence of a US-led international drug control regime: World War II and the early Cold War. Scholars have demonstrated that Nixon's drug war dovetailed with a 1970s backlash against the civil rights movement that witnessed the rise in prominence of "law and order"–based political campaigns, as well as the public's overreaction to accounts of drug use among soldiers in Vietnam; yet it relied on institutions, beliefs, and regulatory principles established much earlier.[2]

Historians who have studied US national and international drug control initiatives have shown that concerted efforts to police the flow of drug commodities began earlier than is frequently recognized. Such initiatives date back at least to the beginning of the twentieth century, when US reformers joined with British officials in an attempt to regulate the opium trade.[3] Since the 1914 passage of the national Harrison Narcotics Act, drug control became an integral aspect of federal government power. But even scholars who have studied this longer history of drug control initiatives tend to emphasize, as is evident in the pioneering work of David F. Musto, that "the current drug problem arose in the mid-1960s."[4] Moreover, World War II is largely addressed as an interruption rather than as a critical formative moment when drug control was refashioned in the midst of the unprecedented consolidation of US superpower.[5] In contrast this study suggests the 1940s through the 1960s marked a watershed moment for the reworking of an international system of drug control. The "drug problem" was not a sociological or scientific fact, but rather an historical construction rooted in beliefs and practices that changed over time and in context. Fundamental to this process was US policy during World War II and the early Cold War, which dramatically solidified the contours of a national and international drug control regime structured according to the geopolitical and strategic interests of the US state and private capital. The US government and the US pharmaceutical industry were the driving force behind the establishment of international drug control during this time period, culminating in the creation of the United Nations' Single Convention on Narcotic Drugs in 1961. Locating the origins of late twentieth-century drug control in this mid-century moment sheds light on the interconnection between the growth of domestic and international policing apparatuses on the one hand and the historic rise of US economic hegemony on the other.

This study aims to change the way we conceive of the "drug problem." Our popular understanding of the "war on drugs" is derived from the selectivity of our focus. Contemporary debate over whether excessive and dangerous drug consumption should be approached as an issue of criminal justice or medical disease obscures the fact that drug control for the first five decades of its implementation in the United States was pursued under the authority of the Department of the Treasury's Federal Bureau of Narcotics (FBN). Drug control was institutionalized through market regulations to secure adequate supplies of drugs while limiting and delineating the legal boundaries of their circulation. The domestic 1914 Harrison Narcotics Act and both major international drug conventions that encompass the scope of this project, the 1931 Convention for the Limiting the Manufacture and Regulating the Distribution of Narcotic Drugs and the 1961 Single Convention on Narcotic Drugs, used market controls and monitoring as enforcement measures. They selectively authorized participation in cultivating, manufacturing, and distributing drugs that effectively advanced US geopolitical and economic dominance. While genuine concerns over public health and social well-being have inspired some to embrace the "war on drugs," drug control has also always been about economic power.

From World War II through the early 1960s the process of consolidating US influence over the international flow of select drug commodities, and the systems of domestic policing that emerged in concert, established foundational principles, relationships, institutional structures, and an ideological framing of the "drug problem," which together continue to shape the implementation and discussions of drug policy to the present day. To understand subsequent policies it is key to contemplate the silences and limits of acceptable debate at the moment when the United States emerged as an unparalleled global superpower and led a campaign to extend the reach of a drug control regime. For it was in the 1940s and 1950s that the United States independently, and by means of FBN Commissioner Harry J. Anslinger's powerful position on the UN Commission on Narcotics Drugs (CND), worked to define the parameters of legal—and hence illegal—drug trafficking as a central component of strengthening national political power and extending its global economic reach. In the process drugs and drug control assumed a privileged place in the structures of policing and profit making that animated US capital's expansion and shaped the terms of debate for decades to come.

. . .

In April 1949, "The White Goddess" provocatively headlined the "Hemisphere" page of *Time* magazine. This exposé on the cocaine trade described international police coordination between agents of the US Federal Bureau of Narcotics and Peruvian officials that culminated in the dramatic bust of a smuggling ring stretching from Peru, through Cuba, to the United States. Readers were informed "that the US was swamped with the biggest influx of cocaine in 20 years" and that the source "was unquestionably Peru." The article identified Peruvians as "the No. 1 producers of crude cocaine, and also among its foremost users." Cuba, on the other hand, a stopover point on the illicit drug trade, reappears in a second feature directly beneath the first. One's eye is drawn to a picture of smiling women (a visual counterpoint to the first article's seductive title) "cheerfully" lining up like "eager beavers" behind a young girl receiving a drug vaccination after the "scary discovery" of a different kind of influx: "the first case of smallpox in 20 years." The US Navy had hastily flown in the inoculations to prevent an epidemic, and to "atone for the recent unpleasantness when three tipsy US sailors befouled the statue of Cuban Hero José Martí."[6]

The parallel narrative conventions in these stories mirror the profound interconnectedness of drugs, economic power, and diplomacy on the one hand, and the extension of US power in the hemisphere during and after World War II on the other. These news reports in 1949 already did not question the parameters of legality as enforced through the collaborative efforts of the FBN, the US military, national police, and public health officials. The illicit drug trade in "cocaine"—represented as

FIGURE 1. Nurse vaccinating women and children for smallpox, Havana, 1949 (reproduced on the "Hemisphere" page of *Time*, April 1949) [© Bettmann/CORBIS].

the "white goddess," a seductive and dangerous temptress—is invoked to justify US policing powers: a spectacle of drug raids, detectives, undercover agents, and cooperative local officials. Meanwhile, the licit drug economy—"smallpox inoculations"—provided the soothing antidote for an actual US military presence in an effort to avoid inflaming resentment toward Yankee imperialism (nationalist Martí had been one of its most famous critics).

Implicit in *Time*'s coverage was the contrasting valorization of American-supplied medicines (in this case smallpox vaccinations) and the easy demonization of cocaine and the alleged Peruvian consumers whose indulgence in the "vice [was] out in the open." This does not negate the public health benefits of vaccination campaigns, but it does reveal the way US access to drugs and its capacity to deploy them as diplomatic carrots (and withhold them to carry a big stick) was the result of the historical emergence at that time of a particular international drug control regime. The depiction of women and children happily lining up in Havana for vaccinations glossed over the element of coercion: some two weeks earlier, when a Cuban traveler returned from Mexico with smallpox, the government made vaccination mandatory and the Cuban minister of health, Dr. Alberto Oteiza, warned "that any person not submitting to vaccination for smallpox would be tried by the courts under the penal code."[7] Oteiza then reportedly "urgently" appealed to the United States for additional supplies of the vaccine.[8] US power distorted the market and shaped government pronouncements and public perception about drugs and efforts to police them. The elision of state compulsion in US media accounts of the Cuban vaccination campaign complemented the misleading focus on policing and cocaine in the Andes. Cocaine was not in fact widely consumed in Peru, although the coca leaves that grew on the semitropical slopes of the Andes Mountains provided the raw material for manufacturing cocaine and had been consumed in their natural state in the region for millennia. Unmentioned was the fact that the major consumer (and manufacturing) market for both legal and illegal cocaine at that time was the United States. These accounts collapsed the distinction between coca leaves and cocaine and privileged manufacturing nations' relationship to and beliefs about coca commodities. Drug control was becoming a potent vehicle for institutionalizing an economic order that privileged US pharmaceutical companies' drug production—and by extension, US national power.

The ideological distinction between the licit and illicit drug economies was cemented during the next decade within the structures of an international drug control regime fashioned through the global reordering of political and economic forces of the early Cold War. The third article gracing *Time*'s "Hemisphere" page conveyed this context; the Canadian Parliament voted overwhelming to approve the North Atlantic Treaty to create a "bulwark against Communism." The mutual defense pact, which helped solidify the military fault lines of Cold War rivalries, went into effect later that year. While in 1949 the FBN welcomed Cuban collaboration in the regional policing of the narcotics trade, only a decade later, following the Cuban Revolution, political tensions between the United States and Cuba transformed drug control discourse and policies. After the revolution Cuba joined China as a favorite target of accusations (inaccurate yet symbolically powerful) by US officials—that each was a Communist dope smuggling nation. By 1959 the tactics, policies, and symbolic politics surrounding drug control had become firmly entrenched as pillars of US power. Exercising power over the drug market had evolved into a material weapon for waging war—an essential resource in what might be termed a US "chemical Cold War."

Economic and political interests have historically exerted a commanding influence with regard to establishing the dividing line between legal and illegal, and in this case quite literally created the legal and illegal drug markets. Yet, in the scholarship on the history of pharmaceuticals and drug trafficking, legal and illegal drug markets are rarely considered to be part of one cohesive economic and political system. This book examines the historical evolution of this interconnection. This approach provides an alternative perspective from standard histories and popular debates about drug control that tend to focus on the *illicit* market. National governments, police officials, scientists, and business executives all hoped to embrace the productive power of drugs—and drug control—to consolidate their political authority and secure their interests within an increasingly integrated global political economy. They sought to monopolize the *licit*. The drug control regime that emerged in the 1940s and 1950s was just that—a system of controls, not actual prohibition. Cocaine and other controlled substances straddled the licit–illicit divide, their legal status being dependent on their circulation within the marketplace and on *who* grew, manufactured, sold, and consumed them. This account illustrates the ongoing existence of both legal and illegal coca markets and presents the issue of legality as a political and historical construction rather than a neutral, descriptive category.

There has been a new wave of scholarship attentive to the history of the legal drug industry, with critical studies of cocaine leading the charge. Paul Gootenberg's important 1999 edited collection, *Cocaine: Global Histories,* and his more recent *Andean Cocaine: The Making of a Global Drug,* Joseph F. Spillane's *Cocaine: From Medical Marvel to Modern Menace in the United States, 1884–1920,* along with Michael M. Cohen's work on Jim Crow, Coca-Cola, and cocaine prohibition, all recount the role played by modern pharmaceutical science and European and US-based commercial industries in producing an international market for coca leaves (to be used in the manufacturing of tonic beverages and medicinal cocaine).[9] They provide valuable evidence of the pharmaceutical industry's influence on defining the parameters of a drug control regime, both through direct collaborations with government officials and indirectly through the production and marketing of products, such as cocaine, which in turn ultimately became entangled with cultural panics that backed calls for prohibitions. In all of these accounts the history of cocaine tends to be narrated from its early popular legality to its emergence as an illegal commodity. This book draws upon this research but attempts to overcome the persistent absence of investigation into the ongoing tension around designations of legality.

In fact to this day, while the United States spends billions of dollars attacking "illegal" cocaine, the country remains both the largest importer of coca leaves in the world and the largest stockpiler of "legal" cocaine.[10]

This study is attentive to insights gained from historians working on drug control and culture who have shown the force of cultural prejudice in historically determining which drugs are targeted for control or prohibition. A wide range of drug history scholars including Wayne Morgan, David F. Musto, David T. Courtwright, Doris Marie Provine, and Curtiz Marez have pointed out the central role of race and racism in the evolution of cultural attitudes, laws, and the emergence of a carceral state.[11] David L. Herzberg encourages us to recognize the "constructed division between licit and illicit drugs" in his study of feminists' cultural demonization of valium in the 1970s, a drug he sees as a "boundary case" that exposes "the historical and cultural connections between medicine-cabinet and 'street' drug cultures."[12] Charles O. Jackson describes the relationship between law, medicinal abuse, and popular culture, pointing out that drug panics historically have been "fashioned by fear and nurtured by atypical horror stories."[13] Lee V. Cassanelli usefully explores the status of a "quasi-legal commodity," focusing on the changing patterns of production, consumption, and political symbolism in relation to the qat economy of northeast Africa in the last half century. He points out how the perceived political threat among a subculture of qat consumers was "construed by outsiders to be anti-social in a larger sense" and drove government drug crackdowns.[14]

The importance of culture in shaping drug crackdowns must also be studied in light of the evolving system of cultural values, economic priorities, and political hierarchies that fueled the growth of US capitalist power. As cultural critic Curtis Marez observes, "Historically, drug traffic has fueled imperial expansion and global capitalism," and as such the politics of legality was firmly mediated through ideologies of the market.[15] Taking this insight to heart, this study considers legal pharmaceutical markets as forms of drug trafficking legitimized through the historical emergence of selective policing of participation in the drug trade. The consolidation of an international drug control regime happened alongside the development of US capitalist power. By tracking participation and control over the flow of drug commodities (and the social and political narratives that accompanied them), this book grounds the history of the rise of US imperialism within the international sphere from which it sought raw materials, consumer markets, and political and economic collaborators. From World War II through the early 1960s, the strategic deployment of science, medicine, and technology on behalf of US economic and political expansion ensured that drugs emerged as critical weapons for both the waging of war and the encouragement of particular models of economic development prioritized by US policy-makers for maintaining peace. A drive to promote mass consumption of US-manufactured goods, including drugs, became one basis for securing international dominance, and it depended on a parallel effort to desig-nate and police mass addiction. Certain habits and certain people—sol-diers, the poor, ethnic and racial minorities—were policed and prodded as the raw material for controlled development, which included testing out new drugs and transforming consumer habits.

The drug control regime advanced by US officials locked South American countries into an economic relationship whereby their par-ticipation in the international market was as providers of raw materials and consumer-importers of US-manufactured goods. The economic dependency and vulnerability this produced in Latin America extended an ongoing process of "underdevelopment" as these nations became further tethered to the global capitalist system. As Andre Gunder Frank pointed out in 1970, with the growth of US power "not only is there now a greater degree of economic dependency, but the entire social and political structure of these 'sovereign' states is tied to metropolitan needs and prevents economic and social development or political free-dom for Asia, Africa and Latin America."[16] Drug control further institu-tionalized inequalities between nations, which refracted through ine-qualities among peoples within nations. The emergent system of drug control differentially affected various groups of people connected to sites of drug production, distribution, and consumption. While the fruits of drug control accrued to powerful economic and political elites cen-tered in the United States, the burdens of the system fell disproportion-ately on indigenous communities of the coca growing regions in Peru and Bolivia and on poor communities and racialized minorities living in the United States. Studying drug control efforts reveals more than the evolution of unequal integration into a global capitalist system; drug control depended on the historical and cultural construction of ideas about physiological and social "danger" that came to be associated with drugs like cocaine and filtered through and perpetuated social, eco-nomic, and racial inequalities.

From the 1940s through the early 1960s, the scope of this investiga-tion, the United States was the largest importer of coca leaves in the world and the largest legal retailer of coca-derived goods. Coca commodities flowed through circuits oriented toward the manufacture of an array of drug products. The definition of a "drug," and more particularly a "narcotic drug" like cocaine, was mediated by cultural politics, economic regulations, and the power of pharmaceutical laboratories to alchemically alter drug raw materials (coca leaves) into a variety of controlled substances (cocaine), and other products that conveniently exited the regulatory gaze (Coca-Cola). In medical science the category "narcotic" attaches to opiates or synthetic drugs that mimic opium's psychoactive properties. The historical deployment of the term "narcotic," however, has been attached to the legal status of a given drug. Thus, opium and coca leaves were integrated into national drug legislation in 1914 as the two primary categories of controlled "narcotics." By 1937, with the passage of the Marijuana Tax Act, cannabis attained that status. While this books charts efforts to regulate the flow of coca commodities as they moved through national and international markets across the Andes and the United States, this story is necessarily situated within a larger context of the production, regulation, and consumption of an array of pharmaceuticals. The historical labeling of a given substance as a "dangerous drug" was rooted not in scientific objectivity but in the political economy and cultural politics of US drug control—as the growing contemporary embrace of "medical marijuana" usefully illustrates.

This study is anchored by the geographic circuits through which coca commodities flowed, but it situates regulatory efforts to control coca within the larger context of a burgeoning drug control apparatus that was guided by the economic and political priorities of the US government and pharmaceutical industry writ large. For instance, during World War II, US efforts to limit Andean exports of coca to Axis powers were paired with a broader campaign to monopolize drug raw material exports and drug distribution networks in the region for the benefit of US corporations and government war mobilization. The determining influence of the US government and pharmaceutical industry was similarly evident in postwar efforts to stamp out indigenous Andean chewing of coca leaves while seeking to create new consumer markets for an array of US-manufactured drugs. Following the trail of coca, and the various drug markets that historically intersected with it, offers an exceptional window onto US-led efforts to determine the parameters of legal and illegal participation within a burgeoning international drug economy. Coca constituted one of only two raw material targeted by drug control campaigners (the other being opium) that was situated squarely in a US sphere of geopolitical influence—what some US politicians continue to derisively refer to as "America's backyard."

The history of efforts to control the flow of coca commodities forces us to contend with the physical production of valued drugs and how efforts to police and regulate their circulation were subsidized and contested by various public and private players. These material conflicts were often refracted through and reinforced by cultural narratives that recast social and political conflict in terms of scientific and legal assessments of the dangers accompanying the twentieth century's therapeutic revolution; the rhetoric of drug control easily reconfigured social, economic, and political dissent as disease, social dysfunction, and criminality.[17] Studying the history of drug control entails tracking the incredible power of drugs' symbolic currency. Beyond the ascribed physical impact of drugs, drug control proponents trumpeted the seemingly transcendental impact of drugs on human subjectivity, wherein their power to harm or heal extended into the social and cultural life of the community and often provided the evidentiary basis for discrediting (or glorifying) people, states, cultural practices, political movements, and alternative systems of value.

Moving from US economic warfare policies during World War II through Cold War "defense mobilization," this book examines the rise to global dominance of the American pharmaceutical industry, the extension of markets for US drug commodities overseas, and the selective criminalization of drug production and consumption within an international capitalist economic system where the aggressive marketing of *some* drugs, to *some* people, was encouraged. In the name of public health, national security, economic development, and collective defense, the government has played a crucial role in establishing access to foreign raw materials and markets for the major US-based pharmaceutical manufacturers. Through state-to-state collaboration among national police and military personnel, scientists and corporate executives, through international organizations such as the United Nations, the World Health Organization (WHO), and the Pan American Sanitary Bureau (PASB), the US government has been deeply involved in regulating, subsidizing, and promoting the US-based pharmaceutical industry as a critical pillar of the nation's global power.

The book begins with an examination of the impact of World War II on the international flow of drugs. The success of US economic warfare initiatives helped position the country as the preeminent global producer of pharmaceuticals and as the major advocate of international drug control by war's end. Chapter 2 explores the ways in which drugs were demobilized after the war and rapidly remobilized as essential for national security and for maintaining a permanent state of war readiness. It looks at government efforts in conjunction with the private pharmaceutical industry to define and police the legitimate flow of drug commodities, to ensure adequate stockpiles for national defense, and to facilitate the export of US-manufactured drugs as diplomatic and economic emissaries of the benefits of allying with the US capitalist system. Chapter 3 examines the subsequent US-led effort, both independently and through the United Nations, to police all of coca's circulation outside of the political economy envisioned by the designers of the drug control regime. This entailed a prohibitive assault on indigenous coca leaf chewing in the Andes, accompanied by a determination to secure adequate supplies of the plant for export to the United States. The chapter describes a US-chaired UN commission sent to the Andes in 1949 to study the "coca leaf problem," how its mission was received, and how the regulatory recommendations it made constituted an attack on indigenous traditions while promoting models of modernization and development premised on integration into a global capitalist marketplace. Chapter 4 examines the seeming contradiction in American capitalist consumer culture that depends in part on cultivating drug consumption while aggressively policing drug "addiction" as a socially and historically constituted crime. The testing and marketing of new drugs became vehicles for both the pharmaceutical industry and the US government to augment their power, police wayward populations, and encourage select consuming habits and economic practices in both the Andes and the United States. These efforts simultaneously sought to cultivate cultural practices and beliefs that would supply and sustain a market for US-manufactured goods. The final chapter considers US and international drug policy and drug control rhetoric as they became tools for confronting economic and political challenges to a US capitalist hegemony in the context of the civil rights movement, global anticolonial struggles, and the Cold War.

It is the dialectical power of drugs to harm or to heal that makes them enormously valuable in varied and historically changing ways. The productive power of drugs includes their very real capacity to physiologically impact the human body, along with their symbolic capacity to mobilize people's deepest prejudices, fears, dreams, and desires. Drugs in this sense might be both "destructive" and "productive" depending on what cultural, economic, and political metrics provide the basis for judgment. The US government has considered the productive value of drugs as both a threat and an opportunity. The power of drugs to cure, alleviate pain, stimulate action, fire the imagination, and dull or amplify the senses has been the subject of spiritual, scientific, and social inquiry for millennia. The material capacity of drugs to make someone wealthy or make someone feel good, their power to mend and to injure, are all part of this story—so too is their symbolic currency for historically constructed beliefs about the body politic and the economy of survival.

The drug industry emerged from World War II as one of the most profitable industries in the United States. The (North) American people have been (and remain) the largest consumers, producers, and exporters of drugs in the world. At the same time, the selective policing of drug production and consumption became an integral objective of US domestic and foreign policy. This history and the ongoing war on drugs it produced has filled domestic prisons with nonviolent drug offenders and contributed to human and environmental devastation, particularly for poor and indigenous communities across the Americas. President Barack Obama's administration continues to escalate the drug wars of previous administrations, despite a rhetorical shift eschewing that terminology, and US-led militarized drug control initiatives continue to fuel national and regional conflicts.[18] The last national election cycle in the United States witnessed the unprecedented legalization of marijuana for recreational, not the more narrowly construed medical, uses in two states, signifying a groundswell of support for alternatives to the current drug control regime. At the same time there is a growing challenge both from within and outside the nation. In 2012 the leaders of Guatemala, Mexico, and Colombia issued a "Joint Declaration" to the United Nations calling for a "new paradigm" for drug control in light of the many failures of current policy—which they identify as an escalation rather than a reduction in drug abuse, an escalation in violence and criminal activities, and the attendant corruption of police forces and governments.[19]

Recognizing the way in which power has shaped the intersection between national security, public health policies, the provision of medicines, and the policing of drug consumption is a necessary step in overcoming the conflicts and misunderstandings surrounding drug policy. Examining the history of the selective enforcement of drug control and its imbrications in hemispheric structures of unequal economic and political power can provide an alternative framework for creating a more just drug regulatory regime. This includes dismantling an approach that targets predominantly poor and racialized minority populations for policing and incarceration, and creating the foundations for improving hemispheric political relations in the future. I hope this book makes a small contribution to the national and international effort that is already underway to promote more humane and effective drug policies in the service of people rather than state and corporate power.

CHAPTER I

"The Drug Arsenal of the Civilized World"

WWII and the Origins of US-Led International Drug Control

World War II was waged in part as a war for control over commodity flows. As one contemporary expert in economic warfare observed, "in a *total* war practically every commodity entering into foreign trade is important, directly or indirectly, to the war effort."[1] Even before the United States officially entered World War II, the president authorized economic measures such as export and shipping controls, the freezing of foreign assets, blacklisting, and foreign aid programs to strengthen the Allied cause and weaken the Axis capacity to wage war. Some of the commodities targeted for control were deemed vital to war making; for instance, rubber was needed to make bombers, tanks, and gas masks, and tin was used to manufacture everything from circuit boards to the millions of cans provisioning food for Allied troops. The strategic value of other commodities, including items as diverse as beef, coffee, and cacao, lay primarily in the indirect calculus that US purchasing and stockpiling of such goods could offset war-caused trade disruptions that had the potential to generate economic and political instability, especially for Latin American raw materials export-oriented economies cut off from the transatlantic trade.[2]

In this context US officials wrestled to control the international circulation of one uniquely valuable group of commodities: pharmaceuticals. The US approach to drug control over the course of World War II constituted a defining moment in the longer history of US efforts to influence the international pharmaceutical trade, to pave the way for US corporate power, and to establish the nation as a formidable political player on the world stage. While World War II was far more than a conflict over commodity flows, the institutionalization of economic warfare policies in relation to the drug trade provide a revealing, if understudied, account of the convergent rise of American power, the war-making capacity of the state, and the economic and political foundations of the US-led "war on drugs" that remains a central feature of US foreign and domestic policy.

The modern history of international drug control dates back to the first decades of the twentieth century, when representatives of European and American colonial powers sought to establish regulatory mechanisms to monitor and channel the international drug trade in directions they deemed essential to their economic, social, and political security. The United States helped spearhead the effort, perpetually contentious, that led to the first international drug control convention in 1912. The International Opium Convention was merely the first in a long line of international agreements (some more widely adhered to than others), and it marked the beginning of what would become a century-long saga driven by drug manufacturing countries to gain widespread geopolitical acquiescence to the notion that their vision of drug control was a critical obligation of not only national but international governance.

While the contest to control the international drug trade preceded and outlasted World War II, the war marked a profound watershed. The war set the stage for a new era of drug control; since then, wars waged *with* drugs have persisted as the flip side to the misleadingly named "war on drugs." World War II and the US wartime mobilization altered the balance of power among drug manufacturing countries and between manufacturing countries and states that produced raw materials for the international drug trade. The United States emerged from the war a global drug giant, the largest manufacturer, producer, and distributor of pharmaceuticals in the world. This gave it unprecedented leverage over former allies and enemies alike. By the war's end, the country's primary prewar manufacturing competitors, Germany and Japan, found their drug industries largely destroyed and under American occupation. In coca growing countries such as Peru and Bolivia, the war's impact was also dramatic as the United States consolidated its position as the primary purchaser of drug raw materials, primary supplier of much-valued finished goods, and influential advocate for the aggressive regulation of the drug market. In the process, drug control became a powerful weapon for advancing American imperial might.

This chapter tells the story of these transformations by tracing the US government's effort to control one particular group of drug commodities, those derived from the coca plant, as an anchor for a broader description of how the geography and political economy of the international drug trade was disrupted by the war, how US government economic warfare initiatives sought to capitalize, and how this shaped interactions with countries like Bolivia and Peru, both important players in the longer history of drug control. If we date the drug war to this era, almost a full three decades before President Richard Nixon famously declared a "war on drugs," it becomes clearer how the drug war itself and the economic order it entrenched helped fuel the rise of an American empire.

DRUGS AND DEFENSE MOBILIZATION

The importance of drugs to war mobilization was self-evident to contemporary government officials and to representatives of the private sector pharmaceutical firms with whom they collaborated. Two days after President Franklin Delano Roosevelt called on the US Congress to declare war in response to the bombing of Pearl Harbor, the head of the Federal Security Administration (FSA) addressed members of the American Pharmaceutical Manufacturers' Association (AmPharMA) at the prestigious Mayflower Hotel in Washington, DC. The FSA was tasked with managing health and safety programs related to national defense. In his speech, Administrator Paul V. McNutt celebrated previous government foresight in acquiring ample stocks of opium, quinine, and other drugs deemed essential to war making, such that by December 1941 the Treasury Department's vaults stored a three-year supply of opium. Existing stockpiles were impressive, but not sufficient. The war threatened to disrupt the supply of "key drugs hitherto imported from abroad," McNutt explained, and highlighted the urgency of developing new sources of supply, particularly in the Western Hemisphere.[3] Earlier that year the FSA administrator had already called on drug manufacturers to emulate the armaments industry and work together to make America "the drug arsenal of the civilized world."[4] McNutt explained the direct importance of drugs for war: "Medical munitions these might be called; for they are munitions in just as true a sense as any held by our Government in military arsenals . . . they are as much a part of preparedness as tanks and planes and guns."[5]

This description of drugs, as a weapons arsenal for advancing an American model of civilization, attests to the enormous value drugs held in 1941 for both state making and war making. War had always provided a stimulus to technological innovation in the drug field, but twentieth-century world war spawned what business historian Alfred Chandler has termed a "pharmaceutical revolution."[6] By the 1940s, this revolution produced a "cornucopia of new drugs," with government-subsidized research and the mass production of vitamins, hormones, sulfonamides, penicillin, and other antibiotics radically changing wound healing, treatment for infectious disease, and government and corporate collaboration in the pharmaceutical industry.[7] The war also galvanized research for synthetic drug alternatives to "replace natural products from the tropics" in an effort to avoid international dependency on materials deemed essential to public health and national power.[8] Such vulnerabilities, for instance, spurred German research during the war that led to the creation of Demerol, a potent painkiller and synthetic substitute for opium. The US Army Medical Corps seized this research in Germany in 1945 and delivered it to American "chemists, pharmacologists and other medical scientists."[9] Access to pharmaceuticals (and industrial secrets) was one critical determinant of a nation's capacity to thrive. War caused injury, hunger, and disease. Drugs promised to alleviate pain, cure infection, and stimulate a greater capacity of productive labor, whether in the mines, the factories, the fields, or on the battlefront. One contemporary neatly captured this widespread sense of the holistic interdependence of societal well-being and pharmaceuticals: "Competent protection of fighting men from disease demands the competent protection of civilians."[10]

The US government began accumulating a drug arsenal as early as 1935, when the eventual thirty-year reigning head of the then five-year-old Federal Bureau of Narcotics (FBN), Commissioner Harry J. Anslinger, created government stockpiles of narcotic drugs in anticipation of war.[11] These stockpiles ensured against shortages that occurred when international drug supply networks were disrupted by hostilities. They also contributed to US economic and diplomatic leverage, for example, when the nation "virtually cornered the opium market during the war years," driving the price up by some 300 percent.[12] As early as December 1939 Commissioner Anslinger reported that sufficient narcotics were stored in Treasury Department vaults to supply domestic demand and to "take care of the whole Western Hemisphere."[13] When the United States officially entered the conflict in 1941, these enormous stocks were already being used to "take care of the medical needs of a lot of our friends." As Anslinger informed Congress: "I mean South America, particularly.

FIGURE 2. World War II propaganda poster for the construction of a pharmaceutical manufacturing facility.

We have helped out the Netherlands Indies, Russia, and other sections of the world which were formerly supplied by the manufacturing countries of Europe. I do not know what the sick and injured of some of these countries would do if it had not been for our reserve stock."[14]

This testimony, just ten days after the bombing of Pearl Harbor, revealed how war preparation and war increased the US government's influence over the international drug trade. Anslinger echoed FSA Administrator McNutt when he rhetorically queried drug industry officials: "But is it our job—the job of you and our government—merely to supply the continental United States? Or will we become the arsenal for medical munitions on the public-health and medical front for all the Americas?"[15] The capacity to supply drugs and enforce regulatory compliance was both a source and manifestation of economic clout in the drug market.

This economic influence was upheld in part through seeking enforcement of international drug treaties. The US FBN had taken measures to ensure "that treaties will not fall apart during the war," in part by continuing to monitor the international narcotics trade through a system of import and export certificates. Moreover, "Being the only manufacturing nation in this hemisphere, we are able to keep international control functioning on this side of the Atlantic."[16] Wartime exigencies transformed what had previously been an international regulatory effort to control a few select pharmaceuticals, into a far more expansive effort premised on a vision of total mobilization. The FBN's original mandate was to ensure adequate supplies of narcotic drugs for domestic scientific and medical uses and to police the unlawful importation and circulation of narcotic drugs.[17] War brought other priorities to the fore. When the war broke out, opium was one of two primary categories of "narcotics" targeted for control by both national and international authorities. The term "narcotic" in this context was derived from a history of legal controls rather than medicinal qualities.[18] Since the first international drug convention in 1912, "narcotic" drug control had targeted poppy plants, coca leaves, and drugs derived from them, including opium and cocaine. Following the ratification of the Convention for Limiting the Manufacture and Regulating the Distribution of Narcotic Drugs (also referred to as the 1931 Geneva Convention), this expanded to include a growing number of synthetic substitutes like codeine.[19] In terms of the "narcotic" drug arsenal, along with its virtual opium monopoly, by early 1942 the FBN reported the United States had similarly secured adequate supplies of coca and rapidly became the primary supplier of cocaine to Allied nations and "liberated territories."[20] Relatively early in the conflict the United States secured adequate stocks of narcotic drugs with which to supply its own and Allied countries' war efforts, while being in a formidable position to deny enemy access to these valuable commodities— something the FBN was actively doing.

However, the war dramatically expanded the reach of drug control to include an array of pharmaceuticals that, while not classified as narcotics, were nevertheless deemed crucial for waging war, and the FBN's influence grew well beyond its previous jurisdiction. The National War Productions Board granted it authority over drug allocations for national defense and Commissioner Anslinger was directly involved in setting "wartime policy for the procurement of all drugs" and in decisions regarding "Allied drug requirements."[21] When asked to clarify his concerns over wartime budgetary constraints and whether the FBN's activities were "not especially related to the war effort" but rather "national welfare," Anslinger was quick to point out the interconnectedness: "Our work with respect to critical and strategic materials all ties into the war effort."[22] As the leader of a relatively young bureaucracy, Anslinger successfully argued the importance of drug control to national security and, in doing so, added to the FBN's (and his own) growing influence.[23] The labels "critical" and "strategic" were defined by the Army and Navy Munitions Board as being materials "essential to national defense," with the strategic category referring to materials whose supply was dependent in whole or in part on sources outside the United States, while critical referred to materials essential for war but for which supply was not foreseen to be "as great a problem." This directly influenced the government's approach to the drug market. While world supplies of opium came from British India, Turkey, Asia, and Yugoslavia, the existing surpluses in US government stockpiles rendered the drug "critical" rather than "strategic." The only drug appearing on the list of strategic materials was the antimalarial quinine, essential for inoculating soldiers deployed to tropical areas. Before the war 95 percent of the raw materials used to manufacture quinine, cinchona bark, was grown in the Dutch East Indies (now Indonesia) and concern over supply disruptions were well founded.[24]

In practice, contemporary officials considered a wide array of pharmaceuticals, both narcotic and nonnarcotic, to be essential to war mobilization, and the terms "strategic," "critical," and "defense material" were often used interchangeably to describe a wide array of drugs deemed important to maintaining national health, economic power, and strategic advantage. In addition to narcotics stockpiles accumulated under Anslinger's early reign, in 1941 the US government identified a number of essential drug raw materials for stockpiling, including "50,000 pounds of aconite root, 200,000 pounds of belladonna leaves and 60,000 pounds of roots, 200,000 pounds of ergot rye, and 675,000 pounds of red squill."[25] The production, stockpiling, and market controls involving drugs during the war were driven by pharmaceuticals' medicinal powers, but more importantly the focus and orientation on certain drugs was dictated by concerns over ease of access to raw materials prioritized for government war mobilization.

WAR AND THE WORLD DRUG MARKET

The war wrought a profound shift in the geography and political economy of the drug trade, and the US government and pharmaceutical industry gained the advantage. The principles and logic of international drug control became firmly tied to US national security and expansionist economic priorities. Before the war the world's pharmaceutical markets were dominated by colonial powers—particularly the United States, the Netherlands, England, and Germany—that were dependent on the steady flow of raw materials from regions across the global South. From the coca-rich Andes of Peru and Bolivia, to poppy fields in India and Turkey, to cinchona plantations in the Philippines and the Dutch East Indies, drug raw materials grew in regions that were especially vulnerable to wartime trade disruptions; some were outright colonies, others were dependent on exporting cash crops to pay for the importation of many basic goods, including medicines. The war disrupted and transformed these trade networks. In the first months of 1942, Japan's rapid military advance into the Philippines, Malaysia, and the East Indies cut off European and American access to raw materials from their colonies in the region, leaving them scrambling for alternatives, or languishing without drugs. In the West, the Allied blockade and German submarine warfare further impinged on a once-robust transatlantic pharmaceutical trade.

Examining the impact the war had on the circulation of one particular set of drug commodities—coca leaves and the various manufactured goods derived from them—offers a revealing account of the intersection of war, drugs, and US power. The war facilitated the consolidation of US control over all coca-derived commodities circulating on the international market, engulfing in particular German and Japanese competition. As one of two categories of narcotic drug targeted for international controls before the war, there is uniquely rich historical documentation recounting the international flow of coca commodities before, during, and after the war that provide insights into war-wrought change. Moreover, as one of two categories of narcotics located firmly in the Western Hemisphere, and with Latin American resources being newly valued as critical to US war mobilization, examining shifts in the coca market also provides perspective on the nature of US economic and political expansion at mid-century. Finally, while this account traces the circulation of coca commodities from the cultivation of coca plants through to the distribution and consumption of goods derived from them, it also offers insight into how any particular drug's value was embedded in broader social, political, and economic visions that increasingly relied on laboratory-manufactured drugs to advance economic development and national power.

In the 1930s coca leaves had been circulating on the international market for more than half a century and constituted the basic raw material for the manufacturing of three other commodities: crude cocaine, cocaine hydrochloride, and a soft drink flavoring extract manufactured for the Coca-Cola Company.[26] Despite competition from Japanese and Dutch farming on colonial plantations in the Pacific, the largest national cultivators of the coca leaf remained within the geography of coca's origins, in the semitropical slopes of the Andes Mountains of Peru and Bolivia. When the war began, the Netherlands East Indies, Bolivia, and Peru produced an estimated four-fifths of the total world trade in coca leaves.[27] Bolivia cultivated coca leaves primarily destined for a regional market sustained by indigenous peasant communities and mine workers. Peru also supplied the Andean market with coca leaves. The circulation of coca leaves in the Andes reflected patterns of traditional use and consumption, interwoven with the impact of the market value of the leaves internationally. In the Andes, coca was typically consumed in its natural leaf state. Coca leaves were chewed, steeped as maté infusions, constituted components of ritual practice, and circulated at times as currency, both in the form of wages or as payment in exchange for goods. The vast majority of coca leaves being cultivated were consumed in this market.[28] Unlike in Bolivia, however, substantial quantities of Peru's coca leaves were cultivated for export. Peru was the largest exporter of coca leaves on the world market and those leaves were exported primarily to manufacturers in the United States.[29]

Although most Peruvian coca leaf exports went to the United States, Peru was unable to export any crude or refined cocaine to the US market.

US narcotics law, since the passage of the 1914 Harrison Narcotics Act, limited national imports to raw materials (coca leaves) and excluded refined drugs (cocaine hydrochloride) and semirefined drugs (crude cocaine)—the manufacture of any narcotic drug for the US market had to be done in the United States by registered importers and manufacturers monitored by the US government. Peruvians did have some limited participation in the manufacturing and export of crude cocaine to Europe, where pharmaceutical companies refined it. Thus, when the war began, the Andean coca leaf market was characterized by the production of raw materials for regional consumption, as in Bolivia, or, in Peru's case, as also a primary supplier of raw material exports (coca leaves and crude cocaine) to US and European drug manufacturers.

Outside the Andes, coca leaves grown on colonial plantations in the Pacific were the primary source of supply for all major drug manufacturing countries except the United States, namely Germany, Japan, France, and the United Kingdom. Japanese cultivation of coca leaves on colonial plantations in Formosa (Taiwan), Okinawa, and Iwo Jima supplied that nation's pharmaceutical industry. Dutch-controlled Java, Borneo, and Sumatra furnished the bulk of coca leaves imported by European manufacturers (along with limited quantities to the United States). While the Andes was the ecological home of coca leaves, nineteenth-century Dutch colonists experimented with transplanting coca seedlings to the fertile soils of the East Indies (now Indonesia) and stumbled across a strain of particularly high-alkaloid-content coca leaf that they cultivated for export. These leaves were uniquely suited to manufacturing cocaine hydrochloride and rapidly came to dominate the international trade geared toward the manufacture of medicinal cocaine.[30]

Nevertheless, in the 1930s the United States remained the largest manufacturing global importer of coca leaves, and these came primarily from Peru. In terms of the North–South distribution of economic power, Europeans and North Americans controlled the manufacturing and international distribution of products derived from coca leaves grown in South America and Southeast Asia. But Americans could claim the most robust market for coca leaves since imports were destined not only for the manufacturing of pharmaceuticals, but also for the large-scale production of a flavoring extract for the Coca-Cola Company. In the United States, only two pharmaceutical companies were legally authorized to import coca leaves: Merck & Co., Inc. and Maywood Chemical Works. Merck imported coca leaves from both Peru and Java, which the company's chemists used to manufacture pharmaceutical-grade cocaine. Maywood imported coca leaves exclusively from Peru, and after extracting and destroying the cocaine alkaloid (to comply with federal narcotics law), the pharmaceutical company transmuted the remainder into a "nonnarcotic" flavoring extract for Coca-Cola. A combined effort by lawyers for the pharmaceutical industry, the Coca-Cola Company, and Commissioner Anslinger of the Federal Bureau of Narcotics secured this concession for "special leaves" in the 1931 Geneva Convention, an exceptional regulatory moment when the legal uses of coca in the drug trade were defined internationally as encompassing both medical and scientific needs, as well as production of a coca-based flavoring extract for the iconic soft drink.[31] By WWII, coca leaves imported into the United States for this purpose consisted of almost twice the volume of leaves imported for medical or scientific use. In both the United States and Europe coca-derived commodities were manufactured for domestic consumption and for reexport. And only at this last stage of the coca commodity circuit did Andean countries reenter as consumer markets for these finished goods, whether as medicinal cocaine, or in bottles of Coca-Cola.[32]

World War II disrupted and transformed the trade circuits through which coca leaves, crude cocaine, pharmaceutical-grade cocaine, and Coca-Cola all flowed. The Japanese occupation of Java, combined with British and American naval blockades of the Atlantic, cut off the European market from supplies of coca leaves and crude cocaine. Germany, the largest European manufacturer and wartime target of naval blockades, was hit hardest. Allied intelligence reports speculated that even reserve stocks inside Germany were being depleted: "Since 1941, Germany has certainly not been in a position to procure coca leaves . . . stocks must have been drawn upon in order to meet requirements in the years 1941 and 1942."[33] From 1936 to 1939, the European continental countries imported an average of 71 tons of coca leaves each year from South America and Asia; however, by 1941 the only trade consisted of a scant few kilograms reexported from one European country to another. By 1943, the League of Nations reported "the countries of the continental group" were unable to procure coca leaves.[34] Europe's access to crude cocaine was similarly disrupted. Before 1939, Europeans were importing from Peru an average of 1168 kg of crude cocaine annually, and German manufacturers constituted the largest market. By 1942 only Spain was reporting any imports, a relatively small 136 kg per year, and by the end of the war, the US commercial attaché in Peru reported that the "great bulk of the exports" were going to Allied countries, primarily England, "with Spain in second place."[35]

With the Dutch East Indies under Japanese occupation, Peru remained the only producer of coca leaves for the world market, and cut off from Europe, the state found itself increasingly dependent on US purchases and subject to the US legal proscription against importing manufactured narcotics. In turn, the United States emerged from the war as the world's largest importer of coca leaves and the largest producer and distributor of cocaine. The United States used this new leverage to dictate the scale and scope of the trade and to exert political influence. In doing so, the United States implemented the structures of its vision for drug control as a constituent element of its wartime policy, and guaranteed its dominant position in the international drug trade in the war's aftermath. Two central animating principles seem to dictate US wartime policy toward the Peruvian coca trade. First, the United States insisted on retaining its manufacturing monopoly and refused to import anything other than coca leaves from the Andes. Second, in the broader effort to undermine Axis economic power and capacity to wage war, the United States interpreted any signs of ongoing Axis trade with South America as evidence of criminal conspiracy and threatened coercive measures to punish those responsible.

Despite mounting stocks of both coca leaves and crude cocaine in Peru, the United States denied repeated requests from Peruvian exporters to sell leaves that had already been converted into cocaine. The war placed the United States in a powerful position to hold onto its drug manufacturing monopoly and further entrench a relationship whereby Andean raw materials remained the region's primary export. The US drug industry depended on an array of Latin American basic supplies: "Important items from Latin America include cinchona bark for quinine; ipecac, valuable for its alkaloid emetine; stramonium, an important substitute for belladonna and also a valuable source of scopolamine; coca leaves for cocaine; fish livers for vitamins, glandulars (thyroid, pancreas, and so on); and cocoa beans, of which the shells and residue are important for the production of caffeine."[36] This was a phenomena exacerbated by the war, but had historical roots in the impact of the 1931 Geneva Convention, which the Peruvian minister of finance and commerce complained had cut Peru's share of the international cocaine market from 40–50 percent to as low as 3–4 percent.[37] In 1940 the Peruvian commercial attaché appealed to the Federal Bureau of Narcotics, which had "the power to determine from which states US firms could buy raw material and to which countries American manufacturers could export," to authorize more US companies to import

EUROPE

40% of world production
1433 lbs cocaine
France 653 lbs
UK 441 lbs
Switzerland 194 lbs
Czechoslovakia 141 lbs
Finland 4 lbs

100% of world production
Coca leaf "flavoring extract"^

USA

56% of world production
2,070 lbs cocaine

Colombia

1.5 % of world production
210 tons of coca leaves
100% consumed domestically

Perú

60% of world production
8,000 tons of coca leaves
95% consumed domestically/regionally
3% exported to the United States
2% exported to Europe as
crude cocaine

Bolivia

38% of world production
5,000 tons of coca leaves
100% consumed
domestically/regionally

Ⓥ Coca leaf cultivator

⊙ Cocaine manufacturer*

🍾 Coca-Cola flavoring extract manufacturer

* the remaining 4% was produced by other countries
^ Quantities are unavailable as proprietary information of the Coca-Cola Company
Source: The market statistics are based on indicative, although rough and incomplete,
estimates for 1946 as published in the UN's *Report on the Commission of Enquiry
on the Coca Leaf, May 1950* and the annual reports of the Permanent Central Opium Board.

1946

S.Araya, 2013

MAP 1. Coca leaf cultivation and derivative manufacturing, 1946.

Peruvian coca leaves.[38] The FBN rejected the request and refused to grant any new import licenses on the grounds that it would make drug control more difficult, in effect a justification for maintaining a US manufacturing monopoly. It also dangled a thinly veiled threat by suggesting the United States had already done Peru a favor by ending a Department of Agriculture project to grow coca in Puerto Rico so as to "prevent upsetting the economic status between the United States and Peru." This project, the FBN official noted, could be easily resumed.[39]

The war only strengthened the international drug manufacturing hierarchy the United States sought to entrench. Thus, when Peruvian Minister of Finance David Dasso argued in 1942 that Peru should manufacture its own cocaine for the US market and proposed that the United States "should buy cocaine instead of the cocoa [*sic*] leaf from Peru since processing the leaf for cocaine was a relatively simple matter," he was resoundingly rejected.[40] In response to Peruvian efforts to expand access to the US market, the State Department declared, "It would seem the answer to Mr. Dasso should be that it is up to Peru to make the concessions, not the United States." This claim was backed by the US accusation that any increase in Peruvian drug manufacturing "would merely go into the illegal trade," which at the time was defined as a willingness to "sell illegally to Germany and Italy, which are in desperate need of cocaine." Characterizing Peruvian export practice—meeting an acknowledged medical need (and hence Axis country strategic import)—as "illegal," the State Department reframed an economic and political struggle into a language and practice of delineating (and ultimately prosecuting) criminality. The United States even threatened to cut "Peru off from all sources of narcotic drugs" and "stop its purchases of coca leaves" to force Peruvian compliance.[41] Thus the United States was able to use its economic and political leverage to entrench a particular economic order that incorporated a definition of criminality premised on political loyalties.

But the US government also made some concessions. The US-Peru Trade Agreement, signed in May 7, 1942, lowered the import duty on coca, increasing profits for Peruvian exporters. When the FBN complained about this loss of tax revenue (a key component of its budget), the Treasury Department explained, "there were overpowering considerations from the point of view of policy which guided the Committee in approving the concession."[42] As this episode shows, profit was not measured exclusively in economic terms; the United States also sought to maintain control over the drug trade to secure the political stability of its trading partners and establish the long-term alignment of Latin American countries like Peru with the United States.

Drug control then had multifaceted value: at once economic, medical, and diplomatic. At the most basic level it promised to supply or obstruct the flow of medicinally valuable pharmaceuticals in the context of a widespread spike in demand generated by war. Cocaine, for example, was valued in part as an unparalleled local anesthetic. When Peruvian exporter Andrés Soberón's crude cocaine stocks began to accumulate with the loss of access to the Italian and German markets, he invoked the drug's wartime medical value in his failed bid to the US State Department and the FBN to sell his semirefined drug to the United States for further refining: "Cocaine is indispensable for attending to those injured in the War and we are sure, based on letters we've received from Europe, that in Russia and all European countries there is a great demand for this product."

Soberón appealed on behalf of the war-injured, even while making an economic entreaty by suggesting this Peruvian-US trade would enhance the capacity of the United States to meet European and Russian "demand." The United States was adamant in its refusal to import Peruvian crude cocaine, although it did flex its diplomatic muscle and offer to put Soberón in touch with interested buyers in the "Government of the Soviet Socialist republics."[43] A year later, Soberón expanded his appeal through an invocation of the trade's importance for maintaining hemispheric solidarity: "[W]ishing to contribute to the defense of America, I offer 600 kilos of crude cocaine." Again his request was rejected.[44]

The war augmented US power in the international drug trade, and officials did not need to circumvent or renegotiate the national drug regulatory framework's long-term orientation toward protecting the interests of US manufacturers. This was especially true in relation to the coca leaf and cocaine market. The United States continued to import coca leaves from Peru, despite shunning Peruvian crude cocaine. Peru remained the "principal source" of US imports of coca leaves and the war boosted the volume of this trade.[45] In March 1942, one week after the Japanese conquest of Java, the commissioner of the FBN gave an update on the state of the coca market: "As you know, coca leaves, an important defense material, are used in the production of cocaine, a narcotic drug which is indispensable in the treatment of diseases and injuries to the eyes. No substitute for cocaine has yet been discovered."

Anslinger wrote that despite the war-caused disruptions to Merck's supply of coca leaves, "We now obtain from Peru a quantity of coca

TABLE I   US COCA LEAF IMPORTS AND USES, 1936–1943 *(in kilograms)*

	Peru		Java (Dutch)	Bolivia
	Cocaine	Coca-Cola	Cocaine	Cocaine
1936	67,607.416	69,533.820	34,248.398	—
1937	67,372.775	88,213.869	34,012.587	—
1938	67,042.560	107,540.455	33,999.660	—
1939	67,037.931	140,676.296	56,100.499	—
1940	67,817.004	206,011.141	78,372.399	—
1941	67,463.968	292,950.105	59,974.825	—
1942	67,911.549	270,806.401	21,849.974	87.997
1943	207,408.941	239,987.450	—	—

SOURCE: The table was compiled with information from the cited correspondence, supplemented by statistics provided in US Treasury Department, Bureau of Narcotics, *Traffic in Opium and Other Dangerous Drugs for the Year ended December 31, 1936–1943* (Washington, DC: US Government Printing Office, 1937–1944).

NOTE: 1942 was the last year of any reported imports from Java, the small amount of coca leaves imported from Bolivia that year were most likely for research, and the remarkable increase in the quantity of cocaine on hand in 1943 seems to correspond with Maywood halting destruction of the alkaloid in the process of manufacturing a flavoring extract for Coca-Cola.

leaves sufficient to replace the amount formerly imported from Java." As with the government-directed accumulation of other raw materials deemed valuable to war mobilization, and even though it anticipated "no shortage for the duration of the war," the FBN authorized the expansion of coca leaf stockpiling. Anslinger reported, "The Bureau of Narcotics has instructed Maywood Chemical Works to recover all of the raw cocaine obtained from coca leaves." In other words, even though existing stocks of raw materials could easily meet normal annual demand for medicinal cocaine, the FBN authorized Maywood to stop destroying cocaine alkaloid extracted in the process of making a flavoring extract for Coca-Cola. In this striking move, the United States invoked wartime necessity to stockpile quantities that exceeded the annual quotas it was entitled to hold under the 1931 Geneva Convention, and tapped large supplies of coca leaves that were easily accessible because of the "special" status Maywood's leaves had been granted under the international treaty. The raw cocaine that could be obtained from these leaves imported for the express purpose of manufacturing a soft-drink flavoring extract, Anslinger reported, amounted to "approximately four times the normal medical needs of the country."[46]

As raw material stockpiles began to accumulate, this reserve supply of drugs put the United States in a powerful economic and political

TABLE 2 COCAINE EXPORTS FROM THE
UNITED STATES, 1936–1941 *(in grams)*

Year	Cocaine Export
1936	21,733
1937	17,350
1938	14,184
1939	29,509
1940	18,695
1941	144,405
Total	245,876

SOURCE: The table was compiled with information from the cited correspondence, supplemented by statistics provided in US Treasury Department, Bureau of Narcotics, *Traffic in Opium and Other Dangerous Drugs for the Year ended December 31, 1936–1942* (Washington, DC: US Government Printing Office, 1937–1943). Prices also increased as supplies became scarce: "Normally the price of cocaine has been between 40 and 50 dollars a kilogram. However, due to demand from Germany, Italy and Great Britain, prices being paid since the middle of 1940 have ranged between 75 and 80 dollars a kilogram." Greenup to Secretary of State, Embassy, Lima, December 4, 1941, Dispatch No. 2305; File 0660 Peru, Folder 1, 1926–1941; 71-A-3554; DEA; RG 170; NACP.

NOTE: These statistics were no longer published by the FBN after 1942 in the interest of "national defense."

position as the major world-supplier of cocaine. US manufacturers replaced European producers in the world market, and US cocaine exports increased dramatically. By 1941 US exports had increased by more than 600 percent over quantities exported just five years earlier. Before officially declaring war, the United States had been "manufacturing a large quantity of cocaine for Russia on the Lend-Lease program."[47] By 1944, as Anslinger testified before Congress, the United States was supplying "Russia with all her cocaine needs, both for military and civilian use, because Russia has been separated from her market. We have supplied Russia and India and a number of parts of the British Empire, and in the case of India, we have received in turn an equivalent amount of opium. We insisted upon that to keep from dipping into our reserves too deeply. We have been able to give this help. Now we are confronted with supplying some of the liberated territories."[48]

The international consumer market for American-manufactured pharmaceuticals expanded considerably as US officials worked with private companies to "help" fill a drug vacuum in Europe, the Soviet

Union (USSR), and colonial markets formerly supplied by the British Empire. This was true not only with regards to cocaine, but also in relation to another exceptional coca-derived commodity: Coca-Cola.

Wartime drug control provided an opportunity for select US corporations with an investment in the coca market, such as Merck, Maywood, and the Coca-Cola Company, to align themselves closely with the interests of the US government and benefit from the collaboration. Much as government intervention prevented the importation of crude cocaine into the United States, when the Peruvian commercial chancellor tried to offer the Coca-Cola Company "de-narcotized" coca for sale, the company's president contacted the head of the FBN, suggesting that Peruvian interest in the market might be exploited to pressure for compliance with "international control authorities."[49] Coca-Cola, the drink itself, became officially allied with the national cause. Following Pearl Harbor Robert Woodruff, the head of the Coca-Cola Company, declared that all men in uniform could get Coca-Cola for five cents wherever they were serving. With a Coca-Cola executive appointed to the sugar rationing board, by 1942, "Coca-Cola was exempt from sugar rationing when sold to the military or retailers serving soldiers," while the rest of the soft drink industry was forced to reduce their consumption. Helping to fulfill Woodruff's promise, sixty-four Coca-Cola bottling plants were established "on every continent except Antarctica" during the war, largely subsidized by the US government. Coca-Cola representatives were given the status of "technical observers"—civilians servicing the military—while the army paid for the transportation costs of Coca-Cola and for military technicians who helped construct Coca-Cola plants for the deployed troops. German and Japanese prisoners of war were even assigned to work in these newly constructed bottling plants.[50] The collaboration between the United States and companies supplying American troops on the battlefront was accompanied by an equally striking government program to capitalize on wartime disruptions in neutral countries far from the battlefront. Nowhere was this more apparent than in US efforts to promote the expansion of its pharmaceutical industries into Latin America.

WARTIME MARKET DISRUPTIONS

The war-wrought transformations in the circulation and flow of raw materials destined for North American and European pharmaceutical manufacturers produced fundamental disruptions in the flow of finished drugs. The impact on Germany was particularly dramatic. The world's longest established and most profitable pharmaceutical industry could not acquire drug raw materials, had its industrial production under attack, and confronted US economic warfare campaigns against Germany's drug production and distribution networks in neutral and Allied territories. Entering the war, Germany dominated the international drug market, including an impressive presence in the Western Hemisphere. While Germany trailed behind England and the United States as the third "major trading partner with South America," the country was the region's largest supplier of pharmaceuticals.[51] A report to the secretary general of the League of Nations in 1943 noted the wartime dramatic shift in pharmaceutical manufacturing clout. "Germany, the chief distributor of drugs before the war, now exports only insignificant quantities of narcotic drugs."[52] By the end of the war American military assessments were more blunt. "German Pharmacy Kaput!" reported the Chief of the Medical Branch, US Strategic Bombing Survey after reviewing the impact of bombing on the infrastructure of the once globally dominant German pharmaceutical industry.[53]

Early in the war, however, German dominance of the drug trade was a serious cause for concern. Writer and investigative journalist Charles Morrow Wilson lamented in 1942 that unlike American businessmen, the "Germans took pains to capture Latin-American markets for legitimate medicines and pharmaceuticals" during the first half of the twentieth century. "Even during the war years of 1939, 1940, and 1941 the German position has been maintained. Actually the Nazis have been making use of their drug trade with South America to provide a source of revenue for propaganda and fifth column activity."[54] These frustrations and fears echoed those expressed by US officials dispatched to South America in December 1941 under the auspices of the newly constituted Board of Economic Warfare (BEW). The "entire Latin American economy was part of [the BEW's] concern" because, as the director of the Council on Foreign Relations explained, the region was "a storehouse of strategic raw materials."[55] However, agents rapidly discovered that while Latin American countries for the most part were willing to cooperate with US economic warfare initiatives in the region, they encountered significant obstacles when it came to limiting the flow of German pharmaceuticals. As the US ambassador to Bolivia confided to the Secretary of State in 1943, "Indeed, it is likely that the failure to eliminate the Nazi dominance in the drug field will assist Nazi interests to continue to have their way in other commercialized fields in which they remain powerful."[56]

Whatever success the United States achieved by dominating the drug raw materials market was undermined by its inability to dominate the consumer market for finished goods. As nations battled to control the flow of the world's resources, raw materials and manufactured goods together constituted the critical inputs for maintaining overall societal health; both production and consumption mattered to this equation. Government planners embraced an economic calculus premised on balancing "the allocation of manpower and raw materials" in the service of war. The economic reasoning constituted an ideology that viewed humans and natural resources together as the raw material inputs to national power, and their healthy presence needed to be sustained for profit and national security. In the United States, before the war was over, "the nation's economic machinery had been reorganized throughout, from the acquisition of materials to the final distribution of the end-products among our armed forces, our allies, and our civilians." And to ensure a healthy flow of material inputs, as the US military explained, "it became necessary for us to exercise a stabilizing influence on the domestic economies of countries most affected, particularly in Latin America."[57] Thus economic warfare in the Andes grew out of this grand imperial vision where rivalries between the United States and Germany in the drug field were driven by the value these commodities held for cultivating human and natural resources in the global competition for national dominance.

The war marked a major economic turning point with the United States emerging as a net importer rather than exporter of raw materials.[58] While the United States had always cultivated a hegemonic economic position in the Western Hemisphere, the war provided an unprecedented stimulus to trade when the conflict disrupted the flow of raw materials from Southeast Asia. As one observer commented, "we *must* have tropical products to win the war and to keep the peace . . . [which means] we are seeing the birth of an entirely new inter-American economy."[59] The *Nation's Business* echoed this sentiment: "War needs of the United States have speeded up production in the South American countries . . . [and] we will help in adjusting the national economics of those which responded to the war effort."[60] Some saw the US effort to mold Latin American economic development toward US priorities as potentially coercive and unwelcome: "We must beware of the temptation to convert hemispheric defense into a new streamlined imperialism."[61] However, this did not slow the economic war, as the desire to undermine German power became firmly tied to the long-term development objectives of the United States in the hemisphere.

Battles over the drug trade in the Andes were waged in the context of the overall importance of these economies to the war effort. At the beginning of the war Bolivia and Peru had significant economic ties to both the Allied and Axis powers. As the United Nations would later report, "Before World War II there were substantial investments in Peru owned by German, Italian and, to a smaller extent, Japanese nationals." However, by the end of the war, "the only substantial foreign business investments" belonged to the United States and Great Britain. Even before the war US investments exceeded German, Italian, and Japanese investments, and by 1935 the US mining company Cerro de Pasco Copper was "by far the largest foreign-owned mining concern in Peru." The United States was the primary source of capital behind Peru's mining industry, which accounted for 20 percent of world production. More than half of the total labor force worked for foreign-owned companies, and Cerro de Pasco alone accounted for over a third of the total, producing "more than half the metallic mineral output of the country."[62] In an overview of its raw materials policy in Peru, the US military even drew a comparison with the British Empire's monopoly over tin production in Thailand, noting that in addition to domestic production the United States was intimately involved in the "commercial control over production in other countries" such as the Vanadium Corporation of America, which controlled almost "the entire Peruvian output" of the steel alloy.[63]

In Bolivia "the basis of the country's economy was tin mining."[64] Before WWI, the "Germans [had] acquired a virtual monopoly in several branches of commerce and had made themselves almost indispensable to the economic life of the country." Yet like Peru, the United States was also a formidable power in Bolivia before the war. The Bolivian tin mining industry was the main source of internal tax revenue in the country and the largest company, Patiño Mines and Enterprises, Inc., registered in the United States and financed by US capital, was responsible for 40–45 percent of the national output. Prices for Bolivian tin, which accounted for three quarters of the country's exports, suffered during the Great Depression. "Foreign exchange receipts decreased sharply," and increasing national debts acquired from "substantial borrowing abroad . . . practically all of it from the United States" placed the United States in a position of considerable economic influence. Tin prices recovered throughout the 1930s and shot up further during World War II. In 1940 the United States negotiated a five-year tin contract with Bolivian tin producers, and secured the country's entire output of tungsten and surpluses of antimony, tin, and zinc.[65]

US investments in Bolivia and Peru in extracting antinomy, tungsten, tin, quinine, rubber, and petroleum were heavily influenced by the logic of economic warfare. When American policymakers devised wartime economic policy in the region, ensuring the conditions necessary to sustain these industries was paramount. For instance in Bolivia the United States launched public health programs that specifically targeted rubber and quinine producing regions in the hopes of maintaining a healthy workforce to extract resources essential for US war making.[66] As the Bolivian ambassador to the United States explained, "Tin and rubber were needed for planes and tanks; the factories producing cannons and ammunition needed Bolivian tungsten; and other commodities, mainly foodstuffs for American soldiers, were required. In this way, the manual work of the Bolivian Indians of the Andes suddenly acquired a transcendental dimension for the life and the defense of that great nation."

Minerals including tin, antimony, and tungsten accounted for 98.3 percent of the country's exports, and demand for such metals was "always large during war periods."[67] Bolivia possessed the only hemispheric source of tin and, spurred by war-induced global tin shortages, the United States built a tin smelter specifically for Bolivian ores.[68] Before the war the British had been the primary smelters of Bolivian tin, which they then sold to the United States. The war facilitated the emergence of a US smelting industry and the end of American dependence on British manufacturers.[69] During the war the United States became the sole purchaser of Bolivian minerals, replacing the United Kingdom as Bolivia's primary tin export market, which gave the United States considerable diplomatic leverage particular since wartime US stockpiling meant "that market power had shifted decisively from producers to consumers." While there were rumblings among Bolivian nationalists (particularly strong among the mine-workers organizations) that the "country had become a virtual colony of the United States," Bolivian officials also sought to capitalize on their newfound importance.[70] The BEW mission reported in December 1941 that "Bolivian authorities feel that since Bolivia is contributing to the defense effort by making available vitally important minerals, it is a responsibility of the United States Government to see to it that the mining industry (eighty percent of Bolivia's import needs) is promptly provided with whatever equipment may be necessary."[71] As the Bolivian ambassador emphasized to his US colleagues, the Indian mine worker "was a true soldier of the cause, whose function ran parallel to that of the soldiers who fought in the trenches, defending the ideals and interests of the Allies."[72]

Such appeals gained traction in the wake of what came to be known as the Cataví Massacre in December 1942, when a tin miners' strike demanding "better housing, wages and medical care" was violently repressed by the government, leaving many dead.[73] Historian Laurence Whitehead suggests American officials saw their subsequent intervention as "Good Neighborly" rather than imperial, when they determined that "labor peace in the mines was of urgent concern for those in charge of Allied procurement" and helped organize an investigation headed by a Joint US-Bolivian Labor Commission.[74] The Assistant Secretary of State invited Judge Calvert Magruder to chair the commission, describing its goal as being the "double end of improving conditions of labor in Bolivia and assuring a steady production of strategic materials for the United States."[75] The investigators found the "standard of living is notoriously low" among the mine workers and recommended changes in labor policy, which ultimately led to the insertion of labor clauses into the US tin contract. The report also noted one raw material input (coca leaves) that might be a contributing factor to the paltry conditions: "These leaves contain a small amount of cocaine and their chewing is claimed to deaden sensory nerves, quiet hunger pains, temporarily stimulate energy, increase the power of endurance, but do constitute a degenerating force that markedly reduces efficiency."[76] The issue was set aside as something needing further study (and would be taken up after the war by the United Nations), but the problem of labor efficiency and its dependence on healthy consumption was of central concern to US officials, and the circulation of drugs—deemed healthy or harmful— became central to questions of national security.

In this way, the war highlighted the already intimate connection between the mining and pharmaceutical industries. Increasingly a vital part of sustaining the "transcendental" contribution of Bolivian Indians to the war effort entailed steady supplies of pharmaceuticals. For instance, as part of a Bolivian effort to secure national benefits in an industry dominated by foreign capital, companies like Patiño Mines were subject to the Bolivian "Mineral Code." The code stated that foreign "mining enterprises employing more than 200 workers and located more than ten kilometers from the nearest town must provide living quarters, health services and food to the workers."[77] A healthy industry required healthy workers, and here Germany's early competitive dominance was stark. In the Andes the mining industry constituted the largest "consumer" market for pharmaceuticals and doctors working for the "large mining companies" continued, despite economic warfare proscriptions, to place orders with German pharmaceutical manufacturers. In January 1942, the US Embassy in La Paz lamented, "Bayer, Merck and Schering products had been specifically requested by the doctors working for these organizations."[78]

ECONOMIC WARFARE AND PUBLIC HEALTH

US economic warfare initiatives encompassed a range of practices including the establishment of a blacklist forbidding trade with people and firms deemed to be enemy nationals or cooperating with the enemy, the preclusive buying of raw materials to prevent them from falling into enemy hands, a system of import and export controls designed to maximize trade in strategic goods, and programs geared toward developing new supplies of raw materials, such as the concerted effort to "revive a practically extinct quinine industry in Latin America" after Japanese military advances cut off Southeast Asian sources of supply.[79] Thus, the BEW pursued two primary goals: weaken the enemy's strategic materials arsenal and financial power, and reorient "Latin America's economic activity . . . toward fulfillment of the war needs of the United States."[80]

In the weeks after Pearl Harbor, the foot soldiers of the BEW traveled through Peru and Bolivia to "familiarize members of the Legation staff with the procedure in Washington for handling Proclaimed List problems."[81] In July 1941, Roosevelt had issued a Presidential Proclamation calling for the compilation of a list of people and firms who directly or indirectly aided the "enemy war machine" and participated in trade "deemed detrimental to the interests of national defense." Between 1941 and 1945 the "Proclaimed List of Certain Blocked Nationals" was compiled and US firms and citizens were prohibited from doing business with those listed. In practice the blacklist impacted many enterprises regardless of national origin if they were accused of doing business deemed detrimental to the "national defense."[82] When the Peruvian minister of finance asked (perhaps nervously, being of Italian ancestry) for clarification on who should be put on the Proclaimed List, the BEW personnel explained it included "persons who, by their action and not by birth and such, were deemed to be nationals of Germany or Italy, and persons whose activities were inimical to the hemisphere as a whole."[83] In the effort to gain Andean cooperation, the United States framed its economic warfare policies as encompassing Axis agents, but also as a broad and flexible category that could target anyone deemed vaguely threatening to hemispheric defense.

While largely successful in relation to securing control over drug raw materials, the United States had a harder time intervening in a consumer market that until the war had been dominated by German drugs. The BEW agents discovered that manufactured drugs constituted a difficult front in US economic warfare initiatives in the Andes. Eliminating German business competition could only be effective if national governments—like Peru and Bolivia—were willing to target companies accused of ties to Axis powers, even if this entailed immediate short supplies of medicines deemed essential to public health and the smooth running of the countries' economies. The goal of implementing the Proclaimed List in the Andes was complicated further by the fact that as of mid-1942, US pharmaceutical manufacturers had not yet extensively penetrated the South American market. Drug diplomacy therefore cut both ways. As public health was increasingly seen as a component of national security, allies like Peru could invoke the public interest to resist limitations on their trade with German manufacturers until "legitimate" substitutes could be provided. The Peruvian government refused to prevent the distribution of German and Italian "pharmaceuticals and medicinals," and insisted an exception to the implementation of the US vision for economic warfare made sense "for such operations as might be necessary in the interest of public health and sanitation."[84] As late as February 1943, the US Embassy reported that the Peruvian government refused to cut off foreign exchange to German distributors "until we can supply American products to take the place of German preparations."[85]

Similarly the US Embassy in La Paz reported its failure "to convince the Bolivian Government" to deny Proclaimed List nationals foreign exchange or to prevent the distribution of their drugs. The reason "that such efforts have so far proved fruitless is due, at least in part, to the fact the Germans control the drug trade in Bolivia and continue to import products essential to the country." Cutting off foreign exchange to German importers would mean that the "country's economy would be most seriously harmed."[86] By June 1942, German drug distribution had been disrupted by naval blockades and the closure of German Bayer and Schering drug firms in Brazil.[87] And yet, as in Peru, by early 1943, "no replacement sources have appeared." The US Embassy wrote explaining the gravity of the situation to the State Department: "The present drug situation is therefore most serious to Bolivia, as an absolute shortage of necessary drug products is dangerous to the general health of the country; and to the further prosecution of economic warfare policies because any dislocation of economy due to the war is immediately blamed upon the United States."

Drugs had become critical to "national health" and critical symbols of the potential abuses and limits of US power. The US Embassy lamented, "German interests can effectively force the Bolivian Government to grant them the financial and other facilities they need."[88] The US government concluded: "in addition to being a matter concerning Bolivia's public health, pharmaceutical products become a most important weapon of economic warfare."[89] Three months later, pharmaceuticals still remained the "knotty segment of the supply problem."[90]

Two key objectives emerged in US drug warfare initiatives in the Andes.[91] The first was the push for Latin American implementation of sanctions against Proclaimed List businesses involved in the drug trade. The second, a necessary accompaniment to the first, was the concerted effort to ensure a reliable replacement supply of US-manufactured drugs. The challenge was formidable as new agencies within the US government jockeyed for control over the program, as American drug companies had not yet penetrated the region, and as regional governments resisted taking action until public health (and by extension, economic production) was guaranteed. In his study of economic warfare and the pharmaceutical industry, historian Graham D. Taylor emphasizes bureaucratic wrangling between the State Department and the BEW as generating enormous inefficiency.[92] In fact battles between the secretary of commerce and the vice president over delays in acquiring Latin American sources of quinine led President Roosevelt to dissolve the BEW in 1943 and replace it with the Office of Economic Warfare under new leadership.[93] Despite the infighting, there was considerable agreement on the value of drugs to national security and a shared belief in the need for US intervention in nations across the hemisphere on this account. Government officials and pharmaceutical businessmen also reportedly shared skepticism "about the commercial benefits of contributing to local chemical manufacturing development in Latin America."[94] The program had to be driven by expanding both supply and demand for US-manufactured drugs.

To overcome these obstacles, staff at US embassies in the Andes worked with local governments and businesses to assess drug requirements and asked US pharmaceutical firms to compile and disseminate lists of comparable American drugs.[95] Drug control brought together commercial and strategic interests while creating a network of public and private collaborators. The BEW mission reported, "Our whole program depended upon getting good commercial intelligence," and informed the US commercial attaché in Peru that "he should use every means to get commercial information."[96] This "commercial intelligence" helped the United States gauge demand for pharmaceutical products and implement what it termed a "Drug Replacement Program," a strategy to replace Axis products with US-manufactured drugs. Embodying a logic that continued to shape international drug regulation, it was not the chemical substance itself that made a drug desirable or undesirable, but rather the political and economic affiliations of its manufacturer. Obtaining information about national essential drug requirements was critical to the program since governments were hesitant to cut off German suppliers of pharmaceuticals until the United States was able to provide "Allied" goods—the very same drugs—as substitutes. While it began as a program initiated during the war, this market reconnaissance strengthened the US government's desire and capacity to facilitate the ongoing expansion of US corporations into those markets.

On the Andean government side, the US commercial attaché suggested that the Peruvian Ministry of Finance create a "Commercial Department" to facilitate "greater oversight and control over stocks of drug commodities and their distribution." As of January 1942, this new department "now has a staff of approximately sixteen men who are devoting all their time to gathering information on essential requirements, stocks, prices and related matters." But as they began their work, US representatives complained the estimates they provided were "greatly exaggerated and that the investigating and analytical ability of the Commercial Department is not high." Believing the capacities of US personnel to be superior, and perhaps as a way of gaining greater access to information, the BEW successfully suggested that a US officer "be placed in the Commercial Department not just to advise with but in reality to organize and direct its work."[97] By March 1943 US economic warfare objectives were gaining ground in Peru, although German-manufactured drugs continued to circulate. The Peruvian government remained unwilling to shut down German drug distribution, but did help the United States gather commercial intelligence to facilitate the replacement program. A Supreme Decree required reports from all government agencies to determine essential drug requirements and medicinal needs, and instituted a system of controls to track stock quantities and direct distribution.[98] The Peruvian Ministry of Public Health also delivered product sales information for various Proclaimed List firms, which the US Embassy handed over to US business interests. Despite these efforts some imports of Axis pharmaceuticals persisted until as late as

November 1943.[99] There was no law requiring the private sector to report its drug stocks, and the US Embassy remained frustrated in its efforts to "ascertain the present inventories in Peru of German Drugs."[100]

This type of collaboration was harder in Bolivia. There too the United States believed essential requirement figures were "grossly exaggerated," but unlike in Peru, the BEW lamented, "There is no American community on whom the Legation can rely for help."[101] In a panicked plea to expedite licensing of US drug shipments, an embassy official wrote the State Department in January 1943: "Scarcity of American pharmaceutical products in Bolivia reaching critical stage."[102] However, by April, the embassy in La Paz had a more optimistic assessment of the prospects for economic warfare coordination. Following a brief tour of the US Vice President through the region in an effort to shore up hemispheric solidarity, US Ambassador Henry Ramsey was confident: "It appears almost certain that Bolivia will declare war and if it does we should move quickly to present a comprehensive [drug] replacement program before the country's initial and belligerent enthusiasm abates."

The very next day, April 7, 1943, Bolivia officially declared war on Germany. Viewing war "enthusiasm" as a boon to US objectives, Ramsey went on to suggest that the financial aspects have to be handled "before we will have much bargaining power on the matter of adequate control." To that end, he recommended the Export-Import Bank finance a Bolivian subsidiary bank to fund the drug replacement program, setting aside government funds to help US pharmaceutical firms distribute in the Bolivian market. The campaign to finance the replacement program was taken up by the Bolivian Development Corporation (BDC), established in 1943 to stabilize the Bolivian national economy through US-Bolivian financial arrangements. The BDC was governed by a board, half of whom, including the president and vice president, were appointed by the Bolivian government and the other half, including the manager and assistant manager, by the Export-Import Bank in Washington. In a letter addressed to the US vice president seeking support for the bank proposal they explained, "[The BDC's] most effective field of action lies in the program of economic warfare through which the democracies are attempting to eliminate the financial potency of commercial and industrial interests inimical to the democratic cause throughout the Hemisphere." The BDC, invoking hemispheric solidarity, wanted to be able to "finance Bolivian firms" so that they might take the business of "distributing merchandise throughout Bolivia out of Axis hands and return it to Bolivians."[103]

The United States was especially concerned that Proclaimed List firms were able to continue to operate by using intermediaries to disguise, or "cloak," Axis involvement. As the United States pursued its replacement programs, dispatches continued to lament German use of business intermediaries. For instance, in November 1943 the US Embassy in Lima notified the State Department that a known "cloak for Schering interests" was importing drugs into Peru.[104] In contrast, national affiliation with the United States offered legitimacy in a context where US economic warfare policies drew the line between legal and illegal participation within the economy, and by extension delineated the legal and illegal status of drugs from various origins. The embassy asked Washington for US corporations to devise a list of medicines to replace "undesirable brands" with the "names of American, British and other acceptable equivalents" as a necessary step "prior to the initiation of an offensive against these products."[105] Not only did the promotion of a "national" identity for a drug collapse the international supply networks of raw materials into the ideological property of "national" manufacturers but also, as a consequence, these manufacturers became key players in the field. The most readily available source of US pharmaceuticals necessary to replace German product lines were those manufactured by former subsidiaries of German firms in the United States, most of which had been severed from the parent company after World War I and transformed—via national affiliations—into legitimate, newly "American" companies.

In response to these worries about a German "cloak for Schering interests," the State Department and US Embassy in Lima coordinated efforts to pass on information regarding the annual Peruvian importation of Schering's drug products to its former US subsidiary: Schering Inc., based in Bloomfield, Indiana. The embassy deemed the information "particularly timely and helpful to it in adjusting its production and sales program to the needs of Peru."[106] These efforts clearly showed a process of criminalizing certain economic participants and select proprietary drugs premised on political and economic affiliations. To prevent German Schering from operating through "cloaks," US Schering, a national "cloak" of sorts, was called upon to intervene. A similar policy was pursued in Bolivia. The embassy there notified the US secretary of state in 1943, "From the standpoint of enforcement of Economic Warfare policies, and realizing that the outright expropriation of German Drug interests is impractical at the present time, the only way to overcome the [Bolivian] Government's inertia and to obtain the desired cooperation, is to actively encourage and increase the export of ethical products by United States Drug concerns. . . . Any comprehensive plan in this direction would necessarily also include an increase in exports of the American controlled Merck, Schering and other companies."[107]

Expropriation reflected one wartime tactic for undermining the enemy's economic power, a process that had already transformed both US-based drug houses, Merck and Schering, into legitimate drug providers. The effort to extend the distribution network of US pharmaceutical companies' products (including "ethical" drugs, a contemporary term for drugs that required a doctor's prescription to purchase) reflected another.

US economic warfare initiatives depended on US collaboration with Andean governments, but also on US government and business coordination. The largest obstacle the BEW confronted was the failure of American firms to supply the adequate quantity of legal substitute drugs or "acceptable equivalents." As the US Embassy in Bolivia reported, "The general lack of interest in the Bolivian market which is being shown by American exporters of drugs and pharmaceutical supplies is encouraging continued purchase of German products of this nature." The embassy repeatedly observed that the efforts of Bolivian importers to do business with US firms were thwarted by American pharmaceutical houses "not interested in the Bolivian market."[108] And the lack of American drug replacements undermined US efforts to exert pressure on Andean governments to comply with economic warfare initiatives: "As the [State] Department is aware the Embassy has been promising local merchants an acceptable product to replace German drugs for some time and the Embassy's failure to do so is becoming increasingly embarrassing as the available supply of German drugs dwindle."[109]

To deal with this problem, the embassy called for government intervention and asked the State Department to put pressure on US drug companies to distribute their products as a wartime imperative.[110] The government's outline for overcoming the drug replacement problem seemed to be a combination of a business plan and a national security directive:

1. That American pharmaceutical firms be induced as a patriotic duty to enter the Bolivian market.

2. That American firms already having representatives in Bolivia change to representatives who will push their products.

3. That the Board of Economic Warfare, War Production Board, and War Shipping Administration be shown the critical importance of American pharmaceutical products to the economy of Bolivia and to the economic warfare of the United States, so that provision may be made for shipments of these commodities.[111]

Behind such economic appeals to "patriotic duty" lay the coercive capacity of the state. Just before the formal US declaration of war, the State Department had issued its "Instructions of September 20, 1941," amended on December 13, 1941 after Pearl Harbor, that set out a standard of conduct for US firms that instructed them to stop doing business with Proclaimed List firms and warned them that "strict compliance with such standard was required." The BEW mission brought these "Instructions" with them to the Andes and gave them to US embassies for distribution to "All American concerns." The State Department asked to be kept informed of US companies not cooperating with economic warfare policy, explaining the government was in a "position to exercise a number of sanctions against any American concerns not cooperating."[112]

The US government could force US businesses to comply with economic warfare initiatives; however, there was in fact a considerable degree of collaboration between the government and the private sector in implementing the pharmaceutical replacement program in the Andes. This collaboration came in a number of forms. The US government worked with other governments and industry players in the Andes and the United States to compile lists detailing national medicinal needs, current drug stocks, and competitors' products and delivered this "commercial intelligence" to American pharmaceutical companies.[113] To improve US drug distribution networks, for instance, the government distributed to US manufacturers a list of "firms, organizations, and individuals," including government offices, the Pan-American Sanitary Bureau, and the Peruvian military, that were "interested in importing drugs and pharmaceuticals from the United States."[114] When US firms refused to work with distributors who also handled competitors' products, the embassy tried to get more local distributors to enter the market (in striking contrast to the comparable refusal to diversify drug importers on the US end).[115] Fostering business relations between American and Andean firms was paired with coordination among agencies of the US government. The BEW and the State Department together tracked reductions in German drug sales and kept US companies abreast of increased demand. Government agencies also expedited licensing and drug shipments to tackle the replacement problem.

American companies also coordinated with one another to advance US economic warfare initiatives. In Bolivia, one of the oldest US merchant businesses in South America, WR Grace, offered to transport Parke, Davis & Company drug products to parts of the country where they traveled for their own business. As WR Grace representatives explained, they were "happy to haul" pharmaceuticals "if such would aid the replacement program."[116] Pharmaceutical companies also worked to expand drug sales by cultivating ties with local physicians. Parke, Davis & Co., for instance, hired a "resident representative . . . [for the] sole purpose of acquainting the medical profession with Parke, Davis products," and the US Embassy prodded other US pharmaceutical houses to do the same: "American manufacturers of ethicals will be encouraged to compile and distribute such compendiums . . . [in] Bolivia and other Latin American countries."[117]

These public programs and policies were paired with more covert levels of collaboration between business and government officials. The United States gathered intelligence through business contacts acting as undercover agents across Latin America. Even before the United States officially entered the war, US businessmen had access to extensive market information that they shared with the government.[118] For example, in 1940, responding to a request from the Federal Bureau of Narcotics, Maywood provided information about the state of the coca industry in Peru, including statistics on quantities of cocaine exported as well as a list of cocaine manufacturers in the country.[119] After the BEW's initiative began, these business intelligence networks were more aggressively used. As an expression of his "loyalty to this country," Maywood's Peruvian supplier began providing the company with information on businessmen in the region, and Maywood in turn passed the information on to the US government to facilitate the implementation of the Proclaimed List.[120] The government actively coordinated these covert intelligence-gathering efforts, as recommendations made by the Board of Economic Warfare made clear: "To handle the job effectively for the whole country, however, at least two experienced Spanish-speaking American business-men should be employed for field investigation. It is suggested that these men ostensibly retain their private positions as representatives of American business so that their moving about the country unobtrusively will be facilitated."

These "undercover agents" were only one part of a much larger "corps of unofficial observers" culled from "friendly firms" who monitored Proclaimed List matters for the US government.[121] All of these sites of public and private collaborations ultimately placed the US government and pharmaceutical industry in a decisive position to capitalize on the drug trade and the regulatory principles and powers that traveled with it in the war's aftermath.

SCENE SET FOR DRUG CONTROL

The experience on the ground in Peru and Bolivia during the war served as a laboratory for US-promoted drug control policies around the world. By the end of the war, the economic warfare policies had effectively squeezed German-manufactured pharmaceuticals out of the Andean market, replacing them with the more "desirable" US-manufactured equivalents. In Peru, economic warfare policies not only helped US corporations triumph over German business in the realm of pharmaceuticals, but even before the end of the war the United States "ranked in the first place as a supplier of merchandise" and was "by far the principal source of Peruvian imports," while also being the most lucrative export market for Peruvian raw materials.[122] US pharmaceutical companies gained knowledge and access to the Andean market and acquired a preferential trade status for US "pharmaceutical specialties."[123] Bolivia similarly emerged from the war increasingly dependent on exports to the United States, particularly as the price of tin began to drop and Southeast Asian sources of supply returned to the market. Glenn Dorn has described the testy negotiations between the State Department, the Foreign Economic Administration, large mining companies, and the Bolivian government over a new tin contract, where the desire to maintain labor protections was counterbalanced by the power of large mining companies, the sinking price industrial countries were willing to pay, and the vulnerable negotiating position of the Bolivian government (which would subsequently fall in a coup) ever dependent on tin revenues.[124]

By the end of the war there was a huge influx of US drug companies and products into the region.[125] This was concurrent with the implementation in Peru of a drug control apparatus based largely on that advocated by the United States. While Bolivia had no industrial production of pharmaceuticals, Peru's limited output made regulatory oversight of special concern to American officials. In October 3, 1944, the Peruvian government issued a decree "establishing regulations for the control of the sale and distribution of narcotics in pharmaceutical establishments in Peru." The decree followed the system of control already in place in the United States by making physician prescriptions necessary for sales to the public, closely monitoring distribution, and requiring drug manufacturers to notify an inspector general of pharmacy about levels of output.[126] The logic of drug control promoted by the United States clearly had penetrated the upper echelons of the Peruvian government. While expressing enthusiasm for these measures, the United States maintained its desire to limit the Peruvian manufacturing of narcotics, preferring that Peru remain primarily a provider of raw materials. As the Treasury secretary explained to the State Department in 1944, with regard to an anticipated Peruvian government monopoly for the manufacturing of cocaine, "It would be desirable, however, from the American point of view if the monopoly were confined solely to the production and sale of coca leaves and not the production of cocaine."[127] Seeking to maintain the prewar status quo within the coca commodities circuit, the United States continued in its efforts to ensure that Peruvian involvement was limited to the production and sale of raw materials.

The war also facilitated US dominance in drug manufacturing in other ways. For example, in 1944 the US government asked pharmaceutical manufacturers to help organize "intelligence teams" to travel with troops deployed in Europe. The Drug Resources Industry Advisory Committee (established early in the war and led by the executive vice president of AmPharMA) "set up a committee on intelligence objectives" that organized the military-escorted travel of pharmaceutical representatives from Eli Lilly, Winthrop, Abbott, American Cyanamid, and Dow Chemical, among others, through Europe to assess the drug industry and obtain information regarding "formulae, microfilms, samples of products and other data found in captured German plants or obtained from technicians or other personnel of these plants."[128] In this way drug manufacturers benefited from their close ties to the government, gaining privileged access to knowledge of competitors' products and manufacturing processes, while strengthening the collaborative relationship between US drug manufacturers and the government.

The end of the war also brought about the implementation of US drug control policies in the Allied occupied territories, making the US model the de facto global model for the postwar implementation of an "international" control apparatus. As early as February 1944, the US Department of State was encouraging international support for drug control in former Axis territories: "In view of the possibility that after the war there will be an increase in the illicit narcotics traffic and in drug addiction in Europe as there was after the last war, it would seem desirable that consideration be given to the question of effecting complete control over the narcotic drugs in the areas which come under the military or civil authorities of the United Nations."[129]

And indeed among the first steps taken after the war's conclusion, in the US Zone in Germany and the Allied Command in the Pacific, was the "re-establishment of narcotics control." In Germany, the US proposal to establish a Narcotics Control Working Party was adopted to centralize drug control across the four occupied zones. In Japan and South Korea, US occupying authorities established a centralized supervision of narcotics, and the Permanent Central Opium Board (PCOB) (created by the League of Nations) expressed its "appreciation of the initiative taken by the military authorities responsible for Pacific Headquarters, by the Department of State and by the Commissioner of Narcotics of the US in bringing about this desirable result."[130] As the FBN reported, these initiatives extended beyond occupied territory: "We are cooperating with the Civil Affairs Division of the War Department as they go into liberated territories. They are engaged in reestablishing narcotics control and trying to see that the stocks are properly safeguarded and distributed."[131]

As in South America, what this meant was that the United States became the primary supplier of manufactured pharmaceuticals in each of these regions and a guiding force behind the implementation of a drug control and policing apparatus. For instance, since Germany was experiencing an "acute shortage" of narcotics—an effect largely of Allied warfare policies targeting the German drug industry—the United States began increasing its manufacturing output. The Allied Control Authority also began policing the legitimate market and making arrests for drug "violations." These policies were consolidated under the US's proposed Narcotic Control Working Party, which was constituted under the Allied Health Committee of the United Nations.[132]

In Japan, the US instituted an even more dramatic restructuring of the drug manufacturing economy. As the FBN commissioner testified before Congress: "We sent our best narcotic investigators to Japan, at the request of General MacArthur, and we have, in conjunction with the War Department, briefed about 2,000 civil-affairs officers who went out there to shut down the narcotic plants in Japan, in Korea, and Formosa (Taiwan). General MacArthur has ordered a very strict control over drug producing, manufacturing and distributing."[133]

Among the war crimes leveled against Japan would be the charge of drug trafficking. The UN Commission on Narcotic Drugs (CND) in 1947 accused the Japanese of using revenues from the drug trade "to finance the preparation for waging of wars of aggression" and "to establish and finance the puppet governments" under its control. Such charges attest to the politically charged nature of designating legal and illegal participation within the drug market in a context where arguably all major combatants had sought to capitalize on the drug trade to wage war. Yet, to the victors come the spoils. The United Nations demanded the Far East Commission and Allied Military Authorities allow "no production of raw materials *for the purpose of manufacturing narcotic drugs*" in Japan, adding that "the manufacture or conversion of narcotic drugs shall be prohibited." At the same time, the head of the FBN advised stronger controls. Previously, the commissioner explained, there had been "no limitation as to quantities of narcotics drugs they [Japanese manufacturers] could sell and no records or reports of sales was required. There was no governmental supervision of these plants," no licensing, no inspections, and no safeguarding of stocks. However, he assured the assembled delegates that with the Allied Command, "this situation has been corrected by the installation of brick storage vaults, heavy steel doors and dial combination locks." Moreover, the "American Armed Forces in Japan seized . . . crude and finished narcotic drugs" and as of June 19, 1946, there was the "enactment of legislation similar to the American narcotic law which provides for annual registration, monthly reports, sales by means of order forms or prescriptions, et cetera." As in Germany, the grounds of a drug enforcement apparatus were being laid: "Courts are now meting out five-year sentences which inaugurates a new era in narcotic enforcement in Japan."[134]

The United States continued to pursue its drug market regulatory priorities both independently and through multiparty organizations like the newly constituted United Nations. The war forced the two regulatory bodies that had previously been responsible for monitoring international drug control to relocate from Geneva to Washington.[135] The close relationship this facilitated between drug regulators, US officials, and the pharmaceutical industry persisted after the war when the United Nations became the primary vehicle for multilateral efforts to control the international drug trade. Anslinger himself became the first US representative to the CND where he "dominate[d] deliberations" on international drug control.[136] It was no coincidence that one of the first matters of business pursued by the CND was the effort to stamp out (the vast majority of) coca production and consumption in Peru and Bolivia that was not destined for export to North American pharmaceutical houses.[137] Significantly, the designation of illegality within the drug industry was no longer tied to an enemy national, but broadly and flexibly applied to those who participated in the pharmaceutical industry outside of the drug regulatory regime's sanction.

. . .

In the midst of world war, the US government increasingly valued drugs as a cure-all for everything from keeping soldiers out of pain, energized, and ready for battle, to maintaining the health and well-being of the general population. The ability to provision valuable pharmaceuticals bolstered state authority and cultivated loyalty toward the international networks that supplied them—in this context both the United States and the broader Allied cause. The US military victory gave US drug firms an advantage in the global restructuring of the pharmaceutical industry that came about with the defeat of Germany and Japan in WWII. Securing drug supply networks and disrupting Axis access to the market also meant, in part, interfering in national economies of the Western Hemisphere. At the same time, US troop deployments, and the framing of drug procurement and distribution as critical defense issues, gave US firms a global advantage. Control over the flow of commodities and the power to designate legitimate participation within the drug economy were critical tools deployed by the US government in its wartime efforts, which linked winning the war with US economic expansion. As a result of this process, American-manufactured and -branded drugs were substituted for the same chemical compounds produced by Axis firms, and the legitimate status of any given commodity—its legality—became dependent on the geography of its production and the national, political, and economic alignment of its producers, rather than the inherent properties of the drug itself.

US economic warfare efforts in the drug field laid the foundation for the growing dominance of the American pharmaceutical industry, and the principles guiding the policing apparatus that traveled with it. To ensure steady raw material flows, the state had to establish drug control on an international scale, fusing an economic principle with an imperial ambition. In the anticipations of FSA administrator McNutt, who had called upon the pharmaceutical industry to mobilize for war, "Will our old sources of opium become readily available, or must we be thinking of new sources of supply? And will those new sources be new lands—lands which must then straightaway be integrated into the international controls which hold in check that dangerous drug? Or will research find a synthetic to replace morphine?"[138] The United States needed to pursue global controls even while trying to stay one step ahead of chemical dependence by cultivating domestic technological innovation. The war furthered US goals in relation to regulating both the raw materials and finished goods in the pharmaceutical trade. Drug stockpiling became a critical component of US defense mobilization as the society and economy became oriented toward a permanent state of war readiness and war. Global demand for US pharmaceuticals grew as a direct consequence of the war. Looking back on the decade, the Department of Commerce anticipated that 1949 "will represent the tenth consecutive year in which drug exports will have attained a new peak." Fifty-six percent of those exports went to Latin America.[139] As in South America, what this meant on the ground around the world was that the United States became the primary supplier of manufactured pharmaceuticals and a guiding force behind the implementation of a drug control and policing apparatus. The influence of the pharmaceutical industry and the drug control apparatus that traveled with it persisted as critical components of the projection of US economic and political power on a global scale.

CHAPTER 2

"Resources for Freedom"

American Drug Commodities in the Postwar World

Nations, like men, can be spendthrifts, consuming their substance as fast as it comes to hand. For the individual, such a policy leads to bankruptcy and ruin; for the nation it may spell major disaster. The remedy for both lies in the creation and maintenance of a reserve against the rainy day . . .

Energy, industrial or human, being the item in highest demand in war, can and should be "canned" in peacetime. Stockpiled through wise foresight and carefully planned action, it makes available in a critical hour a greater volume of energy for the business of fighting, the actual prosecution of the war.[1]

—United States Military Academy, 1947

American officials began imagining and planning for a future of war while the embers of World War II devastation still smoldered. For the nation, and its citizens, the accumulation of goods seemingly provided a bulwark against "major disaster" and shored up an economy and economic behaviors intent on being ever ready for the "actual prosecution of the war." This pairing of war preparation with market manipulation became a fundamental characteristic of US policies and power. Mass consumption emerged as a central feature of postwar American society along with a steady stream of advice on how to gain economic advantage; the practice and discourse saturated popular culture and became a defining trait of the emergent national security state. These postwar transformations were evident in consumer culture where the rise in families' discretionary income encouraged the accumulation of goods in the new homes of a burgeoning suburban America, with kitchen pantries readily stocked from the dizzying array of packaged products lining supermarket shelves. They were also central to the policies advocated by the nation's defense planners who, as quoted above, embraced and celebrated the value of the "canned good." Historian Lizabeth Cohen describes this new "Consumer's Republic" where over the course of the 1940s and 1950s, "the mass consumption economy offered an arsenal of weapons to defend the reputation of capitalist democracy against the evils of communism."[2] And indeed, the ready availability of consumer goods became a powerful symbol in the superpower standoff over competing models of economy, governance, and their respective global reach, as famously captured in the so-called "Kitchen Debate" of 1959 between Vice President Richard Nixon and Soviet Premier Nikita Khrushchev.[3]

Beneath such symbolism, there existed for US officials a very material commitment to reorganize national and international patterns of consumption to enhance the geopolitical influence of the US government and US capital. In a striking formulation of this new orientation, researchers at the US Military Academy explained in a 1947 study, entitled *Raw Materials in War and Peace,* the importance of continuing to maintain raw materials stockpiles as "reserve against the rainy day" of war. The military's social scientists warned that a lack of stockpiling preparedness at the outset of World War II had been the foremost obstacle to rapid wartime mobilization and presented a case for the necessary permanence of raw materials accumulation for national security policy. For them, the accumulation of goods constituted a store of reserve energy, "industrial or human," available to be plucked out of peacetime cans at the "critical hour." In fact, through public and private collaborations, the nation's capacity to produce excess stocks of consumer goods became more than a bulwark of emergency preparedness; the goods themselves became an arsenal for exporting US economic and political influence.

This was particularly true in relation to the international drug trade. The combined private and public efforts to accumulate, distribute, and promote the consumption of American-manufactured drugs and pharmaceuticals in the war's aftermath entrenched an economic order and ideological superstructure premised on US capitalism's global dominance. This political economy of US power, in turn, depended on the policing and regulation of the international flow of drug raw materials and finished goods to promote the consumption of American-manufactured drug commodities around the world. In the decade after World War II government efforts to demobilize drugs from the nation's wartime arsenal quickly transitioned into a concerted focus on remobilizing drugs on behalf of national defense and forging a role for them as material and symbolic ambassadors of the benefits of integration into a US capitalist world system. The reorganization of the drug trade through corporate and government collaborations in the 1940s and 1950s reveals how policing and profit making came together to lay the foundations for a US empire. Michel Foucault's observation that in the late eighteenth century "the economy of illegalities was restructured with the development of capitalist society," rings true too for a modified mid-twentieth-century capitalism with the US state and consumer culture at its epicenter.[4]

DEMARCATING LEGALITY

Postwar efforts aimed at "canning" the power of America's drug commodities encountered unique challenges, despite, or perhaps because of, the belief in the remarkable rewards. War-wrought distortions in the international drug trade caused concern for US officials in the war's immediate aftermath. For instance, US policies pursued to consolidate control over drug commodity circuits during the war combined with the sudden drop in military drug consumption in the war's aftermath to generate government narcotics surpluses. As soldiers were demobilized, the hospitals and medicaments that traveled with them were also packed up and, although sometimes sold overseas, were most often shipped back to the United States. For officials, especially the formidable commissioner of the Federal Bureau of Narcotics, Harry J. Anslinger, who had played such an important role directing drug procurement during the war, these dispersed drug stockpiles generated a postwar policing imperative to control their redistribution. Various agencies of the US government staked out authority over surplus goods reallocation, and Commissioner Anslinger moved quickly to assert his bureau's jurisdiction over all narcotic drugs. As the war's end neared the FBN "considered the matter of disposition of surplus narcotic drugs as of the greatest national importance" and quickly secured the authority "to receive and to retain custody of these surplus narcotic drugs for eventual government use."[5] Managing the generation and large-scale redistribution of surplus goods became a structural component of postwar US economic power, and narcotic drugs as both surplus and as controlled substances posed a unique challenge. With fewer troops deployed, the demand for painkillers, especially the potent "narcotic" drugs (which included an array of opiates, cocaine, and a new array of synthetic drugs), diminished and the FBN was anxious to obtain monopoly control over their redistribution and stockpiling. The FBN sought to limit and define the boundaries of the legal flow of drugs through sanctioned circuits and stockpiles and in the process refashion the "surplus" into legitimate, nationally valuable stores of consumable goods once again. In July of 1945, less than a month before the US atomic bombing of Japan hastened the war's end, Anslinger successfully petitioned to make the FBN the sole agency responsible for "the disposition of surplus narcotics" in the United States.[6]

As head of the FBN, the commissioner presented a multifaceted argument before obtaining centralized control over US national and overseas stocks of government-designated "surplus" narcotics. "I consider this to be a very desirable arrangement," Anslinger explained to his superior in the Treasury Department, "as I believe it will eliminate the possibility that narcotic drugs declared surplus by the Army and Navy will find their way into the illicit traffic." There had been, he noted, "considerable trouble in this respect after the last war."[7] Along with the specter of an imminent rise in illicit drug trafficking, Anslinger included in his argument for FBN monopoly control over narcotic drug surpluses an invocation of America's international obligations. He maintained that any narcotics transfers for civilian medical use would "violate the spirit, if not the letter" of international drug control conventions that the United States was signatory to. In particular Anslinger mentioned the 1931 Geneva Convention's proscription against the accumulation of drug stocks in excess of national quotas pegged to legitimate medical and scientific demand (although the United States did not include national security stockpiles in calculating its quota). The FBN believed acquiring sole authority over drug redistribution was necessary to prevent excess drugs from entering the market, guaranteed adequate supplies for national defense stockpiles, and ensured the federal agency's own dominance over narcotics policy.[8] Anslinger had been able to expand the FBN's influence over national drug policy during the war, and he now successfully maneuvered, through invoking the specter of the illicit trade and drug treaty obligations, to have his and the bureau's influence continue to grow in the war's aftermath.

In Anslinger's eyes, coupled with the threat of illicit trafficking were the dangers posed by the (uncertain) qualities of the drugs themselves and the security of locations where they might be stored. Anslinger emphasized the "dubious quality of most narcotics which become surplus." Highlighting the uncertain chain of custody of demobilized drugs, the varied origins and inconsistent storage conditions, and the frequent lack of uniformity and purity of samples, Anslinger declared that the sale of such drugs to "civilian agencies for medical use would be unsafe." The difficulties of surplus drug quality control, he warned, could even "contribute to a disaster in a given hospital." The FBN's position was that hospitals should not be storing drugs in any case, given the inadequacy of their security facilities. In an almost obsessive detailing of the security obstacles accompanying the storage of drugs in hospitals, the bureau cautioned that, unlike "[drug] manufacturers [who] are required to have secure masonry vaults or heavy safes, burglar-resistant by Underwriter's Laboratories' certification, supplemented by A-1 central station, electrical burglar alarms, the usual hospital is notoriously insecure . . . not one in five hundred has an electrical burglar alarm of any kind. Their so-called 'safes' are usually thin metal lockers. Their pharmacies are usually thin tile or plaster walled rooms with common key-locked wooden doors, to which there are several keys."

This emphatic enumeration of security conditions contrasted the supposedly paltry situation at publicly accessible hospitals with the advantages of pharmaceutical manufacturers' private facilities. The FBN asserted that only its own vaults, the government stockpile, and the storage facilities of private drug manufacturers were the most secure locales for drug stockpiling. This hierarchy was indicative of the high-level collaboration between drug companies and the US government that was increasingly central to profitability within the drug market and in the regulatory apparatus designed to sustain it. In this vision, private capital and police agencies of the US government working together were best equipped to overcome the public menace of the potential illicit lurking everywhere: "Orderlies, delivery men, other hospital personnel, and even visitors, pass to and fro about them at all hours. Numerous building entrances stand open or remain unlocked, many times day and night, for the ingress and egress of doctors, nurses, hospital employees, delivery men, visitors, or passers-by. In other words, hospitals are not prepared to take care of dangerous drugs except for small stocks on a current, rapid turnover basis."[9]

The shadow of the illicit functioned as a powerful stimulus for a government-corporate drug regulatory alliance. The FBN argued the only way to ensure that drugs were safely handled, storage vaults were secure, drugs were pure, the United States was fulfilling diplomatic obligations, and it (the FBN) was able to combat the illicit traffic, was to establish its own monopoly within the government, within the nation, and within US-controlled portions of the world over the disposition of narcotic drugs deemed "surplus" to immediate government needs, in close collaboration with the pharmaceutical industry. It also further consolidated the FBN's influence more generally since the bureau was the agency responsible for granting licenses to pharmaceutical firms desiring a role in the narcotics trade. The bureau's arguments were taken seriously, and by 1946 directives went out informing the military that all narcotics deemed surplus to divisions in foreign theaters as well as on domestic soil were to be delivered to the "Drugs Disposal Committee" of the Treasury Department's Federal Bureau of Narcotics.

Anslinger's obsession with security attested to the difficulty of neatly delineating and enforcing boundaries of legality where slippage from licit to illicit drug circuits (and back) was pervasive, and where the regulatory innovations themselves often generated confusion over where the line between legal and illegal lay. The illicit market in a very real way was the productive consequence of government efforts to delineate the boundaries of legality. As a consequence, the history of the emergence of a robust regulatory apparatus is also the history of the identification and targeting of the illicit drug trade, the former the definitional precondition for the latter. As Itty Abraham and Willem van Schendel have observed, "both law and crime emerge from historical and ongoing struggles over legitimacy, in the course of which powerful groups succeed in delegitimizing and criminalizing certain practices." This study takes their counsel to heart: "Students of illicitness must start from the assumptions that states cannot simply be equated with law and order, and that illicit practices are necessarily part of any state."[10]

While the FBN sought to capitalize on the dynamic interplay between the legal and illegal, it frequently found itself challenged by the instability of the boundary separating the two. Take for instance an incident that happened according to one official account, "on or about" July 1, 1947, when a sick prisoner was taken from the Utah State Prison in Salt Lake City and transported to a hospital, where he died. This event, which might otherwise have passed relatively unnoticed, received a considerable amount of attention after the autopsy determined that the prisoner, Henry Spencer McLeece, had "died from the injection of an unknown narcotic drug." The local FBN agent and his district supervisor based in Denver joined the warden and other prison officials in conducting the subsequent investigation. The source of the hypodermic syringe and the drugs fatally consumed by the prisoner, it turned out, had been the Naval Supply Depot in nearby Clearfield.[11] In fact, the district supervisor reported to his boss, FBN Commissioner Anslinger, that the drugs responsible for the prisoner's demise had been procured from stores of government military surplus. Specifically, they had been part of a lot, "a hospital unit sold by the Navy Department through the War Assets Administration to the Utah State Hospital for Poliomyelitis and other Crippling Diseases," a hospital that was being built at the time.[12]

But how had the drugs come to be in the prison? The year prior to this incident the Utah State Hospital had purchased from the Navy a "100-bed naval hospital unit" that had been designated surplus to military needs. With the Navy wanting to deliver the unit and the hospital still being under construction, the hospital's board of directors managed to have the equipment stored in the interim in "an uncompleted cell-block in the new prison on the outskirts of Salt Lake City." In the process of unloading the Naval Supply Depot delivery trucks, about two weeks before prisoner McLeece died, prisoners laboring at the Utah State Prison discovered a crate marked "Bourbon Whiskey 100-proof." They hid the crate under the loading platform and later smuggled it away through "a tunnel under the cell-block." When the prisoners opened the crate, along with whiskey, they found an array of narcotics including 1250 morphine syrettes (disposable injection devices), opium, and opium derivatives in other forms, an eighth of an ounce and 1000 packaged tabloids of cocaine hydrochloride, along with various other synthetic drug preparations, according to an inventory list drawn up by the prison warden.

In official correspondence relating to the investigation, no one at the Federal Bureau of Narcotics, the Utah State Prison, the Naval Supply Depot, the War Assets Administration, which had facilitated the sale, nor the Utah State Hospital seemed surprised by the fact that a "100-bed naval hospital unit" might have narcotics as part of its inventory. Narcotics—which were defined by national and international drug conventions of the times as opium and coca, their derivatives (and a growing list of synthetic substitutes)—were, after all, routinely used as painkillers in general medical practice; the government considered them essential materials in the recently concluded war. Regardless, all of those involved in this particular transaction professed ignorance of narcotics having been included in the lot of surplus military property sold to the state hospital. Perhaps this was connected to the odd packaging. A crate marked "Bourbon Whiskey 100-proof" filled with narcotics might easily be, or appear to be, contraband, not least since official acknowledgment of the narcotics' existence was only provided after a prisoner's death. At what point the drugs had in fact crossed the line and become technically contraband—whether before the crate ever made it into the surplus naval hospital unit, or only once it was removed from the unit by prisoners locked in the Utah State Prison—was not a question any of the government authorities or institutions involved seemed particularly eager to explore. The narcotics had remained in state custody throughout, after all; from the Naval Supply Depot to the state prison, as they were dispersed through the inmates' prison cells and bodies and, finally, at least for a portion of the drugs, coming to rest at the state hospital morgue.

All parties to the business claimed no prior knowledge of the drugs' inclusion in the sale. Yet, in a gesture which calls into question many of the official reported details, the FBN agent submitted a list to headquarters detailing the drugs that had yet to be recovered. The listing was based on an initial inventory inexplicably dated after the drugs had first been delivered to the prison. How an accurate inventory could be compiled after the narcotics' dispersal (and presumed at least partial consumption) within the prison did not seem to matter. The warden confidently claimed he had recovered all the drugs except "those hidden by the dead man" and expressed his willingness to "plow up whole fields" to find the missing stocks. The Narcotics District Supervisor was impressed by what he described as the warden's "energetic investigation," in particular, "that this matter was kept a secret by the Warden and other prison officials as long as possible" in order that the hunt for the last portion of unrecovered drugs be the most effective. With a majority of the "inventoried" stocks recovered and an explanation for how the drugs wound up in prisoners' hands, the district supervisor ultimately concluded, "It is difficult to place the blame for this unfortunate incident."[13]

The contradictions and unanswered questions in the agent's report may have been less important than the fact of presenting some accounting of the "surplus" commodities involved, providing the documentary evidence for the bureau's files (and any further investigations) of having regained a sort of control over the situation. And this control, as embodied by the official actions taken, meant redistributing the recovered narcotics into channels deemed legitimate once again. The drugs seized in the prison were turned over to the FBN. The supervisor of medical supplies at the Naval Supply Depot assured the investigators that any additional narcotics present in the remaining twenty-nine hospital units they had in their custody would be removed "without too much trouble and expense" in the course of a planned transfer of the units to another warehouse. To avoid a similar scenario, the Navy assured the FBN that the remaining units would not be sold, but rather "held in reserve for a possible future war." The only punishments meted out, not surprisingly, were against the prisoner-consumers. In the course of an undocumented number of interrogations by prison officials, at least a few prisoners were threatened with delayed parole. And, two weeks after Henry Spencer McLeece passed away, the FBN district supervisor reported five prisoners "are now in solitary confinement, and their punishment will be decided upon at a later date by the Warden and the Board of Corrections."[14]

The need to reassert some sort of control over the "illicit" narcotics themselves was one thing—accomplished ultimately through the punishment of those with the least amount of control over the drug commodities' circulation. Why the Navy had sold narcotic drugs to a civilian hospital was quite another. Both concerns centered on defining the parameters of legitimate participation in the drug market: who could store, consume, and provide narcotic drugs to whom. While answers to the first matter reverberated primarily in the lives of those incarcerated or who worked in the prison, the second touched on structural questions of authority and control over the legitimate circulation of drug commodities amid national and international economic and political restructurings in the war's aftermath. Working from the assumption that the narcotics had been pilfered from "legitimate" stocks, the FBN wanted to know why narcotic drugs had been transferred—sold—from military to civilian stores, against federal policy directives granting the FBN sole authority and forbidding such transactions. The War Assets Administration claimed the hospital unit was sold before they had received instructions not to "accept declarations for or including narcotic drugs."[15] The Navy Supply Depot, similarly, "had no explanation as to why the narcotic drugs had not been removed," despite having seen the directive. No mention was made—in either case—of the crate's "100-proof whiskey" labeling that gave no indication, in any case, of the box's actual content, which would have made foreknowledge of the narcotics' inclusion by either agency highly suspect. Nevertheless, the FBN seemed satisfied with these explanations for this particular incident. The drugs were accounted for, punishments doled out, and the drugs' circulation was once again in the legitimate realm.

STOCKPILING AND REMOBILIZING FOR DEFENSE

The establishment, control, and policing of national stockpiles of drug commodities became manifestations of the powerful stance of the United States in relation to the rest of the world. So too were the new prisons, hospitals, and warehouses that increasingly stored the nation's capital. The stockpiling of commodities, along with the immense value of the "energy, industrial or human," stored within them, reflected economic and political transformations that far exceeded the immediate postwar concern of handling military surpluses. The FBN's troubled efforts to assert monopoly control over military surplus narcotic drugs occurred amid a profound shift in US national security policy that placed an unprecedented peacetime urgency around preparations for war. Initially inspired by lessons learned during World War II on the strategic importance of controlling the supply and flow of strategic commodities, particularly raw materials deemed essential to waging war, in the five years following the cessation of hostilities these principles guided government defense policy as it sought to remobilize the nation for war against the Soviet Union.[16]

The Cold War merely accelerated what had already become central to US policy: building a US-centered international economic and regulatory order to sustain and extend the unrivaled geopolitical and economic position in which the United States found itself at war's end. As Thomas McCormick said, "By 1945, it had become axiomatic to American leaders that two prerequisites were necessary for the world system to function in an economically efficient and political stable way. First, there had to be a constantly expanding world economic pie. Second, there had to be a hegemonic power capable of enforcing rules of behavior necessary to ensure that expansion, and punishing or isolating those who refused to accede to those rules."[17] A key mechanism for securing this outcome was through US dominance over international market flows. Examining the principles and logic behind the consolidation of this economic vision provides a revealing perspective on the emerging ideological and material foundations of US capital's growing global power and the policing that sustained it. The US public and private capacity to acquire, stockpile, and control the circulation of commodities, especially drug commodities, was quite consciously seen as a way to lessen dependence on market fluctuations and the trade proclivities of foreign powers, as a tool for replacing European and Japanese colonial influence in the Third World, and as a mechanism for countering the real or imagined influence of communism around the globe.

In 1944 both military and civilian officials tackled the question of what to do with material surpluses at war's end. The US Military Academy lamented that the period between the First and Second World Wars had only "witnessed the birth and feeble infancy of a national policy with respect to raw materials." Problems encountered in the acquisition of material resources during the latter war inspired a recommendation to make stockpiling central to long-term strategic planning. By October 1944, Congress, intent that stockpiling become a permanent feature of national defense policy, passed the Surplus Property Act "to aid the reconversion from a war to a peace economy" by ordering the placement of surplus strategic and critical materials in a government stockpile to be available for national defense or emergency.[18] This vision was furthered after the war when officials reformulated the government's 1939 Strategic Materials Act with the passage of the 1946 Strategic and Critical Materials Stock Piling Act that characterized defense stockpiling as a necessary component of peacetime policy. The following year, the same month the FBN scrambled to contain the fallout from the "illicit" circulation of military surplus drugs, President Harry Truman readied the nation for a new type of war. On July 26, 1947, the president signed the National Security Act that reorganized the institutional foundations of national defense by creating the National Security Resources Board to coordinate economic mobilization, along with the Department of Defense, the National Security Council, and the Central Intelligence Agency. These institutional transformations reflected a shift toward a more aggressive foreign policy, propelled by the president's call in March of that year for the global containment of communism (a policy that later came to be known as the Truman Doctrine).

The need for such institutional changes seemed apparent in 1950 when President Truman declared a national emergency in response to Chinese Communist intervention in the conflict on the Korean peninsula. Immediately, as had happened at the outbreak of World War II, the government rapidly sought out the collaboration of the pharmaceutical industry. Just ten days into the state of emergency, *Drug Trade News* reported, "Key U.S. Agencies move to speed up mobilization plans for the drug industry." Federal and state governments responded to the state of emergency in part by allocating increased funds for the stockpiling of drugs. According to the national Civil Defense director, the government "would spend $400,000,000 for stockpiling critically needed civil defense supplies during the next three years."[19] With the first "hot" war of the Cold War underway, more than a year after the Soviets had demonstrated their capacity to build and detonate a nuclear bomb, medicines stockpiles along with bomb shelters and duck-and-cover drills seemed necessary preparation for a potential attack on the American civilian population.

The Cold War helped solidify the policy link between drugs and national security that had been evident for more than a decade since the government began accumulating stockpiles in the 1930s. When federal gold reserves were transferred from the Treasury Department's vaults in Washington to Fort Knox, the vaults were subsequently filled with government-surplus narcotics.[20] This transfer came about after Congress had devalued the dollar in 1934, providing at least a symbolic counterpoint to the steadily increasing value of drug commodities in economic, political, legal, social, and cultural life.[21] In truth, the government moved the gold reserves in an effort to better protect them from a possible enemy invasion.[22] But Anslinger himself emphasized that drug stockpiling had "even more value," or at least the equivalent importance of safeguarding gold. "We could not store it anywhere else, unless it would be in a Fort Knox gold vault," he informed the press, "because a narcotic addict will go to almost any length to obtain opium and a person who could steal even a small part of the supply would have a small fortune." Beyond its dramatic symbolism, the replacement of gold by narcotics in the US Treasury was a very material reflection—locked up in concrete vaults—of the importance the government attributed to controlling drug commodities. Narcotics embodied the growing interdependence of corporate and government power with the government ostensibly storing private companies' stockpiles for future use. Anslinger bragged the government "does not own an ounce of" the stockpiled opium. "Manufacturers and medical supply houses furnished the money to purchase it through the government, and hold the rights to use it under federal sanction for medical uses as needed."[23] Drug commodities, and the public and private institutional networks involved in regulating them, did in fact do much of the work of establishing a new world order, and drugs assumed a powerful place among the transferable assets of capital with their remarkable interchangeable properties.

Storing and controlling the flow of drug commodities bolstered national power, while at the same time becoming more difficult throughout the 1940s as the quantities of drugs in circulation continued to grow. While the Naval Supply Depot in Clearfield, Utah, had apparently not been informed of the government's directives granting the FBN centralized control over drug dispositions at the time of the prison fiasco, many government agencies did comply with its imperatives. There were a number of different ways that drugs made their way to the FBN's Drug Disposal Committee. In addition to drugs received from the War Assets Administration, the FBN itself accumulated drugs it had confiscated in police raids, as well as from stocks of drugs surrendered by retail drug stores that were going out of business. The FBN worked hard to ensure the fate of these drug stockpiles bolstered its own institutional importance in relation to the government's national security efforts, even as the Treasury Department's vaults rapidly proved inadequate for the growing cache.

This was one of the reasons why the FBN was not eager to cooperate with a 1952 US Attorney's Office investigation into an illicit cocaine ring in Washington. In an exposé of the investigation published in the *Saturday Evening Post,* the Assistant US Attorney revealed that the source of cocaine had been traced back to the vaults in the basement of the US Treasury. Since as far back as 1949, a janitor working in the Treasury Department had been supplying "several major narcotics offenders, big operators who had been in business for years." Over the course of two and a half years an estimated thirty to one hundred ounces of cocaine and between twenty and fifty pounds of marijuana had been delivered to the "underworld." The US Attorney's Office and Federal Bureau of Narcotics agents took the indicted janitor, Eddie Gregg, to the Treasury Annex to demonstrate his methods. As the story was told, "The entrance to the room was a heavy grilled-iron door with a section of steel, encasing the lock, across the middle. There was a knob on the inner side of the lock, but none outside. Unless he had had a key, it was difficult to imagine a man getting past this formidable roadblock." So "Eddie looked around and spotted a piece of brown cord, like that used for wrapping packages" (one might wonder how it came to be there for the demonstration) and managed to work the doorknob from the other side. The incident reveals—as does the story of the prison in Utah—the tenuous delineation of legal and illegal commodity circuits, along with the inevitable—and often profitable—slippage that occurs at its boundary.[24]

Eddie's easy entry made a mockery of the Treasury vault's security system and oddly exposed the futility of the Federal Bureau of Narcotics' preoccupation with security and controls. More striking, the chairman of the FBN's Drug Disposal Committee was unable to provide investigators with an accounting of the quantities of drugs stolen. His explanation that "the system used in keeping inventory in the storeroom, losses or thefts could be sustained and yet not be recorded" was vastly inconsistent with the FBN's own directives and warnings concerning the handling of such stockpiles. Whether true or simply told to the grand jury, this inconsistency reveals the uneven expectations of accountability and powers of enforcement in the realm of drug control at that time. In the end, considering the impossibility of determining that any given quantity of drugs had been stolen, the grand jury cited the FBN for "negligence" and was forced to dismiss several of the indictments for lack of evidence.[25]

Commissioner Anslinger, unsurprisingly, preferred to highlight the necessary and valuable role the FBN played in bolstering the nation's defenses. The same year the Treasury vaults began supplying DC's drug trafficking underworld, the commissioner boasted to Congress of the FBN's expertise in handling drug surpluses and the valuable role the institution played with regard to defense mobilization. Appearing before the congressional committee tasked with approving the FBN's annual budget in February 1949, Anslinger described how the bureau had "sent, since the war's end, some 30 express cars" to the "Munitions Board Stockpile," which he estimated accounted for "several million dollars worth of the stuff." The "stuff" in question seemed to include an array of drugs; as the commissioner explained, "the only drugs that we destroy are drugs like marijuana, for which there is no medical need." The commissioner reassured his audience that the FBN handled drugs appropriately to maximize public safety and provide for the national defense. If there was any question over the chemical content of the drugs coming into FBN possession, Anslinger explained, he passed the drugs on to a pharmaceutical manufacturer licensed to work with narcotic "alkaloids," which in turn purified the questionable substances before the FBN sent them on to the strategic stockpile.[26] Drug surplus stocks grew so large that by June 1952 the Federal Bureau of Narcotics was overwhelmed by the quantities of surplus narcotics being transferred into its custody.[27] As a result, the FBN procedure for handling the drugs—having all surplus narcotics pass through the FBN to be recorded, tracked, stockpiled, or released for final disposition—was modified to have drugs shipped directly through the General Service Administration either on to the national stockpile or turned over to authorized manufacturers for reprocessing: "to purify all of this stuff," as Anslinger put it.[28]

The pharmaceutical industry found itself in a unique position, with private drug manufacturers assuming a central role in government defense mobilization as "reworkers" of drug materials. Private drug manufacturers were given the critical task of transforming excess into valuable goods. While the government designated an array of drugs essential to national defense and destined for national stockpiling, of those legally labeled "narcotic" only opium stocks were considered "deficient or insufficiently" developed and were therefore targeted for acquisition by the government.[29] As the regulations outlined, "Opium and opium derivatives, and preparations thereof, (normally strategic and critical material) should be reported to General Services Administration by the holding agency and if acceptable for the purpose should be ordered to be forwarded direct to the stockpile." All such transfers, whether to the national stockpile or the stores of manufacturers, continued to be tracked by the bureau, which made sure these excess narcotics were stockpiled in "adequately safeguarded storage facilities."[30]

Any drugs rejected for the stockpile should be destroyed or sent to a "registered manufacturer" where chemists could "rework the drugs . . . into a suitable form," or exchange them for drugs "acceptable for stockpiling." The bureau went on to specify that for medically valuable "surplus narcotic drug preparations" which were not needed for the national defense stockpile, including drugs such as "cocaine and the synthetics Demerol, Dolophine, etc.," the preferred "mode of disposal" was to exchange them for strategic drugs of an equivalent value.[31] From the government's perspective the value of drugs like cocaine that fell into the FBN's possession resided less in their chemical substance, or a fear of inadequate access to them, but in their exchange value. Thus drug commodities were a critical component of the new defense mobilization, either as nationally stockpiled material for the eventuality of war, or, as in the case of surplus cocaine, as a drug strategically exchangeable through the manufacturer for other narcotics like opium, needed for the stockpile. In the process, pharmaceutical manufacturers were integrated into the effort of defense mobilization as reprocessors, exchangers, and providers of strategic drug materials.

RESOURCES FOR FREEDOM

By the end of the decade the mutable value of drugs and the logic underlying efforts to direct drug market flows in the interest of national defense were important components of a much larger global and economic agenda being advanced by the government with a spirited imperial ambition bolstered by Cold War compulsions. A pamphlet issued by the Executive Office of the President, entitled "The Story of Defense Mobilization: How the United States Is Building Its Might in Order to Avoid a

Third World War," communicated this vision: "The increasing menace of the forces of communist aggression requires that the national defense of the United States be strengthened as speedily as possible." The same day on which Truman declared a national emergency in response to events unfolding on the Korean peninsula, he also created the Office of Defense Mobilization (ODM) to coordinate and oversee all mobilization activities of the federal government. In particular, the ODM had two central aims: one, "to gear the American industry to production for defense," and two, "to back up that mighty effort with a stable economy."[32]

The importance of resource stockpiling to secure this stable economy and American visions for a new world order was clearly illuminated when Truman convened a President's Materials Policy Commission in January 1951: "We cannot allow shortages of materials," the president explained, "to jeopardize our national security nor to become a bottleneck to our economic expansion."[33] The Materials Policy Commission's task was to devise a plan to guide the acquisition and disposition of materials deemed essential to national security, and to assess the adequacy of both government and private industry practices. The president advised that materials surpluses would provide for domestic necessities, and also that national security depended on international economic expansion to generate ever-greater material supplies so as to avoid any "bottleneck" that might obstruct a growing US empire. By the time the commission published its findings and recommendations in a 1952 report entitled *Resources for Freedom*,[34] the problem of controlling the flow of raw materials that had so dominated US concerns during the war, as well as the problems of surplus materials disposition in the war's aftermath, had increasingly been tied not just to control but to a perceived necessity of expanding that raw materials base. In an expression of the circular logic whereby growth was tied to demand which was tied to further growth, fusing the military and economic foundations of US capital's expansion, *Resources for Freedom* explained: "Military security depends heavily on a vigorous and expanding economy to produce the overwhelming quantities of the equipment, machinery, and supplies necessary for modern military strength. On the other hand, healthy economic growth depends importantly on military security to maintain that climate of confidence in the future in which private enterprise flourishes. Neither military nor economic strength can be raised to its highest potential without an abundant and varied flow of materials."[35]

US drug stockpiling and control efforts went forth in the dual context of the need to handle drug commodity surpluses from war demobilization, as well as facilitating the international flow of raw materials and US-manufactured drug commodities to meet the adjusting demands of remobilizing for defense—a cold war of US expansion.

National security was defined in relation to the military's capacity to maintain circumstances where "private enterprise flourishes," which meant the state had a role in facilitating US private capital's international expansion. This expansion was predicated upon generating a demand—a market—for US-manufactured goods, so as to keep the cycle of growth and expansion operative. Working within an ideological framework whereby overseas consumption of US-manufactured goods was presented as the most desirable route to global economic development, the authors of *Resources for Freedom* characterized US expansion as a service, geared toward meeting the "needs" and demands of the world. The global consumption of American goods and resources was the path of the future. The commission explained that the report's "central task [was] an examination of the adequacy of materials, chiefly industrial materials, to meet the needs of the free world in the years ahead."[36] By the early 1950s when *Resources for Freedom* was compiled, the national resources "mobilization" effort had already been largely transitioned from its structural foundations in wartime US policies to a postwar state of permanent "defense mobilization" whose "supreme objective," according to the ODM, was *"not war, but peace."*[37]

This particular "peace" embodied US international ambition and was premised upon the accumulation of raw materials and control over the flow of finished goods, a program that gained urgency from the threat of Soviet competition. The commission described the best interests of the "free world" as dependent on the US extraction and stockpiling of the world's raw materials and their processing, repackaging, and global redistribution as American-manufactured goods. The possibilities for both deploying and expanding the *Resources for Freedom* charter were grand. As the commission concluded, "The less developed nations have the materials; the industrial nations have the capital and the technical and managerial skills. These facts suggest the possibility of a new era of advancement for the world which is dazzling in its promise."[38] But there were obstacles to the implementation of America's promise of global development. In the aftermath of World War II and in the context of global imperial reorderings, the US government worried that "Less developed countries . . . resent the stigma of 'colonialism' which to their way of thinking attaches to economies heavily dependent on raw materials exports." The United States, however, argued that national ambitions to industrialize—at least in the "less developed world"—were impractical to the new world order, dismissing the sentiment as an unproductive relic of resentment toward European colonialism. Looking at the global marketplace, the commission lamented that these countries "are often more intent on industrialization than materials development." The "free world" needed to contribute the raw material resources to hold onto freedom, which in the realm of a sought-after US hegemony meant an accompanying dependency on US-manufactured goods. Thus the US government envisioned the commodity control apparatus as a critical component of securing and extending its powers in the postwar world. This US vision of stability and control required maintaining various countries' unequal participation in the world economy. The commission's answers to the colonial "resentments" of the less developed world was to seek to lessen market "instability" so as to help these countries overcome their fears of vulnerability to market fluctuations in the context of producing a few major materials for export. US ideology promoted market structures that might eclipse (in language quite self-conscious of this) the former colonial might of European countries.

Beyond providing leverage in the global political economy, the Government Commission on Resource Mobilization concluded that stockpiling as a "device" "offers an attractive alternative to subsidies" in federal efforts to generate national production for defense mobilization.[39] Holding materials for future use was cheaper, reduced foreign dependency in times of crisis, and also provided what the commission described as the "security advantage of certain possession."[40] This policy underwrote enormous power and profit for both the government and private producers who gained disproportionate access to commodity stores and significant leverage over material flows within the international marketplace. This advantage did not only reside in having access to the market and use-value of the stockpiled materials themselves. It also freed up labor and other critical resources. In a formulation that echoed the US Military Academy's logic presented in this chapter's epigraph, the president's commission explained, "When materials are stockpiled, other economic resources such as manpower, energy, and transportation are automatically stored with them as constituents of extracted and processed materials."[41] Thus the stockpiles were a reserve supply not only of critical and strategic commodities, but also of the international labor power, energy, supply networks, and other resources that had gone into their production. As globally derived American stores, these stockpiles provided the necessary pool of resources to fuel US capitalism's postwar expansion.

DRUGS AND NATIONAL POWER

The government's overarching vision of the necessary intersection between economic policy, national security, and US global influence was particularly attuned to the central importance of the nation's pharmaceutical industry. As the Commission on Resource Mobilization explained, "Practically every industry is dependent on the chemical industry to a considerable degree, and this is also true of every household and consumer." The array of products churned out by the nation's chemical and pharmaceutical laboratories provided the foundational building blocks for both America's expanding consumer culture and for strengthening the country's capacity to confront challenges in the world. The peculiar qualities of the commodities themselves made them exceptionally adaptive to the changing demands of the time. The commission detailed that the "Chemical industry also, above all other industries, has a great capacity for adapting itself to variations in raw materials, because to a large extent it can work out methods for using raw materials interchangeably. Finally, it has a great capacity for meeting crises."[42]

The report continued, "Examples are many—dyestuffs, fixed nitrogen, medicinals, synthetic rubber, silk, quinine, ivory, camphor." The capacity of the industry to transform substances at the molecular level meant that the largest companies in the market were involved in both pharmaceutical and chemical production. It was the alchemical power of the industry, its capacity to use raw materials "interchangeably," to have laboratory science parse and reconstitute substances into an array of products spanning medicinal, industrial, and even nutritional uses, that made it so valuable to a national defense policy premised on mobilizing production to ensure preparedness for crisis.

The new and special importance of the industry was particularly dramatic when compared to other sectors of national production. From 1939 to 1949, the chemical industry grew much faster than other industries, with its growth measuring almost two times the rate of all other industrial growth combined.[43] The importance of the pharmaceutical industry and drug commodities specifically was evident in the fact that they were stockpiled not only in the national stockpile, but also by the Army's own war reserve stockpile, in the Federal Bureau of

Narcotics' Treasury stockpile, and in the inventory stockpiles of private manufacturers. The government estimated private manufacturers' "inventory building [was] many times greater than stockpile acquisitions" by the federal government. And, in fact, the "Government deliberately encouraged private accumulation of raw materials" through "credit, inventory control, and import policies" as aspects of mobilization for national defense.[44]

The US government's interest in subsidizing expansion in pharmaceutical output had the mutually reinforcing goals of retaining adequate stockpiles of drugs to meet civilian and military needs in response to domestic attack or war, while also providing the groundwork for US expansion. These ambitions were forged through the experience of World War II, were premised on a vision of US global dominance, and became amplified as the Cold War invigorated corporate and government collaboration. The US government and pharmaceutical industry emerged from the war in unprecedented positions of influence. The challenge consequently, as both saw it, was not just to maintain but also to actively expand their authority in the world. The Department of Commerce joined the president and the ODM in articulating this sentiment. In 1949, the department's bulletin, *World Trade in Commodities*, invoked the pharmaceutical industries' wartime expansion in the Western Hemisphere as a model for the future. "Surely with the knowledge acquired in cultivating Latin America," the bulletin opined, "more visionary promotion should be conducive to somewhat comparable per capita results in the Eastern Hemisphere. In conjunction with Western Europeans, perhaps the drug-consuming possibilities of Eastern Europe, Africa, the Near and Far East may be developed as never before. Some United States drug houses are thinking and acting on this premise but many more might profitably do so. . . . As the outstanding medical center and source of efficacious therapeutic products, the world expects us to display this type of leadership."[45]

Segmenting the world into frontiers for US market expansion, the Commerce Department encouraged companies to build from the model of success in Latin America to exploit the "drug-consuming possibilities" of the rest of the world. Pairing a celebration of economic promise with a refashioned version of the white man's burden ("the world expects us to display this type of leadership"), the department's Office of International Trade latched onto another key aspect of the unique capacity of drugs to advance US dominance. The power of drugs to advance human health meant US companies, the primary producers of "efficacious therapeutic products," had a unique role to play as both emissaries of the benevolent goals of US foreign policy and as engines propelling national economic growth.

While the Commerce Department delighted in visions of "cultivating" an expanding market for US pharmaceutical goods, the pharmaceutical trade press celebrated its material realization with the "fantastic growth of the US foreign market." Whereas in 1939 only $22.5 million of pharmaceuticals were exported, by 1954 the figure was anticipated to have "topped half a billion dollars." This phenomenal growth was a low figure at best given the fact that the "biggest U.S. drug companies [had] moved major sections of their manufacturing, processing, and packaging operations to overseas subsidiaries since the war."[46] The trade press joined the Commerce Department in viewing Latin America as having been the initial site of this expansion. Explaining in 1949 the "industry trend" to increasingly export "finished products," *Business Week* suggested, "The war had a lot to do with this, too. It opened up markets once controlled by the German drug industry—particularly Latin America."[47] While international raw material extraction to sustain national defense stockpiles remained a vital aspect of US foreign policy, during World War II the establishment of distributors and the marketing of US-manufactured goods to consumers became a primary policy objective. Increasingly in the war's aftermath, sitting on top of materials stockpiles, the latter aspect of market penetration became an essential instrument of US imperialism. The term imperialism here is deployed as a category of analysis that, as Paul A. Kramer points out, "foregrounds the analysis of power and politics on a global scale." In the context of examining US efforts to control drug commodity flows, the imperial framework is useful for "tracing trajectories from production to consumption in order to illuminate uneven, hierarchical relationships between and within nation states."[48]

The creation of markets for US-manufactured goods became the central object and indicator of US capitalism's success. There had been two principal components behind the effective introduction of US-manufactured goods into Latin America that the government and private industry believed had been critical: decentralization of operations and effective marketing. By the end of the 1940s, the Commerce Department viewed the decentralization of pharmaceutical companies as a measure of US advance. It explained the process had begun in Latin America, was brought by US companies into Europe in the war's aftermath, and was being introduced in the developing world (initially into the geography of the former British empire) with the growing penetration of US capital:

> For the past decade, interest and participation by United States producers in decentralized operation have been focused on the major countries of Latin America. Following the end of the war, however, there has been a progressive focusing upon western European prospects. Since January 1949 pharmaceutical production and marketing teams from the United States, averaging two firms a month, have been investigating the situation in prewar competitive countries, and the trade press has chronicled plans, agreements, and the inauguration of facilities in many instances. Recently this same interest has become evident in Egypt, South Africa, India, and the Philippines.[49]

As this description suggests, the government tracked and facilitated private business connections and exploratory investigations into foreign markets, so as to ensure not just the maintenance, but also the extension of US dominance in global pharmaceutical manufacturing. US manufacturers benefited from the privileged access to markets they gained as a result of war, new alliances and dependencies, and, in the case of Germany and Japan, the postwar occupation of former "competitive countries." While US pharmaceutical houses had already decentralized operations to some extent in the Latin American market, the war provided an opportunity for accelerated US decentralized expansion into Europe—and Europe's former colonial territories.

International decentralization within the pharmaceutical industry helped US companies avoid national tariffs for foreign-manufactured goods, and brought US commodities competitively closer to the sites of sale. It also tended to enshrine the American industry's dominance as local industrialists could rarely outmatch the production capacity of multinationals already established in a capital-intensive industry.[50] Most often decentralization occurred in local packaging and distribution operations for goods that had been manufactured in the United States. In fact, it was the US goods themselves, along with the capitalist toolbox they traveled with, that would be the emissaries of American imperialism. Marketing US-manufactured goods—despite the international origins of the time, labor, energy, and raw materials stored in them—as "American" brought the "Resources of Freedom" to the rest of the world, while the bulk of the profits—ideological, political, and economic—accrued to the nation. Marketing then, the Commerce Department argued in the January 1949 edition of *World Trade in Commodities,* was the other critical tool to be gleaned from successes in Latin America: "It would seem as though our sales grew in proportion to the scope and intensity of promotional efforts. Indicative of this, sales of all commodity groups increased in the Western Hemisphere. . . . In fact, 56 percent of total drug exports are for nearby neighbors numbering about 140,000,000 customers, primarily Latin Americans."[51]

Interestingly this assessment was made as an explanation for why sales in the pharmaceutical industry had not been as strong outside the Western Hemisphere. De-emphasizing other factors—including the majority of the world's lack of access to dollars to buy US goods (the postwar Dollar Gap)[52]—the Commerce Department proselytized that sales of US commodities grew in direct proportion to marketing: "the scope and intensity of promotional efforts." Marketing was critical. Capturing new markets entailed promoting the distribution and consumption of US-manufactured goods, along with the capitalist ideology, operations, and packaging necessary for their dispersal.

The pharmaceutical industry's valued contribution to the nation's "Resources for Freedom" had its origins in the close collaboration between the industry and the government during World War II. After the war, as US global economic ambition confronted a new geopolitical climate, this partnership intensified to the mutual advantage of key industry players and government agencies intent on entrenching an international economic order attuned to a new vision of US national defense. The linking of defense to economic expansion, with the United States acting as the largest global accumulator of key raw materials and primary exporter of manufactured goods, had significant ramifications for growth in the pharmaceutical industry and, importantly, for the elaboration and implementation of a drug regulatory apparatus. The partnership between the government and pharmaceutical companies to sustain stockpiles and penetrate international markets encouraged the growth of concentrated economic power. This model envisioned the United States as the powerhouse behind global economic and political integration, and it relied on an increasingly limited number of private corporations working with the state. This tendency toward monopoly was clearly on display in the pharmaceutical industry, which during the postwar period underwent rapid vertical integration, with firm sizes increasing dramatically and reorienting their expenditures toward research development, and marketing.[53] These organizational changes aligned well with the government's new desire to encourage the creative exploration of raw materials' "interchangeable" properties while advocating increased efforts at marketing and exporting American goods abroad. Significantly, public and private collaboration to these ends required the parallel growth of a regulatory system to police the entire drug commodity chain: the supply of raw materials, the participation in industrial production, and the circulation of the finished goods. The remainder of this chapter examines this process in relation to the post-wars government regulation of coca commodities in collaboration with companies involved in the trade.

COCA COMMODITIES, CORPORATE COLLABORATION, AND LEGAL CONTROLS

The monopoly logic of enforcement, which granted the FBN primary stewardship over the redistribution of government surplus narcotics, depended on FBN collaboration with select companies involved in the drug trade who, as a result of these policies, acquired a de facto monopoly over aspects of drug raw material imports, distribution, and manufacturing. This monopoly conformed largely to key economic relations already established between private and public capital during World War II that helped situate the pharmaceutical industry in an unprecedented position of political and economic influence. Efforts to control the coca commodity circuit in this context—at least to limit participation in the market to that which could be effectively monitored by the government—provides a window onto the regulatory underpinnings of the national security program outlined in the *Resources for Freedom* report. Government collaboration with the three US companies most directly involved in the coca commodities trade, Merck & Co., Inc., Maywood Chemical Works, and The Coca-Cola Company, paired the selling of American drug commodities internationally with expanding the nation's global influence.

Corporate relationships forged with the government during World War II persisted in the war's aftermath, and this was especially true for Merck & Co. When Anslinger testified to Congress that the FBN sent all surplus narcotics unsuited for the national stockpile to an unidentified "alkaloidal" firm, it is quite likely he was referring to Merck. The company was one of only a handful authorized to import narcotic drug raw materials and extract alkaloids from them. It is difficult to determine the exact number of authorized firms since the FBN in 1943 ended its practice of publishing a list of licensed firms in its annual report on the *Traffic in Opium and Other Dangerous Drugs* (perhaps reflecting the general turn toward government secrecy that accompanied defense mobilization). Nevertheless, Merck had historically occupied the unique position of being the only one of five licensed narcotics importing firms authorized to import both coca leaves and opium.[54] As a contemporary chronicler of the US pharmaceutical industry described Merck's unique position, "Almost everything at Merck & Co., Inc. is bigger, better or first." The *Merck Manual of Diagnosis and Therapy* was (and remains) the medical profession's bible for matching drug treatment to diagnosis, and during the war "pharmacists' mates on submarines and paratroop doctors went into action with the *Merck Manual* in their pockets."[55] As the company's official chronicler recounted, "The wartime spirit of cooperation accelerated progress," with the company receiving government support for plant construction and research and development. The new warehouses and accompanying large drug stockpiles ensured that "from the 1940s on, increases in scale cut costs dramatically, increasing demand and transforming the market for medicinal chemicals." At Merck's Stonewall plant, for instance, which was built during the war in Elkton, Virginia, to comply with the government's request that facilities be built at least two hundred miles inland to be protected from enemy attack, annual vitamin output transitioned from grams to tonnage, lowering consumer prices and consolidating the company's dominance in the field.[56] Merck's expansion was tied to the wartime phenomena observed by the Drugs and Pharmaceutical Unit of the Bureau of Foreign and Domestic Commerce: "Under the impetus of gigantic wartime needs, many drug manufacturers have achieved undreamed-of capacity."[57]

The company's leadership included an array of men directly involved in coordinating the government's efforts to mobilize drugs for the nation's defense both during the war and in its aftermath. The line between private and public in this context becomes difficult to disentangle. During the war the firm's president, George W. Merck, "was personally entrusted with one of the most sensitive jobs in the war effort: chairmanship of the United States Biological Warfare Committee. Under his direction American scientists explored virulent strains of human plant and animal diseases so that the United States could be ready to mobilize man's most powerful enemies if the Germans or Japanese used them first."[58] In George Merck's report to the government on this research he advised that while the field was "born of the necessity of war, [it] cannot be ignored in time of peace; it must be continued on a sufficient scale to provide an adequate defense."[59] For this service Merck was later awarded the Medal for Merit. In 1947 *Fortune Magazine* celebrated George Merck for his war service, which also included an unpaid advisory role on the Munitions Advisory Board's Chemical

Advisory Committee. Merck's influence in the government remained evident in the frequent trips the president made "to Washington as a consultant to Defense Secretary Lovett." Merck's vice president, George Perkins, also held a wartime position as "a colonel in the Army's Chemical Warfare Service," and a member of the company's board of directors served as the wartime head of the nation's research and development program. George Merck became the face of the pharmaceutical industry cast as public benefactor, committed citizen, and protector of national health and defense, even gracing the cover of *Time* magazine in 1952, above the suggestive quote "Medicine is for people, not for profits."[60] One year earlier, President Harry Truman appointed him to the National Science Foundation, and President Dwight D. Eisenhower reappointed him.[61] Such ties were widespread; by the end of the decade Vannevar Bush, described by the company as the man who "ran America's entire defense research establishment," became chairman of Merck's board of directors.[62]

These economic and political connections persisted. After the war, as part of the Drug Resources Industry Advisory Committee, Merck executives (along with a number of other major pharmaceutical houses) advised the National Security Resources Board and Munitions Board of the Department of Defense in developing industrial mobilization plans, in particular with regards to the "procurement of medicines, medicinal chemicals, drugs, biologicals, surgical dressings, and antibiotics for the entire civilian economy in time of emergency and for the armed forces, and the production potential of industry."[63] Both these government agencies worked with the FBN to establish civil defense procedures whereby the first response to "disaster striking an area" would be to "alert every wholesale drug house" to provide "what they need for immediate casualties and within half an hour a truck could be dispatched to that point under police escort and have not only enough morphine for pain, but other drugs, and have them instantly available . . . the wholesale druggist would be the key man."[64]

These political connections had profound effects on policy and profitability and helped establish the privileged position of select pharmaceutical companies like Merck within the drug manufacturing business. Merck as a privileged and politically connected importer and manufacturer of controlled substances became an influential policy advisor and central provider of "medicinal chemicals" for the government and other drug manufacturers in the context of defense mobilization. Stockpiling would be critical to maintaining this position. What *Fortune* character-

ized as a "nagging problem of inventory" generated by Merck's "production efficiency" was the need for possession of "a reasonable stockpile of imported raw materials for such products as narcotics and
quinine." The raw materials stockpiles ensured the capacity to produce
more and to do so quickly, since for Merck, "medicinal orders must, if
at all possible, be filled instantly from stock." As a primary provider of
medicines, Merck had peculiar needs to stockpile drugs, much as the
government's own stockpiling policies were broadly conceived in relation to anticipated global demand. The fact that Merck "had (and still
has) about half the U.S. narcotics business, and it manufactured a long
line of high-purity, low-bulk chemicals for pharmaceutical, food, laboratory and miscellaneous industrial uses,"[65] placed the company in a
position of being a primary supplier for the rest of the industry—a mid-
dleman supplying the reworkable raw materials of national drug manufacturing.

The political influence of Merck's leadership, its economic might,
and its capacity to stockpile and supply other drug manufacturers posi-
tioned the firm well to dominate the US export market. *Business Week*
reported in 1949 that across the drug industry common stock values
had increased significantly from before the war to its aftermath. At the
head of the corporate pack was Merck, whose common stock in the
later 1930s had ranged between $0.30 and $1.74, whereas by 1948 it
was rated at $7.34 per share.[66] Merck's powerful domestic position also
made it an increasingly significant player in the global drug trade. Global demand for US drug exports had grown as a direct consequence of
the war. As early as December 1941 *Barron's*, an investor publication,
reported that the "increase in the company's business since 1938 can be
attributed to the war, which has resulted in a stimulation of exports and
large purchases by the Federal Government."[67] Looking back on the
decade, the Department of Commerce described how every year drug
exports reached a new peak.[68] A few years earlier, in 1946, Merck set up
PWR Export Corporation "to handle the growing volume of foreign
sales."[69] As *Fortune* reported on the company's overseas business,
"Before the war Merck had none to speak of. . . . Today, however, it is
quite sizable."[70] Export sales soared by over 700 percent from a total of
$24 million in 1940 to $171 million in 1951.[71] Having been primarily
in the drug wholesale business, after merging with Sharpe & Dohme in
1953, the company fully embodied the vertically integrated powerhouse
whose laboratories churned out an array of pharmaceutical and chemical concoctions for human, animal, agricultural, and industrial uses

with a "new emphasis on global operations." In the wake of World War II's destruction of competitors' plants and markets, Merck embraced a "vigorous return to globalism," and with the formation of Merck North American and Merck Panamerica, export sales grew to some 20 percent of the company's overall revenue by the early 1950s. The new chief executive officer in 1955, John T. Connor, described the firm as a "free world enterprise based in the United States." Over the next six years "total assets in foreign manufacturing tripled," and the international wing of the company was running twenty plants in nineteen countries around the world.[72]

As a privileged player in the narcotics trade, Merck came to have enormous influence over national defense policy in relation to all drugs, and became one of the most formidable players in the international chemical field. The story of Maywood Chemical Works' close collaboration with the government, as the only other FBN authorized importer of coca leaves apart from Merck, further reveals the evolving relationship between the government and select drug manufacturers during this time period. Maywood was the world's largest importer of coca leaves, and in the war's aftermath it was able, with the helpful intervention of the Coca-Cola Company, to maintain a manufacturing monopoly on the production of a nonnarcotic flavoring extract from the leaves. This depended on securing support from the FBN both in terms of limiting participation in the coca leaf import market by means of government licensing, as well as securing adequate stockpiles to sustain the growing international market for America's famous soft drink. Maywood's role in the coca-based commodity market shows more than the increased economic concentration that accompanied drug control. It also reflected the alchemical possibilities of a drug manufacturing process producing end products that could move (or attempt to move) beyond the regulatory gaze in the form of new commodities that were not necessarily policed or controlled substances, but that benefited from the parameters of participation within the legitimate drug market established by the drug control regime.

While it had been during World War I that a number of US subsidiaries of German pharmaceutical houses were first nationalized, World War II also produced a number of confiscations, at least of those portions of corporate assets that continued to be held by "enemy" nationals. In the case of Maywood, the working out of such a seizure and subsequent sale further reveals some of the mechanisms that justified and sustained a limited arena of economic participation in the drug trade.[73] Upon hearing of the upcoming auction of Maywood stocks seized by the Alien Property Custodian during the war, Ralph Hayes, an executive at Coca-Cola, wrote to the US Commissioner of Narcotics in January 1949 to advocate on Maywood's behalf. At that time, Coca-Cola had an obvious stake in the company's future, being responsible for almost half of Maywood's sales income as the sole purchaser of a coca leaf extract manufactured by its chemists.[74] Hayes explained to Anslinger, "It is our frank hope, as one customer of Maywood, that it might be the successful purchaser" of the shares being held by the government. Hayes informed the FBN that he had spoken with the Alien Property Custodian and had determined that aside from Maywood, S. B. Penick Company was the only other prospective bidder. Outlining the grounds that might be used to assess the suitability of potential bidders, Hayes emphasized that "first, naturally, would be [their] financial responsibility, moral reputation and industrial capability." He went on to suggest that restricting ownership would advance the country's drug control agenda, arguing it was necessary to deploy the "same considerations you would have in mind" for those seeking to "import materials of the type brought in by Maywood." In other words, the fact that Maywood imported "special leaves" (the legal category for coca leaves imported for the manufacturing of Coca-Cola) raised security concerns surrounding the importation of controlled substances.[75]

Ultimately, the Commissioner of Narcotics agreed. Apparently having contacted the Office of Alien Property subsequent to receiving Hayes's letter, Anslinger outlined a response to the Coca-Cola Company's concerns. The FBN expressed a particular interest in the matter "from the standpoint of control measures over the narcotic drug traffic; that Maywood has been cooperative from this point of view" and that Penick was "a comparative newcomer in the narcotic production field." Fusing Hayes's arguments regarding industrial capability with concerns over moral responsibility and the dealing in controlled substances, the FBN assented to Coca-Cola's view of the matter. The bureau "would rather see Maywood continue" having total ownership of company stock in light of their record of being "cooperative" with the government in ensuring effective drug control. Policing imperatives, thus in effect, were deployed to justify limiting participation in the manufacturing market.[76] The company particularly was not eager to see Maywood's monopoly over the provision of its product's flavoring extract subject to economic influences outside—and even in potential competition with—their already-established business partner.

By highlighting the need to ensure adequate drug control, Coca-Cola successfully sought—through the government's enforcement apparatus—to eliminate the interference of a potential competitor. Since at least the 1930s Penick had been trying to gain entry into the coca–soft drink market, yet had been unsuccessful in acquiring legal supplies of coca leaves.[77] Their bid to take control of what amounted to almost a quarter of Maywood stock presumably would have given them access to this valuable commodity.[78] While the rivalry, or "Cola Wars," between Coca-Cola and Pepsi-Cola have received considerable attention, for the most part they played out in competition over consumer markets and sales.[79] With regard to the acquisition of raw materials for beverage manufacturing, an argument grounded in the value of drug control worked to the competitive advantage of Coca-Cola and its pharmaceutical supplier of coca leaf extract, Maywood. Later the same year, US officials continued to try to discourage Penick from entering the coca processing business, this time by denying their application to import coca leaves. When Penick tried to argue for their inclusion in the coca manufacturing market, the Chief Counsel of the Treasury Department A.L. Tennyson outlined arguments that might be made to discourage them. Again, drug control imperatives, specifically the "international movement toward limitation of production of coca leaves," became the justification for restricting market participation. Additionally, the Treasury official emphasized other discouraging factors, highlighting the import duty expense, the Internal Revenue tax, "in addition to initial cost, transportation charges, and expense of production."[80] Thus government regulation in and of itself was presented as a burdensome—and from the government's perspective a hopefully prohibitive—obstacle to expanded participation in the drug manufacturing market.

While the number of participants in the coca leaf import and manufacturing market was carefully limited, the scale of production steadily increased. It is in this realm that the convergence of interests in stockpiling for defense and the expansion of concentrated economic power come to the fore. It was during this period that Maywood began to stockpile larger quantities of coca leaves to meet, as Maywood's President M.J. Hartung explained to the FBN in 1948, the increased demand that came with Coca-Cola's expansion and "process improvements." Maywood anticipated its need for coca leaves would almost double in the next decade. In a letter to Anslinger verifying Maywood's authorization to expand importations of coca leaves, Hartung characterized the company's future dependence on stockpiling: "To make operations economical and profitable, MCW [Maywood Chemical Works] must be in a position to extract coca leaves without interruption, and the seasonal availability of leaf in Peru and the uncertain shipping facilities from Salaverry, necessitates the keeping of an ample stock of leaves on hand in this country. We are accordingly now building up a reserve at Maywood and we understand that this has your approval."[81]

To ensure profitability—by supplying coca extract to fuel Coca-Cola's global expansion—Maywood was building a Federal Bureau of Narcotics' sanctioned reserve store of coca leaves. Maywood needed the stockpile, the company suggested, to avoid seasonal fluctuations in coca leaf supply or "uncertain" Peruvian facilities that might adversely affect the company's access to raw materials. South America figured as the "uncertain" aspect of the commodity circuit that stockpiling was intended to overcome. Maywood invoked Coca-Cola's expanding production as an almost naturalized, if not explicitly valorized, aspect of the equation. As stockpiling became increasingly central to national defense, the definition of "defense" came to include policies designed to protect select corporations invested in the US drug market.

As this correspondence suggests, the federal government intervened in the drug market to police the boundaries of legality regarding raw material production, distribution, and manufacturing. This was implemented primarily through limiting the scale and scope of participation within the market—while ensuring an adequate flow of raw materials to authorized manufacturers. The advantages of these collaborations for select private companies extended to other areas of operations. When Commissioner Anslinger received data on the Peruvian coca industry, he forwarded it to Maywood executives. The company's president responded with an expression of his appreciation for the "map showing the coca growing areas and the location of crude cocaine factories in Peru. Because of our connections with Peru these maps are especially interesting to us and I deeply appreciate your having sent them."[82] Mutually advantageous ties were forged between licensed drug manufacturers and the government agencies charged with policing the drug market. This model of drug control produced a convergence of interests that helped establish a relative monopoly over aspects of drug manufacturing, and corporate beneficiaries could invoke their cooperation as justification for maintaining privileged access to the market not merely with regard to raw materials, but also in relation to the worldwide circulation of finished goods.

EXPORTING RESOURCES FOR FREEDOM

The close collaboration between the FBN, Maywood, and Coca-Cola extended into the realm of exporting and marketing America's "resources for freedom," the canned (or bottled) consumer products deemed essential to maintaining and extending US power. Pharmaceutical companies like Merck and Maywood occupied critical roles in economic defense mobilization as processors and reworkers of drug commodities for government and private stockpiles. The third company centrally involved in the coca trade, Coca-Cola (a primary purchaser of chemically reworked coca leaves), assumed the role of reworking labor, marketing, and consumer habits to meet the needs of the company—and American capitalism more generally as it expanded into the world. Fittingly, for the first time in the magazine's history, on May 15, 1950, *Time* featured a branded product on its cover: a giant smiling Coca-Cola logo personified, cradling the head of a thirsty world as it suckled on a Coke bottle. Echoing the message of the feature article contained inside the issue, the cover image caption read "World And Friend," and its subtitle emphasized the monetary and cultural profit to be made from Coca-Cola's overseas operations: "Love that piaster, that lira, that tickey, and that American way of life."

The company had been aggressively pursuing international markets since the 1920s and by World War II, with the help of the Coca-Cola Export Corporation established in 1930, the company had bottling plants in Europe, Asia, and South America. However, it was wartime collaboration with the government to ensure adequate supplies of Coca-Cola for the nation's military that laid the groundwork for the company's subsequent unprecedented international expansion. The company's official biographer described the convergence of patriotism and profit making in her assessment of this history: "The war was history's ultimate drama of good against evil. . . . And when men like [then Coca-Cola President Robert W.] Woodruff at the head of large companies spoke of helping the war effort, of abetting the fighting forces, they can, in the context of the time, be credited with speaking as much out of patriotic as profit motivation." The company was very conscious of the ways in which this dual motivation might be received as an imperial imposition and worked hard to cast its bottling franchise system as a means to "avoid the appearance of the 'ugly American' in foreign countries and to offset American intellectuals' denunciation of 'exploitative,' giant multinational corporations."[83] To this end, in order to feed a thirsty world, the company promoted its commitment to cultivate local ground troops of distribution. *Time* celebrated the company's elaborate training program for future overseas bottlers and distributors that it flew in to be schooled at a training session in New York, where they went on to various US plants and spent time at Coca-Cola's "central Production School" in Atlanta. *Time* promoted Coca-Cola's trainee education as "one of the miracles of organization" that had made the company so successful. In a vision suggesting the hegemonic force and benefits of US capitalism *Time* declared: "Coca-Cola coolly takes hold of Japanese capitalists, German bureaucrats and Bolivian laborers and trains them to do a series of specific jobs in every move and thought the way they are done in America. What's more, the trainees like it."[84]

Specifically, according to H. B. Nicholson, the company's president in 1952, Coca-Cola was training this global labor force "in production and sales promotion." Echoing *Time*'s presumption of the benefits such training brought to the world's laborers, capitalists, and bureaucrats, Nicholson explained, "[T]he basic attraction for Coca-Cola salesmen is the sense of dignity they are given to feel in their jobs. People everywhere are proud, especially in the depressed areas of the world." Becoming the distributors of American goods represented, in this formulation, an opportunity for gaining self-respect through work; it became a mechanism for spreading the American dream to modernize and develop the "depressed" parts of the world. Nicholson explained that this transformation entailed "[a] full-scale industrial education, for there is no telling what stages of development [trainees] will encounter in the various parts of the world. It becomes us to remember that races not knowing anything about refrigeration, for example, may have cradled the world's religions, or art treasures immemorial, or the tradition of freedom, or the pulsating rhythms of primitive song and story. In so small a world, we need all these people as friends."[85]

Describing the Coca-Cola's New York headquarters as "a miniature United Nations," Nicholson preached the advantages of molding those who would help distribute and bottle the company's merchandise into effective capitalist entrepreneurs—so that US products might be appropriately refrigerated overseas. He did not want his audience, the New York Herald Tribune Forum, to overlook the exploitable possibilities of labor everywhere. Coca-Cola's president wanted them to "remember" the value of other "races" of the world, even those at lower "stages of development" ("primitive," "pulsating," "immemorial"). For Coca-Cola, they embodied value both as providers of the world's cultural "treasures"—an expression of paternalistic commodification—as well as, and no doubt more importantly, the raw material for manufacturing Coca-Cola salesmen.

Training salesmen was critical to ensuring the company's successful expansion and built off of an operating structure that Coca-Cola already had implemented in the United States. The company's domestic decentralized operations were mimicked in its overseas operations, although it acknowledged, "not all bottling franchises are in indigenous hands, particularly in underdeveloped countries."[86] As the company president described, "The company manufactured the syrup or concentrate, that goes to make the finished product. With few exceptions, both at home and abroad, the bottling operation is the business of locally owned and locally operated enterprises." Thus decentralization was seen as an effective route toward market penetration, benefiting from the advantages of local participation in distribution. The trainees who staffed these "locally owned" operations were "governed only by an agreement that protects the use of the trademark and the quality of the finished product for the ultimate consumer. Thus it is possible to advertise Coca-Cola as the same drink everywhere in the world."[87] Coca-Cola was branded as a definitively American commodity, but others, the company asserted, benefited from bringing it to market.

The local nature of participation meant that the company advertised its operations as contributing to the economic development of other nations: "In local countries that aren't too highly industrialized, the local bottlers encourage the development of the supplying industries. . . . Since 1945 in Columbia [sic], for example, factories have been established for making CO_2 gas, bottles, crowns, cases, coolers, and outdoor signs. Colombian bottlers can now buy these business requirements in Colombia. What's more, these supplying industries have developed other customers in the Colombian market. When Coke goes on sale anywhere, the business contributes fairly and squarely to the economic welfare of the people there."[88]

The Coca-Cola Company benefited from presenting itself as a motor for other nations' economic development—or "welfare"—while being able to devolve the company of responsibility for those local operations. Thus, Nicholson argued that decentralization had political value as well, particularly in countering challenges to American influence. He described the valuable "national" identities of local operatives: "During the recent events in Egypt, we encountered no difficulties because Coke is an Egyptian business giving permanent employment to 3,000 Egyptians." Aside from the implicit valorization of American capitalism as "giving" employment (rather than, say, extracting profits), Nicholson's comments reveal another critical formation that was exported with US capital. The decentralization of operations helped the US government and US private capital avoid political responsibility for local operations—one consequence of decentralization that is still being hotly contested today.

The economic model espoused by Coca-Cola executives offers a striking example of the way contemporary modernization and development theory genuinely influenced US self-perception and the belief in the benevolent impact of the nation's global market penetration. Their ideological vision seemed to embody the ideas famously advanced in Walt Rostow's *The Stages of Economic Growth*. Rostow depicted a model of economic development that presumed the world's societies passed through identifiable stages of economic development where the highest stage, "the age of high-mass consumption," was incarnate in postwar US society. This economic vision was conducive to US imperialism since it cast the majority of the world's people as inhabiting nations that existed at lower evolutionary stages of economic development and presumed the United States, as the most advanced, had an important role to play in helping them "modernize." Premised on hierarchical national comparisons, advocates of this vision did not acknowledge, as many US policymakers did at the time, that this economic vision relied on other countries' perpetual provisioning of raw materials along with the imposition of sets of legal controls that limited the accumulation of profits to people living on the peripheries of the capitalist world system. Often, the actual historical impact and workings of integration into a US-centered capitalist system might more accurately be characterized, as scholars who challenged modernization theory pointed out, as producing "dependency" and "underdevelopment." The natural resources, cheap labor, and consumer markets that Coca-Cola officials celebrated cultivating overseas, in the context of marketing a product derived in part from the international drug trade, actively integrated those countries into a global political economy and its accompanying regulatory apparatus that bolstered US power and fostered economic vulnerability and dependency in many regions of the world.[89]

Coca-Cola was able to capitalize on decentralizing operations while, importantly for both the company's and the nation's power, firmly retaining ownership over the finished product. This was accomplished in part, as *Time* enthused, by having distributors perform "specific jobs in every move and thought the way they are done in America." More significantly, the company also retained trademark rights over the Coca-Cola drink wherever it was manufactured. Local bottlers and distributors were subject to a contract that controlled the substance in the finished product as well as directing and providing materials for advertising campaigns that indelibly linked the soft drink to the company and American capitalism. The enforced branding of commodities as "American" was one way of securing and promoting US interests abroad. As Coca-Cola executive James A. Farley explained to other business representatives at the annual "Brand Names Day" dinner in New York in April 1952:

> When we speak to a man in another country of democracy, he may or may not understand us. The idea may be beyond his comprehension; or perhaps a poor brand of democracy has been sold to him by somebody else before. But when you give him a ride in your Jeep or offer him a Chesterfield, a package of Chiclets (or even a soft beverage of some kind), this is something he can easily judge for himself. We are therefore in a position where the things that we manufacture—American brand name products—are perhaps the best proof of what we are and the best ambassadors of our country.[90]

Farley described American commodities themselves as the best tools for overcoming cultural difference and representing the wonders of US democracy overseas. Conflating US democracy and capitalism, in contrast to the "poor brand of democracy" on sale elsewhere, US-branded goods embodied "proof of what we are." Thus, American-manufactured commodities—capitalists argued—not only brought good business practices for fueling local economic development, but beyond that, they acted as material "ambassadors" for the US political system.

These ambassadors often traveled under the authority of the US policing apparatus, particularly as they moved into geographies where they were not always welcomed, and especially when they involved controlled substances. For instance, in the aftermath of World War II, there were particular resentments to the dominating US presence in Europe. Sometimes the challenge to this presence took the form of invoking the drug control regulatory apparatus to challenge the legitimacy of US commodities. Thus, in 1946 Portuguese authorities refused to authorize the construction of a Coca-Cola bottling plant until the US government provided certification that all narcotic alkaloids (cocaine) had been removed from the "extracts sold by Maywood Chemical Works" destined for inclusion in the drink.[91] When Ralph Hayes of Coca-Cola brought this to the FBN's attention, Commissioner Anslinger responded with an "official communication" to the Inspector of the Pharmaceutical Division of the Office of the Director-General of Public Health of Portugal providing the necessary verifications, in wording proposed by the company.[92] The FBN worked closely with the Coca-Cola Company—and as a mediator with foreign governments—to help expand the latter's business operations. Along with overseas resistance to US corporate penetration, the very success of American marketing techniques often inspired local opposition. Thus in January 1951, the Narcotics Control Officer for the Office of the US High Commission for Germany contacted the bureau, reporting that: "Beverage manufacturers in most Western European countries have reacted strongly to the competition of Coca Cola and Pepsi Cola. The aggressive advertising campaigns to further sales of American coca drinks in Europe are particularly resented."

These advertising campaigns had sparked efforts in both France and Germany to have legal prohibitions to limit sales of these drinks. The US High Commission anticipated that "interested European groups will try to protect themselves against the onerous competition of American coca drinks by manufacturing similar beverages themselves."[93] In correspondence responding to these developments, Anslinger downplayed the ability of national or international competitors to effectively replicate Coca-Cola's manufacturing process—explaining that the FBN had been "pestered with numerous attempts," but none had had success in their effort to "develop a coca flavor resembling Coca Cola." Anslinger added, "We suggest that for enforcement reasons also you discourage the import of coca leaves for the purpose as much as possible."[94] Thus once again, US officials sought to undermine US manufacturers' competition by invoking the necessities of drug control in order to limit others' access to valuable raw materials.

In a revealing moment, Anslinger went on to argue that the quantities of coca leaf in Coca-Cola were relatively insignificant: "comparing the limited quantities of coca extract manufactured with the huge volume of finished coca cola extract sold and exported, we are convinced that the contribution of the former to the ultimate flavor to be insignificant, and suspect it continues to be used merely to enable the Company to retain the word 'Coca' in the name which it has spent millions to advertise."[95]

The FBN suggested the importance of the leaf to the company was primarily in retaining the word "Coca" as part of its famous brand name. The elaborate policing of the raw materials—and government certification of the finished goods—was constructed around a substance deemed (in this perhaps self-serving formulation) as materially insignificant, but symbolically fundamental to the success of the business operation. The emphasis on marketing as the explanation for Coca-Cola's success echoed the alchemical sleight of hand in Anslinger's disavowal of the "insignificant" coca leaf. While undoubtedly Coca-Cola's international business model was astronomically profitable, questions over the contents of the drink itself deserve more scrutiny as they reveal murky dividing lines between drug foods, controlled substances, and the selective policing of the market to the advantage of US corporations. Coca-Cola, since its invention as a temperance beverage in the 1890s, was marketed "first and foremost—[as] a medicine." Sold initially as a patent medicine, nicknames for the drink inspired a drug lingo still resonant today ("coke," "dope," "cold dope," a "shot," or a "shot in the arm").[96] The company responded to an early 1900s cultural panic fueled by racist fears of the dangers of African American cocaine consumption by having a pharmaceutical firm extract the cocaine alkaloid before utilizing the spent leaves.[97] Nevertheless, the company continued (and continues to the present day) to be hounded by questions over the drink's addictive properties and potentially nefarious health impact. This included weathering criminal charges brought against the company in 1911 by the Chief of the Bureau of Chemistry for the US Department of Agriculture for "marketing and selling an adulterated beverage that was injurious to health because it contained a deleterious ingredient, namely, caffeine."[98] By World War II, keenly aware of the dangers of marketing their beverage as a drug, company officials both hinted at its rejuvenating properties while insisting "Coca-Cola is a nonessential product, if ever there was one." The statement seems ironic since General Dwight D. Eisenhower himself personally intervened to have Coca-Cola plants set up as near as possible to the fighting front of the war in the interest of maintaining the morale of America's GIs," suggesting it was far from "nonessential."[99] Moreover, the company frequently advertised the drink's energizing properties in its sales literature, including a 1942 pamphlet entitled "Importance of the Rest-Pause in Maximum War Effort," which "reproduced a batch of letters from civilian war workers hinting that they could hardly survive without Coke."[100]

In the context of postwar expansion, questions concerning the drink's content (whether it included drug substances that were, or should be, controlled) became a critical terrain for contests over the benefits and hazards of US "resources for freedom." The leadership of the company seemed to embrace its role as the iconic embodiment of America's expansion. In response to "widespread hostility toward Coca-Cola in the Communist bloc countries," the company vice president circulated a memo: "Apparently, some of our friends overseas have difficulty distinguishing between the United States and Coca-Cola. Perhaps we should not complain too much about this."[101] Yet, with Belgian Communists referring to the drink as a "forerunner of Fascism," the French newspaper *Le Monde* decrying the "moral landscape of France is at stake!" in support of French winemakers' opposition to the drink, the Soviets calling it a "brown poison," and the Viennese publication *Der Abend* warning "Ten bottles will make the user a helpless slave of Coca-Cola for life," the drink and its secret properties together came to represent America's imperial ambitions.[102] The company historically was very adept at avoiding sanctions premised on the beverage's chemical content. During prohibition the company marketed its product as a temperance beverage even while benefiting from its use as a "prime mixer." Similarly telling, as E. J. Kahn, Jr. described, "the official Coca-Cola line is that Coke should never perform chemical, or alchemical, function, but when it comes to combining the drink with substances that can be swallowed without harm, the company is fairly indulgent."[103] While the company could not control the uses to which people put its product, it did work closely with the government through the drug regulatory apparatus to retain its unusual monopoly over the nonmedicinal use of coca leaves, to conceal beneath government-backed trademark protections the list of its ingredients, and to facilitate its international expansion.

Coca-Cola occupied a unique place in the growing American empire, as it helped facilitate, in Victoria De Grazia's succinct formulation, "the rise of a great imperium with the outlook of a great emporium."[104] Commercial, and legal, branding helped US companies retain control and secure profits from the marketing and distribution of manufactured goods overseas. The trademark, executives and government officials believed, advertised the proof of the superiority of the American way of life while capturing the nation's individualistic democratic ethos with the personalization of branded commodities. It also enshrined within it the enforcement and policing apparatus that accompanied US expansion, ensuring profits continued to flow back to the United States. For example, in an effort to disarm challenges to Coca-Cola's expansion, company president Ralph Hayes approached the FBN in 1950 to request that the flavoring extract be exported with a stamp bearing US government certification. Together an arrangement was devised whereby officials from the Federal Bureau of Narcotics made regular site visits to Maywood Chemical Works and took samples of Merchandise #5 (containing the coca extract manufactured for Coca-Cola), which was then tested by "Government chemists" who certified that the extract was indeed "non-narcotic." The certification was then prominently displayed

FIGURE 3. Government "certified non-narcotic" seal for exports of the Coca-Cola Company's flavoring extract, 1950.

on the "stainless steel drums" of extract that were intended for export. The Coca-Cola Company commissioned "a commercial artist" to draw the "lettering and design" that appeared on the seal.[105]

Once the design and certification operation had been established, Maywood shipped the government-sealed and -approved Merchandise #5 to Coca-Cola's "plant at Kearny from which our Export Corporation will have it forwarded overseas as required."[106] Responding to international concerns over drug trafficking (and US imperialism), Coca-Cola's private marketing initiatives drew upon government resources to brand their product a "legitimate" US commodity of international trade. The "certified non-narcotic" seal that was attached to drums of Merchandise #5 effectively advertised not only the commodities' content, but also the company's privileged relationship with the US policing apparatus that had facilitated gaining easier access to drug raw materials and the international consumer market.

. . .

Drawing from the model that had been implemented on the ground as far as "cultivating" favorable trade and distribution networks in South

America during World War II, and in the context of an economy geared toward raw materials stockpiling for defense mobilization, US manufacturers involved in the coca commodity circuit marketed their system of unequal participation in the international drug commodity circuit as a capitalist ethic of democracy and freedom. Thus, for example, the Coca-Cola Company exported a model for economic growth along with its flavoring concentrate; a concentrate whose manufacturing process involved the extraction of cocaine from coca leaves (imported from the Andes), performed by the pharmaceutical house Maywood Chemical Works. Coca-Cola's use of coca leaves, along with the business interests of the only other authorized importer, Merck & Co., Inc., had produced extensive relations and collaborations between company executives and various agencies of the federal government, including the Federal Bureau of Narcotics. These relations and the economic visions they shared contributed during the war and in the war's aftermath to the pharmaceutical industry and US economic hegemony's considerable expansion. The invocation of the wonders of American economic growth was promoted by powerful interests in the government, among corporations, and in the media, as proof of the benefits of participating in the US capitalist system—and as the basis for securing and maintaining national defense. Capitalism, they argued, was democracy. And democracy was their "brand" of capitalism, quite literally. In a presentation in 1952, the president of Coca-Cola explained: "The Coca-Cola business has been compared to a pyramid, with the company and its suppliers taking a small share from the top, the bottlers and their suppliers taking a larger middle share, and the dealers who retail the product taking the largest share at the broad base of the business. We feel this working democracy has contributed immeasurably to acceptance of our product overseas. Because the product is profitable to everybody involved with it, everybody subscribes readily to the methods for selling more of it."[107]

This "working democracy" depended on the structural inequalities within distribution (and of course, unmentioned by the president, production) of the commodities themselves. This depiction of the divergent and unequal roles to be played by different sectors of the commodity distribution chain was presented as natural and desirable, even as *the* method for generating democracy through capitalism. Coca-Cola marketed its corporate model of decentralization of distribution—local bottlers and distributors—as a participatory democracy. It was in fact a "working democracy" working for Coca-Cola, an internationally derived, stamped, and packaged "American" commodity. To a certain extent the commodities themselves did the work of enforcing and transmitting not only the material but ideological powers of empire. "Profits" were depicted as the new measure of democratic access and inclusion. An illusion of democratic distribution, Coca-Cola's vision of the popular pyramid buttressing its business success was in fact simply a model of unequal development. This underdevelopment was maintained not only through a trade and regulatory apparatus premised on extracting raw materials for the manufacturing of US goods and a national defense policy premised on the power of stockpiling, but also on the attendant integration of other nations into this system—which included policing of "legitimacy" within it—to service American capital, working as the distributors and consumers of US commodities.

Yet simply producing the consumer goods did not guarantee people would consume them. Coca-Cola executives, for example, had confronted this obstacle for decades. Coca-Cola had been available in the Andes since the first decades of the twentieth century. As the company began to expand more aggressively, bottling plants were established in Peru and Bolivia in 1936 and 1941, respectively.[108] The success of this expansion depended on transforming the consuming habits of local populations. When the US Board of Economic Warfare tracked the coca leaf export market during World War II, they determined that there were "three types of beverages containing Bolivian coca . . . sold under the trade marks of 'Coca Cocktail,' . . . 'Crema de Coca' . . . and 'Coca Kiln,' " in Brazil. The market, however, for such drinks among the indigenous population of Bolivia was initially small in a context where traditional forms of coca consumption persisted: "Coca is consumed by Indians, who chew it, and by people of all classes, in a tea or infusion."[109] The bureau's agents went on to report just two years after the bottling plant had been established: "It is understood that Coca Cola (which is bottled locally on a fairly large scale, employing extracts imported from the United States) contains none of the narcotic element of coca, but it is widely believed among Bolivians who consume it that it does."[110]

Whether Bolivians' alleged belief that Coca-Cola contained "narcotic elements" was due to the soft drink's name or its "legitimate" energizing properties (caffeine and sugar) is hard to know. But the racial and class composition of the potential consumer market—the Indians being the ones that "chew it" whereas "all classes" drink it—was important to the company and reveals a lot about the mechanisms and stages of US consumer capitalism's expansion. As the Coca-Cola Company studied the world for the most lucrative consumer markets, it divided up nations into their constituent racial and national groups. Categories such as "White," "Foreigner," "Indian," "Mestizo," "half caste," "European," "East Indian," and "Maori" were tabulated in a prewar "Expansion Plan" of 1936 to help guide decisions regarding the current regional prospects for successful market penetration. The race of the prospective consumer not only affected estimates of whether they would "have money enough to buy Coca Cola," but also, in countries such as Peru and Bolivia, helped gauge the degree to which the population had been incorporated into a consumer market for imported, mass-produced goods.[111] The plan conveyed Peru's population demographic as "Peru (6,2000,000—600,000 White)" and the country was identified as an earlier candidate than Bolivia for the establishment of a bottling plant, perhaps because of Bolivia's relatively small white population and large percentage of indigenous peoples. Even so, the company believed that the existence of a large Indian population in Peru at that time still cautioned against rapid large-scale expansion: "The colonial influence seems to persist more in Peru than elsewhere in the South American countries. A large part of the population is of pure Indian blood. Coca-Cola can be successfully marketed in Peru, but I think the potential market is comparatively small . . . it would be necessary for us to assign a member of our staff to remain in Lima for two or three months to initiate our method of aggressive marketing and to build up an adequate showing of advertising."[112]

As raw materials were extracted from the world, transformed and stockpiled, these commodity surpluses were "reworked" much as the pharmaceutical industry could rework military surplus narcotics to be sold as new once again. These drug commodities—and the system of control that traveled with them—were repackaged as national "American" commodities. The international raw material and labor power and energy that these commodities stored within them were transfigured into exemplars of American business acumen and ingenuity and as necessities for securing US security and global dominance. The national stockpiles of US-controlled—and -sold—drug commodities, helped lay the foundations for a new American empire, bolstered by a policing apparatus built to enforce its hegemony. Linking US capitalism's successful expansion to the organic health of the globe, US officials enshrined the US economy—and its privileged position in relation to resource extraction, stockpiling, and goods distribution—as a promise of freedom for the rest of the world. As *Resources for Freedom* declared, "The size of future demand, and the adequacy of supplies, will depend upon the rate at which the United States economy and that of the whole free world expands."[113] Yet, as Coca-Cola's fears over market penetration in the Andes foreshadowed, debates about race, class, consuming habits, and colonial conflict consistently accompanied US efforts to dictate participation within the international coca commodity circuit and the pharmaceutical market more broadly, a process described in more detail in the following chapters.

CHAPTER 3

Raw Materialism

Exporting Drug Control to the Andes[1]

The unequal position in which nations found themselves with regard to access and participation in the international drug trade in the aftermath of World War II depended on more than the promotion of an ideology and economic model to advance and justify US global preeminence. It entailed the rigorous design and enforcement of an international policing apparatus. The US government sought to ensure the access of pharmaceutical manufacturers to the raw materials flowing from the global South into US pharmaceutical laboratories, and to promote the consumption and reexport of US mass-produced drugs. This required a concerted effort to implement an effective international drug control regime, including an often contested determination to revise laws and cultural practices in those nations where valuable drug agricultural crops were cultivated. While over the subsequent decades marijuana and an array of synthetic drugs came under the purview of drug control officials, initially the two primary raw materials targeted by regulators included the poppy plant and the coca leaf, used for manufacturing opiates, cocaine, and Coca-Cola. The production of opium involved an international network of economic, military, and political interests invested in a commodity chain spreading raw material from Southeast Asia and the Middle East into Europe and the United States (where it was transformed into pharmaceutical painkillers). The coca commodity chain, on the other hand, was more exclusively situated within a US imperial domain due to the fact that the principal geographic location of coca leaf cultivation was the Andes Mountain slopes of South America; a part of the hemisphere that US interventionists have long enjoyed proprietarily depicting as "America's backyard." Looking at postwar efforts to police the international coca trade offers a unique window onto the workings of US power through its considerable influence in shaping the principles governing international drug control. Advocates of drug control, led by US officials, focused their attention on limiting the cultivation of drug crops according to parameters established by the combined interests of the pharmaceutical industry and US national ambition.

Efforts to police the international drug trade were not new, but the novel balance of power in the postwar world, characterized by the US's unprecedented position of global dominance, ensured that international drug control took on a new character. The determined effort to regulate the international flow of drug commodities was a twentieth-century invention. It was a structure that had been modeled on US domestic policy and it sought to establish regulatory oversight through a system of licensing and taxation to monitor the international trade. Until mid-century, global participation and reporting was haphazard and the drug control regime had relatively limited authority. By the onset of World War II, only in the early stages of implementation, international efforts to maintain the drug control apparatus effectively went into hibernation. At war's end, the drug control functions that had previously fallen under the authority of the League of Nations were transferred to the United Nations, which established the Commission on Narcotic Drugs (CND) to oversee its implementation. The internationally renowned Harry J. Anslinger, the commissioner of the US Federal Bureau of Narcotics who had played a pivotal role in mobilizing and organizing the international drug trade to advance US interests in both war and peacetime, immediately assumed an influential position on the newly constituted CND as the official US delegate to that body. Anslinger's impact on the CND's work cannot be overstated, as he was the most prominent advocate for drug control of the most powerful nation working to steer the new commission's agenda toward US priorities. As World War II transitioned into the Cold War, and with US officials exerting a disproportionate influence on international drug control, pressure grew for Andean countries, especially Peru and Bolivia, to limit coca leaf cultivation according to definitions of legality and illegality being established by powerful interests invested in the drug trade.[2]

The United States and the United Nations were the main architects of the drug control regime that sought to eliminate all production of coca in excess of those leaves grown and processed for what international drug conventions of 1925 and 1931 had designated as "legitimate needs."[3] The conventions defined "legitimate needs" narrowly to include exclusively those leaves destined for "medical and scientific" purposes. US national narcotics law since its inception in the 1914 Harrison Narcotics Act included an additional "legitimate" allowance that Anslinger successfully lobbied for inclusion in international regulations: "special coca leaves" destined for use in the manufacture of a "nonnarcotic flavoring extract"; in other words, for the manufacturing of Coca-Cola (illustrating the already formidable influence on the tenets of international drug control by US private companies and the state). Under the drug control system, first coordinated through the League of Nations, signatory countries submitted annual estimates of their "legitimate need" for narcotics to a board that monitored the trade by overseeing a system of nationally administered import and export certificates. Governments were responsible for granting authorizations to importers and exporters as a way of monitoring the volume of trade to prevent domestic stocks of controlled substances from exceeding a given country's annual estimates. There had been a long history of US unilateral efforts to gain South American compliance with US priorities for the flow of coca commodities, relying particularly on what historian Paul Gootenberg refers to as "coca diplomacy," whereby private corporations with investments in the trade manipulated purchases in collusion with the FBN's efforts to pressure countries like Peru to "adopt US-style drug policies."[4] After the war, these private and national efforts became institutionalized internationally in the policies and priorities pursued by the CND.

THE TURN TO COCA LEAF LIMITATION

Of the various problems facing the Commission in regard to the control of the international traffic in narcotic drugs, that of limiting the production of raw materials needed for the manufacture of such drugs is the most urgent and important.
—UN Commission on Narcotic Drugs, 27 January 1947[5]

At the CND's very first session a reinvigorated focus on international trade was paired with "the most urgent and important" effort to limit and control a particular sector of the drug commodity chain: the production of raw materials. In practice this meant targeting the production of raw materials in the Southern Hemisphere: securing the access of European and American manufacturing countries to these raw materials while locking developing countries into the bottom rungs of global economic production. And to this end, one of the first major initiatives pursued by the United Nations was a push to control the production of the coca leaf—the one of two primary categories of narcotics (the other being opium) that resided firmly within a US sphere of influence. By July 1947, as part of the preparatory work for a conference to deal with "the possibility of limiting and controlling cultivation and harvesting of the coca leaf," the CND noted that while the international trade in coca leaves fell under earlier drug control treaties, "the existing conventions did not attempt to limit the cultivation and harvesting of coca leaves in producing countries." To that end, restricting coca cropping in the Andes to that destined for export became one of the first major projects launched by the CND.[6] The official reliance by drug control advocates on a legal framework of limiting the international drug trade according to regulators' definition of "legitimate needs" entailed recasting the largest legal market for coca leaves in the world as undesirable and illegal, namely the indigenous consumer market for the plant in the region where it originated.

In 1947 the world supply of coca leaves grew primarily on the Andean *cordillera* in Peru and Bolivia. Of those leaves not consumed locally, coca from the Andes was exported primarily to manufacturers in the United States, ensuring that any effort to limit and control the international coca commodity circuit was fundamentally structured by power inequities within and between nation-states of the Western Hemisphere.[7] As described in the previous chapter, the United States refashioned itself in the name of Cold War national security as the primary supplier of global "resources for freedom," and controlling the flow of raw materials into North American stockpiles became a policy priority. In the pursuit of this objective US government officials recognized that the new global order augured new roles to be played by institutions of international governance. In the drug field, US leadership guided priorities as the United Nations became a vehicle for assessing and then controlling the scale, scope, and context of "legitimate" distribution of the coca commodities (which included coca leaf, crude cocaine, cocaine hydrochloride, and coca flavoring extracts). The US unilateral drug control initiatives during the war, which linked control over the drug economy to the military, public health, and political priorities of wartime national security, found a prominent place in a Cold War expansionist vision. A concerted effort, both unilateral and through multinational forums like the United Nations, to extend the reach of narcotics control into countries that supplied the raw material imports for pharmaceutical manufacturing and national stockpiling became a key aspect of the system.

The United Nations may have been viewed by some as a forum for moderating US power—as a place for both weak and powerful countries to assert national interests within a new, rapidly evolving, international order. It was nevertheless structured by the convergence of US capitalism and the colonial legacy of Great Power diplomacy. The CND's attempts to delineate a "legal" coca leaf market by limiting production to selectively defined "legitimate needs" was part of a North–South global dialectic whereby the industrial powers continued to lay claim to the natural resources of the "developing" world, often by means of direct social, economic, and political intervention. The United States independently and through its influence at the United Nations sought to define the "legitimate" market for a natural resource, coca leaves, as exclusively one premised on the leaves being characterized as "raw material" for the manufacturing of other things. This entailed delegitimizing the widespread consumption of coca in its natural state, whether chewed, steeped as maté, or put to other cultural, spiritual, and ritual uses for which the plant was valued among indigenous communities in the Andes. In the process, the United Nations became a mechanism for pursuing US national security policy by extending the international policing of drug flows beyond national borders and into the domestic sphere of countries where coca leaves were grown.[8] Coca leaves and cocaine were not illegal themselves; they—and other substances that came to be regulated and culturally characterized as "dangerous drugs"—straddled the licit/illicit divide, their legal status being dependent on their circulation within the marketplace, that is, on who grew, manufactured, sold, and consumed them. As the multinational reach of the US pharmaceutical industry grew, so too did the international reach of a renewed drug control regime to police participation within it.

The geographic home of coca leaf cultivation, the semitropical slopes of the Andes Mountains, grounded the international routes through which coca-derived commodities flowed. While exact statistics are not available, the vast majority of coca leaves grown in Peru and Bolivia were cultivated for domestic consumption, where the leaf was particularly valued by the Aymara and Quechua communities. In 1946 the United Nations estimated that at minimum 17.5 million pounds of coca were cultivated in Peru and an additional 11 million pounds in Bolivia. This only accounted for coca that was taxed by the respective governments, vastly underestimating the actual amount grown since much coca grown domestically was not tracked or taxed. Of this low-estimated 28.5 million pounds of coca leaves cultivated in the Andes that year, only roughly 4 percent was destined for export to manufacturing countries (all from Peru).[9] The bulk of coca grown in Bolivia was consumed domestically or exported regionally, primarily to northern Argentina and to a lesser extent Chile (along with Bolivian agricultural workers).[10] With the drug control regime now targeting "raw materials" and, in particular, seeking to eliminate the market for all coca that was not being exported to the North American market, Bolivia's position as a producer exclusively for a domestic and regional market of largely coca leaf chewers meant its international leverage was negligible. This was in contrast to Peru, which was the primary cultivator of coca leaf for the international market constructed to meet North American and European demand for coca-infused beverages and pharmaceutical-grade cocaine since the turn of the twentieth century. Chewing and consuming the coca leaf in its raw state were practices limited to the Andes. Once exported from the region, industrial chemical manufacturers invariably transformed coca leaves when they used them as building blocks for other commodities, most notably Coca-Cola and cocaine hydrochloride.[11] Setting aside the regional economy for the moment, the vast majority of coca leaves exported from Peru were imported by manufacturers in the United States.

The United States was the destination for 85 percent of Peru's coca leaves export market in 1946.[12] The United States dominated this market not only because of regional ties but also more importantly because of US narcotics law, which fell under the jurisdiction of the Treasury Department and operated through the taxation of trade. Coca, as a legally designated "narcotic," could only be imported in its raw material state; all finished controlled substances in circulation within the country (or for export) had to be manufactured within the United States. Peru did manufacture small quantities of refined and crude cocaine for export to Europe; however, Peruvian-manufactured cocaine was barred from entry into the dominant US market. The Jones-Miller Narcotics Import Act of 1922 entrenched this system, banning all cocaine imports into the country. Thus national law within the United States already ensured that South American countries could only be suppliers of the raw material (coca leaves) to the largest world manufacturer of coca-derived commodities, despite failed efforts before and during World War II by Peruvian government and businessmen to challenge these limitations.[13]

The pharmaceutical manufacturers Merck & Co., Inc. and Maywood Chemical Works held exclusive government-issued licenses to import coca leaves. Merck imported the leaves for the purpose of manufacturing cocaine hydrochloride to be used by the pharmaceutical industry as a local anesthetic and for research. Maywood extracted cocaine from the coca leaves in the process of manufacturing a "nonnarcotic flavoring extract," otherwise known as "Merchandise #5," a component of the famous soft drink Coca-Cola.[14] While today the illegal cocaine market's scale dwarfs quantities produced for the pharmaceutical industry, in the postwar period the reverse was true. The legal industry's production vastly exceeded quantities of illegal drugs seized, while all drug production appeared minuscule beside the quantities of cocaine destroyed or sold to the pharmaceutical industry as a by-product of processing the coca leaves as a flavoring extract for Coca-Cola. As early as 1931, even before Coca-Cola's international operations expanded during and after World War II, Coca-Cola was using more than 200,000 pounds of coca leaves annually to manufacture some 10,000 gallons of "nonnarcotic flavoring extract."[15] As laboratories worked their magic, these internationally derived commodities were repackaged and sold as "national" American products, celebrated even as embodiments of the medical and entrepreneurial benefits of US capitalism.

The policing of South American coca cultivation worked in tandem with securing raw materials for manufacturing "American" drug products. The North–South hierarchy of national participation within the international coca economy—South America as the producers of raw materials, the United States as the producer of manufactured goods—filtered through power disparities within Peru and Bolivia. This was abundantly clear in the first postwar effort to limit Andean coca cultivation to those leaves destined for export that unfolded under the auspices of the specially convened UN Commission of Enquiry on the Coca Leaf. The CND sent a group of international delegates, chaired by the United States, on a fact-finding mission to the Andes in 1949 to investigate the "problem" of the coca leaf. The UN mission sought to study and ultimately control the Andean landscape of coca leaf production and consumption and in the process was intervening in local conflicts over the terms of national economic development, political participation, labor and land rights, and in particular, the place of the "Indian" in modern society.

Efforts to control and limit the coca trade exposed and in part depended on political, racial, and economic hierarchies in the Andes. In

1946, coca represented 90 percent of the revenue for La Paz's Excise Office, and though of lesser significance in the more diversified Peruvian economy, the coca market was also formidable there.[16] In both Peru and Bolivia the majority of coca was grown by small peasant farmers, the majority of consumers were indigenous communities in both agricultural and mining regions, and a politically powerful landowning elite dominated the export market.[17] The UN investigators themselves struggled to comprehend the complex internal dynamics in both countries, although their goal of regulating the international market entailed collaborating primarily with a local "white" oligarchy. The UN study focused on the supposed nefarious practice of Indian coca leaf consumption: "No study can be made of the sections of the population in Peru and Bolivia which chew the coca leaf without specific reference to the various groups constituting the populations of those countries. These groups are ordinarily designated 'white', *mestizo*, and 'Indian' . . . almost all coca-leaf chewers are 'Indians', though this does not mean that all Indians are coca-leaf chewers. Moreover, the term 'Indian' is not a sharply defined one. The distinction between 'Indian' and *mestizo* is normally based on cultural, social, economic, and linguistic considerations."[18]

Careful to recognize the cultural specificity of racial and ethnic designations, the United Nations nevertheless oriented their drug control initiatives toward the study of "Indian" culture through social scientific method. In the topics covered by investigators, including whole sections of their final report devoted to "geographical considerations," "medical considerations," "methods of consumption," "race degeneration," "effects of chewing," "medico-biological research," "coca-leaf chewing as a characteristic of the Indian's life," "the legal regulation of labor," and the "economic value of coca-leaf production," there was not a single mention that the region was in the midst of experiencing one of the most profound challenges to the centuries-long subjugation, exploitation, and political disenfranchisement of the Andean Indian majority.

Both Peru and Bolivia had large Aymara and Quechua populations, although Bolivia's indigenous majority was unique in the Americas. The United Nations estimated that about half of Peru's eight million population was Indian, and of Bolivia's population of four million more than 50 percent were Indian, 13 percent white, and the remainder *mestizo*.[19] In both countries Indians were denied basic voting rights and political protections and were subject to onerous land tenancy and domestic servitude obligations to a small and powerful landholding oligarchy. As historian Laura Gotkowitz documents, indigenous struggles for land and justice in Bolivia that stretched back to at least the nineteenth century culminated in 1947 in a number of both urban and rural rebellions at the very moment UN drug regulators focused their attention on the region. These indigenous rebellions challenged a political and economic order that produced conditions of extreme subjugation, which many observers and peasant rebels readily decried as slavery.[20] While similar mobilizations for rights would occur later in Peru, it is striking that no mention was made of these upheavals in Bolivia by the commission, especially considering investigators traveled through key regions that had experienced the most violence and turmoil as peasants and mine workers organized to challenge severe labor conditions and profound inequalities in land ownership, where 6 percent of the nation's landowners controlled 92 percent of all developed land. It is not clear how coca and the effort to control it may or may not have figured in to these regional challenges to the status quo, but the characteristics of the assault against Indian coca consumption were definitely embedded in this larger political context. "Between 1944 and 1946, the region witnessed processes of democratization, radical labor movements, and the rise of the Left. This political opening closed down quickly with the shift to cold war containment."[21] The effort to extend drug control was just one component of the reaction against mobilizations for agrarian reform, political rights, and trade union power that oriented attention away from Indian economic grievances and political demands and toward social scientific assessments of presumed cultural practices in need of transformation. Drug control in the Andes began as the province of international "experts" and national economic elites who accrued the greatest profits from coca leaf processing and export. Indians, on the other hand, dominated the cultivation and consumer side of the national economy and as such became objects of study and control. A complicated landscape of cultural, social, and political struggle was reduced to factoring select human lives as national resources, and more particularly labor power, effectively rendering them the raw material for debate about regulating the coca market in the name of the public good. Ostensible medical concerns, "the harmful or harmless" effect on the "human body," in particular the bodies of Andean Indians, were recast as questions for business management and control over commodity flows; that is, as questions tied to "production" and "distribution" of the coca leaf, to the presumed need to modernize and civilize a backward population, and to the policing of new definitions of legality.

The discursive terrain of the UN commission, and its US leadership, reframed an effort to impose an economic and political order as a social scientific "enquiry" that mapped easily onto the deeply embedded racial and class hierarchies which structured Andean society at mid-century. Warwick Anderson and other scholars of US colonialism in the early twentieth century have noted how a new science of public health easily lent itself to a broader effort to refashion the "bodies and social life" of colonized people in a "civilizing process," which was "also an uneven and shallow process of Americanization."[22] After World War II, drug control in particular, and the discourse that traveled with it, similarly became a "scientific" tool for extending US power by targeting the minds and bodies of populations deemed "uncivilized," and promoting an economic order premised on the supremacy of US capitalism, even while these efforts depended on local collaboration and an embrace of a technocratic discourse of social science and public health. It was undoubtedly more palatable for national elites to participate in international initiatives if the most economically vulnerable and politically repressed populations were identified as the site of the "social problem." Still, the UN commission became a battleground among political and economic interests in Peru and Bolivia over the terms of national incorporation into international markets and systems of regulation. While a degree of lip service was paid to coca's historic cultural importance in the Andes, where it had been chewed for at least two thousand years, the commission's prime objective was to bring about its limitation and control. The international emphasis on raw materials as the necessary locus of this control meant that the UN initiative and the Andean response to it consisted of a debate about the coca leaf and, in particular, the land, life, labors, and consumption habits of Andean Indians. Deploying a language of well-being grounded in Western scientific explanations and tools—whether policing strategies, laboratory techniques, models of economic development, or medical assessments— experts in the field of international drug control sought to direct the flow of coca leaves within an international commodities circuit defined and oriented by US priorities.

THE UN COMMISSION OF ENQUIRY ON THE COCA LEAF

The UN commission published its findings and recommendations in 1950, disseminating only the first of many official UN investigations and publications into the matter. The report's publication came at the end of three years of organizational effort, fieldwork, and a considerable amount of debate both within and outside of the commission, in the Andes, and in the United States. These debates, to which we now turn, together with the various organizational structures and ties which framed both the issues at hand and the necessary "expert" qualifications for participation, provide a critical perspective on the parameters of drug control within a US sphere of influence in the mid-twentieth century. They show how racial, class, and national hierarchies inflected the work of experts schooled in the arts of policing, medicine, business administration, and the social sciences, shaping both the framing of "problems" and the proffering of solutions. They show how economic concerns relating to the control over international commodity flows and, in particular, a US-dominated vision for hemispheric development and trade, ensured that certain capitalist assumptions underwrote the logic of the drug control apparatus as well as the social and cultural arguments that it partially inspired.

The disproportionate power of the United States within the hemisphere (and the globe) influenced the leverage of coca growing countries in seemingly international forums like the United Nations, where hemispheric drug control was largely mediated by US actors. Even in the early stages of international efforts to monitor the coca economy, US political and corporate interests exerted pressure for South American compliance. When the League of Nations was having difficulty obtaining statistical information on Peru's coca economy, Maywood Chemical Works intervened by dangling the possibility of the elimination of Peru's coca leaf export economy if the information was not forthcoming. In a reply from Peru, forwarded from Maywood to the State Department and on to the League of Nations Secretariat, Maywood's supplier in Peru, Dr. Alfredo Pinillos, brought the matter to the attention of the Peruvian Minister of Foreign Affairs "in order to forestall the possibility that the exportation of coca leaves may be prohibited—which would be very unjust and unfair, and which would mean the death of one of the most important national industries." This corporate diplomacy had effect. In response, the Peruvian Minister of Foreign Affairs promised national compliance with the system, issuing export certificates and designating specific ports for the coca leaf and cocaine traffic. While Peru agreed to comply with monitoring the international trade, it sought to preserve the domestic coca leaf economy as a strictly national concern. The foreign minister asserted: "Peru as producer of coca leaves and crude coca will not make any concessions to restrict the cultivation and the production of coca leaves, nor prohibit the use of it for its natives, as it is actually a national problem which is now being studied by the Peruvian government."[23]

This early resistance to the supply-side control paradigm being promulgated by institutions of international drug control continued during the UN era, and US importers and manufacturers continued to exert a disproportionate influence. The impetus behind the CND's initiative for controlling raw materials may in part have emerged from concerns of US importers with regard to maintaining their coca leaf supply. Merck & Co., Inc. wrote to FBN Commissioner Harry Anslinger in January 1948: "As you know, we have been having trouble in obtaining adequate supplies of Coca Leaves." Anslinger, who also served as the US representative on the CND, rejected their suggestion of setting up new plantations, emphasizing the drug control imperative of preventing "any further coca leaf plantings." Yet, he reassured them, "I believe that as soon as the United Nations Commission of Enquiry finishes with its study of the coca leaf chewing there will be a tremendous surplus, because the amounts chewed approximate twenty-five million pounds."[24] The head of the FBN confidently anticipated that the success of the UN commission's efforts to eliminate Andean coca leaf consumption would produce surpluses for US importers. Anslinger explicitly saw this projected outcome as a necessary precondition for securing ample supplies of raw material for US manufacturers.

In the context of US pressure and international attention on the coca commodity chain, the immediate pretext for the UN commission's creation and fieldwork emerged in an official petition from the Andes. Andean businessmen, government officials, and scientists collaborated with the drug control apparatus at mid-century. They were motivated by the economic and political advantages of aligning with the United States, as well as by an interest in retaining a degree of control over national economic development and political power.[25] Responding both to an increasingly acrimonious debate among Peruvian scientists as to the relative merits or dangers of customary Indian coca leaf chewing and to the growing international pressure for Peru to enforce and maintain stricter control over their domestic and international coca production and trade, in April 1947 the Peruvian government submitted a proposal that the United Nations conduct a field survey on the coca leaf. Given the prominence of US power in the coca commodity circuit and the CND's inaugural interest in limiting the production of raw materials in producing countries, Peru approached the United Nations in an attempt to moderate the impact of the coca control apparatus that was already being implemented.[26] In a challenge to what many Peruvians and Bolivians believed was the hasty classification of the coca leaf as a dangerous drug, the Peruvian representative Dr. Jorge A. Lazarte explained "his government's reason for making the request," noting the difficulty of handling the situation due to the scale of consumption, the fact that the coca shrub grew wild, and the "highly controversial" nature of the issue. He emphasized the need for further investigation:

> At no time had the Government of Peru been able to carry out an organized enquiry into the physiological and pathological effects of this habit or to ascertaining whether it was necessary to suppress it. The habit had endured for many centuries and the Indian population which indulged in this practice appeared to be healthy and prosperous, capable of very hard work with little nourishment. Many observers had remarked upon their agreeable disposition and healthy condition. The Peruvian Government was therefore faced with the dilemma whether to suppress it or not.[27]

Peru's representative argued coca leaf chewing was a "habit" whose negative mental and physical effects had yet to be determined, even while it had the proven power to sustain workers on little food. Bringing together elite paternalism and an interest in Indian labor-value, Lazarte suggested coca enhanced the "Indian population's" capacity to perform "very hard work," a factor perhaps militating against prohibition. In fact, scientific investigations into Indian pathology and physiology would provide a common ground for proponents in the debate who all saw Indian labor productivity as a measure of coca's impact on societal health and prosperity, even if they drew different conclusions. The leadership of the UN CND endorsed the project while presuming coca leaf chewing's detrimental impact necessitated a focus on policing. The chairman of the CND, Colonel C.H.L. Sharman, the Canadian representative and close friend of the US representative, FBN Commissioner Harry J. Anslinger, "suggested broadening the scope of the study" to include "the possibilities of limiting the production and controlling the distribution of coca leaves."[28] This latter point would in fact become the main objective of the UN commissioners dispatched to the Andes. Looking back on these efforts, the Secretary of the UN Economic and Social Council (ECOSOC) (and later director of the Narcotics Division), Mr. G.E. Yates, declared that contrary to the Peruvian representative's initial request, the commission "was not really a technical assistance mission. It was a mission to persuade or encourage these Governments [of Peru and Bolivia] to change their policy by recognizing that the coca problem was a thing to be tackled, and gradually suppressed."[29]

The Peruvian proposal emerged from the United Nations in modified form. The original framework of public health and labor concerns was reconfigured as an initiative to control the scale and scope of the coca leaf economy, and eliminate the Indian practice of coca leaf chewing. This transformation ensured that along with two medical experts, the CND would appoint "two persons having experience in the international administration and control of narcotic drugs; one of these two members should preferably be an economist."[30] The final composition of the commission reflected the dominant influence of US capitalism on drug control efforts at mid-century. In particular, it embodied the combined interests of the US government and pharmaceutical industry, as well as the international network of "experts" upon whom it relied for legitimization. The president of the UN commission, Howard Fonda, was a US pharmaceutical executive nominated for the task by the head of the FBN, Harry Anslinger. Among other related institutional roles, Fonda was acting director of the American Pharmaceutical Manufacturers' Association, director of the National Vitamin Foundation, director of the First National Bank and Trust Company, and the vice president and director of the pharmaceutical house Burroughs Wellcome & Company. Fonda's directorship embodied the confluence of US financial, pharmaceutical, and manufacturing interests that assumed the helm of UN drug control initiatives in the Andes.

The extensive correspondence between Fonda and FBN Commissioner Anslinger during the commission's fieldwork in the Andes reveals the close relations between the pharmaceutical industry and the international policing apparatus, as well as the formidable US influence on the work of the United Nations. In a typical exchange, Anslinger wrote to Fonda imagining the UN mission to be a welcome respite from his labors as a pharmaceutical executive: "I am sure that you are having a very refreshing experience after your many years in the drug industry." Fonda in turn kept Anslinger informed of the commission's progress, describing how he dealt with internal divisions and obstacles that emerged during the trip, having "in no uncertain terms let them [the other members of the commission] know I was boss." In another dispatch, Fonda praised the work of the commission, highlighting his own role with the cocky nationalism and self-assurance of the successful businessman he was: "If I had not put some good old American salesmanship into this job and spread the honey this gang would have had one hell of a time."[31] The "gang" included three other appointees to the commission: the director of the Narcotics Bureau of France, a US-trained Venezuelan doctor and pharmacologist, and a Hungarian physiologist with ties to the UN Nutrition Division. The commission's work did not proceed without some debate and disagreement, but their approach and conclusions reflected the dominant US influence on the emerging drug control apparatus.

Following the Peruvian representative's petition and the subsequent convening of the commission, the United Nations resolved to send delegates to Peru, as well as to "other countries concerned as may request such an enquiry." Bolivia, the second largest cultivator of coca leaves in the Andes, was the only other country to participate in the UN field survey.[32] Colombia, the one other acknowledged cultivator of coca—exclusively for a small domestic market (reporting some 400,000 pounds compared to the almost 30 million grown in Peru and Bolivia)—had already implemented decrees to abolish the practice, while regional consumption in Argentina, Chile, Brazil, Venezuela, and Ecuador depended on small-scale cultivation or importations from Bolivia and Peru. Bolivia had been wary of international drug control initiatives since ratifying a 1925 International Opium Convention to be administered by the League of Nations, with the explicit disclaimer that "Bolivia does not undertake to restrict home cultivation of coca or to prohibit the use of coca leaves by the native population."[33] When word of the planned UN commission reached Bolivia, the politically powerful organization of coca plantation owners in the Yungas, the Sociedad de Proprietarios de Yungas (SPY), suggested Bolivia participate to prevent the control apparatus from undermining their influence. Across the Andes small peasant farmers grew the majority of coca, yet landowning elites dominated the export market. The SPY sought to ensure "that Bolivian coca not be included in the catalog of narcotic drugs and that, consequently, no restrictions be established regarding its consumption, production and exportation." The SPY's interest in pursuing the industrialization of coca products led the Bolivian government to seek inclusion in the UN enquiry, mistakenly believing the UN work might lead to the elimination of coca from the list of internationally controlled substances, opening up a new international market for Bolivian-manufactured goods.[34]

The head of the UN Division of Narcotic Drugs (which oversaw the CND), Leon Steinig, an American citizen of Austrian birth, revealed a different perspective when he appraised the Andean export economy in light of the pending field survey, indicating an apparent unwillingness to take Bolivia's vision for industrial development seriously. "Bolivia," Steinig declared, "was the only country exporting large amounts to other countries for consumption by addicts . . . all of the [coca] exported by Bolivia had gone to countries where the habit of chewing coca leaves prevailed." Peru, on the other hand, was more favorably assessed, inasmuch as "half of the total [coca exported] went to the cocaine manufacturing countries and most of the remainder to countries manufacturing non-narcotic substances."[35] Thus in a context where international efforts sought to limit both Peru and Bolivia's participation within the international coca commodity circuit to the production of raw materials for export to manufacturers (primarily in the United States), Bolivia as a producer only of "addiction" did not figure into the "legitimate" export vision of the UN commission at all.

The Bolivian government responded by accepting the technical assistance they believed would accompany the enquiry, while echoing Peru's invocation of health and labor concerns: "Coca leaf chewing is not a vice in Bolivia, and no biological defects have been observed amongst chewers. . . . The loss of the coca plant would create a real problem in Bolivia . . . since it is an indispensable element in the subsistence of the agricultural and mine workers."[36]

Reaffirming these concerns, the Peruvian delegate before the United Nations questioned the tendency to equate coca leaves with cocaine, an assimilation that produced the designation of Indians as "addicts" by "stress[ing] the fact that most of the research had been done on the harmful effects of cocaine and very little was known of the effects of chewing coca leaves."[37] National elites may well have been wary of attacking indigenous cultural practices at a time when exploited agricultural and mine workers were mobilizing for greater rights and in the process contributing to political instability; however, they couched their appeals to the United Nations in more moderate terms. Peruvian and Bolivian government officials contested the terms of their incorporation into the drug control regime by challenging whether coca should be regulated as a "vice" and instead emphasized both its potential to fuel national industrialization and its ongoing role in sustaining labor productivity in the fields and the mines. Debates about the harmful effects of the leaf, its role in local and international economies, and the quantities and dangers attributed to the ingestion of the cocaine alkaloid swirled around the commission and became central to the investigators' work. The UN Commission of Enquiry on the Coca Leaf became a battleground for national elites over the terms of incorporation into international economic and control networks. Both Peru and Bolivia argued before the United Nations that coca might propel national economic development and modernization and claimed further study was needed. These debates unfolded for more than two years before, in 1949, the UN Commission of Enquiry on the Coca Leaf traveled through Peru and Bolivia, visiting regions tied to the cultivation, distribution, and consumption of the coca leaf.

FIRST STEPS: CONTROLLING COCAINE

The impact of the UN initiative—and the drug control framework it grew out of and extended—was felt even before the commissioners journeyed through the Andes and compiled their report. A division of labor was built into the hemispheric policing apparatus. The work of UN experts and scientists on the coca leaf "problem" unfolded in tandem with international police collaboration designed to "suppress" and "tackle" cocaine. Cocaine as a commodity—whose dangers, by the 1940s, were less disputed than those of the coca leaf—was quickly regulated in the Andes through the collaboration of Peruvian and US authorities, even while representatives continued to debate the appropriate mechanisms for dealing with the raw material, the coca leaf, on the floor of the United Nations.

By the time the UN commissioners arrived for their expedition in September 1949, the new president of the military junta in Peru, General Manuel A. Odría, had already invoked the work of the commission and the international demand for drug control to justify and explain a number of Supreme Decrees issued earlier that year. These decrees defined the illicit market specifically as the unregistered traffic in "cocaine" and introduced a paradigmatic shift in state-run drug control policy away from a question of public health and toward a new punitive approach centered on aggressive policing and market regulation. Defining and policing the "illicit" was facilitated by the establishment of a national coca monopoly to control "the sowing, cultivation, and drying of coca, its distribution, consumption and exportation," and to limit coca's industrialization, its processing for medicinal purposes, to the government.[38]

The United States publicly and enthusiastically welcomed these initiatives. FBN Commissioner Anslinger publicly praised Odría's efforts in *Time* magazine. Collaboration between the FBN and the Peruvian police had in fact led to a much-publicized cocaine trafficking bust, which along with the pending UN "enquiry," was used as public justification for the new harsher legislation introduced by the Peruvian government.[39] Not mentioning the FBN's involvement (perhaps so as not to inflame political currents opposed to US imperialism), the military government nevertheless situated these initiatives within an international context.[40] *El Comercio,* a popular Lima newspaper and media outlet for General Odría's government and the Lima social elite, reported that these decrees were passed because of the government's "desire to extirpate drug addiction from the country and avoid the trafficking of cocaine by unscrupulous individuals, Peruvians and foreigners, that have assaulted the national prestige."[41]

While previously Peruvian officials had invoked national sovereignty to challenge international efforts to control the domestic coca leaf economy, now Odría invoked the nation's modernization and international prestige to justify consolidation of control over the domestic economy and the deeper integration of this economy into the international drug control apparatus. By instituting these decrees and taking aggressive action against "unscrupulous individuals," Odría was capitalizing on international calls for drug control to garner domestic and foreign support for the new military regime. It also reflected one direct consequence of the UN- and US-inspired heightened policing of cocaine: the "birth of the narcos" whereby a "wholly new class of cocaine trafficker" appeared on the international scene after 1947, connected to a Peruvian cocaine industry that until that point in time had been legal.[42] As the Peruvian economy and social control apparatus were further integrated into a US-dominated hemispheric order, the line delineating licit and illicit markets became a powerful economic and political tool, which relied on the demonization of cocaine and "cocaine traffickers," even while securing supplies of coca leaves for export to US pharmaceutical manufacturers of cocaine.[43]

Political power accrued to those who embraced the drug regulatory regime. The military coup that brought Odría to power in October 1948 ousted José Luis Bustamente Rivera, who had come to the support of the nationalist (anti-imperialist), populist, though explicitly not communist, party Alianza Popular Revolucionaria Americana (APRA). When divisions between Bustamente's government and Aprista dissidents resulted in a naval mutiny in the Lima port of Callao, the military intervened and installed Odría as Peru's new president, foreclosing the possibility of an official political turn leftward. When the founder and leader of APRA, Víctor Raúl Haya de la Torre, sought political asylum in the Colombian Embassy, General Odría argued the request should be denied on the grounds that he was a common criminal rather than political refugee, prompting a case that dragged on for years before the International Court of Justice. He based this charge on information gathered from his collaborations with the FBN in relation to the recent bust of a cocaine trafficker with Peruvian connections in New York.[44] "Cocaine" then, as now, was a fungible commodity. For Odría, the battle against a "cocaine trafficker" (and founder of the socialist APRA party) consolidated his domestic power while augmenting his international political capital with the United States.[45] Odría perhaps learned this not uncommon McCarthy-era tactic from FBN Commissioner Anslinger himself, who regularly invoked the spectacle of the "communist dope-pusher" to advance his agenda.[46] More than simply currency in a play for US support, Odría traded in drug scandal domestically. The frequent spectacle of cocaine trafficking busts reported in the Peruvian media helped to criminalize domestic political dissent while giving legitimacy to the coercive measures the military junta was using to consolidate its control.[47] The political manipulation of criminal enforcement was becoming an increasingly common tactic in the Andes (and throughout the world) as the drug control regime gained traction. It is worth noting that in the early 1960s Bolivian labor leader and Vice President Juan Lechín would be forced into quasi-exile, based on, as historian Kenneth Lehman has argued, "trumped-up charges of cocaine trafficking."[48]

The spectacle of the drug bust was deployed as a political and economic weapon by the Peruvian government as it selectively licensed cocaine manufacturers and pursued criminal investigations to prevent seepage into the newly "illicit" realm. Government legislation and a series of spectacular media reports on criminal cases in the spring of 1949 helped delineate the line between licit and illicit cocaine, throwing former legitimate manufacturers onto the wrong side of the law. In one such incident, El Comercio published the mugshots of fourteen men, finely attired in business suits, accused of the crime of cocaine trafficking. The cocaine had been manufactured at the factory of Andrés Avelino Soberón in Huánuco. Soberón, a licensed manufacturer, was accused of producing cocaine in excess of his government contracts.[49] The chief of police publicly attacked the "traffickers" for their luxurious lifestyles and their "ill-gotten wealth," airing a populist appeal to the masses as the new regime sought to legitimate its rule.[50] As the government consolidated its control, enforcing the new legislation, it literally created the

illicit economy and numerous pharmacists, formerly legitimate manufacturers of cocaine, became embroiled in the "illicit" trade. This gave
the government the power both to determine who could participate in
the legitimate coca-commodities trade and to wield a powerful symbolic weapon attacking "criminality" in the struggle to consolidate
political and economic control.

While the Peruvian military junta joined US efforts to designate and
then crack down on the illicit traffic in cocaine, it sought to reserve a
realm of legitimate production by invoking national heritage in defense
of the coca leaf. The government declared it was the state's duty to
"defend the national heritage, represented by investments in the cultivation of this valuable plant whose application by scientific means produces great benefits for humanity."[51] In the decree that created the
national coca monopoly, the government conceded the dangers that the
chewing habit might have for the Indian population, while insisting that
the taxation and industrialization of the raw material was of value to the
national economy. Both Peru and Bolivia sought to hold on to their sovereign ability to utilize coca leaves as raw material for national economic,
industrial, and scientific development, even if they were more ambivalent
about protecting Aymara and Quechua consuming practices. In this
regard, both governments acceded to the policing of the illicit cocaine
economy, but limiting the raw material—the coca leaf—posed more
obstacles for national elites. Despite these reservations, it became increasingly difficult for Peru and Bolivia to influence the terms of national
participation within the international "legitimate" drug trade once the
entire commodity chain was incorporated into the international drug
control apparatus and economy.[52] This was accomplished on the one
hand through hemispheric police collaboration and on the other hand
through UN mediation. With the intervention of the UN commission,
efforts to restrict coca leaf cultivation to that destined for export into the
"legitimate" cocaine (and Coca-Cola) trade relied almost exclusively on
attempts to control Indian land, labor, and consumption while marginal-
izing the aspirations of Andean country elites to develop their own
industrially produced coca-derived commodities for the world market.

UN INVESTIGATORS AND PERUVIAN
SCIENTIFIC DEBATES

From September through November 1949 UN representatives of the
Commission of Enquiry on the Coca Leaf traveled through Peru and

Bolivia, visiting regions tied to the cultivation, distribution, and consumption of coca. It became clear only moments after the commissioners descended from their New York flight onto the tarmac at Lima's airport that the commission's primary objective, couched in a social scientific language of "development assistance," was to convince the Peruvian and Bolivian governments to structure the Andean coca market according to their emergent principles of international drug control. Howard Fonda, the US pharmaceutical executive and head of the UN commission, announced to the assembled reporters that his goal was to study the negative impact of coca leaf chewing on the indigenous population and determine what needed to be done to eliminate it.[53] The chairman's explicit comments ignited a fire in the Peruvian press; reporters publicly questioned why the UN investigators were there if they already knew the answers to the questions they were purportedly arriving to study. The commission quickly distanced itself from these statements by issuing a press release claiming the UN emissaries held no preconceived opinions; they were there to pursue an objective scientific study of coca's place in society.

The UN delegates' subsequent three months of travel through Peru and Bolivia proceeded relatively smoothly, with the active assistance and cooperation of national government officials and their specially delegated liaisons—the Chief of Narcotics of the Peruvian government and a representative from the Bolivian Ministry of Public Health.[54] The Peruvian and Bolivian governments both established special commissions to study the issue in conjunction with the UN commission's work, and regional newspapers reported regularly on the progress of all parties. The commission's final report, the *Report of the Commission of Enquiry on the Coca Leaf*, outlined its work methods and described how the delegates sought out contact with local civil authorities, military personnel, and with "the medical profession, pharmacists and academic circles . . . in all the localities visited." In addition, "whenever possible the Commission endeavored to make contact with existing agricultural, industrial and other employers' or workers organizations," although it is not clear in trip documentation or the final report how successful these efforts were or what impact they had on the ultimate recommendations of the United Nations.[55] It seems the UN commissioners did not solicit opinions from Indian coca leaf cultivators or consumers themselves—except, as described below, in the form of scientific research into the physiological effect of coca leaves on their bodies.

Due to the paucity of documentation, it is difficult to gauge popular reaction to the UN mission outside official circles. It is clear many communities were very concerned. When Bolivia's Minister of Public Health and Hygiene welcomed the UN commissioners to the country, he was forced to address the widespread alarm that talk of coca eradication had already generated. He assured the public the commission's investigation should proceed, "Without apprehension or nervousness among any social classes, [since] the object [of the commission's work] is to try to determine as final proof, if coca is a great tonic as it is considered to be among our indigenous masses, or a toxin that must be eliminated."[56] Debates among Peruvian scientists about the effects of coca on the Indian body and social development became a critical frame of reference for the UN commission, which drew upon a scientific discourse to pressure for an economically based system of limitations and controls.[57] This focus was not merely an external imposition, but very much a product of local scientists' incorporation into a US-dominated drug research network. These scientists depended on private and public capital to finance their research and to sustain political support for their work. Both Dr. Carlos Monge and Dr. Carlos Gutiérrez-Noriega, the two primary adversaries in the Peruvian debate, had studied and taught at US universities and maintained ties with various North American institutions.

Monge drew upon his work as the director of the Institute of Andean Biology to defend Indian coca consumption as a natural, harmless component of a high-altitude environment inhabited by the racially specific "Andean man." This line of reasoning, grounded in the racial stratification of Andean society, relied on the idea that "the Andean man is a climactic-physiological variation of the human race"[58] in order to challenge the notion that coca leaf chewing reflected pathological behavior. He leveled this argument as an *Indigenista,* paternalistically protecting the Indians from those who would disdain them as uncivilized or backwards. Nominated by the government to preside over the National Committee on Coca, an investigative body created in response to the UN initiative, Monge's views carried considerable weight. Monge's prominence in scientific and political circles in Peru both bolstered and was facilitated by his international connections. Interest and support for Monge's Institute of Andean Biology came primarily from US-owned mining companies, the US Air Force, and livestock breeders of the central highlands, all of whom were interested in maximizing (worker/soldier/animal) productivity at high altitudes.[59] Thus, a nexus of national and international medical, military, and business interests facilitated the scientific research that became so central to debates about coca.

These institutional ties were facilitated by personal contacts. When the UN commission arrived in Lima, Monge was on tour in the United States, where he attended the Congress of Americanists organized by the American Anthropological Association and gave a presentation before the UN Educational, Scientific and Cultural Organization on "Physiological Anthropology of the Inhabitants of the Altiplanos of America." He returned to Peru in the midst of the UN visit to preside over the International Symposium on High Altitude Biology sponsored by Monge's own institute, the Rockefeller Foundation, and the Carnegie Institution. The symposium was convened "to understand the new Andean biology and anthropology and the social and racial conduct of high-altitude man."[60] It attracted not only the UN commissioners themselves who participated in a number of the sessions, but also an array of prominent US officials, including the chief of US Air Force Medicine and the directors of the US Naval Medical Research Center and Army Chemical Center.[61]

Gutiérrez-Noriega, based at the Institute of Pharmacology and Therapeutics of the University of San Marcos, Lima, did his own tour of US scientific circles in 1949, lecturing at the Society of Pharmacology and Experimental Therapeutics and at the University of Wisconsin.[62] His work turned to coca as an explanation for what he viewed as the uncivilized state of Andean Indian society, arguing, for example, that the "influence of the drug through many generations may have some importance as a creative factor in psychological disturbances and racial degeneration."[63] Gutiérrez-Noriega's work fundamentally influenced the UN commission's report and was well received in the United States, even being translated for publication in the popular magazine *Scientific Monthly*. Introduced by the editors as the "first sustained study of [Indian coca use] in English," Gutierrez-Noriega's work asserted that coca leaf chewing was detrimental "drug" consumption: "In general, coca chewers present emotional dullness or apathy, indifference, lack of will power and low capacity for attention. They are mistrustful, shy, unsociable, and indecisive. In advanced stages many of them are vagabonds." This narration began by representing coca leaf chewing as a social dysfunction and flowed easily into its presentation as a veritable reflection of criminal proclivity, making people not just "unsociable," but "vagabonds." Such arguments blurred the line between cultural practice and racially based notions of cultural, or even genetic, supremacy that increasingly were being articulated—in both the United States and the Andes—through the extension of a coercive penal apparatus.[64]

Although circulating in the same institutional networks and sharing a debate centered on Indian coca consumption, Monge and Gutiérrez-Noriega viewed each other as rivals, and indeed, their work approached the question of Indian coca leaf chewing from fundamentally different perspectives. Gutiérrez-Noriega attacked coca as generating Indian pathology whereas Monge saw it as a legitimate cultural practice of a unique—even super—human species. There was, however, considerable room for convergence between these two poles; both scientists relied on either debasing or idealizing the scientifically objectified "Indian." Members of the Peruvian National Coca Commission headed by Monge praised Gutiérrez-Noriega's work while emphasizing the need for more study. Dr. Fortunato Carranza suggested that research thus far had only produced "a state of confusion." He also emphasized a point central to the national and international debate: the role of nutrition. While Monge defended coca chewing as a necessary and beneficial practice of Andean man, Gutierrez-Noriega saw it as fueling a vicious cycle of malnutrition. Carranza took a line somewhere in between, reflecting the spectrum of the debate—and the currency of racialized thought—in Peru. He acknowledged coca's usefulness in dealing with the physiological effects of high altitude, yet claimed it numbed Indians to the hardships of life, robbing them of their initiative to improve themselves: "after chewing coca, one feels compensated for all the frustrations one's had in life."[65]

THE REPORT OF THE UN COMMISSION

In the wake of its consultations with local scientists, government officials, and business leaders the UN commission recommended that national governments implement policies for policing coca circuits not tied to the "legitimate" North American market, creating through legislative action what came to be called the "illicit drug trade": a legal framework for controlling the circulation of *both* cocaine and coca leaves. The United Nations also recommended that Andean governments set about eradicating the widespread indigenous practice of chewing the coca leaf. Despite some resistance, the general tenets of drug control were accepted in the Andes (even though the effort to eliminate coca leaf chewing was never successful and remains practiced and defended by indigenous people to the present day). At mid-century the

Bolivian government agreed with international drug control officials that scientific investigations into chewing coca leaves constituted the appropriate mechanism for resolving the issue. And in Peru, after establishing a national coca monopoly, the government hoped to "to limit, for now, and eradicate in the future, this general custom, in defense of the indigenous population."[66] The "defense" of indigenous peoples through the eradication of age-old cultural practices drew upon an Andean elite paternalism shared by UN regulators who explicitly defined coca's hazards in terms of the racial and economic status of its consumers: "Not all Indians are coca-leaf chewers, though the great majority are. Moreover, chewing is practised among the *mestizos*, although to a much smaller extent. The very few whites who chew coca leaf must be regarded as isolated cases, and not as a social problem."[67]

The UN's report echoed Gutierrez-Noriega's emphasis on coca's alleged production of Indian degeneracy, decrying the negative implications this held for national economic development. The commissioners determined, among other things, that coca chewing maintains "a constant state of malnutrition"; it produces, in some cases, "undesirable changes of an intellectual and moral character" and "certainly hinders the chewer's chances of obtaining a higher social standard." The report emphasized that coca leaf consumption "reduces the economic yield of productive work, and therefore maintains a low economic standard of life," before going on to recommend that Peru and Bolivia institute policies geared toward its eventual eradication.[68]

These conclusions directly responded to officials in Peru and Bolivia who defended coca consumption as being beneficial to national development. Defenders of the leaf argued that coca's "vitamin content plays a part in the nutrition of the Indian," suggesting the leaf was a valuable source of nutrition necessary to sustain Indian economic productivity.[69] When the Bolivian government circulated a report backing up this claim, the head of the UN commission privately wrote to Anslinger dismissing the "Bull-ivian vitamin report."[70] Despite this scorn, tests conducted by the US Treasury Department for the commission seemed to verify the Bolivian position. In particular the Treasury Department found that the "vitamin content" within an estimated quantity of coca leaves consumed daily was "remarkably high," with vitamins B_1, C, and riboflavin figuring most prominently. Nevertheless, the commission's report ultimately concluded: "In spite of this fact, it would by no means be advisable to supply these requirements by coca-leaf chewing because it must be emphasized that the toxicity of coca leaves (due to their cocaine content) would never allow a safe use as a nutrient."[71] It is hard to know if US Merck's pioneering synthesis of vitamin B₁ and its initiation of large-scale vitamin production in 1936 had any direct impact on this recommendation. But, the hegemonic framework of medical science—tied in large part to the production lines and projected consumer markets of major US pharmaceutical companies—obviously influenced the commission's analysis in this regard.[72]

The push for limiting the indigenous coca market focused on stigmatizing Indian consumer habits and asserting coca's negative physiological impact (due to its cocaine content). Arguments for coca eradication stigmatized Indians while proselytizing the need to help integrate them into a model of "civilization" modeled on liberal visions of land ownership and hard work.[73] The UN report explained the "concept of individual ownership is constantly spreading among the native landowning population," while lamenting that "[m]any Indians, however, possess no land, and work for others."[74] Drug control was presented as a tool for advancing a particular vision of societal progress. Drug control officials also had to contend with the fact that coca leaves were a linchpin in the domestic cash economy. Eighty percent of Bolivian tax revenues were "derived from coca,"[75] and according to Gutiérrez-Noriega, the "coca leaf [was] the single most important item of commerce in the Andes."[76] The UN report supported these claims, finding that "except in some cattle markets, business is on a small scale and generally limited to the exchange of products between the Indians. An exception is coca leaf; it is, as a rule, paid for in cash. In such markets coca leaf is sold by the Indian who grows his own crop."[77] Coca eradication thus entailed the radical transformation of the domestic cash economy, including the elimination of many Indians' primary medium of exchange, subsistence, and access to money, outside of the wage-labor sector. In an effort to accomplish this, a medical discourse of addiction accompanied a positivist narrative of economic development. The final report dismissed indigenous claims that "coca-leaf chewing dispels hunger, thirst, fatigue and sleepiness, or gives strength, courage or energy" as "superstition" and attributed this belief to "the Indian's poor living conditions" and "his lack of education."[78]

Controlling the consumption of coca was an integral part of the civilizing and nation building project the United Nations (and the United States) hoped to promote in the region, in an effort to control the export market and stabilize the region for foreign investment.[79] As the commissioners neatly summed it up, "since there is an intimate bond between the individual and the community, it is also clear that the effects of coca-leaf chewing must be considered as socially and economically prejudicial to the nation."[80] Both in the press and before the CND, representatives of the Peruvian and Bolivian governments questioned the UN recommendations and the conclusions that led to them—nearly a year after the initial publication of the UN report and only one week after the Bolivian representative was provided with a Spanish translation of it.[81] Unlike Peru and the United States, Bolivia did not have a representative on the CND and had to respond to the UN report as a guest in the chamber. These national power disparities before the United Nations mirrored the even greater disparities between those made subjects of investigation, the Indian mine workers and peasants whose bodies and lifestyles were the sites of contention in diagnosing the "problem" at hand, and the internationally dispersed medical, military, and political elite the commissioners consulted with and reported back to, during and after their tour. Both Peru and Bolivia, in good diplomatic form, praised the work of the commissioners but suggested that the research had been too hasty and that three months of fieldwork was insufficient to draw conclusions, arguing that more scientific research needed to be undertaken to determine whether or not the practice of coca leaf chewing was in fact harmful.[82]

Despite these apparently irreconcilable differences, however, there were in fact a number of shared assumptions and underlying concerns that seemed to animate all of the various participants. Officials sought to define the parameters of legitimate drug consumption while creating a logical framework for policing its boundaries. Scientific investigation seemed to represent the ultimate authority for determining policies relating to the control, distribution, and consumption of coca commodities. "Experts" in the fields of physiology, pharmacology, business management, policing, and medicine were the privileged participants in these debates. Those people most directly affected and concerned by the practice and the public and political response to it, Aymara and Quechua Indians, were excluded. This was forcefully apparent in a 1949 progress report from US Public Health Service scientists who were in the Andes studying coca chewing under the auspices of the National Institutes of Health (NIH). They constituted just one of an array of missions in South America at the time that collaborated with the United Nations and that together embodied the prominence of scientific investigators' involvement in constructing visions for Latin American development—and in delineating the boundaries of legitimate participation in the coca market. This vision paired the valorization of scientific "objectivity" and "truth" while denying the possibility that the Indian point of view mattered. The NIH's fieldwork at the Volcan Mines at Ticklio, Peru, involved analyzing blood and urine samples obtained from Indian workers to track cocaine absorption in the body. They noted their findings were ongoing and inconclusive, yet one thing was clear: "The statements in regard to the coca leaf habit given by the workers are not reliable."[83] This easy dismissal of the Indian perspective was also evident in the UN commissioners' primary reliance on testimony provided by members of the Peruvian and Bolivian elite: government officials, military authorities, medical professionals, pharmacists, and academics. For the Andean elite and international regulators, the "Indian" embodied the hazards and promise of Andean economic development.

THE INDIAN QUESTION

This silencing of the Indian voice was in sharp contrast to the centrality of the Indian body as a primary object of investigation into the "problem of the coca leaf." As drug control gained momentum, the physical and symbolic body of the Indian became central to the debate. Regulators studied the "Indian" in their attempt to convey the dangers of consuming the raw material coca leaf in its unprocessed form and implement a system of controls gearing all coca leaf production toward the export market. In this context "Indians" were both objects of science and policing and, increasingly, part of a North American popular imaginary about the Andes. Consequently in the effort to delineate new boundaries of legality, Gutiérrez-Noriega, the US public health scientists, and the investigators helping advance the work of the UN Coca Commission performed numerous tests aimed at exploring Indian bodies and minds.

Approaching Indians as almost natural components of the environment, researchers swooped down on mines, into the countryside, or even utilized the captive populations in penitentiaries and asylums, to study the absorption of cocaine alkaloids in the body—drawing blood, testing urine and excrement, and administering numerous IQ and other mental evaluative tests. An entire section of the commission's report entitled "The Chewing of Coca Leaf" was devoted to analyzing what happens to an Indian body upon consumption of coca leaves. Investigators reframed the Indian cultural practice of chewing coca leaves as a

Severin-Three Lions

Indians make merry after enjoying large quantities of coca. They are sliding down the slope half unconscious of what they are doing

FIGURE 4. Photo and caption from a 1946 *Inter-American* article presenting coca leaf chewing as causing irrational behaviors by indigenous people.

process of cocaine ingestion that needed to be eliminated.[84] This scientific faith in finding answers by probing into blood, stomachs, digestive tracks, and brains paralleled the easy objectification of Indians in popular literature, where Indians repeatedly were likened to animals, an eerie echo, perhaps, of the lab rats and dogs upon which Gutierrez-Noriega performed his first cocaine experiments. The provocatively entitled article "The Curse of Coca," published in the *Inter-American* in 1946, exemplifies this contemporary mix of fascination and disdain for the Indian body in the context of criminalizing indigenous coca consumption in the name of drug control. A Swiss naturalist is cited describing a sixty-two-year-old man as walking "as fast as a mule could go, solely on coca," and the coca fields "look too steep to climb, but barefooted men and women scramble up the steps like mountain goats."[85] An article in *Natural History* the following year described how coca leaves in the mouth "reminds one of a chipmunk with packed cheek pouches."[86] Objectification of the Indian body provided common ground for scientists, drug control officials, and a popular imagination that sustained policy initiatives of the time.

The paired silencing of Indian voices and overproduction of Indian bodies in debates about coca provide a unique window onto contemporary ideas about national economic development and the selective policing of drugs. Discussions about coca drew upon long-standing ideological controversies over how best to integrate indigenous people on behalf of Latin American modernization and development. Linking coca chewing, "moral character," and economic growth, drug control advocates drew upon a long colonial tradition of targeting Indians for cultural transformation, while providing a racially inflected social and economic rationale. At the second Inter-American Congress of Indian Affairs, held in Peru the same year as the UN commission's visit, "the topic that raised more debate than any other related to the supposed physical degeneracy of the Indians," an idea dismissed overwhelmingly by the attendees, although the question of the harmfulness of coca "was left undecided."[87] At the moment of this push for drug control, the notion of Indian racial degeneracy was becoming increasingly unpalatable. However, a new scientific language rooted in concepts like "addiction" supplanted more explicitly racialized debates, while re-embedding social, economic, and racial hierarchies through discourses of criminality and social dysfunction. The UN commission explained that it resisted the term racial degeneracy, which it linked to "the continuous outcry, heard all over Peru from the enemies of Coca chewing," and rather suggested that their "analysis did not lead to the result that the Indian is degenerating; rather that mainly as a result of malnutrition, these valuable people addict themselves to coca chewing."[88]

Finally, this recasting of the Indian problem, as a social rather than genetic issue, also was tied to US principles regarding hemispheric trade and economic development. The phrase "These valuable people" was as much an invocation of the commissioner's "respect" for the Indians (as opposed to a caricatured Peruvian racial disdain), as it was an acknowledgment of Indians' critical capacity as laborers and consumers within the postwar global economic order. Along with its other conclusions, the UN report argued that coca consumption "reduces the economic yield of productive work, and therefore maintains a low economic standard of life."[89] Drug control was presented as a means of overcoming economic backwardness. More specifically, the model of drug control advocated by the United States and United Nations tied the Andes into a hemispheric commodity chain in which coca leaves would ideally be grown exclusively for export (primarily to the United States). The Andes, then as the source of raw materials for North American manufacturers, ultimately might be further incorporated into a new international economic order as consumers of manufactured "American" goods. A member of the UN Secretariat overseeing the commission's work articulated this larger economic vision when he suggested the fundamental issue underlying the investigators' work had to do with the "main problem" of creating "a mass of consumers capable of supporting the new envisaged industrial and administrative developments."[90]

MANUFACTURING CONSENT

Among these "industrial and administrative developments" was the increasing presence of US companies and products in the Andes. This was especially true for US manufacturers operating within the newly delineated licit borders of the coca economy that directly influenced the work of the UN commission. At the same time that the commission sought to control the production, trade, and local consumption of the coca leaf, American companies very carefully sought to ensure their field of research and economic interests remained "licit" aspects of the coca trade. The Coca-Cola Company closely watched the progress of the commission's work. In the late 1940s, Coca-Cola executives were wary of the impact that international drug control might have on their own operations and sought to retain a degree of influence on the parameters of new policing efforts. In response to a preliminary presentation made by the UN commission before embarking on its field research, the vice president of Coca-Cola, Ralph Hayes, wrote to the FBN's Anslinger, highlighting the long record of corporate and government cooperation with regard to coca: "It enables everyone concerned to say that, so far as the writ of the United States runs, the movement and processing of coca leaf and the disposition of all products therefrom is under complete control and that the unity of purpose between Government and industry is, in this respect, unqualified."[91]

Hayes believed the United States provided the United Nations with a model of collaboration for ensuring both policing and manufacturing imperatives within the drug economy, exhibiting an exemplary "unity of purpose between Government and industry." Policing and manufacturing priorities might easily come into conflict, however, as the Coca-Cola executives well knew. In the course of the commission's investigations Hayes maintained contact with Anslinger, receiving regular updates and making suggestions to ensure the company's unqualified access to the coca leaf market. For instance, having received and reviewed an early draft of the commission's report, Hayes successfully turned to Anslinger to modify the report so as to include an explicit mention of the licit use of coca for "the production of the coca leaf for a nonnarcotic flavoring extract." After the issue was addressed in the UN chamber, Anslinger reported back to Hayes that the intervention had been successful and that in order to accomplish this end he had "used some of the excellent wording expressed in your letter."[92]

In less direct ways, select US pharmaceutical companies benefited from the work of the UN commission. When Coca-Cola's vice president took note of the commission's finding that the coca leaf contained large quantities of valuable vitamins, he passed this information on in correspondence with Maywood Chemical Works, the company that processed coca leaves for manufacturing the famous soft drink. He stressed the "remarkably high" vitamin content of coca leaves, reiterating the UN findings to a company well equipped to profitably extract and package the nutrients in pill form, even while mentioning the United Nations wisely had rejected the leaves as a source of nourishment for indigenous consumers "due to their cocaine content."[93] Merck & Co., Inc., the other major US importer of coca leaves beside Maywood, also began focusing more attention on the Andes. While before the war Merck had imported coca leaves primarily from Java, by 1948 the company was, according to FBN documentation, interested in developing "in Peru a source of coca leaves with high alkaloid content, similar to those produced in Java. Apparently Merck & Company contemplates sending a technician to Peru and Bolivia to study present strains and growing conditions, to solicit assistance from local growers and research workers, and to distribute small quantities of selected seed."[94]

Private and public collaborations to secure Andean production of coca leaves for US manufacturers were ongoing even as the commission pursued limitations on the cultivation of coca for the Andean market. While it is difficult to assess what, if any, direct influence Merck had on the UN's work, it is clear that drug control priorities and the valorization of Western scientific inquiry that they depended on shaped an international economic order conducive to the profitability of Merck and other pharmaceutical companies.

Merck's research division cultivated close ties to Carlos Monge, the prominent scientist whose work was central to debates about coca and who was also headed the Peruvian National Committee on Coca established to study the issue in tandem with the United Nations. A few months before the UN commission published its findings, Monge on Merck's behalf successfully petitioned the Peruvian Minister of Work and Indigenous Matters to obtain special coca leaf export authorizations for the company and ensured his government's support for research in US laboratories that might translate or be replicated in a high-altitude environment in Peru.[95] In an interesting exchange in 1951 between Monge and Hans Moliter of Merck's Institute for Therapeutic Research, it is clear how the drug control regime itself provided foundations for a "legitimate" realm of international scientific and profit-oriented collaboration in the drug field. Monge's efforts to secure special coca leaf exports to Merck's laboratories were rewarded when Merck in turn shared with him a supply of cortisone, a new drug with varied therapeutic possibilities the company was studying at the time. In subsequent correspondence Moliter asked Monge for an update on his research with the drug and asked whether he had "had any opportunity to try the administration of cortisone to people who are not acclimatized to high altitude." In addition to these research exchanges, Moliter expressed a noteworthy concern over controlling the drug's circulation: "In this country, there is a very bad black market situation with regard to cortisone and in spite of all our efforts to control it, it is getting worse. I should be very interested to learn from you whether a similar situation has also developed in Peru. I am afraid that your answer will be in the affirmative; indeed your country would be a unique and blessed exception from this ugly picture if it were not the case."[96]

Thus, even the most prominent Peruvian proponent of protecting the indigenous practice of coca leaf chewing, Carlos Monge, might be approached by American scientists working on drug development as a presumed adherent to the notion and logical structure of drug control, even if—perhaps especially if—he argued publicly at the time that coca leaves should not be included on the prohibited list.

The Coca-Cola Company similarly sought to ensure drug control efforts would not impinge on their capacity to profit from their famous product. After reading the FBN's *Annual Report* for 1949, that among other things celebrated Peruvian General Odría's collaboration with the FBN to crack down on cocaine, a concerned Ralph Hayes of Coca-Cola wrote to Anslinger. Hayes highlighted a particular part of the report that referred to "the marvelous co-operation of the present Peruvian Government in enacting legal deterrents and eliminating the illicit 'coke' sources . . . [and the] elimination of illegal 'coke' traffic." He requested that future reports avoid the unfortunate conflation of names ("coke") that might jeopardize the reputation of the company's drink. Complimenting the report drafters as no doubt "above criticism," Hayes suggested to the FBN that the "use of the term 'cocaine' when that substance is meant might be preferable, inasmuch as 'coke' is a trade mark registered by the Federal Government and having a distinctive meaning."[97]

. . .

The profits accrued from controlling the coca commodity circuit went to governments and political, intellectual, and economic elites. In the Andes, the burdens of the new drug control regime fell most heavily on Indian communities. As an international network of "experts" squared off, they all grounded their recommendations in a determined application of science to study an objectified indigenous body. These efforts did not seek to understand or take seriously autonomous indigenous cultural beliefs or political and economic concerns, even as their ultimate recommendations attempted to criminalize customary practices. The ensuing social stigmatization and legal assault on select participants within the coca economy, and drug production and consumption more generally, laid the foundation for a next half century of struggle over the terms of drug control and a starkly delineated licit and illicit divide.

The UN Commission of Enquiry on the Coca Leaf echoed both the FBN's vision for drug control and the approach of earlier international drug control agreements, when it defined the terms of "limitation" that framed its investigative approach according to the coca leaves' commodity state and the associated consumer market. However, with the US government leading the call for a reinvigorated drug control regime, and a US pharmaceutical executive at the helm of UN investigations into the coca "problem" in Peru and Bolivia, these drug control efforts took on a new character. Drug control officials directly intervened to structure and police national and regional coca markets in the Andes, the plants' original geographic and cultural home, and sought to restrict coca cultivation to "raw material" for export. Suppression of coca use was never a total objective but rather an effort to structure the Bolivian and Peruvian economy by eliminating the regional coca leaf market—dominated by Aymara and Quechua coca leaf chewers—while securing adequate supplies for export to primarily US manufacturers. This effort was propelled by the collaborative efforts of the US government, the

United Nations, police and military officials in the United States and the Andes, scientific experts, and corporate executives with ties to both North and South America. Dictating limitations on the circulation of raw coca leaves was far more than an effort to corner an international market; it reflected the deep-seated political, cultural, and social forces that legitimized and sustained the inequities of US-directed hemispheric economic development and drug control. The United States and United Nations together determined that coca leaf—as produced and consumed in the Andes—was not a legitimate consumer commodity, but rather exclusively "raw material" for the industrial manufacturing of other goods.

Even as the regional and international circulation of drug raw materials such as coca leaves became subject to increasing restrictions and regulations, the end drug products that might be derived from them along with a vast and growing array of manufactured synthetic substitutes created to mimic their therapeutic potential contributed to a veritable revolution in the drug field both in terms of the scale and variety of drugs being produced. US pharmaceutical companies led this transformation with the help of the US government and a national and international policing apparatus. US involvement in policing the drug trade was not merely about implementing limitations and controls. It also had a productive impact and goal: to sustain the growth and expansion of US power based on the pharmaceutical industry's economic and medical advancement and the corresponding expansion of the nation's global power and influence. The next chapter turns to this convergence to focus on how policing was crucial for maintaining and expanding the US drug industry and national power in a new economic, legal, and technological landscape influencing the parameters of drug control.

CHAPTER 4

The Alchemy of Empire

Drugs and Development in the Americas

In July 1941, a United States Treasury officer checked out a pamphlet entitled "Coca: A Plant of the Andes" from the department's library. Originally published in 1928 as part of the Pan-American Union's "Commodities of Commerce Series," the pamphlet described the coca leaf market with the intent of facilitating US international trade. In 1941, however, the government's interest in the coca leaf had more to do with military applications than trade. The officer had gone to the library at the request of investigators in the US Army, and he returned the pamphlet to the librarian, having penned this lighthearted message: "I suppose the future will find each soldier chewing a wad of coca leaves as he repulses the attack of the invading hordes."

The US Army was interested in exploring the stimulating properties of the coca leaf for potential use by its soldiers. In particular, the Treasury officer explained, "It seems that they have been discussing the stimulating effect produced by eating the leaves, as well as boiling them and drinking the tea."[1] Military researchers on all sides of the conflict during World War II sought to derive from plants or manufacture in laboratories an array of substances to heal, minimize pain from injury, and stimulate soldiers to make them more efficient fighters. Coca was just one of many such promising entities, although it seems that at least in leaf form it never gained a foothold in US military barracks.

The officer's mirth over the humorous incongruity of coca-chewers filling the ranks of the world's most powerful army was indicative of the growing cultural belief in the power of technology to transform raw materials (like coca leaves) into superior, and often more potent, products (like cocaine) and the presumed backwardness of older and simpler practices. This faith in "Man's Synthetic Future" was on display at the annual meeting of the American Association for the Advancement of Science (AAAS) in a 1951 speech of that title delivered by the organization's departing president: "Until half a century ago, medicinal products for treatment of disease were confined chiefly to plant or animal extracts or principles discovered originally through the cut-and-dry methods of the physicians of earlier ages. The chemist has now synthesized many of these principles and on the basis of this knowledge has been able to produce other products superior to the natural."

This evolutionary vision portrayed the industrial world's chemical laboratories as the utopian realization of human triumph over nature and, by extension, the inevitably dominant role the US nation itself must play as the engine behind the creation of "products superior to the natural." Dividing the world into "smaller nations" and "greater powers," AAAS President Roger Adams described a global order where the chemical sophisticate survived: countries "technologically unsuited to a future in a strictly chemical world" must be "grouped" with nations "which through two centuries have shown an innate ability to advance against all opposition."[2] Adams's geopolitical hierarchy was shaped by a faith that the capacity to chemically alter raw materials was a marker of national superiority, and the ideal relationship between powerful and weak nations was one that ensured a steady flow of raw materials into US industrial laboratories.

In the aftermath of World War II, US importation and stockpiling of raw materials was pursued in the name of national security, accompanied by the promise of protection and benefits that US "resources for freedom" offered the rest of the world. The previous chapter described the solidification of the international drug control regime around efforts to limit the production and flow of coca leaves, one such raw material, channeling them into an export market geared towards US pharmaceutical stockpiles. Here the focus is on the "synthetic futures" of these raw materials: upon arrival in North American laboratories, drug control officials sought to channel and contain the productive power of these substances, even as they were chemically altered and synthesized into an array of other products. This chapter describes how the process of chemical transformation itself both extended and to a certain extent transformed policing practices; synthetic manipulations might catapult substances in either direction—legality or illegality—and government and corporate officials sought to capitalize on the need for scientific expertise to certify the "legitimacy" of the end product. It shows how narcotics control brought together efforts to manage the production of new drugs with scientific and government-backed efforts to cultivate the production of new types of people. A faith in the power of alchemy to transform the natural world into superior products linked chemical laboratories to experiments in human engineering as people and communities stretching from the United States to the Andes were drawn into grand projects that linked the testing of new drugs with efforts to transform peoples' laboring and consuming habits as the basis for securing and expanding US hegemony.

COCA'S SYNTHETIC FUTURE

The most formidable obstacle standing between US soldiers and the wad of coca leaves that could keep them active on long missions was the drug control and regulatory framework being effectively institutionalized at that time by the Treasury Department's own Federal Bureau of Narcotics. The US Army's laboratory-driven experimentation with chewing the leaves and making tea infusions reproduced the most common forms of indigenous Andean coca consumption—where the majority Aymara and Quechua communities had consumed coca leaves for centuries as sources of nutrition and energy, as a market medium of exchange, and also as an entity valued as a component of healing, religion, and ritual. And in simulating such activity the Army researchers threatened to undermine one of the central tenets of the emerging drug control regime: that there was no medical value, but rather numerous dangers, attached to the consumption of coca leaves in their natural state. The legal assault on raw materials consumption—the chewing of coca leaves—was a combination of the effects of US narcotics law and its determining influence on UN drug control initiatives. In relation to the legal narcotic drug trade, the US government allowed only the importation of raw materials; all controlled substances in domestic circulation (or for export) had to be manufactured within the country. The UN Commission of Enquiry on the Coca Leaf traveled through the Andes in 1949 and called for the elimination of indigenous consumption of the coca leaf in its raw material state. The "supply-side" control orientation of the increasingly powerful drug regulatory regime meant policing officials sought to confine the circulation of raw materials to internationally designated "legitimate channels." UN and US experts defined legitimacy in this context according to the industrial world's determination of "scientific and medicinal need," entrenching a North–South global order where the industrial powers continued to lay claim to the raw materials of the "smaller nations."

These considerations informed FBN Commissioner Harry Anslinger's opposition to a planned 1950 study on coca leaves and fatigue led by scientists working for the US Office of Naval Research. Dr. Robert S. Schwab was directing the study at the Massachusetts General Hospital, and when he turned to Merck and Co., Inc. to supply him with coca leaves from their stocks, Anslinger intervened to halt the shipment. Anslinger was worried the research would undermine Andean acceptance of the regulatory framework being promoted at that time by the United States and the United Nations (where he presided as the US representative), and wanted to reassert the FBN's influence over national drug policy. He explained his objection by highlighting "the primary aim of our government . . . has been to secure control of these drugs at the botanical source." A series of exchanges between Commissioner Anslinger, Dr. Schwab, and Commander J. W. Macmillan of the Office of Naval Research provide perspective on contemporary debate over the promise of scientific research to American power, the definition of "legitimate" medical and scientific use of narcotics, the imperatives of international drug control, and the dangers of certain sites and forms of consumption. The incident reveals much about the nature and direction of US involvement in the coca commodity circuit and the intersection of science and drug control at that time. As Anslinger explained:

> The fact that a domestic scientific project was in progress in the United States, involving the study of the effect of chewing of coca leaves on fatigue, would have a most unfortunate effect on our efforts to achieve international agreement on limitation of production of the leaves to medical and scientific needs. Accomplishments in this direction have been based on the tentative assumption that the use of coca leaves for chewing is neither medical nor scientific. Without knowledge of the official findings of the Commission of Inquiry, I nevertheless feel strongly that the practice of chewing coca leaves should never be recognized as legal.[3]

His insistence that coca leaf chewing "should never be recognized as legal" sought to shut down that line of scientific inquiry, and despite his use of the word "tentative," due to his friendship with the head of the UN commission which had traveled through Peru and Bolivia in 1949, Anslinger in fact already knew the United Nations planned to recommend eliminating indigenous consumption of coca leaves in their 1950 report. And with this knowledge he argued that the principle of limitation was defined according to select medical and scientific ends, and that the coca leaf in its raw material state, "for chewing," could not be—within the framework established by the drug control regime—a legitimate consumer commodity. Anslinger cautioned that the planned research might be used by proponents of coca leaf chewing to bolster their position: "It seems to me that those disposed to challenge such findings and to seek legal recognition and acceptance of the habit of chewing the coca leaf, would attempt to use your findings if successful, as an argument for their position."[4] Invoking international obligations—and a system of controls the United States did so much to influence—Anslinger argued that chewing the coca leaf undermined the tenets of the international system by appearing to validate claims of the unreworked raw material's potential benefits.

Significantly, the commodity form was directly linked to legitimacy. Then and now virtually all coca leaves (legally) exported from the Andes were imported by US manufacturers. At the time Anslinger was presenting these arguments, the two pharmaceutical houses, Merck and Maywood Chemical Works, that held exclusive government licenses to import coca leaves, were both conducting research on the leaf's active properties, reworking its form, parsing its constituent elements, and repackaging them in other states, or as elements of different commodities, before making them available for consumption. This process, in part, embodied the "alchemy of empire." The raw material coca leaf was to be cultivated exclusively as an input into a North American manufacturing process; coca was to be transformed, derivatives extracted, and new products synthesized in laboratories, before it could become a legitimate commodity. The commodity itself then was presented as the triumphant output of US ingenuity—rather than as the product of the international network of labor and raw material from which it was derived.

The logic of control attached to the commodity form, worked to the advantage of US economic power, and was bolstered and depended on Western scientific authority. This further explains the urgency of the Commissioner of Narcotics to stop the Navy research project: it threatened to give the imprimatur of the most sophisticated scientific laboratories to the age-old practice of coca leaf chewing. The lead researcher on the project, Dr. Schwab, explained to Anslinger that "Merck Co.," his supplier of coca leaves, had forewarned him that FBN objections might arise. "It was for this reason" that the study was carefully designed to be "an essential pharmacological investigation . . . using this drug as a means of ascertaining information and data in the general study of fatigue." Dr. Schwab presented the raw material as a pharmacological input rather than the object of study itself. Drawing attention to the advanced technical equipment available to his lab, in contrast to the "apparatus available" to the UN researchers in the Andes, he suggested his work might have widespread scientific value, could be kept confidential if necessary, and wrote in bold underline to emphasize there was "no intention at any time" to introduce coca leaves "into this country as a remedy for fatigue."[5] Despite this effort at reassurance, it was the very potential for scientific success that threatened to undermine drug control tenets. Anslinger urged the doctor to reconsider; affirming his belief in the research project's limited intent, he emphasized the difficulty in keeping "such work confidential," and argued "the natural consequence" of scientific study into the fatigue-relieving power of the leaf would "stimulate others to a practical application of the proved thesis."

While elaborating the potential unintended consequences of such research, Anslinger's argument exemplified how scientific authority was influencing the legal parameters of the drug control regime's effective domain. While claiming "I deeply respect the importance of fostering rather than deterring scientific research," Anslinger went on to say: "I am fearful of an attempt being made to expand a scientific use such as you have in mind into a so-called legitimate use which is neither medical nor scientific, and which can not fail to prejudice the proposed International Agreement to limit the production of these leaves to medical and scientific purposes only."

The boundaries of legitimacy within narcotics control were defined by assessments of a substance's "medical and scientific" value, even as the FBN sought to limit scientific research that might produce outcomes contrary to its own drug control goals. Coca leaves, according to the parameters of narcotics control, only gained medical and scientific value after being transformed into other substances. The dangers within the leaf could only be contained in this way—a proposition that was tied both to the commodity form and, more specifically, to an effort to channel the leaf's potent alkaloidal content toward specific, controlled ends. What made coca leaves definitively illegitimate consumer items was the "strong probability that the chewing of these coca leaves, containing cocaine, has a potentiality for the establishment of addiction and possibly other deleterious effects."[6] Alchemical power here was twofold.

First, the chemical laboratory exercised the exclusive power to render dangerous raw material legitimate. Secondly, in a circular fashion, the laboratory itself characterized coca leaves as vehicles for delivering the alkaloid cocaine, defined the drugs' promise and peril (cocaine being "addictive"), and galvanized the system of control accordingly.

The scientific logic emerging from laboratories informed narcotic control efforts as regulators invoked the cocaine content of coca leaves to label them unsafe for indigenous consumption in the Andes. This was evident when the UN commission concluded, "the effects produced by coca leaf chewing are to be explained by the action of cocaine."[7] This equation of coca leaf with cocaine became common practice among drug control advocates. The substances valued, parsed, extracted, and synthesized from the coca leaf in the laboratories of industrial countries were imported back into the Andes not only as legitimate consumer goods, but as evidence of the dangers and need for control over the nonsynthetic. At the same time, the power of the laboratory to extract the alkaloid cocaine and channel the substance into "legitimate" medical and scientific channels also meant that the by-product from which the cocaine had been extracted was now safe once again to be synthesized into still other legitimate commodities: the most famous of which was, of course, Coca-Cola. Before returning to the outcome of the Navy research effort, it is worth considering for a moment the other synthetic futures extracted from the coca leaf. In contrast to the hypervisibility of cocaine (even when hidden in miniscule quantities within a leaf), the afterlife of various other alkaloids, vitamins, and flavor-rich substances that together constituted the original coca leaf disappeared from the regulatory landscape and from the public record for researchers probing the archive.

It is striking that at the very moment the United States was leading efforts to consolidate the drug control regime around controlling raw material, the largest single licit consumer of coca leaves at that time, the Coca-Cola Company, fell off the drug control radar. Coca-Cola, unlike raw coca leaves, was a legitimate and even desirable source of energy, and during and after World War II it underwent a massive global expansion, fueling the need for ever greater quantities of raw material for the production of its famously guarded formula. And yet, despite two decades of Coca-Cola's "special leaves" being granted legal exemption for not qualifying as any "medical and scientific use" in international narcotics law, the UN board overseeing the international trade in narcotics reported: "Since 1947, no coca leaves have been used in the United

States of America for the preparation of non-narcotic coca-flavoured beverages."[8] Perhaps the alchemy of empire made this technically true—Coca-Cola did not use coca leaves, but rather substances extracted from the leaves in a laboratory. When the Office of the United States High Commissioner in Germany heard such reports, he wrote to FBN Commissioner Anslinger, asking how Coca-Cola was now obtaining its flavoring extract. Apparently French and German resentment over the company's "aggressive advertising campaigns" was fueling talk that their governments might import coca leaves to manufacture "similar beverages themselves."[9] Anslinger urged the officer to "discourage" such imports on narcotics enforcement grounds, emphasized the many failed attempts of competitors to reproduce Coke's process in any case, and explained the absence of "special leaves" from UN tallies as follows: "[I]t should not be overlooked that flavoring extracts are also produced from the leaves imported for the manufacture of cocaine. In the cocaine extraction process the liquids bearing the alkaloids are separated at a very early stage from the waxes which contain the flavors and each then goes its own way to completion."[10]

Two categories of legitimate uses for coca leaves technically existed in international law: the use of coca leaves for medicinal and scientific purposes and for the production of a nonnarcotic flavoring extract. These categories of legitimacy would persist and would later be consecrated in the landmark 1961 Single Drug Convention. It was an important and revealing transformation in the public administration of narcotics control, however, when in the aftermath of World War II the only "legitimate" nonmedical use of coca leaves (Coca-Cola's flavoring extract) disappeared from the official record. Since the 1931 Geneva Convention, "special leaves" had international legal provision to be used in the manufacturing of a flavoring extract. Under the convention all such leaves had to be reported and verification provided by the FBN that all the resultant active alkaloids had been destroyed under government supervision. However, during and after the war this destruction stopped and all active alkaloids were reprocessed by pharmaceutical manufacturers for scientific and medical use—or relayed to warehouses where they filled a category of narcotics accumulation exempt from the oversight of international drug control: national security stockpiles. Once this occurred, in terms of legal reporting requirements the flavoring extract was strictly a by-product of drug production, left over from leaves that might be accounted for as imported entirely for scientific and medical use. The FBN no longer reported "special leaves" to the United

Nations since they were accounted for within the tally of "medicinal" importations.[11] Thus, with unintended irony, the production of Coca-Cola's coca leaf–based flavoring extract largely disappeared from international regulatory oversight because it was now primarily derived from coca leaves imported for the manufacture of cocaine.

Coca leaf flavoring extract going "on its own way to completion," out of the international regulatory gaze, had a number of important ramifications for narcotics control and for US government and corporate power. Initially the vice president of Coca-Cola worried this absence of tracking might eventually push them out of the legitimate market altogether. He wrote to the FBN, wondering if it would be better to report imports anyway. "My reason for this suggestion is that it would seem advisable to avoid such apparent non-use of the statutory provisions regarding 'Special' leaves as might cause them gradually to fall into an atrophied or inoperative status." Anslinger successfully reassured the company's vice president that there was nothing to fear and that reporting on "special leaves" might make it seem as if the United States was actually concealing medicinal production from international scrutiny.[12] This was no small worry in a context where synthetic drugs were increasingly replacing cocaine in common medical practice, narrowing even further the domain of legitimacy. Soon thereafter, Coca-Cola began capitalizing on this absence of public scrutiny to conceal its involvement in the coca leaf trade.

The shift also had an immediate impact on the pharmaceutical industry. Merck & Co., Inc. stopped importing leaves destined exclusively for cocaine production, ceding the process entirely to Maywood Chemical Works, Coca-Cola's supplier.[13] Furthermore, Coca-Cola's strong market growth across the decade and beyond helped ensure that the United States remained the largest manufacturer of licit cocaine in the world.[14] In the realm of policing the illicit, the consequences were equally profound. The shift effectively eliminated recognition of any legal market for coca leaves outside the chemical laboratories of industrial powers. And so UN officials tracking the narcotics trade could advocate for stricter raw material controls, providing the following as evidence: "The use of coca leaves for medical purposes, namely for the licit manufacture of cocaine, absorbed only a fraction of the output . . . the balance . . . was consumed for non-medical purposes—that is to say, was chewed by certain indigenous peoples of South America."[15] The only reported "licit" manufacture was pharmaceutical cocaine production, and the only recognized illicit, "nonmedical" purpose was Andean coca leaf chewing. Coca-Cola's nonmedical use of coca leaves no longer provided a public caveat to regulators' insistence on "medical and scientific" value, as the company's utilization of the leaves disappeared from FBN and UN annual reports, narrowing the visible landscape of "legitimate" uses of the coca leaf and making it easier for the Commissioner of Narcotics to make his case to the Navy for limiting their research into coca leaf chewing's fatigue-relieving potential.[16]

Dr. Schwab envisioned that his work might "settle for once and for all the mechanism of the reduction of the sensation of fatigue from coca leaves," and, by doing so, advance "fundamental knowledge of this substance."[17] And Anslinger quickly countered by invoking the potential regulatory nightmare such scientific research might provoke, potentially lending credence to claims emanating from the Andes that coca leaves were legitimate items of consumption in their natural state. For Anslinger the very potency of the leaf necessitated a strict system of control. Despite FBN concern, questions of national security influenced priorities within the realm of drug research and development, and it was for this reason that the Office of Naval Research won a rare triumph over Commissioner Anslinger's objections to research on coca leaf in its unreworked states. "By direction of the Chief of Naval Research," Anslinger was informed of the research project's relevance to the country's national security: "I am sure you are aware of the real interest of the military establishment in problems of fatigue," Commander J.W. Macmillan wrote to Commissioner Anslinger. He went on to explain, "It is our belief that only through such programs can advances in naval power and national security be ultimately achieved." Macmillan concluded with a lofty vision to bolster the coca leaf study: "I am sure all of us are interested in the continuation of freedom for our scientists in their efforts to further our understanding of the human organism."[18]

Anslinger seems to have successfully forestalled the investigation until after the UN commission published its report in May 1950, preventing the diplomatic fallout he had feared. It was not until October 1951 that Anslinger personally submitted an order for the coca leaves to Maywood Chemical Works on behalf of scientists conducting "research on fatigue among Air Corps pilots [who need] these leaves for that purpose."[19] It is worth pointing out that while the research scientists had initially placed their order for leaves with Merck, by 1951, perhaps reflecting the industry shift in production which accompanied the shift in regulatory reporting, Anslinger turned to Maywood, Coca-Cola's supplier, to provide the experimental stocks.

The military's ultimate triumph over Anslinger's objections in this case was an exceptional instance, resting on invocations of military necessity, "national security," and scientific freedom. Most research in this field being conducted in the United States at the time involved the ingestion of the cocaine alkaloid extracted from coca leaves, or experiments with synthetic substitutes manufactured entirely in laboratories. Far from focusing on the qualities of the raw material in its natural state, American scientists and doctors, military personnel, company boardrooms, and even the mainstream media looked to the wonders of new drug development and experimentation for the capacity to advance American economic and political might, societal health, and medical knowledge. And this, unlike the Navy's interest in keeping Air Corps pilots awake by chewing coca leaves, conformed completely to the strictures of international drug control within which North American manufacturers were primary transformers of raw materials into legitimate drug commodities for the national and world market.

DEVELOPING "WONDER DRUGS"

Cocaine's important status within the drug regulatory regime was connected to its relatively early synthesis and revolutionary role in medicine. Tests involving coca leaves, cocaine, or synthetic substitutes in this regard were emblematic of the landscape of drug development at mid-century where a whole array of "wonder drugs," including primarily antibiotics, vitamins, painkillers, and stimulants, promised a veritable therapeutic revolution. The introduction of cocaine into medical practice in the late nineteenth century had transformed surgery, being used very effectively as a local anesthetic. While the US Navy had been interested in the stimulating properties of the coca leaf, the cocaine alkaloid extracted from the leaf was most commonly used not as a stimulant but rather as a painkiller. Anesthesia has always been a hazardous aspect of Western surgical practice, liable to produce toxic reactions resulting in death. This toxicity—primarily tied to the dosage given and the variability of human reactions to it—sparked much research into finding less toxic substances. While cocaine continues to be "used as a topical anesthetic by ear-nose-and-throat surgeons," numerous other synthetically manufactured drugs based on cocaine—drugs such as procaine (also called novocaine), lidocaine, prilocaine, and others—have also found their place in Western medical practice. Some laboratory-manufactured painkilling drugs, such as novocaine, continue to be widely used.

Others, such as cinchocaine and bupivacaine, were discarded after discovery of their "considerable level of toxicity."[20]

All of these failures and successes were part and parcel of the methods deployed for the "advancement" of Western medicine. In the 1940s the promise such synthetic substitute drugs offered was great, spanning policing, economic, diplomatic, and medical worlds. Limiting US dependence on raw materials promised to eliminate what William McAllister characterizes as the drug control regime's "excess production dilemma," the overproduction of raw materials that might slip into illicit channels.[21] The Chief of the Addiction-Producing Drugs Section of the World Health Organization (WHO) articulated this sentiment: "Many believe that, from the viewpoint of the efficiency of control, it would even be better to be, for legitimate medical purposes, not dependent on substances manufactured from agricultural products, provided, of course . . . drugs of purely synthetic origin, are at least as good."[22] Limiting the flow of raw material also had the potential to increase US economic and diplomatic leverage if it dominated the production of synthetics. The power of synthetic drug alternatives was evident from the circumstances of their genesis: Allied World War II embargoes that propelled German chemical innovations to overcome raw material shortages. The first generation of synthetic narcotics, hailed as harbingers of a "drug revolution," were all "discovered in Germany during the war."[23] US observers believed that synthetic drugs might reduce dependence on foreign imports while also reducing manufacturing costs. In the war's aftermath, "old sources of supply" had opened up again, but as *Business Week* reported, "labor costs for collecting the plants are higher now. So the trend is definitely toward replacing imported botanicals with US-made synthetics. Manufacturers can often produce these synthetics more cheaply than they can import the plants."[24] And finally, as embodiments of the technological wonders of scientific research and capital investment, laboratory-synthesized drugs seemed to offer a limitless potential of yet to be discovered benefits.

War policy and subsequent defense mobilization illustrated the power of the synthetic drug not merely in political and economic terms, but also, importantly, in terms of their potential impact on the human body. The US military was an important site for drug experimentation as well as a critical consumer market for US-manufactured drugs. Often research that began in the context of helping soldiers overcome ailments would subsequently become incorporated into civilian medical practice. It was often military needs initially that determined which drugs were

FIGURE 5. *Merck and Co., Inc.* Louis Lozowick's artistic depiction of an aerial view of a Merck chemical manufacturing plant, commissioned by the company for an advertisement. The lithographic print captures American modernist infatuation with the machine age and industrial innovation, and the pharmaceutical giant's iconic place within it [Smithsonian American Art Museum, Gift of Adele Lozowick © 1944, Lee Lozowick].

developed and to what ends. Doctors began testing procaine (novocaine) on injured soldiers at Fort Myer, Virginia, to minimize the pain resulting from "acute sprains and strains of ankles, knees and backs." The success of these initial experimental uses of the drug were made public by *Newsweek* as it enthused, "Men who had hobbled and been helped to the hospital were able to walk naturally immediately after treatment and were quickly returned to heavy duty with no ill effects."[25] Research on procaine's possible uses was extensive and offered other advantages beyond its painkilling powers. Dr. Ralph M. Tovell of Yale University and chief of anesthesiology at Hartford General Hospital, "among the first to persuade the Army of the United States to treat soldiers' wounds with procaine," found in his experiments one advantage of the drug was that it "was less habit forming than morphine."[26] Dr. Tovell and other researchers at universities, hospitals, and military clinics, during and after the war, experimented with procaine for a wide range of therapeutic possibilities. By 1947 while "the subject was one on which much work by anesthetists and other doctors must still be done," procaine as described by the president of the International Anesthesia Research Society "gave promise of developing into an aid for sufferers of arthritis, gangrene, diabetes and similar afflictions."[27]

Clearly the ailments such drugs might relieve made them beneficial to realms outside of the military; however, it is important to note that this early emphasis shaped the landscape of drug production and was tied to an anticipated consumer market. Along with the creation of painkillers, the first major breakthrough in synthetic drug manufacturing, hailed as a revolution in pharmacy, was to combat malaria among the armed forces deployed to tropical countries during World War II. In a study of the history of this development the WHO explained: "[W]hen Anglo-American forces landed in North Africa, Indonesia [a natural source of quinine provided by the chinchona tree] was in the hands of the enemy. The health authorities no longer had free choice of drug and so quinacrine was prescribed. . . . It can be said that the 'era of the synthetic antimalarials' dates from that time."[28] The US Office of Scientific Research and Development (OSRD) launched mass production of penicillin during the war as part of the agency's mandate to "initiate and support scientific research on medical problems affecting the national defense." In a report to the US president entitled *Science: The Endless Frontier* (which became the basis for the establishment in 1950 of the National Science Foundation), the director of the OSRD, Vannevar Bush, linked government-sponsored drug production to the success of the war effort. What Bush termed the "physiological indoctrination" of soldiers (with drugs) provided critical support against "the disastrous loss of fighting capacity or life."[29]

As military priorities led to innovations in drug development, the laboratory gained increasing importance as a source for manufacturing drugs synthetically, to avoid dependence on raw material flows which might be disrupted by war or political instability, and to empower soldiers in their work. The production of laboratory-synthesized drugs for military consumption also made them available for other consumer markets. Bush celebrated how the war's "great production program" made penicillin "this remarkable drug available in large quantities for both military and civilian use."[30] In the civilian realm drug control and development priorities also reflected the unequal distribution of power internationally. For instance, while synthetic drug innovation would remain valuable for future military deployments, the same drugs became valuable resources especially for use by other travelers, most frequently tourists or business employees working for North American or European companies.[31] The WHO described how by 1953 synthetic antimalarials made "possible traveling, staying or working in the endemic regions with results equal or even superior to quinine." It was clear the benefits derived from such drugs were not distributed equally. The WHO advised that it was necessary to extend "this protection and not to limit it to non-immune, non-indigenous persons or those working for them." As the study concluded, "Among the indigenous population the children are those who are non-immune. It is certain that so far few children have benefited from preventive medication. . . . Although the era of synthetic antimalarials has arrived, the social position has not greatly changed."[32]

This "social position" of drugs was true of both the sites and bodies upon whom their development relied for testing as well as the populations initially envisioned as their primary consumers. Thus drugs tested on soldiers for soldiers and other military personnel would also become useful to the corporate and pleasure-seeking visitors in colonized or "undeveloped" countries, traveling from the countries out of which the soldiers initially came. The international "social position" of a drug was influenced by the objectives spurring its initial development, and also by disparities in distribution and popular access to it. Until the "distribution problem" was solved in less developed parts of the world, if present conditions were not "greatly changed and if economic development is not accelerated, only temporary and non-indigenous residents will greatly benefit from the advances made."[33] Scientists working in the field at mid-century were aware of inequalities in access to newly manufactured drugs, yet the promise such drugs held was not questioned. This then created an opportunity for drug diplomacy, whereby symbolic and material efforts to redress uneven access, particularly among populations in the non-industrial world, became a central component of US (and increasingly Soviet) efforts to foreground health initiatives as exemplars of benevolent superpower intent.

Public health diplomacy—including the celebration and distribution of wonder drugs as markers of the pinnacle of Western medical advancement—became a prominent public component of projections of American power in the world. In October 1950, Assistant Secretary of State for Economic Affairs Willard L. Thorp declared, "World-health improvement has become a major concern of American foreign policy. Health has become recognized as a major factor in economic and social progress throughout the world—and thus in the preservation of peace." The US surgeon general echoed such sentiments, explaining that US Army and Navy wartime involvement in civilian health problems in "far-flung combat theaters" and in "liberated or conquered areas" provided a strategic precedent for the ways in which the "promotion of world health came to be recognized as a major instrument for attaining our goals of world peace and prosperity."[34] As the United States sought to step into the power vacuums left by World War II and collapsing European empires, public health initiatives provided a seemingly neutral and unimpeachable realm of intervention. In a geopolitical context animated by anticolonial movements and burgeoning Cold War rivalries, drug trade regulations ensured industrial powers' virtual monopoly over the manufacturing of legal drug commodities, while providing a formidable weapon in competitions for global influence.

The wonder drugs were hailed by private and public spokespeople alike as critical tools for gaining allies and securing US power and influence in the world. In 1955, *Business Week* celebrated the "fantastic growth" of US drug sales in foreign markets by emphasizing the humanitarian implications: "Millions of people in the underdeveloped parts of the world . . . have become acquainted with 'miracle' drugs since the end of World War II."[35] The advances of Western science were ultimately (if unevenly) to be exported to the rest of the world to assist in its "development." The article's message was dramatized in a split image where a graph depicting the growth in US exports is directly related to the work of Western medical practitioners in the "underdeveloped" world, in this case with the administration of eyedrops on a small "desert child." The ideology that accompanied US economic expansion often relied on such representations of the benevolent and unquestioned progress US products brought to peoples of the world—people who were depicted as being unable to provide for themselves. While many drugs developed did indeed transform life expectancy and alleviate illness, often the resources invested in them inherently structured drug development not only initially toward helping the ailments of privileged populations, but also toward creating a global dependence on Western manufacturers whose drugs replaced indigenous medicinal plants in the very regions where they were cultivated.

Beyond this structuring of the international drug economy to the disadvantage of raw materials–producing countries and providing powerful diplomatic leverage to drug-manufacturing countries, it also valorized

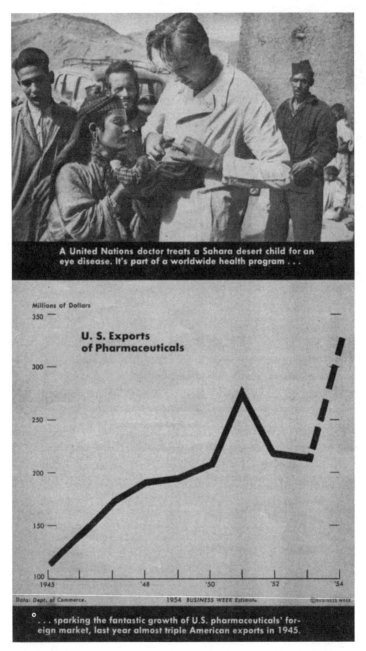

FIGURE 6. Graphics from a 1955 *Business Week* article celebrating the "fantastic growth" of US pharmaceuticals' foreign market.

Western science often in disregard of local belief, custom, and experience. As Marcos Cueto has described initiatives to introduce Western medical practice and medicines in Peru: "In many Andean localities Western medicine was absent; and where it was available, it was applied in an essentially authoritarian way, with an unlimited confidence in the intrinsic capacity of technological resources and little regard for the education of the Indian people. Practitioners of modern medicine . . . assumed that in a 'backward,' nonscientific culture, disease could be managed without reference to the individual experiencing it."[36]

Within an emerging international system for the manufacturing and controlled distribution of drug commodities, such issues were not of central concern to the confident circle of scientists and experts working in the field of development connected to poverty, nutrition, and health. Indigenous populations' own beliefs about the foundations of medicine and health were rarely taken into consideration. Nevertheless, as with the "desert child" invoked above, they often embodied in the US public imaginary proof of the beneficence of US capitalist expansion, even reframing it as bringing health and progress to "less fortunate" parts of the world. The regime not only increasingly entrenched an international economic hierarchy between states but also provided a rationale justifying and perpetuating inequality between peoples within states. The ready objectification of the "desert child" as a site for the performance of Western benevolence and the easy dismissal of alternative cultural understandings of health were indicative of the ways in which drug control policy infused race, class, and geography into a new imperial ideology. While the history of science as a bolstering force behind European and American colonialism stretches back at least into the nineteenth century, as Ashish Nandy has argued, the post–World War II moment marked a shift as science and development became increasingly central categories of national security, and science itself became "a reason of state," potently on display in US Cold War policy.[37] As Shiv Visvanathan further elaborated: "Progress and modernization as scientific projects automatically legitimate any violence done to the third world as objects of experimentation."[38] As scientists, government officials, pharmaceutical executives, and international organizations debated the parameters of drug control, they approached indigenous people of the Third World and the poor and marginalized of the industrial world much like the raw material coca, with a laboratory-like gaze where these people were not considered independent political actors, but rather as (often childlike) malleable objects ripe for socially and chemically engineering other synthetic futures. This dynamic was clear as debates over drug control provided a setting for the working-out of great power rivalries, while reasserting the First World's dominating influence over the economic and political trajectories of "underdeveloped" countries and peoples.

COLD WAR PROTOCOLS

For US and UN officials concerned with international drug control, the profusion of wonder drugs posed a new regulatory challenge as they worked on devising oversight mechanisms to channel manufactured drugs' productive power—their promise and peril—to their own sanctioned ends. The dreamer behind "Man's Synthetic Future," the "scientific statesman" Roger Adams who was deeply involved in advancing chemistry's role in both government and business, having served among many other posts as consultant for the National Defense Research Committee and the Coca-Cola Company,[39] captured the fear lurking at the edges of the wonder: "The future may bring us a series of drugs that will permit deliberate molding of a person, mentally and physically. When this day arrives the problems of control of such chemicals will be of concern to all. They would present dire potentialities in the hands of an unscrupulous dictator."[40]

This dystopian vision of nefarious forces using drugs to manipulate human bodies and social organization was the logical counterpoint to celebrations of their ability to bring "peace and prosperity." Both projections accepted the proposition—at once celebrated and feared—that governments might use drugs to influence society (and implicitly, that the consumption of drugs—the physical impact—had predetermined social consequences). The distinction—one good, one bad—between the US military's reliance on drugs for the "physiological indoctrination" of soldiers and a "dictator's" use of drugs for the "deliberate molding of a person," rested on moral, cultural, and political arguments to justify the regulation and policing of drugs, even while advancing a belief in the power of drugs to transform publics.

Such arguments held enormous weight when drug control officials sought to dictate the trajectory of drug production, distribution, and consumption, from the raw materials through to the finished goods. The "two serious new problems" first identified by the UN Commission on Narcotic Drugs (the primary body governing the international drug trade) stemmed from the "habit of chewing coca leaves" and the new abundance of "man-made drugs." Reporting on the CND's activities for the *Washington Post,* Adelaide Kerr explained how a duality intrinsic to the drug revolution generated the need for regulation: "Rightly used, many of these drugs are boons to mankind, but wrongly used they can wreck health, destroy men's moral sense to such an extent they often turn into criminals, ruin their ability for constructive work, impoverish them, reduce them from producers and wage earners to charity charges of the state and because of these and other reasons, produce extremely serious economic and social problems for their countries."[41]

The belief in the capacity of drugs to improve "mankind" relied on the depiction of drugs as powerful agents: capable of turning people into wage earning, productive members of society, or, in contrast, of transforming them into destructive elements and economic drains on the state. The government had a primary interest in securing economic advantage within the drug trade, which entailed influencing the consuming habits of the population. When framed in this way, the challenges confronting the drug control regime were twofold in the quest to realize "boons to mankind." First was the question of determining which drugs were most valuable. Second was the need to implement regulations and oversight to ensure consumer demand for all drugs remained in legitimate channels. Drug control was not geared towards eliminating dangerous drugs; rather, it was oriented toward harnessing the productive potential of drugs and delegating the relationship of various countries and populations to the "legal" international drug trade. Controlling the flow of raw materials to limit the nature, extent, and geography of manufactured drug production was one component. Controlling the circulation and consumption of manufactured drugs themselves was another. And so, along with initiatives in the Andes to control coca leaf production, a concerted international campaign was launched, spearheaded by US representatives at the United Nations, to extend the regulatory regime's jurisdiction to encompass new synthetic "man-made" drugs.

Public officials attending the United Nations aired these preoccupations in late 1948 when they convened to draft, debate, and ultimately adopt the Protocol Bringing under International Control Drugs Outside the Scope of the Convention of 13 July 1931 for Limiting the Manufacture and Regulating the Distribution of Narcotic Drugs (the 1948 Protocol). This treaty launched international regulation of synthetic drugs—substances previously "outside the scope" of legal supervision. Eleanor Roosevelt, the former president's widow and US delegate in attendance, contributed to the sense of urgency as she recounted how synthetic drug production "was so easy that a single factory could flood the world market with products of that category," and insisted, "the machinery for controlling narcotic drugs should be extended and modernized." Roosevelt reported that the "United States would give its full support to the draft protocol," and delicately tried to overcome a central point of contention among world powers about whether the protocol would apply to colonial and other non-self-governing territories: "It is hoped that the General Assembly would approve the protocol during the current session and that all Governments would apply it without delay in their dependent territories." In a series of exchanges that augured the role drug control would increasingly play in anticolonial and Cold War conflict (addressed more extensively in the next chapter), conflict surrounding passage of the protocol mirrored those accompanying global power realignments.

The source of controversy was Article 8 of the proposed UN protocol, which delegated to imperial powers, including the United States and United Kingdom, autonomous determination over whether the protocol's rules would extend to territories under their nations' control. The Soviet delegates challenged the proposal on a number of grounds. They argued it was a mechanism for metropolitan powers to bypass oversight and it exemplified a negligent lack of concern for "unhealthy conditions prevalent in those Territories." What followed was a back-and-forth verbal exchange in response to this assertion that Article 8 rendered drug control imperially selective and self-serving. British officials defended the clause as protecting the right to representative government in its territories (which could choose to sign on or not), challenged Soviet depictions of it as "an escape clause" (that would allow the United States and United Kingdom to have unregulated drug markets in regions under their control), and explained, "the United Kingdom did not wish and was not able to impose its own point of view on the territories placed under its trusteeship." US representatives supported the British; however, they emphasized the distinctiveness of their colonial administration whereby "in accordance with their usual practice," the protocol would automatically apply "to all territories for the foreign relations of which they were responsible." The Soviets persisted in their opposition, exhibiting their own paternalist ambitions as they accused the United States and United Kingdom of malicious colonial neglect: "The abolition of such colonial clauses would convince the Native peoples that the metropolitan authorities were seeking to improve their administration; their retention, on the other hand, indicated a lack of desire to promote the real interests of colonial peoples."

As the exchange heated up, the fault lines of postwar diplomacy were clearly on display. The symbolic jostling around the concern of superpowers for the peoples of colonial territories reflected a geopolitical division whereby the United States defended its own and England's imperial administration while the Soviet Union postured as an ally of "colonial peoples." All three presumed the superiority of industrial world power and expounded the benevolent possibilities of exporting their own visions of progress to other parts of the world. It was not the system of control being contested, all sides agreeing that drug control "would be of such obvious benefit to them [colonial peoples]," but rather the political principles delineating its effective domain. Symbolic posturing became central to negotiations over drug control. The USSR proposed eliminating Article 8 "based on a desire for equality for all peoples," and the British argued the "steady advance towards independence for non-self-governing peoples" meant they "should be allowed to decide whether they wished the protocol to be applicable to them."[42]

The balance of power at the United Nations ensured that the interests of colonial powers carried the day; the protocol was adopted, including Article 8, despite Soviet reservations. In the midst of postwar reconstruction, colonial readjustments, Cold War tensions, and the political challenge posed by a growing number of newly independent states, drug control efforts provided one way for industrial countries, particularly the United States, to secure international dominance through a selective regulatory apparatus portrayed as an act of international benevolence. The delegate from India remarked on the unprecedented embrace of drug control, comparing it to burgeoning efforts to control atomic power:

> It was easy to imagine the sensation it would cause if the First Committee were to adopt unanimously, after a single day's discussion, a convention for the control of atomic energy. Yet the difference between the two problems was not so great. Both were the result of progress achieved through science, progress which might be put to either good or bad uses. The destruction which the atomic bomb could wreak, though more limited in its extent, was more spectacular, whereas synthetic drugs were able to do great damage insidiously and continuously, on a larger scale. They destroyed the mind before they destroyed the body.[43]

Political, economic, and cultural factors influenced which drugs under what circumstances would fall under the system of control, something implicitly acknowledged in this declaration that scientific "progress" could be put to both "good and bad uses." It was the drug control regime itself that delineated the boundaries of legality—when an individual, official, institution, or government was putting drugs to "good" or "bad" uses—and officials administering the system based these determinations on the authority of Western scientists, inevitably and profoundly shaped by power hierarchies and cultural bias. Arguments over colonial authority exhibited this tendency. So too did the language and categories of enforcement enshrined in the 1948 Protocol, particularly the assignation of the label "addictive." The idea that opium and cocaine were "addictive" provided the foundational justification for the entire drug control regime. The deployment of this term in negotiations over the 1948 Protocol showed the ongoing manipulation of the concept to augment the capacity of industrial countries to influence the lives of people and communities around the world in very concrete ways.

The CND drafted the 1948 Protocol, which introduced regulations to limit the manufacture of and monitor the trade in certain synthetic drugs to be overseen by the Drug Supervisory Body (DSB). It delegated to the WHO the authority to determine which substances should be controlled based on whether "the drug in question is capable of producing addiction or of conversion into a product capable of producing addiction."[44] National governments adhering to the treaty had to report to the UN secretary general the discoveries of synthetic drugs that might prove "liable to the same kind of abuse and productive of the same kind of harmful effects" as those attributed to coca and opium, and the secretary general in turn would notify the CND and the WHO. The WHO made a scientific determination of a substance's potential danger and the CND launched regulation when necessary. The Preamble to the 1948 Protocol summarized the treaty's origin and function: "Considering that the progress of modern pharmacology and chemistry has resulted in the discovery of drugs, particularly synthetic drugs, capable of producing addiction," the treaty placed these drugs "under control in order to limit by international agreement their manufacture to the world's legitimate requirements for medical and scientific purposes and to regulate their distribution." The 1948 Protocol did not apply to all synthetic drugs, but exclusively to drugs deemed to have addictive properties similar to opium and cocaine. The two original "narcotic drugs" subject to international control, the poppy plant and coca leaves and their valued derivatives (opium and cocaine), remained entrenched as the benchmark for all other drugs in determining whether they should be deemed addictive and regulated as "narcotics."

Drug control officials identified "addiction" as the object of their regulatory and policing endeavors, and defining the concept became an important aspect of establishing the regime's effective domain. Determining the "addictive" properties of synthetic drugs became the designated responsibility of the WHO's Expert Committee on Drugs Liable to Produce Addiction, which in 1949 defined its task as follows: "The Expert Committee . . . is to investigate the extremely complicated situation created by the production of a whole group of new synthetic products whose analgesic properties produce an effect analogous to that of morphine and are habit-forming or which lend themselves readily to conversion into drugs capable of producing addiction."[45]

Synthetic opiates were the largest category of drug leaking into illicit channels at that time. Drug control authorities, particularly in the United States, also worried about the illicit circulation of synthetic versions of cocaine. As early as the 1930s, studies were done to help "government chemists . . . identify both cocaine and novocaine separately." This grew out of police anxiety that "illegal cocaine seized by the Narcotics Bureau . . . had been adulterated with novocaine," or even completely substituted by it.[46] In 1945 the FBN failed to secure a conviction for illicit novocaine seized at the border when the defense attorney successfully argued the drug was not a derivative of the coca leaf and consequently did "not come within the purview" of federal narcotic law.[47] Anslinger raised alarm and, concurrent with international efforts to control synthetics, the United States amended its narcotic law to "redefine the term 'Narcotic Drugs' to include synthetic substances which are chemically identical with a drug derived from opium or coca leaves." As an FBN circular described the adjustment to its agents, "it was decided to amend the law so that such distinction [whether synthetic drugs were 'narcotics'] would be unnecessary."[48] According to the FBN, the time for policing synthetically manufactured drugs as "narcotics" had arrived.

Drug control now targeted synthetic drugs believed to mimic the presumed addictive qualities of opium and cocaine. The international drug control regime's emphasis on "drugs capable of producing addiction" bolstered international efforts to limit the circulation of particular substances, like coca, and in the process justified policing people deemed threatening to the social, political, and economic status quo. This was evident when the CND investigated the "problem" of coca leaf chewing in 1949 and turned to the WHO Expert Committee for help. The CND asked to be furnished with "definitions of the terms 'drug addiction,' 'addiction forming drugs,' and 'fundamental structure of addiction-forming drug' . . . to illustrate such definitions by references to appropriate drugs." In response to this request, the Expert Committee explained that essential to defining the notion of "addiction" was distinguishing it from the term "habit-forming." The head of the Expert Committee elaborated this point in an exchange with its US delegate: "In the Paris Protocol of November 1948, and even as early as in the 1931 Convention, the word 'addiction' has been used in preference to 'habit.' In my opinion, 'addiction' corresponds better than 'habit' to the meaning. There are many habits which have nothing to do with addiction. Therefore, 'addiction-forming' drugs might be a more appropriate expression than 'habit-forming.'"[49]

The US delegate, Nathan B. Eddy—who served as a medical officer at the US Public Health Service (USPHS)—concurred and emphasized, "at least for control purposes 'addicting drug' is a more exact term and nearer the meaning intended than 'habit-forming'; as you say, the latter is too comprehensive."[50]

"For control purposes," then, "addicting" was determined to reflect the greater social menace posed by the consumption of certain drugs. The Expert Committee went on to officially "caution against the erroneous characterization as addiction-producing, of such substances or drugs which in fact do not bear a real addiction character, but merely create habituation. The use of tobacco is an example, alcohol is another." The "real addiction characters" of certain drugs as defined by the WHO was unique in many ways "from many earlier ones, given by pharmacologists and psychiatrists, in the sense that they include the social aspect, the harm done not only to the individual but to society."[51] So, the dangerous aspect of drug consumption, according to the parameters of the emerging drug control regime, resided not only in an individual's consumption habits or even the physiological action of the drug on a person's body, but also in the threat these bodies posed to the larger society. As such the definition inherently structured into the drug control regime the power of cultural, racial, class, gender, national, and other biases to influence the determination of what constituted a menace to the community.

Such biases were evident in the work and conclusions of the UN Commission of Enquiry on the Coca Leaf, as discussed more extensively in the previous chapter. It was widely acknowledged at the time, as described in the US publication *Natural History* in 1947, that "the coca

FIGURE 7. A Peruvian peasant in Vicos in 1952 holding a coca leaf bag, lime dispenser (to dip into while chewing the leaf), and a cigarette in his hand. According to drug control officials, tobacco use constituted a "habit" while coca consumption was an "addiction." ["Vicosino Holding Coca Bag, Lime Dispenser." Photograph by Abraham Guillén. Allan R. Holmberg collection on Peru, #14–25–1529. Division of Rare and Manuscript Collections, Cornell University Library.]

habit is more universal among Andean Indians than the tobacco habit is among civilized people."[52] And the fact that the habit of coca leaf chewing, unlike tobacco, was prevalent among a racially distinct and economically impoverished population who were not considered "civilized," made the attack on coca seem all the more necessary. The WHO's logic reflected larger structures of power operative in the world at mid-century. And the parameters of the drug control regime—those drugs (and people) that got targeted—were flexible in defense of this larger vision. When specifically asked to address the question of coca leaf chewing, "The Expert Committee came to the conclusion that coca chewing is detrimental to the individual and to society and that it must be defined and treated as an addiction, in spite of the occasional absence of those characteristics."[53]

Scientists declaring coca addictive, despite "the occasional absence of those characteristics," suggests the definition was more socially than scientifically based, a phenomenon long true in the history of the policing of cocaine.[54] As early as the 1920s scientists drew clear distinctions between the physiologically addictive properties of opiates—where symptoms of withdrawal were manifest—in contrast to cocaine. Nevertheless, cocaine users in scientific and popular representations continued to be identified as "addicts." In a 1929 article in the *Journal of Pharmacology and Experimental Therapeutics* the social aspect of addiction trumped the "absence" of physical symptoms: "Although, therefore, in contrast to morphine, we consider a tolerance to cocaine in the pharmacological sense as unproved, we are compelled to recognize the fact of a passionate addiction."[55] The threat posed by such addiction, first diagnosed among consumers in the industrial world in the 1920s, was similar to that which would animate attacks on coca leaf chewing in the Andes in the 1940s and 1950s. It resided in the perception of the related uncontrolled behaviors deemed "irregular" or socially undesirable. As the author of the textbook *Practical Pharmacology* characterized the threat, cocaine was "a substance to produce complete abandon and an utter disregard for consequences and future . . . the normal person gets no pleasure from injections of cocaine."[56] And elsewhere, "Chronic cocainism produces marked sexual irregularities in man, usually increasing libido by allowing freer play of the imagination; most female cocainists exhibit nymphomania."[57] Beyond the implicit gendered hierarchy of presumed independent thought even among addicts in this particular characterization, the politics of declaring and identifying a "passionate addiction" was rooted in racial, gender, and class conflicts in both the Andes and the United States. The medical concept "addiction" was a category most meaningful among the field of international experts who defined and enforced it, not exclusively as a scientific phenomena, but as a social construction of the object, behavior, or population to be controlled—through imposed isolated or refashioning into productive members of society.

By the 1950s such definitions of addiction drew upon scientific research in both the Andes and the United States. Studies of indigenous coca consumption helped establish the baseline for the drug control regime's policing of "addiction." In the industrial world, other vulnerable populations would become the objects of scientific inquiry into the addictive properties—and attendant need for regulation—of an array of new synthetic substances being churned out by pharmaceutical laboratories.

THE NARCOTIC FARM

At mid-century, drug development and experimentation (particularly when involving the use of human subjects) tended to occur (or at least get documented) within public institutional settings. In both the Andes and the United States the test subjects for such research were drawn primarily from military personnel, prisoners, asylum populations, committed "narcotics addicts," and poor people in need of medical assistance or cash. This was dramatically on display at the US Narcotic Farm run by the USPHS in Lexington, Kentucky. As the Commissioner of Narcotics testified before Congress about the work being done at this institution:

> We are having a drug revolution. New drugs are coming into the field of medicine, all of which, so far, were discovered in Germany during the war. . . . Every country in the world is now going to ascribe to the protocol on synthetic drugs. We will put these new drugs in the same compartment as morphine and heroin and other derivatives of opium and the coca leaf. All of those organizations are looking to one place, and only one place, where we can get accurate information, and that is the work at Lexington.[58]

And indeed, the CND, the National Research Council, the WHO, and a range of pharmaceutical firms all drew upon the work done by scientists working for the USPHS at Lexington to determine the addictive potential of various new substances and, by extension, the reach of drug control. The Narcotic Farm was jointly run by the USPHS and the Bureau of Prisons and it housed a research unit—the Addiction Research Center which was at that time the only research center in the world that was conducting studies on "addiction" using live subjects—i.e., prisoner-patients who had previously been identified as "addicts" and were deemed, as such, extremely valuable for testing the addictive potential of new drugs. FBN Commissioner Anslinger exulted, "There is no question about the research work there. It is the finest in the world. The research is not conducted upon animals, but upon individuals who are themselves addicts."[59]

A new politics of value was being advanced with the growth of American power and it was profoundly on display in the market's influence on laboratory agendas. At Lexington, market and scientific value merged in the efforts to cultivate valuable people and to cultivate valuable drugs. A guiding principle of the research done at Lexington was to develop drugs that might be substitutes for other drugs—value, as with money, relied as much on a substance's fungibility, on the capacity to replace existing drugs with similar, but more strategically valuable versions, than on any intrinsic health benefit. And value in this context was part of a complex diplomatic, economic, and legal calculus.

As the tenets of international drug control were being construed around the policing of "addictive" substances, the National Research Council's National Committee on Drug Addiction made it a priority to collaborate with the pharmaceutical industry in an effort to "systematically set out to review all compounds that promised to achieve analgesic effects without producing physiological symptoms of tolerance and withdrawal." Science and pharmacology promised to relieve social conflict. "The committee maintained that through substitution, industrial production of alkaloids could be 'reduced to a minimum,' thus lessening the police authority necessary to control the situation."[60] Thus the research at Lexington was not so much designed to rehabilitate "addicts," who were largely considered to be unredeemable, but rather to test out new synthetic substitutes being cranked out by American pharmaceutical laboratories. Experimental drug trials for new compounds being put out by companies including Merck, Eli Lilly, Parke-Davis, and many others benefited from the research conducted at Lexington. This research reverberated through the drug regulatory regime. In justifying annual appropriations to continue the work at Lexington, the FBN commissioner reported to Congress in 1947: "Not so long ago I went to get demerol, a new synthetic drug, under control, and I had to prove that it was a habit-forming drug and it was only because of the work at Lexington that I was able to convince the Ways and Means Committee that this drug should be under control."[61]

Demerol was just one of a number of drugs that fell under the purview of the international 1948 Protocol based on research into addiction being conducted at the Lexington Narcotic Farm.[62] The work at Lexington helped establish both national and international definitions of "addiction" that influenced the orientation of international drug control. For a country intent on cultivating mass consumption, the policing of addiction offers a striking window onto the political economy of US power. Not only was the category of "addiction" notoriously difficult to define when detached from social and cultural understandings of it, but as a legal category it structured enforcement according to the power of racial, national, cultural, and other biases to determine whose consumption practices were targeted as a menace to the larger community. Unsurprisingly at Lexington, "The researchers were almost entirely white, upper- and middle-class professional men who experimented on poor, lower- and working-class, ethnically and racially diverse addicts."[63]

This hierarchy was a direct consequence of the seemingly neutral science that had been brought to bear on the definition of addiction. The medical director of USPHS at Lexington, Kentucky, described his research conclusions on the nature of addiction before an audience of the American Psychiatric Association in 1947: "The term 'addiction' need not be confined to the use of substances. Persons who pursue certain practices to their own or the public's inconvenience, harm or peril are sometimes a greater problem than those who misuse a substance. It may well be that internal or external difficulties responsible for the unwise pursuit of a practice and those responsible for the misuse of a substance are similar."[64]

The social and the biological were intimately linked, he suggested, and addiction was a manifestation not merely of a drug's impact on the human body, but of a person who already exhibited socially dysfunctional behavior. It is striking how notions of social conformity rooted in a particular model of consumer capitalism were prominently on display. As historian Nancy Campbell explains, the test subjects at Lexington were deemed socially irredeemable and, as such, incredibly valuable as "research material"—a sobering refashioning of people as human raw material inputs into the chemical laboratories of US capitalism. "Drug addicts, who occupy the social category of unproductive or even antiproductive, were rendered 'useful' through the exercise of scientific discipline at the [Addiction Research Center]."[65] Echoing this logic, the medical director at Lexington testified before Congress in 1948, "Narcotic addiction is a public-health menace inasmuch as without control addiction spreads and persons addicted become submissive, ambitionless and abject." The "typical symptoms of drug addiction" are evident in the "loss of self-control." The doctor went on to describe the promise of social transformation such research might bring about: "In addition to this unconditioning and as a substitute for old habits, new habits must be built up; and for this reason the addict under treatment should be kept busy in some useful way during all his waking hours."[66]

And Lexington provided an experimental context to do just that. As its original title suggests, the Narcotic Farm as a penal-research

FIGURE 8. Federal Narcotic Farm, Lexington, Kentucky. [Photo by Arthur Rothstein.]

institution was also operated as a labor farm. Its institutional name would be changed to "Public Health Service Hospital" when "people began to ask where the narcotics were grown," although it never shook the nickname "Narco."[67] Arguably narcotics were indeed being grown, or at least tested on the premises; however, the confidence behind the entranceway's dramatic inscription ("United States Narcotic Farm") was based on the idea of the redemptive value of productive labor. Inmates at Lexington operated a clothing factory, a furniture factory, a farm, and a patient commissary.[68] The farm was intended to be self-sustaining and the other capital industries produced products "utilized by government agencies."[69] In fact, during the war the Army received articles manufactured at Lexington of "value in excess of $100,000."[70]

With the revolution in drug development underway, synthetic drugs offered the opportunity to replace drugs deemed dangerous (addictive) with nonaddictive substitutes and alternatives (of course, many of the drugs produced like methadone and others turned out to be just as addictive as the drugs, in this case heroin, they were intended to replace). Similarly people deemed "antiproductive" threats to the community (convicted felons) could be put to work and, if not completely transformed themselves, might contribute to the greater social good. The logic of the laboratory was intimately linked to a vision for policing drug production and consumption, and the way this new drug market incorporated people's bodies reveals much about the cultural and social implications of capitalist-driven modernization.

ALCHEMY IN THE ANDES

Policing and regulation were not tied simply to limitation and repression, but also to the positive production of capitalist consumer habits. This was true in both the United States and the Andes, at both ends of the economic circuit through which coca commodities flowed. In particular the policing of drug production and consumption was guided largely by identifying "addiction" as the benchmark for designating select drug consumption "illegitimate." The deployment of a language of "addiction" to attack certain contexts of drug consumption relied on identifying the bodies of people deemed socially threatening to become the test subjects for drug development and social engineering across the Americas. The research conclusions devised from human drug experimentation in the United States would be replicated in US-led Andean projects of social engineering. US national strategic priorities incorporated a commitment to US-manufactured drugs as a component of encouraging specific models of modernization and development, defining the rights of citizenship, and controlling the physical bodies of people targeted for necessary social and cultural transformation in the United States, Peru, and Bolivia. The alchemy of empire consisted of more than simply the control of plants and physical material. It was also a process of cultivating the necessary social order, modeling the laboring and consuming habits of populations to quite literally fuel and sustain the envisioned economic transformations. In this regard, drugs were not merely valued as "commodities of commerce" but were deemed critical tools of international diplomacy and even, for an array of public and private officials, the very basis for pursuing US national security.

American laboratories had an impact on both the logic and material practices of US development policy internationally. The possibilities of laboratory transformation were explored not only in penal institutions in the United States, but also in peasant communities across the Andes where fears of social upheaval were countered by US-oriented development projects. World War II profoundly transformed the pharmaceutical industry with massive government subsidies to this strategic materials sector, fueling new drug developments and the expansion of US pharmaceutical markets around the world. Traveling with troops and aided by agents from the US Board of Economic Warfare, US pharmaceuticals replaced those of their former, now defeated, primary competitors, the Germans and the Japanese. In the aftermath of the war, the task of familiarizing the "underdeveloped" world with American-manufactured drug products assumed an increased urgency in the context of burgeoning Cold War Soviet and US competition over spheres of influence. Many US-backed research institutions, businessmen, scientists, anthropologists, public health officials, police and military personnel, and diplomats aggressively embraced this challenge and grounded it in an ideological vision of US world leadership. As John T. Connor, president of pharmaceutical giant Merck & Co., Inc., warned an audience at the American Management Association in 1958: "The Soviet is at least as well equipped medically as it is economically to match us in underdeveloped countries. . . . And when this well-staffed army sallies forth from its borders— as it will—carrying the nostrums of Communism in its medical kit, it will have a proposal to make that could be quite appealing. Reorganize your state along our lines, the proposal would go, and you, too, can do what we did—make the fastest progress in health achieved by any large nation in modern times."[71]

The fear of a spreading sympathy for communism combined advantageously with the capitalist ambition to profit from social reorganization. These US visionaries found welcome partners among the Andean political and economic elite who embraced US ties and "viewed economic development as a bulwark against communism."[72] In the context of competing Cold War economic initiatives, Merck's president went on to explain what this development entailed: "the Bolshevik planners were right when they decided to pour enormous effort into their human capital on the theory that better health as well as better education would have to precede to better output. . . . This concept of the relation between human capital and economic growth could turn out to be decisive as the Soviet sets forth to meet the rising expectations of Asia, Africa, the Middle East and even Latin America with a program of health, development and Communism."[73]

US programs of health, development, and capitalism were already well underway. In fact, North American advisers had been involved in developing "human capital" in Peruvian and Bolivian "development" projects since the war prompted US advisors to study and recommend economic development programs that continued to influence govern-ment initiatives throughout the 1940s and 1950s.[74] The United States was the region's primary export market, and US public and private cap-ital was the largest source of foreign investment in Peru and Bolivia at the time, particularly in the mining industry—an industry of critical importance as a supplier of material to the US military.[75] The US Office of Inter-American Affairs spearheaded US involvement, pursuing Andean development through defining and institutionalizing "public health." Public health campaigns were launched specifically to prioritize and transform "critical economic sectors."[76] Maintaining healthy mine workers and promoting market-oriented rather than subsistence-based agriculture was the focus of US initiatives. The American representative from the International Cooperation Agency (predecessor to the US Agency for International Development [AID]), John J. Bloomfield, who helped establish national public health programs in the 1940s in both Peru and Bolivia, focused these efforts on promoting "occupational" health in the major export industries.[77] Health and the economy then were becoming mutually constitutive categories of modernization and progress.

Following the coca commodity circuit back into the Andes provides a window onto the capitalist values that structured modernization and development schemes and the way in which these visions targeted indig-enous peoples—much like the coca leaf itself or the prisoner-patients at Lexington—approaching them as raw material in need of transforma-tion to generate greater value. The logic of coca leaf control was embed-ded in debates about the land, life, labor, and consumption habits of Andean Indians. While governments deployed law enforcement to establish a line between licit and illicit cocaine, regulating the coca leaf would prove more complicated. In many ways this reflected a much longer colonial and imperial history. Historian Kenneth Lehman has argued that the twin exploitation of "silver and Indians" drove Spanish colonial policy in the Andes and continued to characterize post-inde-pendence governments' structural exclusion of Indians from "national life."[78] This marked only the beginnings of an ongoing imperial encoun-ter where local European-descended elites joined with foreign and, by the mid-twentieth century, primarily US-based interests to approach the native population as "vital resources of revenue."[79]

The UN focus on controlling the coca leaf (or "supply side" of the market) ensured that this aspect of international drug control consti-tuted an intervention in local conflicts over the terms of national economic development and, in particular, indigenous peoples' envisioned contribution to the larger society. Centuries-long debate had swirled around Indian coca leaf consumption that, until these UN initiatives, was accepted as a necessary, if vexing, aspect of assuring indigenous labor capacity.[80] Neither national nor international elites particularly worried about transgressing Indian cultural traditions, yet there was considerable interest in maintaining control over the labor force by acknowledging both customary usage and the leaf's central role in the wage-labor economy. As late as 1940, the Bolivian government decreed that coca was "an article of prime necessity" and ordered its compulsory sale in mining and railway companies.[81] The UN Commission of Enquiry into the Coca Leaf's report in 1951 (see the previous chapter), and the national and international experts with whom it consulted, successfully shifted the regulatory landscape to identify coca leaf chewing as an obstacle to national development.

Arguments for coca eradication stigmatized Indian practices while proselytizing a model of "civilization" based on liberal visions of land ownership, hard work, and consumer capitalism.[82] The attack on coca entailed the transformation of individual habits, as well as a general restructuring of the national economy (to secure the export market and stabilize the region for foreign investment).[83] Coca was a source of government revenue and a linchpin of the informal market. As noted earlier, Gutiérrez-Noriega estimated the "coca leaf [was] the single most important item of commerce in the Andes."[84] The UN commission supported these claims, finding that "except in some cattle markets, business is on a small scale and generally limited to the exchange of products between the Indians. An exception is coca leaf; it is, as a rule, paid for in cash. In such markets coca leaf is sold by the Indian who grows his own crop."[85] Coca eradication thus entailed the radical transformation of the domestic cash economy including the elimination of many people's primary medium of exchange, subsistence, and access to money, outside of the wage-labor sector. As one of an array of international development missions warned in 1951, "it must be constantly remembered that from one-half to two thirds of [Bolivia's] people still live practically outside the money economy on a more or less self-sustaining basis."[86] The drug control agenda called for the eradication of coca leaf chewing as central to the process of dispossession required to create a wage labor–based consumer economy in the Andes.

An array of development schemes sought to tackle the issue. One such example was the ambitious "Andean Indian Project" coordinated by the "Expanded Program of Technical assistance of the UN and the specialized agencies." Beginning in 1952 this broad effort brought scientific "experts" to Bolivia, Peru, and Ecuador, "to raise the health, nutrition, housing, education, working and social standards of the *altiplano* people and to integrate them into the social and economic life of their countries."[87] A number of dramatic initiatives were launched, including crop replacement and expansive resettlement programs designed to relocate Indians from their traditional lands in the high Andes to lower, more tropical regions where the conditions for large-scale commercial agriculture were imagined to pertain. As Enrique Sánchez de Lozada, the head of the International Labor Organization program, pointed out, these experts believed that solving the agrarian problem must take the Indian into account who "by the very weight of his number is the most important factor in the economy."[88]

These programs fused visions of eradicating communities' cultural habits with effecting modernization, "integrating" the native into national society, and coca was central to these concerns. Cornell University anthropologist Allan Holmberg, an important figure in experimental modernization schemes, articulated the ways in which coca in the Andes was fundamentally a marker of "Indianness": "A person who speaks an Indian language, wears homespun dress, and chews coca will be classed as Indian. If the same person speaks Spanish, wears Western dress and does not chew coca, he may be classed—depending on other characteristics such as family name, occupation, education, and health— as either *mestizo* or white." Interestingly he went on to explain, "In a biological sense, at least, Peru has no racial problem. Its so-called 'racial' problem is largely a cultural one."[89]

Perhaps embracing a postwar reluctance to accept race and biology as an explanatory framework for inequality, and also reflecting the way in which sociocultural factors had always shaped "Indian" identity in the Andes, such arguments blurred the line between cultural practice and racially based notions of cultural, or even genetic, supremacy that increasingly were being articulated—in both the United States and the Andes—through the extension of a policing apparatus that accompanied modernization and economic development schemes. Such arguments helped justify an attack on indigenous communities. This involved outright criminalization of traditional practices (such as the banning of coca leaf chewing among soldiers and among laborers on certain large-scale agricultural projects) but also a larger attack on indigenous culture and society as these scholars sought to remake indigenous peoples into "productive" members of modernized nations. The *United Nations Review* echoed these sentiments when it described a scene of an unknown Andean woman holding a baby in a marketplace: "Though poverty and ignorance have been the woman's lifetime companion, there is a chance the baby she holds on her lap will lead a totally different kind of life."[90]

Officials debated the best ways to make Indians modern. In Bolivia for instance, officials worried that "considerable economic dislocation would be caused if its production [of coca] were suddenly to be discontinued. It is suggested, therefore, that the transfer from coca to coffee should be gradual." Replacing one stimulant with a more civilized other, coffee, was part and parcel of the economic logic that valued the unthreatening substitute: "In connection with the possible replacement of coca, priority should be given to tea together with coffee and a pilot project for tea similar to that proposed for coffee should be put into operation."[91] Development efforts depended on Andean indigenous labor to reconfigure the agricultural landscape, and they also included initiatives to cultivate consumer markets in the Andes for "North American" manufactured goods. This reworking of human raw material was to be pursued in the fields as well as the mines. In fact dispensaries run by mining companies were the largest purchasers and distributors of US pharmaceuticals and employed a labor force that might easily be sold, if adequately educated, other commodities like Coca-Cola (something the company was aggressively pursuing at that time).[92]

The vision behind a Cornell University agricultural development experiment on a hacienda in Vicos, Peru, embodied the almost missionary quality that often accompanied US Cold War initiatives in social engineering. The project's director, Allan Holmberg, explained, "Cornell University undertook a systematic program of research and development in order to determine how an Indian population would respond to a concerted effort to introduce it to a more modern way of life."[93] The Cornell Peru Project in collaboration with the Peruvian Indian Institute was viewed by its program managers—men who assumed the role of *patron,* a boss and patriarchal figure that could demand labor from peasants on the hacienda—as a "natural laboratory."

> We were trying to manipulate and control large and complex blocks of reality (environment, society, and culture) in their natural setting. At the same time, we were trying to conduct our experiments and our interventions by dealing with substance that has a real meaning to the Vicosinos (like potatoes, cattle, land, or health). And we were trying to deal with this substance

within the total context of culture. This, of course, is not experimentation in the laboratory sense of the measurement of the precise effect of a single variable, but rather the development of a strategy for the manipulation and control of systems or sets of variables in the direction of meaningful and purposeful ends.[94]

The "purposeful ends" in this context was indigenous participation in capitalist development. Vicos was a community in Peru whose people, as labor, were owned by the land lessee—a lease bought by Cornell University that it administered during the 1950s in collaboration with the Peruvian government (with help from US AID, Carnegie, the Peace Corps, and others). Cornell's researchers oversaw the Vicos Hacienda for five years before allowing Indian self-government, taking advantage of forced labor requirements to facilitate the transition to commercial farming. All the while these researchers introduced what they described as revolutions (in pesticides, drugs, and general consumption) in a self-conscious effort to stave off a real social revolution. Looking back on the project in 1964, one anthropologist-participant explained: "we similarly regard the late Allan R. Holmberg as a truly revolutionary anthropologist. Whereas [African independence leader] Kenyatta worked with native activists to confront colonial authorities and wrest power from them by force, Holmberg chose to prove a prototype for peaceful social reformation."[95] The program's experimental ambition was to prevent revolutionary upheaval through liberal development schemes.

The seemingly neutral science of economic development, deploying Western expertise to bring about economic and cultural transformation, masked the very real political struggle being waged by indigenous communities in the Andes seeking to redress their ongoing marginalization from economic and political power. Thus, in the Andes, the fear of revolution was responding not merely to international communism, but rather to ongoing indigenous mobilizations, as Holmberg himself explained the desire to avoid a "pan-Indian or pan-peasant movement, as in Bolivia, which would usurp the power of the government and initiate drastic reform."[96] The revolution in Bolivia in 1952 did bring about the radical redistribution of land and power in the country, although by the end of the decade, most scholars agree, the conservative bourgeois faction of the leadership had effectively consolidated their control, in part through the embrace of US economic development programs.[97]

As Vicos researchers sought to transform subsistence farmers into wage laborers who manned large-scale export-oriented farms, native

FIGURE 9. Cornell graduate student teaching a Vicosino the application of chemical pesticides. ["Mario Vazquez and a peasant spraying the crops with DDT." Photograph by Abraham Guillén. Allan R. Holmberg collection on Peru, #14–25–1529. Division of Rare and Manuscript Collections, Cornell University Library.]

communities fought back to preserve some of their customary rights and cultural practices. One example was the negotiation over "traditions" that actually stemmed from peonage rather than cultural practice, such as trying to eliminate coca leaves as wage payment and challenging workers' customary coca-chewing breaks or rest and rejuvenation time which from the perspective of the patron seemed a marker of "laziness" but for the "Vicosino on the other hand this was a social period, characterized by conversation and joking."[98] While "[c]ontrary to early expectations, there ha[d] been little resistance to the acceptance of modern medical practices or even to the purchase of modern drugs," these experts were frustrated by the persistence of cultural values that seemed to undermine the preeminence of the cash and export-oriented economy.[99] "More often than not, increased economic benefits are channeled through traditional value and social systems, intensifying old imbalances ... for example, that additional income derived from economic development may be spent in gaining prestige through staging more elaborate religious *fiestas* rather than be put to productive uses."[100] These experts echoed the vision of a UN technical mission in Bolivia that identified "the *fiesta* and the habit of coca leaf chewing" as the source of "nonessential expenditure [which] is directly harmful to health and working efficiency," and recommended that "education on the evils of the present habits should be accompanied by an increased supply of household and other goods suitable for popular consumption."[101]

. . .

The legacy of these initiatives is mixed, although it does help explain some of the structural delineation of legal and illegal drug economies— as well as the conflicts they engendered. Holmberg would look back on the work done at Vicos with pride: "The traditional system is now being subjected to many inroads. Today there are few communities that have not been touched, however lightly by the technological revolution. Coca-cola, the tin can, penicillin, and even the wrist watch and radio have penetrated to the most remote *haciendas* of the Andes."[102]

Interestingly all of the products mentioned may have been manufactured from raw materials—coca, tin, chinchona—exported from the Andes, although clearly here rhetorically the technological revolution is one being exported into—not out of—the region. Looking at the alchemy of empire at mid-century, considering substances, people, and communities affected by drug control initiatives, provides perspective on the logic and structures that facilitated the expansion of US capitalism. Healthy bodies and societies came to be defined in terms of their capacity to sustain a market hierarchically structured to promote North American–manufactured goods—and unhealthy, threatening bodies were targeted for experimentation and transformation. The unequal power between nations and within nations in the hemisphere translated

FIGURE 10. Photograph, "General store in Vicos selling alcohol and coca," 1951. [Photograph by Abraham Guillén. Allan R. Holmberg collection on Peru, #14–25–1529. Division of Rare and Manuscript Collections, Cornell University Library.]

into the unequal roles that various peoples would play in the fashioning of a new world order.

While the therapeutic revolution embodied the privileged priorities of the manufacturing countries, this era that has been referred to as "the golden age of drug discovery" brought new challenges for policing, along with new possibilities for profit making. Scholar James Le Fanu has aptly pointed out that "the dynamics of the therapeutic revolution owed more to a synergy between the creative forces of capitalism and chemistry than to the science of medicine and biology."[103] To this must be added not merely the creative force of capitalism and chemistry, but the power of the state to coerce participation within the new structures being lauded as the promise of the future. The success of US drug development depended not only on the ability to procure and transform the raw material, but also on the capacity to test and market the reworked commodity as a desirable consumer item.

For prisoner-patients at Lexington, their drug crimes stripped them of their human rights, making them valuable inputs into the drug development process as raw material. In the Andes, indigenous communities with even fewer recognized rights were approached as objects for the study of social transformation: laboratory objects for the production of a modern, productive citizenry. Concepts like "addiction" and the regulation and policing such labels justified were selectively deployed in an effort to transform the habits and lifestyles of people not fully invested in—indeed often in active political, cultural, and social opposition to—the cultural and economic hegemony of the United States. In the context of the US-Soviet Cold War rivalry, and the attendant American interest in expanding the capitalist marketplace, these projects took on a peculiar urgency. The extension of the drug control regime provides perspective on the era's "development economics," which scholars Veronica Montecinos and John Markoff have argued "blossomed as the Western powers, especially the US, sought to continue and extend the now-established tradition of state-run economic management, with an eye to warding off Third World revolution."[104] The seeming contradiction of a capitalist system dependent on mass production and mass consumption targeting overconsumption or "addiction" was reconciled through cultural narratives grounded in scientific market logic. Implicit notions of cultural superiority profoundly shaped the scientific rationale behind the selective attack on coca leaf chewing and the process of designating legitimacy within the system out of which it emerged. The logic of institutional and popular scientists, including their awkward efforts to protect tobacco and alcohol from regulation while targeting coca leaves, reflected the larger structures of power operative in the world in the postwar era and, in particular, the determining influence of US capitalism. The fear of revolution and desire for US power combined to create powerful cultural narratives around drug control that continued to animate the chemical cold war, as will be seen in the following chapter.

CHAPTER 5

The Chemical Cold War

Drugs and Policing in the New World Order

While anthropologists involved in social engineering projects in the Andes hoped their work might forestall upheavals in the mold of African liberation struggles, similar fears resonated on the floor of the United States Congress. During January 1952 annual appropriations hearings for the Federal Bureau of Narcotics, a World War II and Korean War veteran, and member of the House of Representatives, Alfred Sieminski, warned that international collaboration was urgently needed to prevent drugs being deployed as the fuel firing up global revolution: "I wonder, inasmuch as our fleet now, for the first time in history, is refueling in the Mediterranean, and great bases are being built in Africa and since Africa becomes of some interest to us, if you could pass on to your British counterparts that an Oxford graduate, later schooled in Moscow, is behind the colored unrest in the Kenya area and is no doubt the Kremlin's No. 1 man to lead a race rebellion on that continent with the aid of drugs as fuel."[1]

Rep. Sieminski's vision, while misrepresenting Kenyan independence leader Jomo Kenyatta's biography, nevertheless embodied the convergence of fear and global ambition that animated US discourse linking drugs to the Cold War, civil rights, and "race rebellion" in the 1950s and beyond. Persistent in this focus, Sieminski would later simplify his expression of concern: "Let us put it this way. Are drugs playing any part in the Mau Mau movement which seeks to throw the white man out of Africa?" FBN Commissioner Harry Anslinger confirmed that "riots" in Kenya had been traced to the "use of dagga, which is the same as hashish or marijuana, [and] has become widespread in Nairobi where the Government established a commission to look into the situation."[2] Referring to a recent article in *Life* magazine, the congressman explained his line of questioning was motivated by the worry that "American magazine and printed opinion deal well with the problem of communism and race tensions, yet little is said of the influence, if any, of narcotics in spreading both movements; in easing infiltration to carry out missions of plunder, torture, degeneration, murder and death."[3]

This pairing of narcotics with communism, racial tension, violence, and political rebellion was widespread in US public life and helped drive the passage of increasingly coercive drug laws and enforcement measures at both the national and international level throughout the 1950s. Examining this heightened policing of drugs shows new mechanisms of social control that depended in large part on monopolizing the power of laboratory-manufactured commodities in both material and symbolic form.[4] This discourse selectively linked narcotics to criminality in confrontation with an increasingly empowered politics of social change. The congressman's invocation of Kenyatta depended on sets of associations increasingly articulated in a white American reaction to the threat posed by African liberation movements at home and abroad. While in fact Kenyatta did not attend Oxford (he graduated from the London School of Economics), did not use drugs to fuel rebellion (as reporter J.A. Rogers said, "They don't need it. The indignities and the injustices they suffer are enough to drive them on,"[5]) and was neither a Communist nor the leader of the Mau Mau (the Kenya Land and Freedom Movement), in London he did meet with Pan-Africanists such as civil rights leader Paul Robeson, whose passport had only recently, and very publicly, been revoked due to his criticism of US foreign policy in Korea. Extensive coverage of the anticolonial uprisings fueled white fears and mobilized black solidarities. So for instance, jazz drummer Art Blakey's "A Message from Kenya" paid tribute to the rebellion through Afro-Cuban musical forms, in a decade where the coercive powers of the state, mobilized in no small part through the pairing of drugs and war, confronted Soviet and Chinese Communism, the civil rights movement, "Negro" and Puerto Rican youth, jazz musicians, and Cuban revolutionaries.[6]

In the early 1950s, as the Cold War turned hot in Korea and the superpowers jockeyed for global influence across the nationalist, anticolonial Third World, the material and symbolic power of drugs was both celebrated and feared. The belief of diplomats, scientists, and pharmaceutical executives in the productive power of new drug developments was accompanied by intensified national and international efforts to identify and police the perceived dangers posed by these drugs circulating outside these authorities' sphere of influence. The "wonder drugs," described in the last chapter, when viewed as migrating beyond the reach of direct control, easily devolved into mediums for transmitting social and political unrest, a phenomenon frequently described by recourse to a language of disease, contagion, social dysfunction, political subversion, and criminality. This chapter follows US officials' policing of the drug market as a constitutive element of efforts to consolidate a US-dominated capitalist economic system in the face of domestic and international challenges to its hegemony. It charts the role that "drug warfare" played in regulatory debates at the United Nations, in justifying the introduction of the first mandatory minimum sentences in the United States, and in shaping Cold War confrontations. The research reveals how a seemingly neutral logic linking science, law, health, and national security empowered policing officials to pursue perceived threats to the dominant cultural, political, and economic order. The selective policing of drugs became an important regulatory tool and rhetorically charged framework invigorating and defining the pursuit of US power.

COLD WAR DRUG WARS

World War II cemented the status of drugs as strategic materials and weapons of war. As alliances shifted in the war's aftermath, the access of nations and people to participation within the legal market and their vulnerability to accusations of illicit trafficking, reflected the persistent power of drugs as tools for acquiring economic and political influence, as well as their symbolic importance in Cold War struggles over global dominance. By the early 1950s, US leadership at the United Nations Commission on Narcotic Drugs had established the centrality of the global drug control regime's focus on the control of raw materials as well as ensuring that narcotic drugs, and synthetic substitutes for them, were subject to international controls. The work of the Commission of Enquiry on the Coca Leaf paired with ongoing diplomatic, political, and economic collaboration between the US and Andean nations produced in the early parts of the decade a sense of triumph at the FBN in relation to efforts to control the production of cocaine. This in turn prompted a shift in focus of US global drug policy toward efforts to extend a similar system of control over opium producing nations, nations that did not fall exclusively within a US sphere of influence. At the end of the decade when new threats to US hegemony would appear in the hemisphere, particularly Cuba, specific accusations tied to cocaine trafficking and hemispheric subversion would reemerge as central to drug policy and discourse. In the interim, the logical foundations of drug control, established during the previous decade with its alchemical power to target different substances, peoples, nations, and enemies, would be refined in polemical debates animated by Cold War and imperial rivalries.

These public debates about drugs, as agents of warfare and medicinal progress, provide a window onto the ideology of US imperialism. They also suggest the ways in which imperial ambition at mid-century, among both the United States and the Soviet Union, was articulated through a new logical framework that prioritized technological progress, scientific expertise, and economic productivity.[7] The explicitly race-based arguments that had previously justified colonial conquest and genocide were increasingly replaced by arguments grounded in policing, public health, and the social sciences as the great powers battled for control and influence across the colonial and postcolonial world. The convergence of chemicals and the Cold War was on dramatic display when the United Nations convened in New York in the spring of 1952. The national and international press reported on debates at the UN General Assembly and in the US Congress as the United States, Soviet Union, and China publicly traded heated accusations over the deployment of chemical weapons in the context of the Korean War.

During the early years of the Cold War, the United Nations became a public international forum for the Soviet Union, United States, and their respective allies to articulate competing ambitions and political conflicts within a bureaucratic institutional setting where rules of procedure rather than battlefield tactics predominated. A new imperial rivalry was on display, for example, when the Soviet Union persistently challenged the seating of the Nationalist Chinese (Kuomintang) representative [exiled to Formosa (Taiwan) after defeat by the Communists in the civil war] in place of a delegation from the People's Republic of China, and the United States defended the same. In 1952, the representative of the Union of Soviet Socialist Republics began the UN's Economic and Social Council's First Special Session with a point of order declaring the presence of Kuomintang representatives "illegal" and "requested that that they should be expelled and replaced by accredited representatives of the Central People's Government of the People's Republic of China." The US representative retorted by reiterating his country's consistent opposition to Soviet efforts to unseat the "the Nationalist Government of China," arguing that the proposal "should not even be considered in view of the fact that the Chinese Communist Government, in its international behaviour, and specifically in Korea, was showing open disrespect for the principles upheld by the United Nations."[8]

Referring to the ongoing conflict on the Korean peninsula where US and UN forces battled the North Korean and Chinese armies, this confrontation embodied the rhetorical backdrop to a growing reliance on proxy war and the enfolding of liberation struggles within a US-Soviet bipolar global conflict. Allegations of drug trafficking played a surprisingly central role. The United States, whose influence in 1952 at the United Nations far superseded the USSR's, triumphed through procedural maneuver, preventing the Soviet proposal to seat the Chinese government from coming to a vote. Not, however, before the USSR exacted public revenge. The Soviet representative noted "It was well known that the Kuomintang represented nobody but a group of mercenaries in the pay of the United States Government." Furthermore, his government was "surprised to hear the United States representative mention the current situation in Korea as an argument in support of his proposal." Countering, "As a matter of fact, it was rather the question of the bacterial warfare waged in Korea by the United States which should be discussed in the Council."[9]

The United States disputed this allegation of deploying bacteriological warfare in an official report through the CND to ECOSOC only two months later, and countercharged the Chinese and North Koreans with smuggling heroin into South Korea and Japan.[10] Standing accused of bacterial warfare, the United States suggested it was the accusers who sought to infect the West with dangerous substances: narcotic drugs. While on the surface there might seem to be a fundamental categorical distinction between narcotic drugs and agents of bacteriological and chemical warfare, the line in fact was quite murky when research and researchers explored the productive and destructive powers of various natural and synthetic substances; studying the destructive potential and how to cure infectious disease went hand in hand, and involved both natural and laboratory-manufactured agents.[11] Moreover, Cold War rhetorical combat often relied on the implicit connection between the two.

China denied using heroin as an offensive weapon, backed by the Soviet representative's denunciation of this "slanderous falsehood," and attempted to have read into the record a refutation supplied by the People's Republic of China (PRC), which being excluded from the commission, could not "defend itself against such accusations."[12] FBN Commissioner Anslinger later boasted in US congressional testimony, "I did not permit the Russian delegate to read the Chinese propaganda in the meeting. I called him on a point of order." Anslinger contested allegations of "the use of gas and bacteriological warfare by American troops," and the Soviet contention that when speaking of heroin, "under the barbarous conditions of United States warfare—including the blockading of Communist China—no smuggling in or out of China was possible unless conducted by the Americans." This back and forth over the warring powers' interest in controlling an array of scientifically synthesized substances, including narcotic drugs, became an attention-grabbing aspect of Cold War conflict. As control of chemical and biological entities became increasingly central to superpower rivalry, politically volatile debates joined market and military power to mimic the magic wrought by laboratories: one's medicine became another's poison as the celebrated potential of drugs also made them fearful weapons of war. For US officials involved in policing the domestic drug economy, as Anslinger explained, there "is a good answer to their charge of bacteriological warfare, because we can show that it is chemical (heroin) warfare which is being carried on."[13]

Cold War conflict brought to the fore the power of natural and synthetic compounds to wreak havoc, whether overtly deployed as part of a military arsenal or covertly used to infect the social order and undermine military discipline of enemy nations. Simultaneously, these substances became increasingly valued for their potential to advance health and national prosperity. The physical substances deployed in chemical or bacteriological (or even atomic) warfare were distinct and varied; however, there was a widespread belief in both the promise and peril of technological innovation for human health and disease at mid-century. Bacteriological and chemical warfare had been deployed to devastating ends during World War II. While Nazi experiments have received much attention, the Japanese Imperial Army's Unit 731, led by physician and Lieutenant General Ishii Shiro, also experimented with human subjects to develop and spread biological warfare agents in China. As Ishii later testified to US interrogators, "bacterial bombs had been made and tested and rather sophisticated efforts made to breed and employ disease vectors as well."[14] On the Allied side, the United States dropped incendiary bombs filled with magnesium and napalm, which "caused more widespread devastation in Japan than the atomic bomb." As historian Ruth Rogaski chillingly assesses these policies, "Japanese citizens, like vermin, perished through the application of chemical technologies."[15] The charges of narcotics drug warfare also pertained. The US Army accused the Japanese during World War II of war crimes for peddling drugs in conquered territories.[16] Citing information supplied by the United States, the CND announced it was "profoundly shocked by the fact that the Japanese occupation authorities in Northeastern China utilized narcotic drugs during the recent war for the purpose of undermining the resistance and impairing the physical and mental well-being of the Chinese people." The UN narcotics body recommended to ECOSOC, "that the use of narcotics as an instrument of committing a crime of this nature be covered by the proposed Convention on the Prevention and Punishment of Genocide."[17]

This back and forth augured the increasing centrality of drugs to contests over power in the decades following WWII. In fact it was the well-publicized US refusal to prosecute Lieutenant General Ishii at the Tokyo war crimes trials, in the interests of capitalizing on his research for the US government's own biological warfare research program, which stoked Chinese suspicion that the United States was deploying bacteriological weapons in the Korean War.[18] The conflict escalated to the point of becoming, according to the US Army Center of Military History, "among the more remarkable episodes of the Korean War" when "North Korea, China, and ultimately the Soviet Union [attempted] to convince their own citizens and mankind at large that the United States was engaged in biological warfare (BW). Then and later American officials denied the charge and accused the Communist states of embarking on a propaganda campaign in an attempt to conceal their inability to control actual epidemics. The debate played a prominent part in the ideological struggle for world opinion that accompanied the fighting."[19]

Drugs were powerful tools in modern warfare and the specter of the deliberate spreading of disease, the potential "inability to control actual epidemics," was accompanied by public campaigns to reassure populations of their governments' preparedness. The US government contended with these issues in part through promoting pharmaceutical industry experimentation with concoctions that could be used as weapons or alleviators of deliberately spread devastation, whether biological or chemical. George W. Merck, as the head of the government's biological warfare unit during World War II, described the nebulous line between "biological and chemical agents" that might be used to attack humans or crops, and could "prove of great value" to agricultural development, public health, and preparedness in case of postwar attack.[20] The US countercharge that infection spread from Communist states' "inability to control actual epidemics" rather than US biological warfare attacks, whether accurate or not, did demonstrate the new significance of drugs to national security. While there has been much disagreement over the legitimacy of biological warfare accusations, the belief in their accuracy fueled the massive expansion of vaccination and public health campaigns in China, Korea, and the United States.[21] US newspapers broadcast the possibility that the Korean War "situation might be considered by the Soviets as a good one in which to stage a trial of such a weapon" and reassured the public that "mass immunization . . . is one of the weapons we are actively forging against germ warfare." *Science News Letter* described the interest of "scientists and pharmaceutical manufacturers" in US nationwide polio vaccination trials in 1954 "as practice for what might have to be done if BW is ever let loose on the land."[22]

This early 1950s US fear of future Communist biological warfare was accompanied in public accounts by a belief in the already immediate dangers posed by "chemical (heroin) warfare." As the *New York Times* suggested in an editorial in 1953, the perception was widespread that Communist China was capitalizing on the revenue derived from the illicit sale of opium while also using "narcotic addiction as a weapon against the societies in which it can get a foothold": "Opium as a secret weapon is considerably older than the Communist hullabaloo about bacteriological warfare. . . . This is not the time for timidity and soft words. . . . When we get the next bit of nonsense about [US] bacterial warfare the retort should be the documented charge against the Soviet Union and its puppets concerning something that is more deadly and that does not happen to be imaginary."

In a portrayal of the culpability of drug users in helping fund the nation's enemies (a tactic that became common to US antidrug campaigns through the early twenty-first century), the paper decried Communist strategy "when teen-age addicts in New York are helping to pay for the shells that kill American boys in Korea."[23] Similarly a Los Angeles police sergeant entitled a chapter of his memoir, "Dope Versus the Atom Bomb," implicitly contrasting "free world" arsenals to those of "Communist saboteurs," as he declared, "Red China is engaging 'warfare by dope'," infecting US teenagers to "undermine the moral strength of the nation."[24] Such interpretations illuminate how the narrative of criminal drug deployments shifted with the ebb and flow of diplomatic alliances. Until recently China had been the widely acknowledged victim of drug warfare dating back to European encroachment and the opium wars of the nineteenth century, culminating in the Japanese invasion during WWII. Cold War politics radically transformed this narrative in the wake of the US occupation of Japan and in response to the Chinese Revolution of 1949. Suddenly the United States recast the Chinese as purveyors of addiction, and Japan (as an occupied ally, rather than Axis enemy recently accused of peddling drugs as a wartime atrocity) joined the United States as victims of the nefarious drug warfare of Chinese Communists. In a "reverse irony" not lost on some members of Congress, US officials accused "Chinese Communists" of "a fantastic plot to ruin the US armies in Korea and Japan through the cheap peddling of heroin."[25]

COLD WAR IMPERIALISM AND THE UNITED NATIONS

Anslinger, as head of the FBN, strategically deployed drug warfare allegations to influence drug control policy at both the national and international levels, particularly with regard to his championing of international passage and national ratification of the 1953 Protocol for Limiting and Regulating the Cultivation of the Poppy Plant, the Production of, International and Wholesale Trade in, and Use of Opium (the Protocol). Described by William McAllister as the "high tide of the original drug-control impetus," the Protocol brought together the harsher aspects of US narcotics regulatory efforts, extending them to opium producing countries.[26] With the two primary coca producing countries already collaborating to varying degrees with the drug control regime, Anslinger sought to extend its reach beyond the Western Hemisphere. The ongoing focus on securing the production and distribution of raw materials took on global proportions and might be viewed as a proving ground for the reach of US imperial ambitions in the midst of the decline of the European colonial empires. Politicized accusations of dope peddling unfolded in a global context where an East–West rivalry between capitalism and communism increasingly filtered through disparities in wealth and power between the industrial and nonindustrial world, and where a North–South divide was being transformed by widespread upheaval as colonized yellow, brown, and black peoples challenged and overthrew white colonial power. Exemplifying this dynamic, when

FIGURE 11. Harry J. Anslinger testifying before the US Senate Foreign Relations Committee, 1954. [Library of Congress, Prints & Photographs Division, reproduction number, LC-USZ62–120804.]

Anslinger appeared before the Senate Subcommittee on Foreign Relations advocating US ratification of the Protocol, the chairman of the committee depicted the global nature of the problem: "And we, of course, are well aware that North Korea, or the Chinese in North Korea, simply have been the satellites of the Kremlin. Now, is there any place where the Kremlin has penetrated elsewhere, Guatemala or any of the other places that they have utilized the drug that you know of—[?]"[27]

Acknowledging a hierarchy of proxy control, North Korea by the Chinese and the Chinese by the Kremlin, Anslinger denied direct knowledge of the scope of Soviet penetration around the globe. Yet, the image of the Kremlin's covert influence over "satellites" or "puppets" in relation to political subversion or, as with the earlier-described Mau Mau, fostering drug-induced rebellion, provided an ideological framework that at once represented the Third World as dangerously malleable, even unfit for self-government, while providing the rationale for US imperial expansion. Just twenty days before this testimony a US-backed military coup had successfully ousted the democratically elected government of Guatemala.

While drug control was only one ideological and institutional weapon in the Cold War arsenal, following these efforts does provide a perspective on the forces propelling the larger struggle for global influence. The Protocol incorporated many of the provisions of previous treaties and was designed to consolidate them under one instrument with escalated powers of enforcement.[28] It limited raw opium production to seven states (a "closed list" including Bulgaria, Greece, India, Iran, Turkey, the USSR, and Yugoslavia) and limited purchases of drugs exported from these states based on national estimates of legitimate demand—estimates that would be set even for states not party to the convention. This was arguably an imperial effort to meet (and regulate), as Anslinger described, "the medical needs of the world" by targeting source, or supply-side, countries as the foundational tenet of drug control, and limiting the scale of the trade according to Western definitions of medical value.[29] Along with the power to effect on-site inspections, *any* state "impeding the effective administration" of the Protocol could be subject to embargo.[30] The treaty purported to introduce "the most stringent drug-control provisions yet embodied in international law." It extended reporting provisions to raw opium and, in a "victory for Anslinger," stipulated that opium be "restricted to medical and scientific needs," a definition with built-in exemptions whereby "in a manufacturing country like the United States" military stocks were excluded from the estimate.[31] Three of the seven Protocol-identified legitimate world suppliers of raw opium had to ratify the convention before it came into force, an event that did not happen until 1963 in the midst of heated UN debates over whether the Protocol or an alternative agreement known as the 1961 Single Convention on Narcotic Drugs (the Single Convention) should dictate international control efforts.

The Protocol embodied the core prohibitionist principles embraced by the United States, and, in the words of David R. Bewley-Taylor, "was symbolic of US prominence within the UN control framework."[32] The USSR refused to participate in the proceedings regarding the Protocol. Instead, Soviet officials threw their weight (with the support of many former colonial countries) behind efforts to devise another instrument, ultimately realized as the Single Convention, which slightly weakened, although did not fundamentally transform, the control model advanced in the Protocol. The decade-long process of unifying existing international drug control law under a single convention culminated in a standoff between Anslinger's reluctance to weaken any provisions proposed by the Protocol and the ultimately more widely accepted Single Convention.[33] Amidst superpower wrangling, drug control provided a platform for Cold War campaigning. Competing power blocks, largely aligned with the drug manufacturing countries on one side and drug raw material exporting countries on the other, negotiated to advance their own interests.

Anslinger, through some wily diplomatic maneuvering in the midst of negotiations over the terms of the Single Convention, succeeded in using economic and political pressures to have the necessary number of three opium-producing countries ratify the Protocol, which accordingly went into effect in March 1963. Anslinger wrongly hoped this would undermine the Single Convention, which went on to receive the necessary number of ratifications (Kenya provided the critical fortieth accession) and went into effect in December 1964. Once ratified, the Single Convention superseded the Protocol as the prime instrument of international drug control. Despite Anslinger's initial chagrin, by the end of the decade he was urging Congress to ratify the Single Convention as an effective international enforcement tool, which it did in 1967.[34] There were differences between the two treaties, yet both entrenched the fundamental tenets of supply-side control and, as a US Public Health Service officer explained, the Single Convention "continue[d] essentially the previous international controls restricting production, distribution and use of narcotics drugs to medical and scientific purposes."[35] Moreover, in a triumph for a central principle of drug control, long advocated by Anslinger himself, US prohibitions against marijuana consumption (first introduced in national legislation in 1937), and any other nonmedical consumption of organic raw materials (coca, opium), were solidified in the international treaty. The final outcome ultimately reflected "US dominance in the UN control system [and] ensured that the Single Convention created a Western-oriented prohibitive framework for international drug control."[36] However, the initial standoff at the United Nations over the US representative's support for the Protocol and Soviet support for the Single Convention shows how a new geopolitical context infused drug regulatory conflicts with symbolic power.

Soviet strategy was to align with Third World countries (including many producer states that saw the Single Convention as the lesser of two evils, and as an opportunity to push back against some of the more onerous drug regulatory provisions emanating from the industrial world) and to publicly challenge the considerable US influence at the

United Nations where it initially enjoyed a voting-bloc majority.[37] Debates about the mechanisms necessary to institutionalize drug control must be understood in relation to the anticolonial revolutions of the era. The United Nations, in and beyond the CND, had rapidly become a forum for US and Soviet denunciations of each other's imperial ambitions. Soviet representatives depicted US initiatives as a replacement for European colonial control, and the United States countered with accusations focused on the Kremlin's alleged expansionist designs. The US delegation to the United Nations reported, "Increasingly, both the United States and the Soviet Union are coming to see that the outcome of their struggle may be determined largely by what happens in the uncommitted nations," as debates over sovereignty unfolded concurrent with efforts to regulate the international drug marketplace.[38] In the first decade of the UN's existence, the USSR could only level symbolic challenges to US domination. The US ability to gain passage of the Protocol occurred in a context where the "Soviet bloc" was excluded from "all committees established to deal with colonial disputes." The United States, on the other hand, as one contemporary observer explained, "has been deeply involved in most aspects of the UN's work concerning colonialism, and it has been extremely influential."[39] Mobilizations for political independence confronted contested international models for economic development when "the colonial powers and their allies and associates retained a very strong position in the UN" and as the Cold War facilitated the transition of these allies into an international anticommunist bloc.[40] US influence at the United Nations offered a welcome framework to "avoid drifting in the dangerous currents of colonial rebellion," as one contemporary international relations scholar explained, "filtering an act of intervention in colonial affairs through an international organization may transform what would otherwise have been labeled 'an imperialistic act' into an action recognized on every side as necessary and fair to all parties."[41]

Chapter XI, article 73, of the UN Charter recognized the principle of equal rights and self-determination of all peoples, ensuring the international body became a forum where the implications of these terms were debated. This was reinforced in 1952 with the passage of Resolution 637 (VII), reiterating "The Right of Peoples and Nations to Self-Determination."[42] The United Nations included thirty-five member states in 1946; by 1970 national decolonization movements swelled that number to 127 member states. As the march of successful independence movements began to shift the balance of power in the United Nations across the decade, the United States consistently voted with other colonial powers to resist intervention in what they viewed as "domestic" disputes that came before the Security and Trusteeship Councils (which had jurisdiction over colonial and trust-territory issues respectively).[43] There were a number of factors influencing the US position. While the United States increasingly used economic and political pressure to exert influence, with drug control just one prominent example, the country continued to have both colonies and trust territories under its jurisdiction.[44] It is worth noting that the lack of representational government in places like Puerto Rico and the Trust Territories of the Pacific made them particularly valuable sites for conducting tests of the new atomic, chemical, and biological weapons so critical to US Cold War arsenals. US economic and military alliances with European powers also militated against stances embracing anticolonial positions. While the United States ostensibly opposed imperialism in the name of democracy and the right to self-determination, such "principled U.S. positions were tempered by having to deal with the ongoing economic weakness of their European allies." Furthermore, anticolonial movements often challenged the terms of foreign investment which placed the United States on the defensive, as did the resulting perception that they fostered instability and threatened the establishment of US military bases (a key component of its Cold War strategy). As historian Henry Heller argues, "anticolonialism was one thing, but opposition to economic imperialism by third world leaders was quite another matter so far as Washington was concerned."[45] Finally, with the USSR assuming the role of "most outspoken critics of colonialism at the United Nations," US foreign policy became driven by anticommunism, a priority that often necessitated procolonial politics.[46] The US representative on the Trusteeship Council, Mason Sears, explained this prophylactic vision, "We ensure freedom tomorrow by blocking Communism today."[47] This diplomatic maneuvering was widely perceived as the superpower struggle that it was. US delegates reported back to the Senate Committee on Foreign Relations that an emerging Afro-Asian bloc "wish[es] to keep 'colonialism' from being a 'cold war' issue. The Asian and African countries do not wish to give these European powers a chance to hide behind an attack on Soviet Imperialism and thus perhaps divert attention from their duty to promote self-determination pursuant to article 73 of the charter."[48]

The United States used its disproportionate power to influence struggles defining and asserting self-determination. In 1952, for example, after most of the leadership of the nationalist forces had been killed or imprisoned, a constitutional convention established Puerto Rico as a US Commonwealth. Recognized by the United Nations, Puerto Rico's status constituted a new category apart from the original interpretive framework outlined in the UN Charter, having ended colonial rule in a manner that "involved neither full independence nor full integration." Puerto Rico's semi-independent status became a model for European colonial territories such as Suriname, the Netherlands Antilles, and French Togoland among others.[49] In terms of recognizing the power of newly independent states, the United States also played an important role in determining the international balance of power. Responding to growing domestic resentment over US expenditures on the United Nations, US officials "conceded that on an ability-to-pay basis we would owe in the neighborhood of 38 percent, but averred, in effect, that other states had better start showing some sense of sharing the burden." The General Assembly "grudgingly" accepted in 1957 that "no state should pay more than 30 percent of the budget."[50] It was demonstrated at the time that relative to GNP the US payment was in fact "abnormally small" and that across the 1950s the "less-developed states" increased their contributions far more rapidly than the developed states, with African states in the period from 1946–69 contributing the most in relative terms.[51] Nevertheless, the absolute value of the US contribution fueled US congressional disillusionment with the United Nations, particularly when votes did not go its way. In what might be seen as an updated version of nineteenth-century Euro-American paternalists chafing at the burdens of colonial administration, small states were accused of not paying their "share" in discussions over how to apportion representation in this international forum. Sovereign equality did not imply economic equality and, at least in terms of international governance, US representatives believed all states were not in fact equal.[52]

While the General Assembly could not dictate policy with the force of the veto-empowered Security Council (whose five members were the victorious Allies in WWII: the United States, United Kingdom, Soviet Union, China, and France), as an international public forum that included representatives from all UN member states it did exert considerable political and symbolic influence. By 1960 state membership at the United Nations soared to 114 states, and the new members, all former colonies (35 from Africa, 15 from Asia, 11 from the Middle East, and 2 from the Caribbean), constituted a solid two-thirds majority that often garnered support from the Soviet bloc.[53] Contests over drug control unfolded in the midst of these revolutionary shifts in power, and fueled US skepticism towards the United Nations. In 1960 Soviet Premier Nikita Khrushchev launched an opening salvo calling for a UN declaration demanding immediate independence for all non-self-governing countries that ultimately evolved into a more moderate, yet nevertheless significant resolution passed by the General Assembly in December 1960: "The Declaration on the Granting of Independence to Colonial Countries and Peoples." Calling for the end of all armed action against liberation movements, declaring colonialism a violation of people's human rights and right to self-determination, and demanding "immediate steps to be taken . . . to transfer all powers to the peoples" of dependent territories, the declaration echoed sentiments first expressed by the non-aligned Afro-Asian world at Bandung, Indonesia, in 1955.[54] Despite a moderating clause that stated any attempted "disruption" of the territorial integrity of a country went against the principles of the UN Charter, the major imperial powers (including the United States, the United Kingdom, France, Belgium, and Australia) all abstained. But they could not prevent the resolution's adoption by the General Assembly.[55] A special committee, known as the "Committee of 24," was established to oversee the declaration's implementation which, despite its lack of enforcement powers, managed to dominate much of the debate on the floor of the General Assembly across the decade and produced a number of resolutions on behalf of anticolonial forces. According to a former US representative to the Committee of 24, resolutions were "normally . . . worked out by a group of communist members and anti-Western African and Arab States," often with the support of "Latin American" members who sought a middle ground so as not to alienate US officials. This inability of the United States to mobilize a majority in a context where "self determination is equated with independence" fueled public confrontation over US imperialism, such as when the delegate from revolutionary Cuba denounced US control over Puerto Rico and the US representative resigned from the committee in disgust.[56]

While the Committee of 24's work is beyond the scope of this chapter, it is indicative of the ways in which anticolonial movements by the 1960s were forcing the United States to reconsider its approach to international diplomacy, including narcotics control. Only a few months after the General Assembly issued the Declaration on Colonial Independence, the United Nations circulated the 1961 Single Convention on Narcotic Drugs for ratification. Describing the convention as a Soviet ploy to win anticolonial alliances, FBN Commissioner Anslinger initially advocated against US ratification, although with the sufficient support of other states it went into effect in December 1964.[57] The Single Convention, from Anslinger's perspective, reflected a Communist victory: a dangerous example of drug policy intersecting with Cold War and anticolonial politics. When Anslinger argued before Congress against ratification he characterized the elimination of the closed list of raw material–producing states (the major distinction behind his preference for the Protocol over the Single Convention) in stark terms:

> The Soviet bloc took the bit in its teeth with the assistance of the neutrals and the newer African nations emerging into independence, by holding out the idea that they might be able to participate in this legitimate traffic. . . . The Soviet bloc even held out the proposition to the African nations, "You vote with us and you can produce opium." That was not the worst of it. . . . The Soviet bloc made reservations as to the countries not there for political reasons. . . . I think Communist China forced the Russians into this position . . . the Russians felt the people who were not there should not be bound. . . . The Communist Chinese were always complaining about the fact Formosa was making the estimate for all these people. . . . What they are trying to do with these reservations, they are trying to break out of this tight control.[58]

In this dramatic accounting, Anslinger tapped into sentiments that held widespread appeal, reorienting conflicts over access to participation in the global drug economy toward questions of political legitimacy.[59] Drug control as Cold War conflict marginalized the Third World challenge to the dictates of the industrial world, deploying a logic—embraced to a certain extent by both the United States and the USSR—whereby the alleged immaturity of the "neutrals and the newer African nations" made them vulnerable to bribery and political manipulation. US Congressman John R. Pillion (NY) responded by urging newspapers and television media to "publish [Anslinger's] recital" about the Single Convention in order "to prove to the world that the Communist Soviet apparatus is primarily responsible for this proposed United Nations action." He lamented the "consolidation of political voting power shifting from the United States and the free world into the control and direction of the Communists in the Sino-Soviet bloc."[60] In a context where the United States lined up with other colonial powers to contain the implications of "self-determination," the fervent invocations of the need for US-guided drug control to protect "free nations" reflected Cold War competition and the anticolonial challenge to US dominance at the United Nations. The primary architect of the international treaty, Adolph Lande, was a US international civil servant, Anslinger's close friend and confidant in the UN secretariat overseeing narcotic drugs, and by the early 1970s a representative of the American Pharmaceutical Manufacturers' Association, echoed these concerns. At the United Nations Lande lamented challenges to US dictates, which he couched in racist assertions of cultural superiority when he worried that "the UN drug control apparatus was being staffed increasingly by non-Westerners," and complained that their frequent opposition to the US prohibitionary stance was due to their "low intellectual level" and "violent anti-Americanism," especially among Africans.[61]

Despite this (mostly symbolic and revealing) furor, the Single Convention consolidated into one treaty drug control mechanisms that had worked and would continue to work to US advantage. It incorporated the basic tenets of drug control that had been promoted by the United States since World War II: it institutionalized inequalities between the industrial and nonindustrial world, oriented control toward raw material–producing states, and privileged a capitalist international economic framework as the guiding principle behind it. By 1967, with Anslinger's approval, the US government ratified the Single Convention to ensure, in the words of President Lyndon B. Johnson, the country continued to play a "leading part in international cooperation for the control of narcotic drugs."[62] For all the heated US-Soviet posturing, the drug control regime weighed most heavily on Third World and producing nations. The newly consolidated regime extended international efforts to control the production and circulation of raw materials backed by two key principles. First, it called for the main manufacturing countries, mostly colonial powers (including the United States, England, France, Germany, Switzerland, and Holland), to fulfill their obligations to the control regime by limiting drug output to global "legitimate" needs. As Anslinger explained the new thrust of the drug control regime, "Today, every one of those countries is fulfilling those obligations in relation to manufacturing. So instead of the manufacturing countries being the culprits today, it is the producing countries." This then led to the second guiding tenet: that countries in the industrial world were "the principal victims of overproduction."[63] Even while industrial world laboratories churned out drugs on an unprecedented scale, the logic of drug control emphasized the need to control production in the nonindustrial world, embedding within it a new imperial framework for securing hierarchical economic flows, while invoking victimization to legitimize the extension of First World police oversight.

These were the substantive stakes behind disagreements described earlier over the seating of the Chinese Representative at the United

Nations. Due to its ongoing support from the United States, the exiled and defeated Chinese nationalist government in Formosa (Taiwan) represented all of China at the United Nations, meaning it was responsible for submitting estimates on drug requirements for the continent ruled by the PRC. These estimates formed the basis for judgment on compliance and potential sanctions. This was why the PRC was "always complaining" that it was bound by drug-needs statistics submitted by a hostile regime. Political affiliations clearly influenced designations of legality and "legitimate" participation in the international drug trade. Since the PRC government was not granted political recognition, it had been denied a "legitimate" role in negotiating the drug market. As historian William O. Walker describes, Anslinger diligently sought to "cast the Chinese as international outlaws on the subject of opium."[64] When the Chinese government legally tried to sell stocks of opium, which had been seized from factories run by Japanese occupation forces during World War II, the US-led Western economic embargo against Communist China ensured its exclusion from the legal market. As Anslinger said, "They offered that legitimately, but no country would take it on."[65] While scholars have pointed to the lack of evidence behind heated accusations of illicit Communist dope pushing during the Cold War, they have tended to overlook the fact that by virtue of Communist exclusion from the narcotic drug market, *any* opium the PRC might produce for export was predestined for illegality according to the logic and regulations advanced by the international drug control regime.[66] Drug control in this context offered both an ideological framework for challenging the readiness of colonized peoples for self-determination, limiting the economic and political power of Communist countries, while structuring participation and designating legality within the marketplace according to the interests of capitalist countries.

POLICING THE CRISIS

Cold War posturing and colonial conflict animated tensions at the United Nations in debates over competing visions for international drug control. These international dynamics also shaped US national drug policy, informing people's beliefs about the threat posed by narcotics and people who consumed or trafficked in them. Fears of communism and racially inflected ideas about self-determination filtered into and fueled domestic anxieties producing a veritable "moral panic" in the 1950s about drug crimes. Stuart Hall and colleagues detailed how such panics are social phenomena and are "about other things than crime *per se*" when he detailed how the heady mix of race, youth, and crime became an ideological conduit for the widespread belief in Britain in the 1970s that the social order was disintegrating and "slipping into a certain kind of crisis," which generated in turn an authoritarian consensus around the need for "law and order." Two decades earlier, the United States was gripped by a similar sense of crisis with analogous ideological underpinnings that sparked a crackdown on drug "crimes." The social construction of these crimes, the way they were understood and defined, as well as the social forces that were constrained or contained by, or benefited from, them, are essential for understanding the origins and underpinnings of the subsequent decades-long US "war on drugs."[67]

As people lined up before Congress to testify in support of US ratification of the 1953 Protocol, the chair of the Senate Subcommittee of the Committee on Foreign Relations deployed a paranoid discourse increasingly common to Cold War public culture:[68]

> First, if our American people can be made aware of the fact that Mao Tze-Tung is engaged in undermining the health and the morale and the strength of our boys in the services, and secondly, if they can get, as you say, a picture of this dirty business, that it is not just a few skunks around the corner that are handling it, but that it is the result of people in high places, like Mao Tze-Tung, who is using it [opium] as a weapon to deteriorate the morale and health of this country, then the people of this country will become aware that we have to "stop, look, and listen" and think about it.[69]

The Chair of the Committee on Foreign Relations, Alexander Wiley, warned the "American people" of subversion lurking in their midst, advising that they "stop, look, and listen" and be on guard against drugs being used as a weapon to attack "this country." He invoked international enemies to call for internal vigilance and policing. A parade of witnesses echoed these sentiments, with a journalist testifying that "dope warfare" was an "instrument of policy with Red China," followed by a New York City Police Department inspector, the president of pharmaceutical giant Merck & Co., Inc., and the Secretary of State for UN Affairs, all warning of the dire need for aggressive drug controls. Mrs. Duncan O'Brien of the New York Federation of Women's Clubs cut to the chase: "Our Communist enemy has invaded. They are shooting our youth with drugs instead of bullets."[70] As the United States promoted its drug regulatory vision internationally, such images were mobilized in the 1950s behind the passage of extraordinary legislation that vastly expanded domestic police powers. In a decade marked by dramatic conflict over racial equality and civil rights, the social panic and attack on drug "crimes" could be used to recast dissent and nonconformity as dangerous "contagions" threatening the very fabric of American society—rhetoric grounded in the power of modern drug technologies and public health concerns regarding the spread of disease.[71]

Religious leaders, the media, teachers' organizations, youth congresses, and state and local officials all echoed congressional fears that the "drug cancer operating among troops of the United Nations in Korea" was only one site of a broader illness infecting US society: "Red treasuries swell as free world consumption of drugs mounts. The social aspect of the menace is evident in its degenerating effects upon our youth, here at home."[72] Cardinal Archbishop Francis Spellman and evangelist Billy Graham both visited US soldiers in Korea and decried the "frightfully high number" of narcotic addicts among them.[73] Journalists sought out firsthand testimony at places like the Stateville-Joliet prison in Illinois where almost half the inmates were veterans, the majority "Negroes," and a significant minority "admitted addicts." One Korean war veteran at Joliet, "who shall be called James, a Chicago negro, 26," when interviewed explained, "I believe the Chinese Reds are to blame for making 'junk' so cheap and easy to get. . . . It's one way to undermine the enemy soldiers. A lot of my friends thought so too, but we kept on using it."[74] The acknowledgment of enemy treachery raises interesting questions as to the private, political, or other reasons soldiers "kept on using it," but for readers of the *Daily Defender,* the story ended there. Appealing to a similar curiosity, the *New York Times* tracked the number of soldiers sentenced and discharged "on narcotics charges."[75] The FBN reassured the public it was working to contain the threat returnee soldiers might pose by getting "the Army to notify the chiefs of police, where the boys return to their home communities, so that they do not become sources of infection and start peddling."[76]

Depicting veterans as potential "sources of infection" was indicative of a broader tendency to link (illicit) drug consumption with the potential for criminal delinquency. There emerged a widely remarked-upon relationship between drugs, delinquency, racial identity, and social pathology. As one NYC prosecutor explained, "addiction, then, is a disease of high social contagion that not only may produce criminality . . . but also tends to attack those persons whose resistance to anti-social activity is, for a multitude of reasons, notoriously low." He tellingly left it to "psychiatrists and sociologists" to explain its high incidence "among the negroes and Puerto Rican" youth.[77] A Times Youth Forum meeting in Los Angeles on how to "improve the welfare of youth in the United States" illustrated the reach of this emerging consensus. Teenagers aired their belief that without a "happy home," spiritual and vocational guidance, and good role models, "Communism will be used to fill in the gaps, narcotics to numb the sting of discouragement and delinquency as the counterweapon to fight the world."[78] The director of Chicago's Crime Prevention Bureau, Dr. Lois L. Higgins, warned an audience at the National Biology Teachers' Association: "While we join other free nations to resist the threat of Communism in other parts of the world, our Communist enemies are waging a deadly and tragically successful war against us here at home. Narcotic drugs are some of the weapons they are using with devastating effect."[79] At a health fair in Chicago, Higgins simplified this message: "Youthful narcotics addiction is one facet of the hydra-headed threat of crime and communism."[80] The image of corrupting forces threatening American youth was deeply embedded in the racial politics of the era. A 1956 article in *Reader's Digest* entitled "We Must Stop the Crime that Breeds Crime!" warned readers: "Formerly concentrated in the Negro, Puerto Rican, Mexican and Chinese sections of a few large cities, addiction has spread during the last ten years to smaller metropolitan areas and taken in youths of every race."[81]

Drug control in this context recast domestic upheavals as foreign infiltration while elaborating a strengthened system of social control and policing that particularly targeted African American, poor, and immigrant communities. It eschewed the language of race with a seemingly neutral and socially beneficial discourse of protecting (white) "youth" against criminal contagion.

Jacquelyn Dowd Hall describes that by the early Cold War, "antifascism and anticolonialism had *already* internationalized the race issue and, by linking the fate of African Americans to that of oppressed people everywhere, had given their cause transcendent meaning. Anticommunism, on the other hand, stifled the social democratic impulses . . . narrow[ing] the ideological ground on which civil rights activists could stand."[82] Much as red-baiting sought to sever black American political mobilizations from the international context out of which they came, so too did accusations of criminality. The Ku Klux Klan attacked integration as communist-inspired and attacked acts of civil disobedience as amoral flaunting of the law. A full decade before presidential candidates like Barry Goldwater and Richard Nixon would run on political platforms invoking "law and order" as a not-so-veiled appeal to white supremacist resentment towards black civil rights, a "rhetoric linking crime and race" had already become "fused in the public mind."[83] While officials distanced themselves from the position that crime was caused by biological or racial factors, the social sciences provided a seemingly race-neutral framework for explaining the preponderance of crime among certain racial groups. This slippage was a critical component of a new large-scale policing and prison system that grew in tandem with the victories of the civil rights movement. Appealing to fears of contagious subversion, law enforcement measures worked to recast cultural, racial, and political manifestations as criminal threats to public safety. Scientific presumption that pathology caused crime functioned as a mechanism for perpetuating the politics of Jim Crow segregation, denial of political rights, and the maintenance of economic inequality within a liberal articulation that elided its white supremacist foundations. This was nowhere clearer than in the manufactured drug crisis that led to unprecedented policing, escalation of criminal penalties, and the targeting of poor, immigrant, and especially black communities during the 1950s.

Drugs and war fused in domestic politics as the public and government responded fiercely to sensational portrayals of the "narcotics menace," and as the FBN successfully linked projects of international and domestic drug control. By the 1960s, congressmen celebrated Commissioner Anslinger as "the No. 1 American general in this fight against narcotics addiction in our United States," along with the new "legislative weapons necessary to win this war."[84] Just a decade earlier, when the Welfare Council of the City of New York pursued an investigation "for the purpose of determining the nature and extent of 'teen-age' drug addiction in New York City," the purported crisis of "teen-age" addiction was not common knowledge: "The project committee encountered difficulty in obtaining statistics from public agencies and soon discovered that most public agencies have not kept very close check of the incidents of 'teen-age' addiction. This failure was principally due to the fact that there was no such awareness on the part of most public agencies of the existence of such a situation."[85]

A spate of local and national hearings and investigations helped raise "awareness" of the alleged crisis as part of an effort spearheaded by the FBN and fulfilled by Congress to revise the nation's drug laws. Sensational media coverage fueled public uproar. As *Newsweek* reported in June 1951, "Last week the verbatim confessions of teen-age addicts filled up more newspaper columns than the MacArthur hearings." Such youth testimonials of arrest for using "marijuana, heroin, morphine, or cocaine" underwrote the buildup to legislative action.[86] By 1951, the crisis inspired radical proposals: "Recent disclosures of teen-age addiction may result in the passage of more stringent laws. Already there are demands for legislation which will make the sale of narcotics to minors punishable by death."[87] When a congressional committee held hearings that year to revise narcotics legislation, the chairman declared, "A drug addict is something more than a criminal. Because he is enslaved to dope he is, in a sense, also a 'disease' spreader. . . . Because their moral fiber has been destroyed, victims of dope, like victims of smallpox, must be quarantined for their own protection and for the protection of the rest of society."[88] The fear of an "epidemic of narcotic addiction among younger people" had a profound impact on national drug policy.[89]

Between 1951 and 1956, as historian John C. McWilliams notes, there was "a dramatic increase in the number of Washington legislators who proposed federal statutes for the greater control of narcotics," with twenty-six bills presented in 1951 alone. The passage of the Boggs Act in 1951 introduced mandatory minimum sentences for narcotics law violations as well as a number of measures to "make it easier for prosecuting attorneys to secure convictions."[90] A radical law enforcement tool, the mandatory minimum sentence undermined judicial discretionary power and rapidly "more than doubled the average prison sentence of federal narcotics offenders."[91] Even prior to the Boggs Act, the FBN boasted that with only 2 percent of "Federal criminal law enforcement personnel," bureau arrests accounted for "more than 10 percent of the persons committed to Federal penal institutions."[92] Between 1946 and 1950, a 20 percent decrease in people sentenced to federal prisons was accompanied by a 20 percent increase in those "sentenced for narcotic violations."[93] Five years later the Narcotics Control Act in 1956 once again escalated penalties dramatically. Selling narcotics to juveniles now carried "a maximum sentence of death upon recommendation of the jury," and the act maintained mandatory minimum sentences, while extending their maximum duration: "For the first possession offense, the penalty was two to ten years' imprisonment with probation or parole. For the second possession or first selling offense, there was a mandatory five to twenty years with no probation or parole; and, for the third possession or second selling and subsequent offense, the violator was sentenced to a mandatory term of ten to forty years with no probation or parole."[94]

State laws largely mirrored the regulations adopted at the national level, with some dissent. In 1958, Missouri lowered penalties for a first-time drug conviction since, as the circuit attorney in St. Louis explained, "We found that juries simply would not send a man up for two years on the strength of a marijuana cigarette found in his possession." Yet this incident, according to a journalist for the *Nation*, "marked the rare occasion when an agency of any government questioned the authority or wisdom of Anslinger" (who, it might be noted, quickly retaliated by withdrawing the bulk of FBN officers from the state).[95]

The escalation of penalties for illicit drug consumption had deeper roots than the sensational coverage that directly preceded the passage of legislation.[96] While congressional testimony and media coverage seemed to confirm a popular demand for action, the FBN itself was a critical force cultivating the perception of a crisis. Statistics regarding the national incidence of addiction were based upon police reporting of arrests for narcotics law violations. All persons arrested for illicit narcotics possession were classified as "addicts," and the increased number of arrests created the perception of an increasing incidence of criminality. As enforcement—and reporting—escalated, so too did the incidence of crime, leading in a circular fashion to the perceived need for more policing. In the wake of public hearings on addiction in New York in 1951, "the size of the Narcotics Squad was doubled."[97] With the passage of the Boggs Act in 1951 and the Narcotics Control Act in 1956, the FBN received the two largest budget increases in its history.[98] The expansion of police powers was also connected to the presumed race of narcotics law violators. The FBN targeted "the teen-age problem [that] is in New York, Chicago, and Los Angeles" and focused most of its policing in the predominantly poor and black neighborhoods of those cities.[99] As a consequence, throughout the decade, charts submitted to Congress to justify narcotics enforcement budgets reinforced the association connecting minorities, addiction, and crime.

In an era when the explicit deployment of race as an explanation for social inequality became increasingly unpalatable, congressmen delicately pointed to the overrepresentation of black "addicts" in FBN reports. A year after the passage of the Narcotics Control Act, Rep. Gordon Canfield (NJ) fretted, "I wonder if it is proper—if I am treading on dangerous ground I hope you will tell me—but I note in your charts presented today that the dope peddlers of the United States apparently prey to a large degree on our Negro population, and that I am sorry to hear."[100] In the midst of mass African-American protests, sit-ins, and

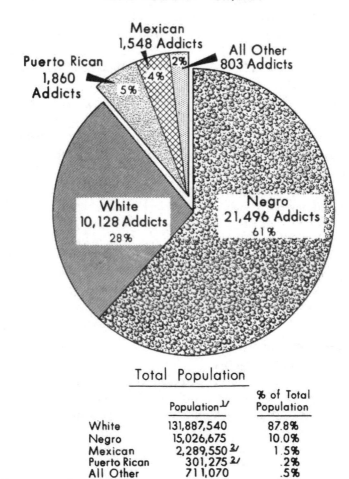

DRUG ADDICTION
Composite Total For Calendar Years
1953 —— 1956

Total Addicts   35,835

Mexican
1,548 Addicts

All Other
803 Addicts

Puerto Rican
1,860
Addicts

2%

.4%

5%

White
10,128 Addicts
28%

Negro
21,496 Addicts
61%

Total Population

	Population[1]	% of Total Population
White	131,887,540	87.8%
Negro	15,026,675	10.0%
Mexican	2,289,550 [2]	1.5%
Puerto Rican	301,275 [2]	.2%
All Other	711,070	.5%

[1] 1950 Census.   [2] Estimated by Bureau of Census.

FIGURE 12. Federal Bureau of Narcotics chart representing drug addiction statistics for 1953–1956, differentiated by race.

marches for economic, political, and social equality, many congressional representatives knew that black people were disproportionately being charged with narcotics violations. It is clear from congressional exchanges that many sought to studiously avoid addressing race directly, even while presuming black criminality. The record of congressional hearings themselves reproduced this avoidance of race, even while it was clearly being given serious weight, as is evident in the notable frequency that conversations about race and drug use proceeded "off the record." Rep. Otto E. Passman (LA) emblematically exclaimed: "I am not making any racial implications at all, but when you have statistics of this type, then there should be some explanation as to why there are five colored addicts to one white addict." In response, before going off record, the Commissioner of Narcotics reiterated a frequent explanation that crime was "confined to certain police precincts where you have very bad social and economic conditions," assuring the Louisiana congressman that "negro" addiction was not a problem in the South (as opposed to the North) —echoing perhaps a frequent assertion that increased levels of freedom for blacks brought increased levels of crime.[101]

Such attitudes in the 1950s and 1960s bolstered funding for the FBN, and fueled the dramatic expansion of police powers. The Cold War tendency to pursue national security through international covert operations had a domestic counterpoint in the shift toward undercover narcotics enforcement. As Anslinger explained, "We decided to take advantage of the men and the money and the Boggs Act—we had all three—so we stepped into the underworld. We put most of our new men right out into the underworld."[102] By 1957, the commissioner testified that the vast majority of narcotics agents "work undercover. Even our supervisors, we try to have them work undercover."[103] This shift to undercover work depended on a number of transformations including the FBN need to "recruit Negro, Sicilian, and Chinese agents."[104] Along with changes in police personnel came the weakening of civil rights protections. Early in the decade Anslinger described a New Jersey law as "an excellent thing" for enabling officers to arrest "an addict as a disorderly person just like a common drunkard." He lamented that in Washington, DC, "there is nothing that the police can do. They do not have the power to pick up a man because he is an addict. They must have probable cause. We have a search-and-seizure restriction in Federal jurisdiction."[105] Voicing a common complaint, police frequently demanded "the right to arrest without warrant; the right to search for and seize contraband before and after a valid arrest." Without them, since 1950 the police had pursued other tactics to "offset some of these handicaps." Undercover officers increasingly "shifted enforcement emphasis to the purchase of drugs from violators—a method which is slow, costly and inefficient by previous standards, but designed to avoid judicially imposed disabilities."[106] These tactics tended toward the apprehension of low-level violators. As the new drug policy's most vociferous public critic, a professor of sociology at Indiana University, Alfred R. Lindesmith, described, "penalties fall mainly upon the victims of the traffic—the addicts—rather than on the dope racketeers."[107] Nevertheless, in 1956 many of these "obstacles" were removed. Anslinger celebrated the introduction of "witness immunity" in narcotics cases, explaining, "We never got this type of an informer who is now willing to trade his long-sentence term for turning in his connections."[108] And the Federal Bureau of Narcotics was "given the authority to carry firearms, serve search warrants, and make arrests without warrants" in their pursuit of narcotics law violations.[109]

To some contemporaries, the connection between racism, policing, and opposition to black political mobilizations was clear. In a Pulitzer Prize–winning series, reporter Gene Sherman remarked: "The methods of narcotics officers have come under fire lately by some moralists, attorneys and vociferous proponents of civil rights."[110] In a remarkable statement submitted to the newly constituted Federal Civil Rights Commission which the petitioners shared with the *Los Angeles Tribune,* the "Fellows of Tank 12A-1" of the Los Angeles County Prison protested that narcotics squad police tactics violated their "Constitutional guarantees, railroading men and women to the penitentiary." Offering an indictment of the powers granted under narcotics legislation, these prisoners suggested their due process rights were violated by the use of secret informers against whom defendants had been denied the right of subpoena. Moreover they argued undercover agents used bribery, in the form of drugs and the promise of reduced sentences, to gain informers' collaboration, a tactic openly celebrated by the FBN. Explaining that agents deliberately targeted "slum areas" to achieve their "specific goal," they protested being made "objects for political popularities and gains," and implored the Civil Rights Commission "to help save what the Constitution guaranteed us."[111] Drug laws were powerful, oppressive tools in a city where the police force "protected its white constituency, [by] keeping in check," in Police Chief William H. Parker's words, the "primitive Congolese."[112] This was true across the nation. In striking testimony, Cook County state's attorney John Gutknecht described the racial politics and legal consequences of narcotics enforcement in his jurisdiction, which included the city of Chicago. Remarking on "the prevalence of Negro defendants among those charged" and noting police operations tended to target people who "operated mainly in the lower/middle branches of the illicit traffic," the state's attorney believed: "The white race is responsible for the distribution of narcotics in America, and let's not kid ourselves. The others are the victims." The perception that drug enforcement was a tool for maintaining white supremacy, while not popularly embraced, nevertheless seemed to lie just beneath the surface of policy debates. The governor of New Jersey drew upon this reservoir when, in the context of numerous states "passing laws which match or exceed the rigor of the national laws," he vetoed a narcotic bill passed by the state legislature, "characterizing it as an example of a lynch law."[113]

The racial logic behind the expansion of policing drew upon a seemingly apolitical professional consensus forged among sociologists, psychologists, and other experts that identified specific drugs with certain "types of people" and communities. The incredible expansion of new drug commodities propelled a public health debate about the relationship between habit, addiction, crime, and disease, which along with prison demographics, represented economic, racial, and cultural bias even while asserting scientific neutrality. When asked before Congress, "from what strata of society would you say the largest number of addicts come—the low, middle class, or upper crust?" the FBN commissioner replied, "Unquestionably from below. . . . These fellows mostly have been criminals first and then addiction follows. The type of people they live with, that is where you get addiction. You don't see addiction where the individual has a good school, a good home and a church."[114] Suggesting poverty bred crime along with the absence of "good" schools and homes clearly appealed to the normative power of white middle-class beliefs. The definition of addiction devised by the World Health Organization for international drug control officials, which emphasized not its impact on the individual body but rather the threat that body posed to the broader community, was adapted to social control initiatives in the United States. Dr. Harris Isbell, the director of the Addiction Research Center of the USPHS, and Nathan B. Eddy, his colleague and former member of the WHO's Expert Committee on Narcotic Drugs, clarified the intent behind the definition of addiction and its relevance for drug control:

It was not meant to be pharmacological, nor strictly speaking scientific, but practical, and was intended to include the diverse substances currently under international narcotics control. State and national narcotics laws and regulations and international narcotics conventions are designed to prevent or at least limit abuse of cocaine and marihuana as well as of opium and the potent analgesics. Though all of these substances are commonly and loosely termed narcotics, their properties differ so widely that they are similar only in being subject to abuse *and in creating social dangers*.[115]

This focus on "social dangers" left room for discriminatory application of the law according to subjective representations of what constituted a threat to the dominant social order. This definition led to the targeted policing of specific communities, and enabled the ongoing production, testing, and consumption of drugs by other people. Citing studies conducted on inmates at the USPHS narcotics farms, these scientists warned that the new synthetic drugs varied in their potential to generate addiction and implored a "need for flexibility" so as not to hamper research into a "nonaddicting pain-relieving drug." They also went on to advise that "the amphetamines, the barbiturates, or other sedatives" not be subject to control since their "clinical experience leads us to believe that most persons will handle and use these drugs as prescribed."[116] These allowances for drugs most widely consumed at the time by white middle-class housewives or teenagers studying for exams speak to social bias. The hoped-for power of the laboratory to create nonaddictive painkillers was paired with the "clinical" belief that some drugs (and by extension, some people) did not pose a social danger.[117]

Debates about addiction sharply reveal this duality. Embedded in the process of designating legality was the recognition of the power of drugs to effect positive change *and* to pose threats, a calculus profoundly influenced in any given circumstance by the broader context of cultural, racial, and political conflict. One common fear was the alleged power of drugs to incite people to frenzy and economic depravity, as expressed by Senator Mike Mansfield of Montana: "As I understand it, the drug addicts, once they get into the habit, will do anything to get the drug, and that means of course, they will steal, they will rob, and they will do anything," to which Anslinger responded, "That is very true, Senator, because they do not work. They just live a life of crime."[118] Such sentiments fueled belief in a drug crisis and sustained fearful enthusiasm for extreme coercive measures. In the words of a federal judge: "What would they do if a man came in bringing tuberculosis germs and infected the public with tuberculosis germs? A person like that should be executed. And yet by bringing narcotics in this country they were bringing in something worse than tuberculosis germs. I think the death sentence would not be an inappropriate sentence."[119] In another example, a prosecutor's vision neatly contained the productive and destructive potential of drugs in a simple plan: "The plan calls for the hospitalization of addicts on a massive scale . . . some of these . . . might be work camps; others might be on farms . . . others—more immediately available— would be existing institutions, such as mental hospitals with beds that have been emptied through the miracle of tranquilizers and improved therapy, or tuberculosis sanitariums vacated by the new wonder drugs." A clear line existed in this critic's mind between the wonder drugs and those producing addiction: In "good conscience" the state "ought not engage in administering narcotic drugs to individuals for indefinite periods, when such drugs, ultimately . . . will impair health, and when, by lulling patients into euphoria, they will destroy ambition and industry."[120]

Countering demands for harsher penalties were people such as Dr. Hubert S. Howe, who headed a New York Academy of Medicine study questioning the criminalization of drug consumption. Howe argued it was the withholding of drugs and the black market itself that turned drug users into criminals: "The public has yet to grasp the fact that addicts are dangerous when they are without drugs, not when they are with them. . . . The only way to get rid of the black markets is to undersell them."[121] Such arguments sought to reposition the addict as threats to themselves rather than to the larger society; and by extension cast "addiction" as an illness that should be treated through the controlled disbursement of medicaments rather than the controlled confinement of bodies. When such arguments were presented to Senator Price Daniel's Narcotics Subcommittee in the 1950s, *Time* reported on the subsequent discussion asking, "Should dope addicts get their dope free from the government?" The magazine described how "The proposal split the experts—doctors and law enforcers—right down the middle."[122] Even affirmative arguments still drew upon the logic of legality embedded in the drug control regime by characterizing government-regulated disbursement of drugs to addicts a "legitimate medical use." However, the social origins of the notion of "addiction," which had been embraced by scientists and policymakers alike, militated against disentangling the disease from the criminal. The perceived negative social impact of "addiction" was what had come to define the phenomenon. The subcommittee declared, "any provision of low-cost drugs to uncured users was immoral and that it had failed in all countries that have tried it."[123] The "immorality" of the "provision of low-cost drugs" might promote rather than undermine "addiction." For these policymakers it was addiction—the consumer—that generated the illicit traffic in drugs and social dangers, not the other way around.[124]

Such debates persist to this day, but their translation into policy persistently reflected the historical construction of ideas about collective well-being. This explains in part the sympathy accorded to the physician addict, a group that reportedly accounted for the "highest incidence of narcotics," in stark contrast to the sensational accounts of social dysfunction used to describe its manifestation in policed communities.[125] In a typical example, the *Science News Letter* dismissed the phenomenon: "Most doctors need a good night's sleep, more vacation time, and release from tension. Without it, they are in greater danger from temptation than any layman, because of their easy access to the drugs."[126] These exceptions extended to classes of drugs themselves, such as the tranquilizers and barbiturates, increasingly common antidotes for white suburban anomie. Explaining to Congress why such drugs were not covered by the Narcotics Control Act, Anslinger said, "the control would be so tight that I think it would cause hardship . . . we see those drugs do more good than harm to people with so much tension in the country today."[127] The line demarcating legality, and the productive and destructive power of drugs, was culturally determined. The same Congressman Sieminski who linked drugs with race rebellion in Africa responded to FBN statistics by advocating the value of drug consumption in certain contexts: "I hope that when people . . . see your figures, they will take a genuine interest in helping their own kind. . . . This is a challenge for man all over. Tranquilizer pills seem to be an approach in this direction. They say, it is helping man integrate himself into society."[128] In emblematic contrast, one psychologist described the pathology of drug use in black culture: "the specific drug used by [black] musicians is reflected in their music and is related to the degree of their acceptance by society. Alcohol was often used by early Dixieland musicians with their raucous rhythms, marijuana was linked with musicians playing the more sensitive and lighter swing music, and heroin use is associated with the complexities and emotional flatness of the 'cool' music of today. This music is described by musicians as being 'way out'—the same expression they use to describe the effect of heroin."[129]

REBEL MUSIC

Training a boy to blow a horn no longer insures that he will not blow a safe. It may well blow him into delinquency, for who can deny the close association between jazz and delinquency?[130]

Threads of anticommunism, white hostility to civil rights, expanded police powers, and an awareness of international dimensions to domestic upheavals came together in the public linking of jazz and narcotics. By 1957, "If the average man in the street was asked what sort of people take dope, the chances are he would give 'jazzmen' as one of the answers."[131] Jazz's groove, the antiracist, anticolonial politics of many of its luminaries, as well as its appeal to racially mixed audiences, placed it at the vanguard of protest movements, sparking considerable fear, hostility, and violence from forces defending the status quo. A surprising number of social scientists probed what ethnomusicologist Alan Merriam and sociologist Raymond Mack referred to as "the Jazz Community," drawing attention to the interplay between musicians and their audience. Recognizing the music's revolutionary potential, they acknowledged, "The anxiety felt about jazz in the dominant white culture stems further, in the view of a number of writers, from the fact that jazz is a music of protest." Yet as they survey the literature on jazz they describe the frequency with which notions of immaturity and social pathology (echoing the terms used to stigmatize other cultures in the service of "development" initiatives) were used to stigmatize the music. For example, an article entitled, "A Theory on the Psychology of Jazz," described how "there are few, if any, other causes (with the possible exception of Communism) which can satisfy the needs of the adolescent so fully ... because of basic psychological correlations between their needs and what the jazz community offers them."[132] The deceptive neutrality of academic inquiry nevertheless provided ideological justification for very material attacks on jazz musicians. Describing police responses to jazz performances in Los Angeles at mid-century, trumpeter Art Farmer explained, "The police started really becoming a problem. I remember, you would walk down the street, and ever time they'd see you they would stop you and search you." Farmer described jazz's racial transgressions as particularly threatening, "The police ... the only thing they saw anytime they saw any interracial thing going on was a crime ... it was a crime leading to prostitution and narcotics."[133] Bassist Charles Mingus had similar impressions of New York City in 1959: "the Police Department really enjoys harassing any club where a healthy integrated feeling is a little too out in the open."[134]

Many jazz musicians felt compelled to publicly respond to the situation.[135] At the Newport Jazz Festival in 1957, George Shearing, Stan

Getz, Dizzy Gillespie, Specs Wright, and others convened a panel on "Music and the Use of Habituating and Addicting Drugs." While the panel faced criticism that it might contribute to the general perception of a connection between drug addiction, black people, and jazz music, the panelists believed that a "factual discussion would help clear the air." Among other things, the musicians decried the targeting of their community by the police.[136] They denounced the Philadelphia police's "special habit" of "rounding up all nearby jazz musicians at random in dope raids." While these raids accounted for 2700 arrests between 1953 and 1954, they had resulted in "only 960 convictions." They condemned discrimination in New York City where having an "arrest" record (not necessarily a conviction) was grounds to be denied a music license to "perform in restaurants or night clubs in the city."[137] In a more subversive vein, in the mid-1950s a group of jazz musicians approached by psychologist Charles Winick who was studying the "connection between drug use and jazz musicians" told him they all smoked marijuana and at a benefit concert for a police narcotic group had performed songs "which had synonyms for narcotics in their titles": "Tea for Two," "Tumbling Tumbleweed," and "Flying Home."[138]

In the midst of such protests, investigators like Winick helped to establish policing and medical science as the terrain for understanding, identifying, and combating the "narcotics problem." Winick became the director of the Musician's Clinic in New York City, established with proceeds from the Newport Jazz Festival, "which provide[d] psychiatric treatment for jazz musicians."[139] A participant on the drug panel organized at Newport, Winick had served as secretary of the National Advisory Council on Narcotics and as a consultant to the US Senate Subcommittee on Delinquency. His assessment of the first few years of the jazz clinic's operation captures the public mood: "From the epidemiological point of view, which would regard addiction as a contagious disease, the world of jazz contains a large number of potential hosts to the disease of addiction and a number of carriers, some of them enjoying high status. The environment is a uniquely favorable one for the spread of contagion."[140]

This representation of the character and creative potential of jazz as "contagious disease" was intimately tied to the politics implicitly associated with the genre. As Winick explained elsewhere, "Rebellion and experimentation are related needs found in some addicts."[141]

In one of many events where this politics came to the fore, jazz artists Charles Mingus and Max Roach, self-proclaimed "Newport Rebels," organized a protest concert to run concurrent with the 1960 Newport Jazz Festival, which in their minds had become "too big, too square and too interested in box office instead of music."[142] An array of prominent musicians joined the rebels, protesting the commercialization of the festival, the trend toward "standard, conventional type music" along with the fact that the organizers had been "capitalizing on our efforts and not paying the musicians any money," by moving to an alternative venue down the street from the main event.[143] Mingus suggested the Newport Festival organizers had "lost their true identity with jazz" and jazz critic Nat Hentoff noted "the occasional Jim Crow at Newport," while a *Time* correspondent reported on the rebels: "This is like an extension of the sit-ins. I called it a sit-out."[144] At the beginning of the weekend, more than twelve thousand college students who had shown up for the main festival broke out in "drunken rioting," triggering the deployment of the police, National Guard, and US Marines and the cancellation of the festival.[145] Langston Hughes, organizer of the festival's blues session, tried to distance jazz musicians from the violence: "The rioters were not lovers of jazz, but young beer drinkers who had nothing better to do than throw their beer cans at cops," while feeling compelled to add: "(Incidentally according to the police records there was not a single Negro among them: and the riots had no racial angles)."[146] In contrast, the Mutual Broadcasting System, a major national broadcast radio networks, linked events at the jazz festival to political subversion: the "riots had not been spontaneous, but like those in Japan, Korea and Turkey, had been Communist inspired." New York's *Journal America* noted the incident did not conform to public presumptions: "The Newport rioters were definitely not delinquents with holes in their pockets. They were 'good' boys and girls from 'better' families and colleges." Jazz journalist Nat Hentoff noted the Soviet mouthpiece *Izvestia* tried to capitalize on the incident by pointing out, "'the savage beat of the drum and the howl of the trumpet' so often used in recent years as 'a cold war propaganda weapon' in support of 'Western Civilization' had been decisively unmasked."[147]

By the late 1950s, jazz had indeed been established as a "propaganda weapon" in the US Cold War arsenal, although the messages delivered by musicians traveling in the State Department–sponsored cultural diplomacy tours were as mixed as interpretations of "riots" and "rebellions" at Newport. As Penny Von Eschen has argued, the "jazz ambassadors" tours opened "an avenue for pursuing civil rights, solidarity, and musical exchange . . . with those behind the Iron Curtain, as well as a new embrace of Afro-diasporic connections and a deep interest in African independence."[148] During the Cold War, jazz, much like drugs, functioned in many ways as a floating signifier: it was hailed as proof that the United States could transcend its Jim Crow foundations and embody the spirit of the free world against Communism, while at the same time providing a vehicle for expressions of black political solidarity and the associated danger of revolutionary action. This led at times to incongruous intersections of music and politics. For instance Dizzy Gillespie, a former card-carrying member of the Communist party, joined many of the Newport Rebels, including Charles Mingus and Ornette Coleman, on international tour under the State Department banner.[149] The "infectious" power of jazz was embraced in this context as a Cold War weapon of containment. Such jazz tours not only pulled in big-name performers, but also groups like the Paul Winter Sextet, a college jazz band which in 1962 toured twenty-two Latin American countries, "intended primarily to reach students, the sextet played for many non-student audiences, including Indians in the Andes, who applauded with as much vigor as the jazz-initiated audiences of Buenos Aires, Santiago, Rio de Janeiro or Montevideo." In Quito, Ecuador, the group played a benefit for "a splendid anti-Communist student group," while elsewhere they encountered "leftist agitators" including a group in Colombia who "tried to portray jazz as a product of Africa, something the United States had "stolen." However, overall, the *Music Journal* reported, "The group encountered less resistance from left-wing groups than they had anticipated—partly, it is believed, because three of its members are Negro, and to demonstrate against them would have put the Communists on awkward ground, in view of their claim to be the 'friend' of minority groups."[150]

REVOLUTION AND REACTION

Even while jazz was depicted as fertile ground for drug contagions and communist infiltration, news reports mimicked State Department propaganda in celebrating that "Jazz Battles Communism" abroad. Drugs occupied this alchemical diplomatic realm. The international policing of drugs became a double-edged sword the United States unleashed in the Cold War battle. Just three months after the college jazz sextet returned from their Latin American tour, the Cuban Missile Crisis marked a crescendo in the ongoing racial, political, and diplomatic turmoil sparked by the Cuban Revolution, and signaled the culmination of the decline in relations between the United States and Cuba since Fidel Castro's arrival in Havana in January 1959. This deterioration was also evident in US-Cuban narcotics control diplomacy, revealing again the material and symbolic power of drugs and drug enforcement to projections of US power. Much as had happened with the Chinese in the midst of Cold War diplomatic realignments, the US government was quick to deploy accusations of illicit drug trafficking as a weapon against Fidel Castro's regime, accusations whose intensity grew in tandem with the broader diplomatic fissure.

Just days after Fidel Castro replaced Fulgencio Batista as leader of Cuba, on January 12, 1959, Anslinger sent his deputy FBN officer Charles Siragusa to Havana to establish contacts with the new regime. Siragusa shortly afterward wrote a book where he detailed Cuba's failings in drug control. It is difficult to disentangle distortion from facts in his self-aggrandizing account of his own heroic antinarcotic efforts, but portions of his narrative were serialized in a popular magazine, speaking to the public's fear and fascination with the drug trade in the midst of Cold War rivalries. Siragusa recounted that when he arrived at the Havana Hilton to meet an old informant he was surprised to find, "The revolution had turned the mousy [Juan] Gonzalez into a tiger. Instead of the ill-fitting 'zoot' suit he had worn in New York, he now wore the green uniform of the day. Even he packed a .45." Evoking the image of the gun-toting, army-clad revolutionary that became so central to American imaginings of Cuba, the much-feared revolutionary potential of urban youth culture was materially embodied in Gonzalez's transformation from awkward rebellious urban youth culture to a full-fledged revolutionary soldier—although here the FBN agent hoped to harness it for collaborative drug policing. He claimed to have provided Cuban officials with a report detailing a number of mafia-led trafficking operations the United States had been following in Cuba, telling them "that honest cooperation between our police forces would enhance relations between Cuba and the United States, for my government considered the unhindered flow of cocaine over its borders a pressing problem."[151] As the new Cuban government established itself, narcotics enforcement constituted one of the very first sites of potential diplomatic collaboration, and very rapidly augured a decline in relations as Cuba pushed back against US dictates.[152]

Two weeks after Siragusa's encounter at the Havana Hilton, Commissioner Anslinger expressed his dismay with the new Cuban government's failure to act on US intelligence. He told Congress, "We never got any response," which launched a diplomatic scuffle and mutual recriminations over whether a list of drug traffickers had ever exchanged hands. The commissioner explained that while the United States was "willing to help them suppress this traffic," it would do so with preconditions; that prosecutions follow arrests, that foreign "hoodlums" be deported, and that Cuba cooperate more extensively with UN drug control.[153] These warnings were printed in both Cuban and US newspapers and predictably inspired a firm response. In the March 18, 1959 issue of *Prensa Libre,* Castro attacked Anslinger and questioned US motives: "What happens is that the American Bureau of Narcotics has not heard that there has been a revolution here and that gangsterism, racketeering, interventionism and similar things have stopped."[154] Still, one month later on an unofficial visit to Washington, Castro dispatched an emissary to meet with FBN officials but failed to stem the hostile drift.[155] Siragusa lamented "the strong stench of communism had begun to permeate [Castro's] government" and implied an increase in cocaine trafficking (measured by two large seizures in Miami and New York) could be attributed to Cuban neglect: "If this was Castro's idea of cooperation, I sincerely hoped he would forget the whole thing."[156] While a decade earlier a dope bust in Cuba had been invoked as evidence of successful collaborations, now drug seizures provided proof of Cuban duplicity.[157] By January 1960, Anslinger's position solidified. He announced to Congress "there is probably more cocaine traffic in Cuba than all the rest of the countries of the world put together," before continuing the conversation off the record.[158] Politicized allegations of Cuban drug criminality were also on display at bilateral and regional drug control efforts in the hemisphere.

In March 1960, the First Inter-American Meeting on the Illicit Traffic in Cocaine and Coca Leaves convened in Rio de Janeiro, Brazil. The first of three Inter-American conferences held between 1960 and 1962 brought together policing and public health officials from the United States and Latin America (including Argentina, Brazil, Chile, Colombia, Cuba, Ecuador, Mexico, Paraguay, Peru, and Venezuela) and representatives from the UN CND and the European police agency Interpol. FBN agent Siragusa Chaired the US delegation and triumphantly reported back to his superiors that the final acts and resolutions adopted were "almost entirely ours," and "virtually guaranteed" that harsher law enforcement mechanisms and stricter controls over the legal drug trade would be implemented in Peru, Bolivia, and Brazil because of the delegation's close contact with "their high ranking police representatives."[159] A number of these representatives, including the Peruvian Chief of

Criminal Investigations, Dr. Alfonso Mier y Teran, had been trained at the US Federal Bureau of Narcotics training school, created by the 1956 Narcotics Control Act.[160] By the following year's Second Inter-American meeting, eight additional police officials from Ecuador, Peru, Bolivia, and Venezuela had all graduated from the FBN training school, smoothing the integration of US policing priorities across the Americas. Connections forged at the First Inter-American conference brought FBN officials to Bolivia to participate in counternarcotics operations that culminated in the passage of a law modeled on US drug enforcement, introducing "minimum mandatory sentences ranging from one year to life imprisonment for various types of trafficking offenses."[161]

As the US government pursued hemispheric police collaboration outside the UN framework, designations of legality remained politically powerful tools. The United States used Inter-American drug forums to try to discredit the Castro government. In preparation for the 1960 conference, Siragusa wrote to Brazilian officials "regarding our mutual problem represented by Peruvian and Bolivian cocaine. This cocaine is smuggled into your country, and large quantities are also smuggled into the United States via Cuba."[162] US officials expressed concern at the persistence of the "coca-chewing problem" in the Andes, and anxiously reported "with the spread of the knowledge of chemistry . . . the flow of crude cocaine towards the outer world seems now at a critical point."[163] A US representative informed Latin American police officials, "Cocaine paste, smuggled into Cuba from Peru and Bolivia . . . is converted into cocaine. Consequently, this excessive coca leaf production is ultimately responsible for the cocaine entering the United States traffic from Cuba."[164] The North–South hierarchy of legal production was being disrupted and rendered illicit by alleged Cuban intermediaries. The US delegation reported that while "several years ago the use of illicit cocaine in the United States appeared to be a thing of the past," with the Cuban revolution, "The picture has changed radically and today it is disturbing."[165] In the months following these accusations of Cuban involvement in the illicit drug trade, economic relations between the United States and Cuba would hit an all-time low as the United States cut off its sugar imports and the Cubans retaliated by nationalizing parts of the industry.[166] Disputes over drug control must be viewed as part of a larger confrontation through economic warfare, one which very effectively mobilized a narrative of criminality in an effort to politically isolate the Castro regime that was increasingly challenging the terms of US economic dominance in the hemisphere (and within its own economy).

Cuba represented more than an economic threat. The Cuban Revolution, in part because of its widely broadcast antiracist and anticolonial sympathies, garnered much support in Africa and its diaspora.[167] In July 1960, a few months after the regional narcotics conference, The Fair Play for Cuba Committee organized a trip to Cuba of prominent black activists, writers, and poets. Black nationalist and Afrocentric jazz critic LeRoi Jones returned from Cuba advocating a politics of active engagement, impressed by the revolution's grassroots base. Jones reported that Castro declared himself neither communist nor anticommunist, but rather a "radical humanist."[168] Castro's initial self-identification relied on the language of the non-aligned movement and was also adopted by some African American activists in the United States who challenged the Cold War consensus. When Castro traveled to New York to attend the UN General Assembly meeting in 1960, which had witnessed the revolutionary shift in power toward an Afro-Asian bloc, a downtown hotel offensively demanded thousands of dollars from Castro in advance while the New York tabloid press maligned the *fidelistas* as "uncouth primitives" that "killed, plucked, and cooked chickens in their rooms at the Shelburne and extinguished cigars on expensive carpets."[169] In protest, Castro moved his delegation to Harlem, where the Hotel Theresa welcomed him as an honored guest. Prominent civil rights advocates Robert Williams and Malcolm X, as well as international political leaders such as Jawarharlal Nehru of India, Gamal Abdul Nasser of Egypt, and Nikita Khrushchev of the USSR, all made the journey uptown for high-profile visits. Khrushchev's visit and, more significantly, the visits of Nasser and Nehru, both prominent leaders of the Third World Non-Aligned Movement, symbolically linked the US civil rights struggle to anti-imperialist struggles around the globe and Soviet propaganda efforts to capitalize on them. The US delegation to the General Assembly lamented the US media's "ill-informed" attack on these leaders' presence in New York, warning that the non-aligned leaders' seeming symbolic victory was far less "serious" than the need of US delegates to be "acutely conscious" of the way racial discrimination undermined US diplomacy: "All the explaining and apologies in the world will not erase the injury to an African delegate who is turned away from a restaurant."[170]

Two years later, responding to the Bay of Pigs invasion, Cuban foreign minister Raul Roa read aloud to the United Nations a telegram from Robert Williams challenging the US government to live up to its professed concern for "people willing to rebel against oppression" by responding to the urgent request from Southern blacks for weapons and manpower to help "crush the racist tyrants who have betrayed the American Revolution and the Civil War." Roa added his own twist: "I would like to ask Mr. Stevenson what would happen if the government of the United States, which claims to be champion of democracy, dared to arm not only the Negroes of the cotton fields of the South, but the Negroes right here in Harlem?" The roaring applause and the red face of the US ambassador challenged Cold War bipolar understandings with an acknowledgment of common cause between civil rights and challenges to US imperialism.[171] While Castro by this point was openly embracing Cuban ties to the USSR, Cuba's economic and political challenge to the United States continued to embody a Third World and anticolonial challenge to US hegemony. This was on display at the 2nd Inter-American Conference on drug control convened in Brazil at the beginning of December 1961, while the United States still chafed at the Bay of Pigs fiasco. The Cuban delegate sparked a diplomatic row when he dismissed US allegations of Cuban drug trafficking and sought to shift participants' critical gaze toward the United States by circulating a pamphlet with a section entitled, "United States Imperialistic Penetration of the Economic, Agricultural and Health Phases of Cuban Life, before the Castro Regime." Attempting to resituate the struggle over drug control as a battle over sovereignty and the healthful use of national resources, the Cubans declared "all American countries have a common enemy in the United States in their struggle for a better health standard."[172] While the determined effort by US officials to implement their vision of drug control had been bolstered by the persistent effort to limit the circulation of drugs for medical and scientific needs, this Cuban challenge effectively questioned the political underpinnings of public health invocations, even while trying to claim the mantle of an alternative model to that being advanced by the United States. The US delegation believed Cuba's main goal at the meeting was to "win friends for their Communist regime," and the confrontation inspired US allegations of Cuban drug trafficking that persisted into the next century.[173] By 1961 the FBN identified "Cuban nationals" as the force behind drug trafficking in the United States, and despite evidence that it was Cuban exiles rather than Castro loyalists behind the trade, deliberately cultivated the perception of Cuban government complicity, including a salacious report of narcotics seizures in an apartment "bedecked with pictures of Fidel Castro and the Cuban Communist flag."[174] One US congressman went so far as to suggest a more intimate connection between the revolution and narcotics: "It is my personal opinion that Castro himself must be a mighty good customer for this stuff by the way he carries on."[175]

. . .

Drugs and war came together in unique ways as the growing influence of the United States confronted Cold War and anticolonial opposition at mid-century and beyond. New drugs brought promise as well as peril, and while the US government and corporations sought to secure access to raw materials and control over the manufacturing of drug commodities, they devoted considerable attention to policing drug production and consumption outside of their envisioned system of controls. National and international drug control initiatives across the decade of the 1950s implemented unprecedented legal sanctions for drug crimes that was bolstered by the historically constructed belief in a drug crisis that linked select drug users to communism, the spread of disease, social subversion, racial revolt, and criminality. New legislation introduced mandatory minimum sentences and capital punishment for drug violations and became a new and potent pillar of the US government's coercive power to police at home and abroad.

In the context of the Korean War, the civil rights movement, and revolutionary upheavals in the Americas, drug warriors selectively identified the "drug menace" by targeting groups deemed threatening to the economic and social order. In practice, the cry of "dope pushers" was leveled against the Cold War Communist enemies of the United States and mobilized domestically to limit the impact of black cultural expressions and political challenges to white power. When the media, public officials, and scientists labeled those who were arrested as "addicts," they effectively concealed the political and cultural biases built into the new system of policing and controls, rendering the targeted communities "criminal" and empowering new instruments of class- and race-based social control in a language of scientific neutrality. A new vision of the hazards of uncontrolled drug production and consumption became a critical weapon in the US Cold War arsenal as it sought to secure its hegemony on a global scale.

Conclusion

When the Committee on Appropriations of the United States Congress met in March 1963 to review the annual budget for the Treasury Department's Federal Bureau of Narcotics, the session began with a series of effusive tributes in honor of the agency's first and recently retired leader, Commissioner Harry J. Anslinger. After more than three decades at the helm of the FBN, Anslinger had stepped down from his post, although he remained active in the field of drug control through his ongoing appointment as US representative to the UN Commission on Narcotic Drugs. Congressmen from Virginia, Louisiana, New York, Massachusetts, and Oklahoma joined in a chorus of praise: "It has been largely through his influence and his unswerving devotion to duty that control over narcotic addiction has been achieved in the United States." The accolades to his dedicated service in transforming the domestic policing of drugs were reinforced by homages to his international profile: "As the first Commissioner of Narcotics, Harry Anslinger became a world renowned figure in the regulation of the production and distribution of narcotic drugs. Always aware of the legitimate use of narcotics, he has throughout his long and enviable career protected the application of those drugs to their necessary use." Special mention was made of the fact that he had been the 1962 recipient of the American Pharmaceutical Association's "coveted Remington Medal," awarded to the "individual who has done the most for American pharmacy." A jury consisting of past presidents of this organization of professional pharmacists honored Anslinger for his work as an "humanitarian and international servant of the people, for his outstanding contribution to the public health and to the profession of pharmacy through control and suppression of illicit traffic in and use of narcotic drugs and for able representation of the US government in international affairs."[1]

The nature of the occasion lent itself to hyperbole and overly optimistic projections: US "control over narcotic addiction" had not in fact been achieved, and the policing, prosecution, and consumption of (legal and illegal) drugs escalated throughout the remainder of the twentieth century—a consequence in part of the policing and profit-making apparatus the FBN helped build in the 1940s and 1950s. The contemporary praise for Anslinger's role in institutionalizing both national and international drug control suggests that by the 1960s the FBN commissioner had cemented his historic reputation as the nation's first drug czar. More significant than Anslinger's public prominence and recognized leadership, the tributes spoke to deeper structural factors, particularly the economic and political interests that made drug control such a viable vehicle for consolidating and expanding US power. The US government had been concerned with drug control since the early decades of the twentieth century, but it was not until World War II and the early Cold War that the nation wielded sufficient political and economic influence to dictate the regulatory logic and economic hierarchies of an assertive international drug control regime. Celebrations of Anslinger attest to the consensus among policymakers and pharmaceutical industry representatives of the material and symbolic importance of drug control to national security, public health, and private profit making. And while the first commissioner of the Federal Bureau of Narcotics is most famous for his strident public condemnations of illicit drugs, drug users, and infectious enemy drug traffickers, congressmen joined with pharmaceutical industry representatives in emphasizing his contributions to the legal drug industry, praising his efforts on behalf of "American pharmacy" and the promotion of the "legitimate use of narcotics." They explicitly tied the health of the country and the legal drug industry to the enforcement and regulation of self-interested definitions of illegality.

Only a decade and a half before these public tributes, the FBN commissioner had warned Congress of a new and troubling development. In 1947 a "tremendous quantity of cocaine" had surfaced in Peru after the "cocaine traffic had been practically nonexistent for more than 15 years." It is likely that the perceived spike in cocaine trafficking was a result of heightened policing rather than supply or consumer demand, but by 1950 Anslinger attributed a minor reduction in cocaine seizures to effective "enforcement activity of the Peruvian Government."[2] The US government sponsored hemispheric policing in the named pursuit of drug control, and launched an assertive campaign to implement an international drug control regime through the regulatory authority of the United Nations. The 1961 Single Convention on Narcotic Drugs was one culmination of this effort: a treaty that to this day delineates the definitions and reach of international drug control policy.

The principles enshrined in the Single Convention reveal the persistent and defining influence of particular US-based economic and political priorities on the global policing of drugs. Even though Anslinger initially opposed the Single Convention, for what he viewed as its lax enforcement powers and potential to inflame Soviet and anticolonial ambitions in countries where drug raw materials were cultivated, he worked to ensure US corporate and government interests were enshrined within it. US pharmaceutical companies exercised considerable influence over the parameters of national and international drug control. When the CND met to discuss an early draft of the convention in 1955, attendees were invited to a "luncheon" at Merck and Co., Inc.'s laboratory in Rahway, New Jersey, with transportation provided by the company.[3] Even without a record of what transpired when UN representatives working on drug control lunched at Merck's facilities, the sustained lines of access to regulatory officials, the sharing of social spaces, and mutual work devising drug policy exemplified US economic and political dominance. FBN officials also pursued formal interventions on behalf of US companies. Consistently throughout the negotiations, Anslinger spoke for the interests of Maywood Chemical Works, Coca-Cola's supplier, informing executives from both companies that he had succeeded in securing the "desired language" in the Single Convention—specifically he had "proposed an additional sentence to insure that the use, etc., of the coca leaves for decocainized flavoring extract be considered a legitimate purpose . . . which I hope will be satisfactory, as recognizing the legitimate need for Coca Cola."[4] The principles that guided the delineation of legality were carefully constructed so as to sustain a legitimate market for US manufacturers while stigmatizing other uses as "illegitimate." The vice president of Coca-Cola wrote Anslinger in gratitude: "It is most fortunate that you intervened in the Commission's proceedings as deftly and decisively as you did and that your position was sustained. . . . It need scarcely be said that your action is most warmly gratifying."[5]

Even more striking, during a series of meetings and conferences geared toward gaining widespread acquiescence to the Single Convention's implementation, FBN officials actively intervened to guarantee sufficient quantities of raw material be available to US pharmaceutical manufacturers. Establishing a political economy of legality tied to North American economic priorities entailed more than simply enshrining favorable definitions of legality in the language of the treaty. When some delegates saw the treaty negotiations as an opportunity to pressure Andean countries to reduce the quantities of coca leaf being grown, anxious US representatives agreed but wanted assurance that the reduction would not affect coca fields being grown for export to US manufacturers. FBN officials specifically demanded not a reduction but an expansion of coca fields being grown for Maywood, to secure "sufficient quantity of coca leaf for the needs of this important industry."[6] After negotiations among Maywood representatives and US and Peruvian officials, the chief of the UN CND, also on the scene, approvingly observed that he "believed deliveries of these commercial supplies, intended for flavoring extract, would naturally reduce the availability of leaves for chewing."[7] By 1962, securing the interests of manufacturing countries in drug control was thus presented as a mechanism for "reducing the availability" of raw materials that might be used to other ends—specifically in this context it presented an attack on indigenous communities' consumption and use of the leaves on their own terms.[8] Definitions of legitimacy were entrenched within an unequal hemispheric hierarchy whereby the countries that produced raw materials were encouraged to steer national production exclusively toward an export market geared toward the industrial nations, reflecting and exacerbating not only the unequal relations between nations involved in the coca trade, but also contributing to hierarchies of political and economic power among different peoples within those nations. Drug control became a mechanism for extending US influence into the domestic and international life of its allies and enemies alike.

The trajectory of drug control implementation in the Andes is particularly revealing in this regard. In 1960, as a "result of the enactment of the Legislation on Narcotics," the Bolivian government came into the possession of 130 kilos of cocaine. Bolivia contacted the Pan American Sanitary Bureau (PASB)—an institution which by then served as the World Health Organization's regional control center for the Americas[9]—which in turn contacted the WHO in Geneva asking for advice: "The Government would like to find a legal way of selling the Cocaine and has asked our advice as to the procedure to be use[d] in this case."[10] By 1960, countries like Bolivia that had been especially targeted by the drug control apparatus as producers of raw materials for the manufacturing of narcotic drugs were forced to bargain for inclusion in the international marketplace within the framework established by the control regime. Both Bolivia and Peru had resisted elements of the drug control regime's implementation. They were nevertheless forced to contend with its logic not merely as gestures of international diplomacy, but as a prerequisite for a viable position in an economic order increasingly dominated by the United States. In this particular instance, Bolivia was seeking to transform into legitimate commodities drugs that the government had seized from "illicit" channels, searching for "a legal way of selling Cocaine."

The drug control regime, however, effectively excluded Bolivia from participating in the marketing of manufactured drugs. The WHO responded to the PASB petition and explained, "Bolivia may grant an authorization to export the cocaine to a country which has issued a prior import authorization." Yet, in an international drug marketplace where import and export authorizations were hard to come by for a nonestablished manufacturer, it was highly unlikely that Bolivia was going to obtain the necessary certificates. The most logical outlet for the cocaine, the United States, as a matter of policy only imported the raw material in any case. Under the terms of the 1931 Geneva Convention's regulatory provisions, which would soon be reproduced and subsumed by the 1961 Single Convention's ratification, the relevant article for contraband drugs that had been seized was "interpreted to permit domestic use for medical or scientific purposes of drugs appropriated by a government, but not the export of such drugs."[11] This meant that once rendered "illicit," drugs could only be channeled back into legal domestic markets, presumably since the quotas and limits within the legal international market would be exceeded if "illicit" drugs were added to the field. Bolivia, as a primary producer of drug raw materials in a regulatory climate oriented toward supply-side controls, was a particularly precarious petitioner for inclusion in the international cocaine trade.

The hierarchies of participation within the coca commodity chain— and international drug markets more generally—were firmly entrenched by the time of this incident. Those countries that might participate in given stages of drug production and manufacturing had been codified in international policy. Countries that cultivated the raw material, the coca leaf, were locked into a system where they were effectively excluded from any significant participation within the market for manufactured drug commodities, except as consumers of North American or European manufactured goods. Even while Bolivia and Peru persisted for the next half century in defending domestic coca leaf production and chewing, they recognized the authority of the international control regime, as was evident in Bolivia's petition to the PASB for guidance, as well as in both countries' ratification of the 1961 Single Convention, even while expressing official reservations regarding a provision that required the complete elimination of coca leaf chewing within twenty-five years of ratification. Participation within the international market was predicated upon acceptance of the authority of the international policing apparatus and the categories of legitimacy and criminality that traveled with it. So, in the Andes where domestic consumption of the leaf persists, indigenous growers and consumers continue to operate at the precarious borders of legality.

The Single Convention was designed to "replace all the existing multilateral treaties in the field . . . and extend full international control to the raw materials of narcotic drugs." This purpose depended on the careful delineation of what constituted the legal, and defining at what stage and in whose hands raw materials became contraband. The WHO, which acted in a scientific advisory capacity to the CND, called for the coca leaf to be subject to the tightest regulatory controls. Moreover, reflecting the previous two decades of drug control initiatives, those working toward the convention's implementation envisioned only three legitimate uses of the coca leaf, namely: "(a) the production of flavouring agents; (b) the medical and scientific needs, (c) chewing wherever it is a licit practice." Then, of momentous import, the WHO added a caveat, "It should be borne in mind that of these three legitimate purposes, only the first is likely to remain permanent because the therapeutic value of cocaine is more and more put in question and because chewing may only be permitted for a limited period of time—up to 25 years after ratification of the Convention by a country."[12]

In 1961, the WHO predicted that of the three then recognized legitimate uses of coca leaves, only one under the Single Convention would retain its legitimacy into the future: coca's use as a "flavouring agent" for the manufacturing of Coca-Cola. Even as increased production of Coca-Cola was contributing to the status of the United States as the largest stockpiler of cocaine (a by-product of the flavor manufacturing process), the WHO's assessment of the gradual disappearance of the second "legitimate purpose," the extraction of cocaine for "medical and scientific need," reflected general scientific sentiment. The impact of a dreamed-of future dominated by synthetic drugs, along with a growing faith in the wonders of laboratory science to create better, more potent substitutes, was apparent in the common perception of the time that the medicinal market for cocaine would disappear. Not all contemporaries embraced this prediction. When Dr. James W. Brown encountered a report in a 1969 article in *U.S. News and World Report* that echoed the WHO's vision when it suggested that there was "no accepted medical use" of cocaine, he worriedly contacted the government:

> I find cocaine one of the two or three most basic drug needs in my practice as I do a lot of nasal surgery under local and topical anesthetic. I have used it for twenty-one years and do not feel the drug is hazardous if properly used. I concur in its strict control but I do not feel that those of us who find it essential to their practices should be deprived of its use. . . . I have tried numerous other synthetic topical anesthetics and have found nothing to compare with its efficacy, both as an anesthetic and as a shrinking agent.[13]

Dr. Brown argued for cocaine's critical and incomparable value to medical science, even while he conceded the need for "its strict control."

The drug control apparatus directed the flow of commodities, such that the same drug might be licit or illicit depending on the context. Forecasts of cocaine's disappearance were in fact inaccurate: to this day "medical and scientific" uses of cocaine have persisted even while the prominence of cocaine as a target of various US government administrations' "wars on drugs" has meant that many people are largely unaware of the continuing legitimate uses for goods manufactured from the coca leaf—or the political, economic, cultural, and racial biases that historically produced the multiple legal designations and ideological significations. While indigenous coca leaf growers and consumers in the Andes are forced to defend against assaults on their cultural practices, the field of US corporate participation in the coca leaf and cocaine trade seems to have grown. In 2012 the US Drug Enforcement Agency (DEA), the contemporary successor to the FBN, registered at least four authorized importers of coca leaves, five companies authorized to import cocaine, and fourteen companies authorized to manufacture it. From the limited information revealed in the filings, the end products derived from coca leaves and their potential productive powers are varied. One company, Stepan Pharmaceutical (which acquired Maywood in 1961 and continues to provide coca leaf flavoring extract to the Coca-Cola Company), as the DEA explained, "plans to import the listed controlled substance [coca leaves] to manufacture bulk controlled substance for distribution to its customer." Other companies planned on using the leaves both for distribution to customers and for "research and analytical standards." Companies manufacturing cocaine similarly seem to do so for a variety of not always publicly clarified purposes: "for the manufacture of reference standards," for "sale to researchers and analytical labs," for use in "clinical, toxicological, and forensic laboratories," and mysteriously for manufacturing "the listed controlled substances in bulk [cocaine] for sale to its customers."[14] According to the most recently available annual statistics compiled by the UN Drug Supervisory Body (responsible for overseeing the international system of import and export controls designed to limit the market to "legitimate" medical and scientific demand), the United States in 2010 was the world's only importer and utilizer of coca leaves and the "main reason for utilization was to manufacture a flavouring agent, while cocaine and ecgonine were obtained as by-products."[15] Nevertheless, the belief in the 1960s that the "therapeutic power of cocaine is more and more put into question" was also indicative of the general impact of a drug control logic through which a commodity itself came to embody all sorts of dangers, even if inevitably these associations continued to vary according to consumers and context.

Finally, when we turn to the third "legitimate use" of the coca leaf enshrined in the Single Convention, the hierarchies of nation, class, and cultural bias in the operations of drug control are starkly apparent. The Single Convention presented a new challenge to coca growing countries and particularly their indigenous peoples. For years Peru and Bolivia had responded to the drug regulatory priorities of industrial countries with compromise and resistance. Bolivia had signed onto an early League of Nations convention in 1925 and Peru had ratified the 1931 Geneva Convention; however, both countries did so with specific reservations that they would not try to limit domestic consumption of the coca leaf.[16] The 1961 Single Convention required that all parties to it abolish the practice of coca leaf chewing within their countries within twenty-five years of their national ratification of the treaty. Peru ratified it in 1964 and Bolivia in 1965. Both countries continued to resist this provision even after the transitional period had passed. The issue remains contentious and, in fact, the fate of the status quo was called into question with a twenty-first-century Bolivian government proposal to have the ban on coca leaf chewing completely removed from the Single Convention, and barring this, Bolivia would denounce and withdraw from the convention, and re-accede without recognizing the criminalization of coca leaf chewing. In January 2011, at the very end of the UN-mandated eighteen-month wait period for such proposals to either be challenged or become law, the United States and a few other countries submitted formal objections. Bolivia subsequently withdrew its accession of the treaty and only in 2013 re-acceded with a firm reservation that it did not recognize coca leaf chewing as criminal. The events have promoted a broad public debate internationally about the wisdom of the ban on coca leaf chewing, the exclusion of countries like Bolivia from participating in the international trade for coca-derived products, and the heavy toll drug control takes on poor and indigenous communities confronting prohibitions on traditional and nonexport market-oriented uses of the coca leaf.

The president of Bolivia, Evo Morales, argued the ban violated the recently adopted UN Declaration on the Rights of Indigenous Peoples, in particular that "indigenous peoples have the right to maintain, control, protect and develop their cultural heritage, traditional knowledge, and traditional cultural expressions."[17] Bolivia's casting of this drug control debate as a question of indigenous sovereignty and defense of tradition has garnered support for its challenge to the UN Single Convention from around the world, and most significantly across South America. This unprecedented challenge issued by the first Aymara president of a nation comprising the world's largest population of indigenous coca leaf chewers to the General Assembly of the United Nations reflects an important moment in the history of international drug control, whatever the outcome. Unfortunately the petition and the limited scope of its objective (it is not a call for decriminalization or for fundamentally challenging the tenets which guide the political economy of drug control) reflects the persistence of the logic and practical foundations of international drug control that remains wedded to the powers and interests of the United States and the global capitalist system its influence has sustained.

Nevertheless, increasingly vocal criticisms of the drug control regime persist both nationally and internationally in the face of its obvious failures in curbing drug use, in generating unprecedented levels of violence stretching from Mexico, through Central America and South America, and in devastating countless numbers of lives through mass incarceration for drug consumption. While important, many of these debates get trapped within the deceptively neutral logic of the drug control regime itself, for instance by focusing on the question of whether drug use should be treated as a crime or an illness (in the midst of the aggressive cultural and medical promotion of legal drugs), or whether some drugs, like marijuana or coca leaves, should be removed from regulatory oversight (as if the drug properties themselves have been the primary determinant of legal status). The so-called drug problem will not be eliminated until the political economy of drug control and its origins in the logic and structural hierarchies sustaining US global power are directly addressed. There seems to be some promising movement in this direction with organizations such as the Global Commission on Drug Policy arguing that criminalization has fueled rather than reduced a global drug pandemic, and in a June 2011 report, the commission cited Bolivia's challenge to the UN ban on coca leaf chewing as a welcome frontal assault on "drug control imperialism."[18]

The drug control apparatus emerged as a mechanism for policing and protecting selectively designated "legitimate" drug production—and created a seemingly neutral, medically backed, and socially promoted framework for the policing of people and activities that seemed to threaten the envisioned social and economic order. In the United States, drug manufactures, pharmaceutical executives, and scientists collaborated with the Federal Bureau of Narcotics and the United Nations to secure their markets while limiting and controlling the parameters of others' participation. Modern laboratory science created a whole new array of products that helped propel the United States into a dominant global position as the primary supplier of mass-manufactured drugs and medicines. The capacity to refashion raw materials seemed limitless. The process of securing and limiting to the industrial world access to raw materials used to manufacture finished drug commodities emerged with the establishment of a US-led policing apparatus that enforced and legitimized the boundaries of legality. US political and economic leaders proffered the country's unique ability, role, and function as the preeminent global suppliers of manufactured drugs, as seeming proof of the advantages of US capitalism not just for the country but also for the world. The logic of drug control was such that these same goods became dangerous when their production, distribution, and consumption were not confined to "legitimate" sites and participants. The construction of this legitimacy was influenced by national, social, racial, and economic biases. As with coca leaves and laboratory chemicals, certain groups of people too became part of the landscape of raw material, to be refashioned, "developed," and guided along a path toward appropriate participation within the marketplace, or even isolated from the general populace so as not to spread antisocial disease.

The US pharmaceutical industry grew in tandem with the rise of US political power and depended on the concurrent fashioning of a regulatory and policing apparatus to secure their mutual dominance. The production of drug commodities and their valorization as harbingers of a future relieved of illness through technological breakthroughs became a foundation for the expansion of US capitalism, and often provided a seemingly objective explanation for obstacles to its success. At mid-century in the Andes, elites paired with international experts to stigmatize indigenous coca leaf consumption by characterizing it as an impediment to Indian development, societal progress, and modernization more generally. Similarly, the escalation of criminal penalties in US domestic politics was a direct response to the political turmoil presented by the intersection of the Cold War and the civil rights movement; in particular, the threat posed by African American challenges to white cultural and economic hegemony. The public mobilization of fear and cultivated sense of crisis attributed to Communist dope-pushers and an infectious black criminality led to the dramatic escalation of criminal penalties associated with drug consumption and distribution and the disproportionate incarceration of African Americans. From the human guinea pigs who filled US Public Health Service narcotic farms and provided valuable research material for pharmaceutical development and experimentation, to the Andean peasant farmers subject to anthropological and social experiments that degraded traditional culture (including coca) in the service of producing modern, wage-earning citizens, the burdens of the enforcement regime have been carried by the poor, racialized minorities and the politically and economically disenfranchised. The history of the establishment of the international drug control apparatus and the particular history of the coca leaf within it together reveal the twentieth-century dynamics of American imperialism. US dominance over policing and the political economy of the international drug trade was predicated on the production of drug commodities and consuming citizen-subjects as raw materials for fashioning a US-centered capitalist world.

Acknowledgments

This project would never have come to fruition without the incredible guidance, support, and confidence bestowed on me by mentors, friends, family, and colleagues. It is an honor to be able to express my appreciation for all the people whose encouragement over the years has made this book possible.

I began working on this project as a doctoral student at New York University in the late 1990s—a magical place populated and inspired by a brilliant assembly of faculty and students. A special thank you to Jamie Wilson and Mireille Miller-Young, who went through the program with me and whose joy for life, intellectual camaraderie, and friendship have anchored me ever since. For sharing the fun of intellectual community and exchange, thank you Valeria Coronel, Betsy Esch, Christopher Winks, Kim Gilmore, Dayo Gore, Bryant Terry, Forrest Hylton, Jasmine Mir, Peter Hudson, Eric McDuffie, Orlando Plaza, Rich Blint, Daniel Inouyé, Adria Imada, Julie Sze, Grace Wang, Victor Viesca, Hillina Seife, Sobukwe Odinga, Michelle Chase, Dan Rood, David Kinkela, Seth Markle, Ted Sammons, Khary Polk, Njoroge Njoroge, and Kobi Abayomi.

I am deeply indebted to Robin D. G. Kelley for his generosity of spirit, intellectual rigor, and political commitment—a beautiful person whose example since my undergraduate days has shaped the kind of scholar I aspire to be, and whose support has helped me get to where I am today. A warm thank you to Sinclair Thomson for consistently believing in the value of this work, and for his gentle guidance as I grappled with my ideas and sought out people and archives in Peru and Bolivia. Marilyn Young, Greg Grandin, Michael Gomez, Ada Ferrer, Allen Hunter, and Jeremy Adelman all provided mentorship and models of scholarship of worldly consequence.

Walter Johnson's graduate seminar on American capitalism provided the critical space for this project's genesis, and a decade later being a fellow at Harvard University's Charles Warren Center for Studies in American History for a year under his and Vincent Brown's able stewardship helped me transform the research into this book—I am grateful for both. Our wonderful cohort of fellows—Patrick Wolfe, Marisa Fuentes, Kristen Block, Paul Kramer, Joshua Guild, Cynthia Young, Gunther Peck, and Edward Rugemer—brought good humor, intellectual imaginings, lunchtime bonding, and dance-filled evenings that sustained my efforts and continue to fortify and inspire. And thank you to Larissa Kennedy and Arthur Patton-Hock for taking such good care of us during our residency.

I have benefited from participating in both formal and informal exchanges with numerous scholars whose own work, insightful comments, critical questioning, and interest in the project challenged me in important and productive ways—while some of those providing this feedback did not agree with my premise or conclusions, the book has benefited enormously from many moments of lively intellectual discussion and debate. For all of this I need to shout out, in no particular order, Pablo Morales, Michael Fox, and Christy Thornton of the North American Congress on Latin America, Nikhil Pal Singh, David Roediger, Laura Briggs, Linda Farthing, Jesse Freeston, Mary Renda, Adam Rothman, Brian DeLay, Amy Greenberg, David Kazanjian, Joseph Nevins, Mark Weisbrot, Rachel St. John, Sven Beckert, Alison Frank Johnson, Bruce Schulman, Brooke Blower, Bethany Moreton, Stephen Mihm, Shane Hamilton, Colleen Dunlavy, Sarah Haley, Allan Kulikoff, Jessica Lepler, Steve J. Stern, Francisco Scarano, Jeremi Suri, William Cronon, Florencia Mallon, Alfred W. McCoy, Nan Enstad, Stephen Kantrowitz, Brenda Gayle Plummer, Mark G. Hanna, Christine Hunefeldt, John Marino, Luis Alvarez, Daniel Widener, Takashi Fujitani, Everade Meade, Michael Monteon, Michael Parrish, Nathaniel Lee Smith, Matt R. Pembleton, Daniel Weimer, Jeremy Kuzmarov, Jonathan V. Marshall, William B. McAllister, William O. Walker III, Brian O'Connor, and the anonymous reviewers of my book manuscript.

I am thankful for the support and intellectual stimulation I received from a wonderful group of friends and scholars that I have met at the

University of Hawai'i Mānoa, including Cyndi Franklin, Matt Romaniello, Ned Bertz, Becky Pulju, Marcus Daniel, Vina Lanzona, Noelani M. Arista, Wensheng Wang, Shana Brown, Rich Rath, Kieko Matteson, Mimi Henriksen, Bob McGlone, Herb Zeigler, Jim Kraft, Jerry Bentley, Dick Rapson, Matt Lauzon, Kim Lauzon, Ned Davis, David Chappell, Leonard Andaya, Yuma Totani, David Hanlon, Karen Jolly, Jun Yoo, Elizabeth Colwill, Peter Arnade, Vernadette Gonzalez, Robert Perkinson, Mari Yoshihara, Ming-Bao Yue, Wimal Dissannayake, John Rieder, Christina Bacchilega, Laura Lyons, Richard Nettell, Craig Howes, Ruth Hsu, Yun Peng, John Zuern, Monisha Das Gupta, Hokulani Aikau, Lois Horton, Johanna Almiron, Anthony Johnson, Jonathon Osorio, Joy Logan, David Stannard, Patricio Abinales, Mari Matsuda, Charles Lawrence, John Charlot, Loriena Yancura, Paul Holtrop, Paul Lyons, and Monica Ghosh.

I am especially grateful to Niels Hooper at the University of California Press for his backing of this project, along with the staff there whose skills have made the editing process smooth and enjoyable — Kim Hogeland, Wendy Dherin, and Kate Hoffman, thank you. Thanks to Paul Tyler for his editing prowess, and to Sebastaian Araya for sharing his considerable talents as a cartographer. Thank you to all the people who helped me acquire the necessary permissions for images contained in the text, especially Richard Sorensen of the Smithsonian American Art Museum, Eisha Neely of the Division of Rare and Manuscript Collections, Cornell University, and Annie Rothstein-Segan, who graciously allowed me to reproduce a photograph from her father's collection.

In addition to the sources already mentioned, this project was made possible with financial support from numerous institutions including New York University's Graduate School of Arts & Sciences, NYU's Department of History, NYU's Center for Latin American and Caribbean Studies, NYU's International Center for Advanced Studies' Project on the Cold War as Global Conflict, and the King Juan Carlos I of Spain Center. I am also grateful for grants received from Princeton University's Committee on Research in the Humanities and Social Sciences, the University of Hawai'i Mānoa's University Research Council, and support received from UH's Department of History. These funds enabled me to visit numerous archives, libraries, and private collections in Europe, the United States, and South America. I am forever indebted to the amazing librarians and archivists who deftly helped me navigate the historical record. Of special note are Fred Romanski and Tab Lewis at the US National Archives and Records Administration, who brought to my attention the records of the Board of Economic Warfare, and Mr. P. Massaoutis at the World Health Organization in Geneva, who let me occupy his office pouring over records for hours. I am also thankful for the warmth and generosity of Marcos Cueto, who welcomed me into his home and personal archives in Lima, Peru, at a critical formative stage of the work. Thanks are also due to Silvia Rivera Cusicanqui, whose home in La Paz is an important oasis for activists and scholars working to decriminalize coca and advocate for indigenous rights. Thank you to Dr. Fernando Cabiesis, Dr. Uriel García Cacerés, Jaime Durand, Rafael Fernández Stoll, Rossana Barragán, and Alison L. Spedding, for taking the time to speak with me about their own historic involvement with the politics of coca and drugs in the Andes. Much respect to my fellow traveler and friend Hernan Pruden, who showed me the living archive of the coca market in Bolivia, introduced me to the art of coca leaf chewing, and brought me to *fiestas* where life in the Andes is constantly renewed.

It is a great pleasure to acknowledge the immeasurable sustenance I have received from friends and family over the years. I would like to say a special thank you to Giovanni Vitiello for his friendship, sense of humor, and the joy and laughter he so easily keeps alive. Thank you to Christy Ringor and Greg Chun for keeping it realer, for feeding me, and for bringing a beautiful future revolutionary into the world. Thank you to Katti Wachs, Meredith Sterling, Will Lara, and Haik Hoisington for believing in me and for friendships I will always treasure. Thank you to Stan Pyrzanowski and the Rhythm Method for all the music and good times. Thank you to the Njoroge family for all the support. Thank you to my mother, Jean Reiss, and my brothers, Matthew and Justin, for indulging my intellectual explorations and sharing in the love and hilarity of life. Thank you to Patricia Hilden, whose political passion and astute eye have always inspired and guided my own belief in the power of academics to make a real difference in the world. Thank you to my amazing father, Timothy Reiss, who taught by example the value of hard work, and whose love has always given me strength. And thank you to Njoroge Njoroge, the love of my life.

Notes

CMM   Carlos Monge Medrano Papers (in the possession of Dr. Marcos Cueto, Instituto de Estudios Peruanos, Lima, Peru)

DEA   Drug Enforcement Administration Library and Archive (Washington, DC)

HUA   Harvard Law School Library, Harvard University Archives (Cambridge, Massachusetts)

LNA   League of Nations Archives (Geneva, Switzerland)

MRECB   Archivo del Ministerio de Relaciones Exteriores y Culto (La Paz, Bolivia)

NACP   US National Archives (College Park, Maryland)

PAHO   Pan-American Health Organization (La Paz, Bolivia)

RFA   Rockefeller Foundation Archives (Tarrytown, New York)

RWL   Robert Woodruff Library, Emory University (Atlanta, Georgia)

UNANY   United Nations Archive (New York, New York)

WHOA   World Health Organization Archives (Geneva, Switzerland)

INTRODUCTION

1. Richard Nixon, "Special Message to the Congress on Control of Narcotics and Dangerous Drugs," July 14, 1969, online by Gerhard Peters and John T. Woolley, *The American Presidency Project,* www.presidency.ucsb.edu/ws/?pid = 2126; Richard Nixon, "Telephone Remarks to Students and Educators

Attending a Drug Education Seminar in Monroe, Louisiana," October 4, 1971, online by Gerhard Peters and John T. Woolley, *The American Presidency Project.* www.presidency.ucsb.edu/ws/?pid = 3179.

2. For two examples, taken from a vast literature, that reflect this focus on the late 1960s forward as the critical formative moment in the drug war, see Dan Baum, *Smoke and Mirrors: The War on Drugs and the Politics of Failure* (New York: Little, Brown, 1997); Jeremy Kuzmarov, *The Myth of the Addicted Army: Vietnam and the Modern War on Drugs* (Boston: University of Massachusetts Press, 2009)

3. William O. Walker, *Opium and Foreign Policy: The Anglo-American Search for Order in Asia, 1912–1954* (Chapel Hill: University of North Carolina Press, 1991).

4. David F. Musto, *The American Disease: Origins of Narcotics Control* (New York: Oxford University Press, 1973), vii.

5. H. Wayne Morgan, *Drugs in America: A Social History, 1800–1980* (New York: Syracuse University Press, 1981), 143–44; Douglas Clark Kinder and William O. Walker III, "Stable Force in a Storm: Harry J. Anslinger and United States Narcotic Foreign Policy, 1930–1962," *Journal of American History* 72, no. 4 (March 1, 1986): 912.

6. "Peru: The White Goddess," "Scare with a Smile," and "Clear Voice," *Time,* April 11, 1949, 44.

7. "Cuba Enforces Vaccinations," *New York Times,* March 24, 1949, 10.

8. "Navy to Fly Vaccine to Cuba," *New York Times,* March 29, 1949, 22.

9. Paul Gootenberg, ed., *Cocaine: Global Histories* (New York: Routledge, 1999); Paul Gootenberg, *Andean Cocaine: The Making of a Global Drug* (Chapel Hill: University of North Carolina Press, 2008); Joseph F. Spillane, *Cocaine: From Medical Marvel to Modern Menace in the United States, 1884–1920* (Baltimore: Johns Hopkins University Press, 2000); Michael M. Cohen, "Jim Crow's Drug War: Race, Coca-Cola and the Southern Origins of Drug Prohibition," *Southern Cultures* 12, no. 3 (Fall 2006): 55–79.

10. United Nations, *Narcotic Drugs: Estimated World Requirements for 2012—Statistics for 2010* (New York: UN Office on Drugs and Crime, April 2012), 206–7.

11. Musto, *American Disease;* Morgan, *Drugs in America;* David T. Courtwright, *Forces of Habit: Drugs and the Making of the Modern World* (Cambridge: Harvard University Press, 2001); Doris Marie Provine, *Unequal under Law: Race in the War on Drugs* (Chicago: University of Chicago Press, 2007); Curtiz Marez, *Drug Wars: The Political Economy of Narcotics* (Minneapolis: University of Minnesota Press, 2004).

12. David L. Herzberg, "The Pill You Love Can Turn on You," *American Quarterly* 58, no. 1 (March 2006): 82.

13. Charles O. Jackson, "The Amphetamine Democracy: Medicinal Abuse in the Popular Culture," *South Atlantic Quarterly* 74, no. 3 (1975): 323.

14. Lee V. Cassanelli, "Qat: Changes in the Production and Consumption of a Quasi-Legal Commodity," in *The Social Life of Things: Commodities in Cultural Perspective,* ed. Arjun Appadurai (New York: Cambridge University Press, 1986), 242.

15. Marez, *Drug Wars,* x.

16. Andre Gunder Frank, "The Wealth and Poverty of Nations: Even Heretics Remain Bound by Traditional Thought," *Economic and Political Weekly* 5, nos. 29/31, special number (July 1970): 1184.

17. The term "therapeutic revolution" is taken from Morgan, *Drugs in America,* 10.

18. Suzanna Reiss, "Beyond Supply and Demand: Obama's Drug Wars in Latin America," *NACLA Report on the Americas* (January/February 2010): 27–31.

19. "Declaracíon Conjunta," October 1, 2012, www.guatemala.gob.gt/index.php/2011–08–04–18–06–26/item/1656-declaraci%C3%B3n-conjunta.

1. "THE DRUG ARSENAL OF THE CIVILIZED WORLD"

1. Percy W. Bidwell, "Our Economic Warfare," *Foreign Affairs* 20, no. 3 (April 1942): 423.

2. Percy W. Bidwell, "Self-Containment and Hemisphere Defense," *Annals of the American Academy of Political and Social Science* 218, Public Policy in a World at War (November 1941): 179. For US economic warfare during World War II, see also Howard Daniel, "Economic Warfare," *Australian Quarterly* 15, no. 3 (1943): 62–67; Jonathan Marshall, *To Have and Have Not: Southeast Asian Raw Materials and the Origins of the Pacific War* (Berkeley: University of California Press, 1995); Donald G. Stevens, "Organizing for Economic Defense: Henry Wallace and the Board of Economic Warfare's Foreign Policy Initiatives, 1942," *Presidential Studies Quarterly* 26, no. 4 (October 1, 1996): 1126–39.

3. "Ample Opium, Other Drugs Stored, McNutt Declares," *Washington Post,* December 10, 1941.

4. Luis Galluba, "Pharmacy and the War," *Vital Speeches of the Day* 1, no. 3 (November 15, 1944): 90.

5. Paul V. McNutt, "How Do We Stand on Medical Drugs?" *Domestic Commerce* 27 (April 10, 1941): 333, 335.

6. Alfred D. Chandler Jr., *Scale and Scope: The Dynamics of Industrial Capitalism* (Cambridge, MA: Belknap Press of Harvard University Press, 1990): 164. For histories that deal with drugs and war, see David T. Courtwright, *Forces of Habit: Drugs and the Making of the Modern World* (Cambridge, MA: Harvard University Press, 2001); Roger Cooter, Mark Harrison, and Steve Sturdy, eds., *Medicine and Modern Warfare* (Atlanta: Rodopi, 1999).

7. James Le Fanu, *The Rise and Fall of Modern Medicine* (New York: Carroll & Graf, 2002), 206–17.

8. Daniel R. Headrick, "Botany, Chemistry, and Tropical Development," *Journal of World History* 7, no. 1 (Spring 1996): 15. See also Peter Neushul, "Science, Government, and the Mass Production of Penicillin," *Journal of the History of Medicine and Allied Sciences* 48 (October 1943): 371–95; E.F. Woodward, "Botanical Drugs: A Brief Review of the Industry with Comments on Recent Developments," *Economic Botany* 1, no. 4 (October–December 1947): 402–11.

9. "Morphine Substitute," *Science News Letter,* August 16, 1947, 98.

10. Charles Morrow Wilson, *Ambassadors in White: The Story of American Tropical Medicine* (New York: Kenikat Press, 1942), 324.

11. Apparently the surgeon general of the US Army had been granted authority in 1925 to stockpile opium that had been seized by authorities to be held in case of national emergency, but it is unclear whether these stockpiles were consolidated with those under the authority of the FBN. See US, Joint Army and Navy Munitions Board, *The Strategic and Critical Materials* (Washington, DC: Army and Navy Munitions Board, 1940), 26.

12. John C. McWilliams, "Unsung Partner against Crime: Harry J. Anslinger and the Federal Bureau of Narcotics, 1930–1962," *Pennsylvania Magazine of History and Biography* 113, no. 2 (April 1989): 221–22.

13. US House, Committee on Appropriations, *Treasury Department Appropriations Bill for 1941, Hearings before the Subcommittee on Appropriations for Treasury and Post Office Departments,* 76th Cong., 3d sess., 11–16, 18–19 December 1939, 4, 12 January 1940, 432.

14. US House, Committee on Appropriations, *Treasury Department Appropriations Bill for 1943, Hearings before the Subcommittee of the Committee on Appropriations House of Representatives,* 77th Cong., 2d sess., 6, 15–18 December 1941, 7–8 January 1942, 160.

15. McNutt, "How Do We Stand on Medical Drugs?" 333.

16. US House, *Appropriations Bill for 1943,* 163.

17. US House, *Act to Create in the Treasury Department a Bureau of Narcotics,* Public Law 71–357, 71st Cong., 2d sess., June 14, 1930.

18. Medical science defines narcotics as drugs derived from opium or opium-like compounds.

19. For overviews of international drug regulation, see William McAllister, *Drug Diplomacy in the Twentieth Century: An International History* (New York: Routledge, 2000); Arnold H. Taylor, *American Diplomacy and the Narcotics Traffic, 1900–1939: A Study in International Humanitarian Reform* (Durham, NC: Duke University Press, 1969); William O. Walker III, *Drug Control in the Americas* (Albuquerque: University of New Mexico Press, 1981); David F. Musto, *The American Disease: Origins of Narcotic Control* (New York: Oxford University Press, 1999); David R. Bewley-Taylor, *The United States and International Drug Control, 1909–1997* (New York: Pinter, 1999).

20. Anslinger to Morlock, March 18, 1942; File 0480–11, Drugs: Coca Leaves (1933–1953); 170–74–4; DEA; RG 170; NACP; US House, Committee on Appropriations, *Treasury Department Appropriations Bill for 1945, Hearings before the Subcommittee of the Committee on Appropriations House of Representatives,* 78th Cong., 2d sess., 29–30 November, 1–4, 6–9 December 1943, 539.

21. Douglas Clark Kinder and William O. Walker III, "Stable Force in a Storm: Harry J. Anslinger and United States Narcotic Foreign Policy, 1930–1962," *Journal of American History* 72, no. 4 (March 1, 1986): 919–20.

22. US House, Committee on Appropriations, *Treasury Department Appropriations Bill for 1944, Hearings before the Subcommittee on Appropriations for Treasury and Post Office Departments,* 78th Cong., 1st sess., 10–12, 14–16 December 1943, 8, 18 January 1944, 487.

23. For an overview of Anslinger's career see John C. McWilliams, *The Protectors: Harry J. Anslinger and the Bureau of Narcotics, 1930–1962* (Newark: University of Delaware Press, 1990). For Anslinger's own self-aggrandizing perspective see Harry J. Anslinger and William F. Tompkins, *The Traffic in Narcotics* (New York: Arno Press, 1981 [1953]); Harry J. Anslinger, *The Protectors: The Heroic of the Narcotics Agents, Citizens, and Officials in Their Unending, Unsung Battles Against Organized Crime in America and Abroad* (New York: Farrar, Straus, 1964).

24. US Senate, Committee on Military Affairs, *Strategic and Critical Materials and Minerals, Hearings before the Subcommittee of the Committee on Military Affairs*, 77th Cong., 1st sess., May–July 1941, 7, 16. By the end of the war the government collapsed "strategic and critical materials" into one category with subsets A, B, and C contingent on availability, explaining that "it had become impractical to differentiate clearly between the pre-war classifications." Within Group A, for which ongoing stockpiling was deemed essential, were included the drugs iodine, opium, quinidine, quinine, castor oil, emetine, and hyoscine. See US Military Academy, Department of Social Sciences, *Raw Materials in War and Peace* (West Point, NY: USMA AG Printing Office, 1947), 131, 159–61.

25. Dennis B. Whorthen, *Pharmacy in World War II* (New York: Haworth Press, 2004), 7.

26. For good historical overviews of the coca market see Paul Gootenberg, *Cocaine: Global Histories* (New York: Routledge, 1999); Paul Gootenberg, *Andean Cocaine: The Making of a Global Drug* (Chapel Hill: University of North Carolina Press, 2008); Joseph F. Spillane, *Cocaine: From Medical Marvel to Modern Menace in the United States, 1884–1920* (Baltimore: Johns Hopkins University Press, 2000); Steven B. Karch, *A Brief History of Cocaine* (New York: CRC Press, 1998).

27. "Coca Leaves," November 5, 1943; File 0480–11, Drugs: Coca Leaves (1933–1953); 170–74–4; DEA; RG 170; NACP.

28. There is an extensive literature on coca's role in Andean society from precolonial times to the present. A useful selection includes: Madeleine Barbara Léons and Harry Sanabria, *Coca, Cocaine, and the Bolivian Reality* (New York: State University of New York Press, 1977); René Bascopé Aspiazu, *La Veta Blanca: Coca y Cocaine en Bolivia* (La Paz: Ediciones Aquí, 1982); Joan Boldó i Clement, ed., *La Coca Andina: Visión Indígena de una Planta Satanizada* (Coyoacán, Mexico: Instituto Indigenista Interamericano, 1986); Deborah Pacini and Christine Franquemont, eds., *Coca and Cocaine: Effects on People and Policy in Latin America*, Cultural Survival Report 23 (Peterborough, NH: Transcript Printing, 1991); Fernando Cabieses, *La Coca ¿Dilema Trágico?* (Lima: Empresario Nacional de la Coca, 1992); Edmundo Morales, *Cocaine: White Gold Rush in Peru* (Tucson: University of Arizona Press, 1996); Silvia Rivera Cusicanqui, *Las Fronteras de la Coca: Epistemologías Colonialies y Circuitos Alternativos de la Hoja de Coca* (La Paz: Instituto de Investigaciones Sociológicas "Mauricio Lefebvre," Universidad San Andrés y Ediciones Ayuwiri, 2003).

29. In 1934 Bolivia's export market consisted of Argentina and Chile and a very small amount (probably for research purposes) in 1930 and 1932 to

Germany. UN Box 8070, Coca Leaf; R4945, 1933–1946; 12/8070; RG 8; Registry Files; LNA.

30. Gootenberg, *Andean Cocaine,* 125–28.

31. Oral history interview, Oscar R. Ewing, April 29, 1969, pp. 57–64, Truman Library, Independence, MO. The Coca-Cola Company was the only company as far as my research has shown to ever be granted permission by the FBN to use this coca-based flavoring extract; in effect the law was written exclusively for them.

32. Even though Peru had some limited legal production of cocaine hydrochloride for domestic consumption, there is evidence that, as in Bolivia, manufactured cocaine was in fact exported from Europe and the United States to Peru. Julian Greenup, Commercial Attaché, US Embassy Lima to Secretary of State, May 19, 1944; Folder 2, 1942–1944; File 0660, Peru; 71-A-3554, DEA; RG 170; NACP.

33. "Narcotic Drugs—Supplies, Stocks and Requirements," Report to Secretary General, January 20, 1944; UN Box R5031; RG 8, 749; Folder 12/41702/41702 "Post-War Drug Control in Territories of the US of A in Berne under the Jurisdiction of the Authorities of the United Nations"; Registry Files: 1933–1946; LNA.

34. "Continental Trade in Narcotic Drugs: General Observations," 1943; UN Box R5031; RG 8, 749; Folder 12/41702/41702 "Post-War Drug Control in Territories of the US of A in Berne under the Jurisdiction of the Authorities of the United Nations"; Registry Files: 1933–1946; LNA.

35. "Excerpt from Report, Dated April 27, 1938, from the American Consulate General at Callao-Lima, Peru"; Folder 1, 1926–1941; File 0660, Peru; 71-A-3554; DEA; RG 170; NACP; "Continental Trade in Narcotic Drugs: General Observations," 1943; UN Box R5031; RG 8, 749; Folder 12/41702/41702 "Post-War Drug Control in Territories of the US of A in Berne under the Jurisdiction of the Authorities of the United Nations"; Registry Files: 1933–1946; LNA; Julian Greenup, Commercial Attaché, US Embassy Lima to Secretary of State, May 19, 1944; Folder 2, 1942–1944; File 0660, Peru; 71-A-3554; DEA; RG 170; NACP.

36. T.W. Delahanty, "Drugs," *Domestic Commerce* (January 1944), 17.

37. Julian Greenup, Commercial Attaché, US Embassy Lima to Secretary of State, December 18, 1941; Folder 1, 1926–1941; File 0660, Peru; 71-A-3554; DEA; RG 170; NACP.

38. McAllister, *Drug Diplomacy,* 98.

39. Anslinger to Treasury Department, Memo, November 19, 1940; Folder 2, 1942–1944; File 0660, Peru; 71-A-3554; DEA; RG 170; NACP. For another reference to the "destruction of several thousand coca leaf plants on the island of Puerto Rico which were being grown for experimental purposes to determine whether the plant would thrive on this island and to supply the United States with its coca leaf quota, if this were found possible," see Anslinger to McClintock, Director, Division of Commodities and National Resources, Council of National Defense, February 27, 1941; Folder 1, 1926–1941; File 0660, Peru; 71-A-3554; DEA; RG 170; NACP.

40. "Joint Report of Messrs Ravndal, Nitze and Mann," Lima, January 3, 1942; File 459693; A1/Entry 500B; BEW; DEA; RG 169; NACP.

41. Memo, "Narcotics in Peru," Department of State, Division of the American Republics; Folder 2, 1942–1944; File 0660, Peru; 71-A-3554, DEA; RG 170; NACP.

42. Mr. White, Department of Monetary Research, Treasury Department, to Mr. H J Anslinger, Commissioner of Narcotics, May 23, 1942; Folder 2, 1942–1944; File 0660, Peru; 71-A-3554; DEA; RG 170; NACP.

43. State Department to the Bureau of Narcotics, September 4, 1941; Peru; Folder 1, 1926–1941; File 0660, 71-A-3554; DEA; RG 170; NACP.

44. Andrés A. Soberón, Huanuco, Peru, to BEW, Miscellaneous Commodity Division, October 26, 1942; Folder 2, 1942–1944; File 0660, Peru; 71-A-3554, DEA; RG 170; NACP.

45. Mr. White, Department of Monetary Research, Treasury Department, to Mr. H J Anslinger, Commissioner of Narcotics, May 23, 1942; Folder 2, 1942–1944; File 0660, Peru; 71-A-3554; DEA; RG 170; NACP.

46. Anslinger to Morlock, March 18, 1942; File 0480–11, Drugs: Coca Leaves (1933–1953); 170-74-4; DEA; RG 170; NACP. Note: There were in fact substitutes for cocaine, although apparently none of them had been integrated into medical practice on any significant scale. See for instance Yvan A. Reutsch, "From Cocaine to Ropivacaine: The History of Local Anesthetic Drugs," *Current Topics in Medicinal Chemistry* 1, no. 3 (August 2001): 175–82.

47. Mr. White, Department of Monetary Research, Treasury Department, to Mr. H J Anslinger, Commissioner of Narcotics, May 23, 1942; Folder 2, 1942–1944; File 0660, Peru; 71-A-3554; DEA; RG 170; NACP. Lend-lease funds were also used to gain diplomatic leverage; as one reporter explained, "It is no secret that these funds have been used to bring sometimes reluctant nations to our side and to break Axis ties which were rather strongly laid in some South American countries." O.K. Armstrong, "Lend-Lease in War and Peace," *Nation's Business,* August 1942, 25.

48. US House, *Appropriations Bill for 1945*, 539.

49. Ralph Hayes, Coca-Cola Company to Colonel Harry Anslinger, Commissioner, Federal Bureau of Narcotics, March 22, 1944; Folder 2, 1942–1944; 71-A-3554; DEA; RG 170; NACP.

50. Mark Pendergrast, *For God, Country and Coca-Cola: The Definitive History of the Great American Soft Drink and the Company that Makes It* (New York: Basic Books, 2000), 195–200.

51. Graham D. Taylor, "The Axis Replacement Program: Economic Warfare and the Chemical Industry in Latin America, 1942–44," *Diplomatic History* 8, no. 2 (April 1, 1984): 147.

52. "Continental Trade in Narcotic Drugs: General Observations," 1943; UN Box R5031; RG 8, 749; Folder 12/41702/41702 "Post-War Drug Control in Territories of the US of A in Berne under the Jurisdiction of the Authorities of the United Nations"; Registry Files: 1933–1946; LNA.

53. Cortez F. Enloe, MD, "German Pharmacy Kaput!" *American Druggist* (June 1946): 82–83, 174, 178, 180.

54. Charles Morrow Wilson, *Ambassadors in White: The Story of American Tropical Medicine* (New York: Kenikat Press, 1942): 41.

55. Stevens, "Organizing for Economic Defense," 1130; Bidwell, "Self-Containment and Hemispheric Defense," 178.

56. Ambassador Pierre de L. Boal, US Embassy La Paz to Secretary of State, February 13, 1943; File 21324; A1/Entry500B; BEW; FEA; RG 169; NACP.

57. US Military Academy, *Raw Materials*, 99, 101, 108.

58. "By 1940, the United States was consuming 60 percent of the world's rubber, 45 percent of its chromium, 40 percent of its tin, and 36 percent of its manganese, mostly or entirely purchased from foreign supplies." For an overview of US dependence on Asian raw materials and how this shaped economic warfare policy, see Marshall, *To Have and Have Not*, 2.

59. Charles Morrow Wilson, "New Crops for the New World," *Nation's Business*, August 1943, 96 [emphasis in the original].

60. Julius B. Wood, "War Remakes South America," *Nation's Business*, April 1945, 23.

61. Bidwell, "Self-Containment and Hemispheric Defense," 185.

62. United Nations, Economic and Social Council, "Foreign Investments in Peru," Economic Commission for Latin America, 4th Session, 7 May 1951. E/CN.12/166/Add.11.

63. US Military Academy, *Raw Materials*, 79.

64. James F. Siekmeier, "Trailblazer Diplomat: Bolivian Ambassador Víctor Andrade Uzquiano's Efforts to Influence U.S. Policy, 1944–1962," *Diplomatic History* 28, no. 3 (June 2004): 389.

65. US Military Academy, *Raw Materials*, 95.

66. Kenneth D. Lehman, *Bolivia and the United States: A Limited Partnership* (Athens: University of Georgia Press, 1999), 78.

67. Victor Andrade, *My Missions for Revolutionary Bolivia, 1944–1962* (London: University of Pittsburgh Press, 1976): 24. By 1952 tin mining "provided around 95 percent of the Andean nation's foreign exchange"; see Siekmeier, "Trailblazer Diplomat," 389.

68. Lehman, *Bolivia and the United States*, 75–76, 79. Other major Bolivian exports included chinchona bark for making quinine, tungsten, zinc, and lead.

69. John Hillman, "Bolivia and British Tin Policy, 1939–1945," *Journal of Latin American Studies* 22, no. 2 (May 1990): 289–315.

70. Laurence Whitehead, "Bolivia," in *Latin America between the Second World War and the Cold War*, ed. Leslie Bethel et al. (Cambridge: Cambridge University Press, 1992), 131–32. For an overview of Bolivian foreign policy during the time period, see Emmett James Holland, "A Historical Study of Bolivian Foreign Relations 1935–1946" (PhD diss., American University, 1967).

71. "Joint Report of Messrs Ravndal, Nitze and Mann," La Paz, December 29, 1941; File 450423; A1/Entry500B; BEW; FEA; RG 169; NACP.

72. Andrade, *My Missions*, 29.

73. Victor Andrade, "Boliva—Past and Future: Economic Diversification Necessary to Avoid Chaos," *Speeches of the Day* 23, no. 2 (November 1, 1956): 62. See also Glenn J. Dorn, *Truman Administration and Bolivia: Making the World Safe for Liberal Constitutional Oligarchy* (State College: Pennsylvania State University, 2011), 15.

74. Whitehead, "Bolivia," 132.

75. Papers of Calvert Magruder, 1920–1965. Dean Acheson, Assistant Secretary of State to the Honorable Calvert Magruder, Telegram, January 20, 1943; Speeches and Other Professional Activities; Folder 40–6; HUA.

76. Papers of Calvert Magruder, 1920–1965. *Labour Problems in Bolivia, Report of the Joint Bolivia–United States Labour Commission* (Montreal: International Labor Office, 1943), 39–40; Speeches and Other Professional Activities; Folder 40–4; HUA.

77. UN, "Foreign Investments in Bolivia," 7 May 1951.

78. "Difficulty in Obtaining Drug Shipments from the US," US Embassy La Paz to Secretary of State, Dispatch No. 1605, January 22, 1942; File 450424; BEW; A1/Entry500B; FEA; RG 169; NACP.

79. Martin Williams, "Foreign Economic Administration Activities in the Chemicals Field," *Chemical and Engineering News* 23, no. 24 (December 25, 1945): 2323.

80. David Green, *The Containment of Latin America: A History of the Myths and Realities of the Good Neighbor Policy* (Chicago: Quadrangle Books, 1971), 87.

81. "Joint Report . . .," December 29, 1941.

82. George M. Lauderbaugh, "Bolivarian Nations: Securing the Northern Frontier," in *Latin America During World War II*, ed. Thomas M. Leonard and John F. Bratzel (New York: Rowman & Littlefield, 2007), 113; Percy W. Bidwell, "Our Economic Warfare," 427.

83. "Joint Report . . .," January 3, 1942.

84. US Embassy, Lima to Secretary of State, Dispatch No. 3321, April 9, 1942; File 21147; A1/Entry500B; BEW; FEA; RG 169; NACP.

85. Richard Turner, US Embassy Lima, to Dewey Anderson, BEW, State Department, February 1, 1943; File 453737; A1/Entry500B; BEW; FEA; RG 169; NACP.

86. US Embassy La Paz to Secretary of State, Dispatch No. 1158, January 19, 1943; File 20027; A1/Entry500B; BEW; FEA; RG 169; NACP.

87. "Six Firms Taken Over," *New York Times*, March 14, 1942, 7.

88. US Embassy La Paz to Secretary of State, Dispatch No. 1158, January 19, 1943; File 20027; A1/Entry500B; BEW; FEA; RG 169; NACP.

89. Richard Turner, US Embassy Lima, to Dewey Anderson, BEW, State Department, February 1, 1943; File 453737; A1/Entry500B; BEW; FEA; RG 169; NACP.

90. Henry C Ramsey, US Embassy La Paz to Theodore Tannenwald Jr., Department of State, April 6, 1943; File 27096; A1/Entry500B; BEW; FEA; RG 169; NACP.

91. Despite the focus here, it is worth noting that BEW initiatives encompassed more than pharmaceuticals. Both countries were reluctant to crack down on German drugs, but they did give general support to US economic warfare efforts. Bolivia was initially more reluctant than Peru to embrace US economic warfare policy. "Unfortunately," BEW officials declared in December 1941, "the realization that an economic war is being fought has not yet reached Bolivia." In contrast, "The cooperation which we have received from the Peruvian Government in the matter of economic warfare is eminently satisfactory." Yet in

both countries steps had been taken—at least formally—to enact some of the economic warfare policies promoted by the United States. Although Peru did not officially recognize the Proclaimed List, after January 1942 it took "no steps to prohibit or hinder its publication." Monitoring the situation, the BEW reported that while some firms "are feeling the pinch . . . none as yet are in desperate circumstances," and "no serious unemployment or disruption of manufacturing seems to have resulted yet." In Bolivia, meanwhile, a Supreme Decree on December 11, 1941, froze German, Japanese, and Italian assets and made "their enterprises subject to control." The decree identified those who fell under its purview as: "Japanese, German and Italian individuals and firms included in the black lists adopted by American countries." Even while these moves were significant, both countries resisted enforcing the Proclaimed List in relation to the pharmaceutical industry on the grounds of public health. "Economic Background Report," December 1, 1941; File 450421; A1/Entry500B; BEW; FEA; RG 169; NACP; "Joint Report . . .," December 29, 1941; "Joint Report . . .," January 3, 1942; "Foreign Investments in Bolivia," 7 May 1951, United Nations.

92. Taylor, "Axis Replacement Program," 155.

93. Walter Wood, "Quinine Supply Sufficient for Bare Needs," *Washington Post*, November 10, 1943, 9.

94. Taylor, "Axis Replacement Program," 161.

95. In the archives it became apparent there were many obstacles to this task, as staff complained they needed better lists because certain "chemical items" on a US list of anticipated essential requirements were not found in "pharmacopeia and are untranslatable in Spanish." See, for example, "Joint Report . . .," January 3, 1942. In both Peru and Bolivia this was a problem. People at Legation in Bolivia requested "clearer definitions of the commodities on which estimates are requested to be furnished to the mission. Some of the chemical items are not found in the dictionary or pharmacopoeia and are not translatable into Spanish. It is not clear what is to be included in some of the more important items." As an early example of the confusion arising from this pairing of commodity distribution with politics, this shows how it was not even clear to many what the parameters of essential requirements in fact were. See, for example, "Joint Report . . .," December 29, 1941.

96. "Joint Report . . .," January 3, 1942.

97. "Joint Report . . .," January 3, 1942.

98. US Embassy Lima to Secretary of State, Dispatch No. 131, March 27, 1943; File 86068; A1/Entry500B; BEW; FEA; RG 169; NACP.

99. "Importations into Peru of Schering Products for the Years 1937 to 1942, Inclusive," US Embassy Lima to Department of State, Dispatch No. 8383, November 22, 1943; File 72591; A1/Entry500B; BEW; FEA; RG 169; NACP.

100. "Importations into Peru of Bayer Products During the Years 1937–1942, Inclusive," US Embassy Lima to Secretary of State, Dispatch No. 8464, December 1943; File 75322; A1/Entry500B; BEW; FEA; RG 169; NACP.

101. "Joint Report . . .," December 29, 1941.

102. Richard Turner, US Embassy Lima, to Dewey Anderson, BEW, State Department, January 30, 1943; File 451399; A1/Entry500B; BEW; FEA; RG 169; NACP.

103. Henry C. Ramsey, US Embassy La Paz to Theodore Tannenwald Jr., Department of State, April 6, 1943; File 27096; A1/Entry 500B; BEW; FEA; RG 169; NACP.

104. "Importations into Peru," Dispatch No. 8383.

105. US Embassy, Lima to Secretary of State, Dispatch No. 3321, April 9, 1942; File 21147; A1/Entry 500B; BEW; FEA; RG 169; NACP.

106. "Importations into Peru," Dispatch No. 8383.

107. US Embassy La Paz to Secretary of State, Dispatch No. 1158, January 19, 1943; File 20027: A1/Entry 500B; BEW; FEA; RG 169; NACP.

108. "Difficulty in Obtaining Drug Shipments from the US," US Embassy La Paz to Secretary of State, Dispatch No. 1605, January 22, 1942; File 450424; A1/Entry 500B; BEW; FEA; RG 169; NACP.

109. Boal, US Embassy La Paz to Secretary of State, Telegram, December 31, 1942; File 420498; A1/Entry 500B; BEW; FEA; RG 169; NACP.

110. For just two of many examples, see "Difficulty in Obtaining Drug Shipments from the US," US Embassy La Paz to Secretary of State, Dispatch No. 1605, January 22, 1942; File 450424; A1/Entry 500B; BEW; FEA; RG 169; NACP; and "Drug Situation in Bolivia," US Embassy La Paz to Secretary of State, Dispatch No. 531, September 10, 1942; File 497452; A1/Entry 500B; BEW; FEA; RG 169; NACP.

111. Richard Turner, US Embassy Lima, to Dewey Anderson, BEW, State Department, February 1, 1943; File 453737; A1/Entry 500B; BEW; FEA; RG 169; NACP. It was apparently harder to encourage US companies to move into the Bolivian market than elsewhere because, as the US Embassy in Bolivia acknowledged, for US drug firms the "Bolivian market . . . [was] admittedly small and economically weak by comparative standards, [but it] is of vital importance and concern to Bolivians." US Embassy La Paz to Secretary of State, Dispatch No. 1951, July 6, 1943; File 41575; A1/Entry 500B; BEW; FEA; RG 169; NACP.

112. "Joint Report . . .," January 3, 1942.

113. Turner to Anderson, February 1, 1943

114. "List of Peruvian Firms, Organizations and Individuals Interested in Importing Drugs and Pharmaceuticals from the United States," File 62096; A1/Entry 500B; BEW; FEA; RG 169; NACP.

115. US Embassy La Paz to Secretary of State, Dispatch No. 1951, July 6, 1943; File 41575; A1/Entry 500B; BEW; FEA; RG 169; NACP.

116. Henry C. Ramsey, US Embassy La Paz to Secretary of State, Dispatch No. 2052, August 5, 1943; File 49109; A1/Entry 500B; BEW; FEA; RG 169; NACP. This is an interesting example that again shows how the drug industry was integrated into the larger national economy and how this economy was very much connected to US and German warring for imperial access and technological advantage. WR Grace was transporting "high octane gasoline from Cochabamba to Santa Cruz to service Panagra planes." Panagra was Pan American Grace Airways, a US airline, which during World War II replaced the services of German-controlled SEDTA in Ecuador and Lufthansa in Peru and Bolivia.

117. Henry C. Ramsey to Secretary of State, Dispatch No. 2052, August 5, 1943.

118. Leslie B. Rout and John F. Bratzel, *The Shadow War: German Espionage and United States Counterespionage in Latin America during World War II* (Frederick, MD: University Publications of America, 1986); see also Martha H. Huggins, *Political Policing: The United States and Latin America* (Durham, NC: Duke University Press, 1998), 60–66.

119. M.J. Hartung, Vice President, Maywood Chemical Works to Mr. E.C. Brokmeyer, Attorney, National Press Building (forwarded to Anslinger at the FBN), April 15, 1940; Folder 1, 1926–1941; File 0660, Peru; 71-A-3554; DEA; RG 170; NACP.

120. Hartung, Maywood to Anslinger, FBN, May 12, 1942; Folder 2, 1942–1944; File 0660, Peru; 71-A-3554, DEA; RG 170; NACP.

121. "Joint Report . . .," January 3, 1942. The BEW discussed the work of the undercover businessmen with the "Coordinating Committee" in Lima, which was a group of local businessmen who worked with the embassy carrying out the program of the Coordinator of Inter-American Affairs. The Coordinating Committee assured the BEW its "100% cooperation." The members of the Coordinating Committee included "W.R. Grace & Company, Cerro de Pasco and the International Petroleum Company" who were among the largest "American business interests in Peru." See "Joint Report . . .," January 3, 1942.

122. US Embassy, Lima to US Secretary of State, February 1943, Dispatch No. 203, "Peruvian Foreign Trade in February, 1943"; File 33013; A1/Entry500B; BEW; FEA; RG 169; NACP.

123. "Regulations for the Registration and Reregistration of Pharmaceutical 'Specialties'," US Embassy Lima to the Secretary of State, Dispatch No. 7875, September 17, 1943; File 63611; A1/Entry500B; BEW; FEA; RG 169; NACP; US Embassy Lima to Secretary of State, Dispatch No. 183, April 27, 1944; File 102195; A1/Entry500B; BEW; FEA; RG 169; NACP.

124. Dorn, *Truman Administration and Bolivia*, 61–66.

125. Embassy Lima to Secretary of State, Dispatch No. 436, October 2, 1944; File 129227; A1/Entry500B; BEW; FEA; RG 169; NACP.

126. "Legal Narcotics Control," Julian Greenup, US Embassy Lima to Secretary of State, October 6, 1944, Dispatch No. 1631; Folder 2, 1942–1944; File 0660, Peru; 71-A-3554; DEA; RG 170; NACP.

127. Herbert Gaston, Assistant Secretary of the Treasury to George A. Molock, Office of Far Eastern Affairs, Secretary of State, June 15, 1944; Folder 2, 1942–1944; File 0660 Peru; 71-A-3554; DEA; RG 170; NACP.

128. "U.S. Industry to Get Technical Drug Data Dug Out of Germany: American Pharmaceutical Industry and Government Joined Forces to Organize Intelligence Teams," *Drug Trade News,* September 10, 1945.

129. Leland Harrison, Minister of the US of A in Berne to Sean Lester, Acting Secretary General, League of Nations, February 16, 1944. Folder: "Post-war Drug Control in Territories Which Come under the Jurisdiction of the Authorities of the United Nations"; 12/42326/41702; Box R5031, RG 8, 749; LNA.

130. UN, CND, "Report to the Economic and Social Council on the First Session of the Commission on Narcotic Drugs Held at Lake Success, NY, from 27 November to 13 December 1946" (United Nations: 27 January 1947): E/251, 26.

131. US House, Committee on Appropriations, *Treasury Department Appropriations Bill for 1946, Hearings before the Subcommittee of the Committee on Appropriations House of Representatives,* 79th Cong., 1st sess., 17 January 1945, 150.

132. United Nations, "Report on the 1st Session," 79.

133. US House, Committee on Appropriations, *Treasury Department Appropriations Bill for 1947, Hearings before the Subcommittee of the Committee on Appropriations House of Representatives,* 79th Cong., 2d sess., 12 November, 1945 (Washington, DC: US Government Printing Office, 1946), 94.

134. United Nations, "Report on the 1st Session," 65–70 [emphasis in the original].

135. The Permanent Central Opium Board was created by the 1925 International Opium Convention, and the Drug Supervisory Body was created by the 1931 Convention for Limiting the Manufacture and Regulating the Distribution of Narcotic Drugs.

136. Kinder and Walker, "Stable Force," 922. For a similar argument about the war's role in making the United States "the dominant force behind narcotic control," see David R. Bewley-Taylor, *The United States and International Drug Control, 1909–1997* (New York: Pinter, 1999), 44.

137. UN, CND, "Report to the Economic and Social Council on the First Session of the Commission on Narcotic Drugs Held at Lake Success, NY, From 27 November to 13 December 1946" (United Nations: 27 January 1947): E/251, 11.

138. McNutt, "How Do We Stand on Medical Drugs?" 334–335.

139. United States, Department of Commerce, Office of International Trade, "Overseas Sales of United States Drug Products," *World Trade in Commodities* 7, part 3, no. 19 (Washington, DC: US Government Printing Office, January 1949).

2. "RESOURCES FOR FREEDOM"

1. US Military Academy, Department of Social Sciences, *Raw Materials in War and Peace* (West Point, NY: USMA AG Printing Office, 1947), 129–30.

2. Lizabeth Cohen, *A Consumer's Republic: The Politics of Mass Consumption in Postwar America* (New York: Vintage Books, 2004), 124.

3. For more sources on postwar consumer culture, see George Lipsitz, *Rainbow at Midnight: Labor and Culture in the 1940s* (Chicago: University of Illinois Press, 1994); Elaine Tyler May, *Homeward Bound: American Families in the Cold War Era* (New York: Basic Books, 1999).

4. Michel Foucault, *Discipline and Punish: The Birth of the Prison* (New York: Vintage, 1995), 87.

5. A.L. Tennyson to Mr. Wood, Memo, January 11, 1946; "Surplus Narcotics" File 0450–7; Box 62; 170–74–4; DEA; RG 170; NACP.

6. Secretary of Commerce to Mr. H.J. Anslinger, Commissioner, Bureau of Narcotics, July 24, 1945; "Surplus Narcotics" File 0450–7; Box 62; 170–74–4; DEA; RG 170; NACP.

7. H J Anslinger to Mr. Gaston, Inter-Office Communication, Treasury Department, July 25, 1945; "Surplus Narcotics" File 0450–7; Box 62; 170–74–4; DEA; RG 170; NACP.

8. A.L. Tennyson to Mr. Wood, Memo, January 11, 1946; "Surplus Narcotics" File 0450–7; Box 62; 170–74–4; DEA; RG 170; NACP.

9. Director, Personal Property Utilization Division to Administrative Officer, FSS, Office Memorandum (draft), August 14, 1953; "Drug Disposal Committee: Procedures File" File 0450–7; Box 62; 170–74–4; DEA; RG 170; NACP.

10. Itty Abraham and Willem van Schendel, "Introduction: The Making of Illicitness," in *Illicit Flows and Criminal Things: States, Borders, and the Other Side of Globalization,* ed. Willem van Schendel and Itty Abraham (Bloomington: Indiana University Press, 2005), 7.

11. The Clearfield Naval Supply Depot, built in 1942, was the Navy's largest inland distribution center. The location was chosen because of the large amounts of land available, distance from potential enemy air attacks, and the access to highways and railroads that made it a hub of production for the Pacific fleet.

12. James J. Higgins, District Supervisor to H.J. Anslinger, Commissioner of Narcotics, July 16, 1947; "Surplus Narcotics" File 0450–7; Box 62; 170–74–4; DEA; RG 170; NACP.

13. Ibid.

14. Ibid.

15. Ibid.

16. Thomas G. Paterson and Robert J. McMahon, eds., *The Origins of the Cold War* (Boston: Houghton Mifflin, 1999); John Lewis Gaddis, *The United States and the Origins of the Cold War, 1940–1947* (New York: Columbia University Press, 1972); Melvin P. Leffler and David S. Painter, *Origins of the Cold War: An International History* (New York: Routledge, 1994); Henry Heller, *The Cold War and the New Imperialism: A Global History, 1945–2005* (New York: Monthly Review Press, 2006); Odd Arne Westad, *The Global Cold War: Third World Intervention* (New York: Cambridge University Press, 2007).

17. Thomas McCormick, "'Every System Needs a Center Sometimes': An Essay on Hegemony and Modern American Foreign Policy," in *Redefining the Past: Essays in Diplomatic History in Honor of William Appleman Williams,* ed. Lloyd C. Gardner (Corvallis: Oregon State University Press, 1986), 205.

18. US Military Academy, *Raw Materials,* 82, 168.

19. "Key U.S. Agencies Move to Speed Up Mobilization Plans for the Drug Industry," *Drug Trade News,* December 25, 1950.

20. Committee on Appropriations, *Treasury Department Appropriation Report for 1943, Hearings,* 77th Cong., 2d sess., 1943, 160, as cited by John C. McWilliams, *The Protectors: Harry J. Anslinger and the Federal Bureau of Narcotics, 1930–1962* (Newark: University of Delaware Press, 1990), 96.

21. See James Willard Hurst, *A Legal History of Money in the United States, 1774–1970* (Lincoln: University of Nebraska Press, 1973), for an extended discussion of monetary policy history in the United States.

22. Associated Press, "50 Armored Trains to Carry Federal Gold," *New York Times,* August 8, 1936, 1.

23. Associated Press, "Opium Put in Vaults of Treasury," *Deseret News,* March 8, 1940, 2. Some of the stores must have in fact been owned by the government, particularly those seized from the illicit trade, although they did solicit manufacturers at times to purify those stores, under unclear terms of proprietorship.

24. Thomas Wadden Jr., "We Put the Heat on Washington Dope Peddlers," *Saturday Evening Post,* October 3, 1953; Joseph Paul, "Theft of Drugs from Treasury Is Revealed," *Washington Post,* May 24, 1952, 1–2. The exposé and incident are also discussed in McWilliams, *Protectors,* 122–23. The *Washington Post* piece also drew comparison to the "'missing marijuana' of the John R. Weatherbee case" of the previous year where local police seized 193 pounds of marijuana but reported it on official records as 94.02 pounds and never explained the discrepancy.

25. Wadden Jr., "Heat on Washington Dope Peddlers."

26. US House, Committee on Appropriations, *Hearings before the Subcommittee on Appropriations for Treasury and Post Office Departments, Treasury Department Appropriations Bill for 1950,* 81st Cong., 1st sess., 26–28 January, 1–4, 9 February 1949, 275–76. Since 1937 under revised domestic drug laws marijuana had been included on the list of substances falling under the jurisdiction of the FBN; however, with no recognized medical or scientific uses, there was deemed to be no legitimate market for the drug.

27. H. J. Anslinger, Commissioner of Narcotics to A. J. Walsh, Commissioner Emergency Procurement Service, General Service Administration, September 8, 1952; "Drug Disposal Committee: Procedures File" File 0450–7; Box 62; 170–74–4; DEA; RG 170; NACP.

28. US House, *Appropriations for 1950,* 276.

29. Jenner G. Jones, Colonel, MC, Chief Supply Division, Department of the Army to Commanding Officers, AM, LV & SL Medical Depots, Medical Supply Officers and AT & SY General Depots, April 29, 1952; "Drugs Disposal Committee: Procedures File" File 0450–7; Box 62; 170–74–4; DEA; RG 170; NACP. After the passage of the 1937 Marijuana Tax Act, cannabis would be included in the narcotic control regime as well within the United States, and at US insistence, would fall under international drug control convention of 1961. See David R. Bewley-Taylor, *The United States and International Drug Control, 1909–1997* (New York: Pinter, 1999), 85.

30. H. J. Anslinger, Commissioner of Narcotics to A. J. Walsh, Commissioner Emergency Procurement Service, General Service Administration, September 8, 1952; "Drug Disposal Committee: Procedures File" File 0450–7; Box 62; 170–74–4; DEA; RG 170; NACP.

31. H. J. Anslinger to A. J. Walsh, September 8, 1952.

32. United States, Office of Defense Mobilization, *The Story of Defense Mobilization: How the United States Is Building Its Might in Order to Avert a Third World War* (Washington, DC: US Government Printing Office, 1951).

33. "The President's Letter—Jan 22, 1951," in *Resources for Freedom* (see following note), June 1952, vol. 1.

34. United States, The President's Materials Policy Commission, *Resources for Freedom: A Report to the President by the President's Materials Policy Commission* (Washington, DC: US Government Printing Office, 1952).

35. *Resources for Freedom,* vol. 1, 153

36. *Resources for Freedom,* vol. 1, 1.

37. US, *Story of Defense Mobilization,* 21 [emphasis in the original].

38. *Resources for Freedom,* vol. 1, 16.

39. *Resources for Freedom,* vol. 1, 158.

40. *Resources for Freedom,* vol. 5, 138.

41. *Resources for Freedom,* vol. 1, 163.

42. *Resources for Freedom,* vol. 2, 103.

43. *Resources for Freedom,* vol. 2, 105.

44. *Resources for Freedom,* vol. 5, 148.

45. US, Department of Commerce, Office of International Trade, "Overseas Sales of United States Drug Products," *World Trade in Commodities* 7, part 3, no. 19 (Washington, DC: US Government Printing Office, January 1949).

46. "U.S. Drug Makers: Overseas in a Big Way," *Business Week,* February 5, 1955, 94.

47. "Drugs Stage a Recovery," *Business Week,* May 7, 1949, 81. The novelty of the US postwar position seems to have been widely commented upon: "Back in 1939 the U.S. was a minor factor in foreign markets. Germany did about 75% of the business outside the United States The rest was divided largely among French, Swiss and British producers." "U.S. Drug Makers," *Business Week.*

48. Paul A. Kramer, "Power and Connection: Imperial Histories of the United States and the World," *American Historical Review* 116, no. 5 (December 2011): 1391, 1375–76.

49. US, Department of Commerce, Office of International Trade, "Cultivating Health Products Manufacturing Opportunity—Abroad," *World Trade in Commodities* 7, part 3, no. 76 (Washington, DC: US Government Printing Office, November 1949).

50. For a more detailed managerial analysis of pharmaceutical industry practices and their role in the Third World, see Gary Gereffi, *The Pharmaceutical Industry and Dependency in the Third World* (Princeton, NJ: Princeton University Press, 1983); Milton Silverman, Mia Lydecker, and Philip Lee, *Bad Medicine: The Prescription Drug Industry in the Third World* (Stanford, CA: Stanford University Press, 1992); Barbara Freese and Charles Medawar, *Drug Diplomacy: Decoding the Conduct of a Multinational Pharmaceutical Company and the Failure of a Western Remedy for the Third World* (London: Social Audit, 1982).

51. US, "Overseas Sales of United States Drug Products."

52. McCormick, "Every System Needs a Center Sometimes," 205–6.

53. Peter Temin, "Technology, Regulation, and Market Structure in the Modern Pharmaceutical Industry," *Bell Journal of Economics* 10, no. 2 (Autumn 1979): 433.

54. The five firms in 1943 in the business of extracting alkaloids from drug raw materials included Merck & Co., Inc., Maywood Chemical Works, Mallincrodt Chemical Works, New York Quinine & Chemical Works, and Hoffman-LaRoche, Inc. These companies were bound to submit quarterly and monthly returns to the FBN accounting for imports, manufacturing output, and dispositions to ensure no production in excess of quotas established under the 1931 Convention and that the subsequent circulation of all drugs legitimately produced was tracked and accounted for. See US Treasury Department, Bureau of Narcotics, *Traffic in Opium and Other Dangerous Drugs for the Year ended*

December 31, 1943 (Washington, DC: US Government Printing Office, 1944), 34.

55. Tom Mahoney, *The Merchants of Life: An Account of the American Pharmaceutical Industry* (New York: Harper & Brothers, 1959), 191–92.

56. Louis Galambos, *Values and Vision: A Merck Century* (Rahway, NJ: Merck & Co., c1991), 110–13.

57. Evelyn Schwartztrauber, "New Markets from New Drug Products," *Domestic Commerce*, April 1944, 13.

58. Mahoney, *Merchants*, 197.

59. George W. Merck, "Official Report on Biological Warfare," *Bulletin of the Atomic Scientists* 2, nos. 7/8 (October 1, 1946): 18.

60. "Merck," *Fortune* 35, June 1947, 107–9; "What the Doctor Ordered," *Time*, August 8, 1952, 44.

61. Fabian Bachrach, "George W. Merck Dies at Age 63," *New York Times,* November 10, 1957, 86.

62. Galambos, *Values and Visions,* 87.

63. "Drug Industry Held Prepared for War Task," *Drug Trade News,* July 24, 1950. Members of the committee included the pharmaceutical manufacturing houses, Merck, Parke, Davis, Squibb, Sharpe & Dohme, Abbott, Penick, Pfizer, and Mallincrodt.

64. US House, Committee on Appropriations, *Hearings before the Subcommittee on Appropriations for Treasury and Post Office Departments, Treasury Department Appropriations Bill for 1952,* 82nd Cong., 1st sess., 8, 9, 14–16, 19, 20 February 1951, 281.

65. "Merck," *Fortune,* 185.

66. "Drugs Stage a Recovery," 81. Other drug companies stock value increases provide a comparative context: Parke, Davis stock went from $1.77 to 1.89, by 1948 at 1.98; Abbott went from between 1.05 and 1.3 up to 5.95; Sharpe & Dohme went from .17-.41 up to 4.16; and finally Squibb grew from .65-1.23 up to 2.02.

67. "Growth Stocks and the Investor," *Barron's* 21, no. 50 (December 15, 1941): 13.

68. US, "Overseas Sales of United States Drug Products."

69. "Drugs Stage a Recovery," 81. Interestingly while US Merck had been severed from its German counterpart during WWI, connections persisted between the companies—particularly with regard to partitioning up the global market. This apparently ended during WWII when an agreement Merck had with Merck Darmstadt—to divide up the world and have rights to market products under the Merck name—was cancelled in 1945 ("by a consent decree growing out of an anti-trust suit").

70. "Merck," *Fortune,* 187.

71. Leon Gortler, "Merck in America: The First 70 Years from Fine Chemical to Pharmaceutical Giant," *Bulletin for the History of Chemistry* 25, no. 1 (2000): 7.

72. Galambos, *Values and Vision,* 12, 17, 19, 125.

73. As per the announcement of the pending auction, "The Alien Property Custodian, under the authority of the Trading with the Enemy Act . . . found

that the following shares of Maywood Chemical Works were the property of nationals of a designated enemy country (Germany), and vested such shares in himself to be held or sold in the interest and for the benefit of the United States." And the details of breakdown of stock quantities and categories were as follows: 23.10% common stock, 29.28% participating preferred stock, and 32.85% cumulative preferred stock. See "Statement of Terms and Conditions relating to Public Invitation for Bids for Purchase of [Stock] of Maywood Chemical Works, Maywood, New Jersey," Office of Alien Property, Department of Justice; "Drugs Beverages 1947–1959" File 0480–9; Box 63; 170–74–4; DEA; RG 170; NACP and "Announcement with Respect To [Stock] of Maywood Chemical Works," Attorney General of the United States; "Drugs Beverages 1947–1959" File 0480–9; Box 63; 170–74–4; DEA; RG 170; NACP.

74. It was estimated that 42.5 percent of Maywood's income from sales between 1945 and 1948 was from sales to Coca-Cola. "Statement of Terms and Conditions relating to Public Invitation for Bids for Purchase of [Stock] of Maywood Chemical Works, Maywood, New Jersey," Office of Alien Property, Department of Justice; "Drugs Beverages 1947–1959" File 0480–9; Box 63; 170–74–4; DEA; RG 170; NACP.

75. Ralph Hayes, The Coca-Cola Company to Hon. H. J. Anslinger, Commissioner of Narcotics, January 11, 1949; "Drugs Beverages 1947–1959" File 0480–9; Box 63; 170–74–4; DEA; RG 170; NACP. Aside from their coca leaf business, Maywood manufactured and sold other chemical products including: "Acetanilid, Aromatics (Ionones, Iraldeines, etc.), Cesium Salts, Caffeine Alkaloid, Cocaine, Coumarin, Flavors, Maypons (Lamepons or detergents), Lithium Metal, Lithium Salts, Rare Earth Salts (Cerium, Lanthanum, Neodymin, etc.), Rubidium Salts, Theobromine Alkaloid, Thorium Salts, Vanillin," which while originally all pharmaceutical production, in the "past quarter of a century" had supplied various industries including "Air conditioning, Ceramics, Cosmetics, Electrical, Food, Glass, Metal, Textiles [and] Soap." "Statement of Terms and Conditions relating to Public Invitation for Bids for Purchase of [Stock] of Maywood Chemical Works, Maywood, New Jersey," Office of Alien Property, Department of Justice; "Drugs Beverages 1947–1959" File 0480–9; Box 63; 170–74–4; DEA; RG 170; NACP.

76. "Memo: Maywood Chemical Works; Suggestion of Mr. Ralph Hayes of Coca Cola Company," January 28, 1949; "Drugs Beverages 1947–1959" File 0480–9; Box 63; 170–74–4; DEA; RG 170; NACP.

77. An example of S.B. Penick Company's earlier effort to gain entry to the market is also filed in the FBN records at NACP. When the Coca-Cola Company successfully lobbied in order that the "Narcotic Drug Import and Export Act be held not to apply to the exportation of decocainized extract of coca leaves" (April 2, 1937), Penick unsuccessfully tried to import them under the same principle. Maywood brought these efforts to the FBN's attention, prompting an investigation in February 1942. The FBN found "that there is a difference between decocainized extract [Coca-Cola's Merchandise #5] in so far as the definition is concerned, and decocainized leaves ... such raw material still retains its identity as coca leaves," a controlled substance. And, the FBN would not authorize Penick to import these controlled commodities on the grounds

that it posed a threat of creating excess that might slip into the illicit trade. Coca-Cola since the writing of national drug control legislation had always benefited from its close ties to the drug enforcement apparatus. Even before its collaboration with the government during World War II, as discussed in the previous chapter, Coca-Cola's economic interests in the coca trade had shaped the writing of national legislation. Ultimately, the question was turned over to the "opinions section" of the Treasury Department that, in April 1942, backed up this decision forbidding imports of decocainized coca. E.H. Foley, Jr., General Counsel to H.J. Anslinger, Commissioner of Narcotics, April 19, 1942; File 0480–17 "Decocainized Coca Leaves (1930–1956)"; Box 64; 170–74–4; DEA; RG 170; NACP; and Chief, Narcotic Section to Mr. Cairns, Mr. Tennyson, February 6, 1942; File 0480–17 "Decocainized Coca Leaves (1930–1956)"; Box 64; 170–74–4; DEA; RG 170; NACP.

78. Note that the designation of enemy, or "German" nationality as illegitimate, supplied a source of government revenue (the auction price), even if not fundamentally altering company operations.

79. J.C. Louis and Harvey Z. Yazijian, *The Cola Wars* (New York: Everest House, 1980).

80. Mr. Tennyson to Mr. Cunningham, Office Memorandum, June 13, 1949; File 0480–9, Drugs—Beverages, 1947–1959; Box 63; 170–74–4; DEA; RG 170; NACP.

81. Compared to the 250,000 pounds of coca leaves used in the company's operations in 1948, Maywood anticipated that in the next decade the annual demand for coca leaves would be 400,000 pounds per year. M.J. Hartung, President, Maywood Chemical Works to Hon. H.J. Anslinger, Commissioner, Bureau of Narcotics, July 30, 1948; File 0480–10, Drugs—Cocaine (1933–1962); Box 63; 170–74–4; DEA; RG 170; NACP.

82. M.J. Hartung to H.J. Anslinger, December 2, 1948; File 0480–11, Drugs: Coca Leaves (1933–1953); Box 64; 170–74–4; DEA; RG 170; NACP. These types of collaborations are also examined in chapter 1, in particular in relation to covert activities and information gathering during World War II.

83. Pat Watters, *Coca-Cola: An Illustrated History* (New York: Doubleday, 1978), 164, 198.

84. "Coca-Cola: World and Friend," *Time*, May 15, 1950, 30.

85. H.B. Nicholson, "The Competitive Ideal: The Economic Route to Friendship," *Vital Speeches of the Day* 19, no. 5 (December 15, 1952): 152. The speech was delivered by Coca-Cola Company President H.B. Nicholson at the New York Herald Tribune Forum in New York City on October 20, 1952.

86. Watters, *Coca-Cola*, 198.

87. Nicholson, "Competitive Ideal," 152.

88. Nicholson, "Competitive Ideal," 152.

89. Walt Rostow, *The Stages of Economic Growth* (New York: Cambridge University Press, 1960). For foundational work on dependency and underdevelopment, see Fernando Henrique Cardoso and Enzo Faletto, *Dependency and Development in Latin America*, trans. Marjory Mattingly Murquidi (Berkeley: University of California Press, 1979); Andre Gunder Frank, *Capitalism and Underdevelopment in Latin America: Historical Studies in Chile and Brazil*

(New York: Penguin Book, 1971); Immanuel Wallerstein, *World-Systems Analysis: An Introduction* (Durham, NC: Duke University Press, 2004).

90. James A. Farley, "Brand Names: A Basis for Unity, Our Greatest Hope of Expanding World Trade," *Vital Speeches of the Day* 18, no. 15 (May 15, 1952): 473. The chairman of the board of Coca-Cola Export Corp. presented this speech at the annual *Brand Names Day* dinner, New York City, April 16, 1952.

91. Ralph Hayes, The Coca-Cola Company to Commissioner Harry F.[sic] Anslinger, Bureau of Narcotics, April 25, 1950; File 0480–9, Drugs—Beverages, 1947–1959; Box 63; 170–74–4; DEA; RG 170; NACP.

92. H.J. Anslinger, US Commissioner of Narcotics to Augustu R. Arruda, Esq., Attorney, Lisbon, Portugal, April 29, 1946; File 0480–9, Drugs—Beverages, 1947–1959; Box 63; 170–74–4; DEA; RG 170; NACP.

93. Charles B. Dyar, Narcotics Control Officer, Office of the US High Commissioner for Germany to Mr. H.J. Anslinger, Commisisoner of Narcotics, Treasury Department, January 2, 1951; File 0480–9, Drugs—Beverages, 1947–1959; Box 63; 170–74–4; DEA; RG 170; NACP. It is worth noting that Pepsi did not include coca extracts in its drinks.

94. H.J. Anslinger, Commissioner of Narcotics to Mr. Charles B. Dyar, Foreign Relations Division, OMGUS, Office of Political Affairs, January 10, 1951; File 0480–9, Drugs—Beverages, 1947–1959; Box 63; 170–74–4; DEA; RG 170; NACP.

95. Ibid.

96. Louis and Yazijian, *Cola Wars,* 16, 33.

97. Michael M. Cohen, "Jim Crow's Drug War: Race, Coca-Cola and the Southern Origins of Drug Prohibition," *Southern Cultures* 12, no. 3 (Fall 2006): 55–79.

98. Ludy T. Benjamin, Jr., Anne M. Rogers, and Angela Rosenbaum, "Coca-Cola, Caffeine, and Mental Deficiency: Harry Hollingworth and the Chattanooga Trial of 1911," *Journal of the History of Behavioral Sicences* 27 (January 1991): 42.

99. Watters, *Coca-Cola,* 198, 162.

100. E.J. Kahn, Jr., *The Big Drink: The Story of Coca-Cola* (New York: Random House, 1960), 15.

101. Louis and Yazijian, *Cola Wars,* 13.

102. Kahn, *Big Drink,* 20–33, 98.

103. Kahn, *Big Drink,* 159–60.

104. Victoria De Grazia, *Irresistible Empire: America's Advance Through Twentieth-Century Europe* (Cambridge, MA: Harvard University Press, 2005), 3.

105. H.J. Anslinger, Commissioner of Narcotics to Ralph Hayes, April 12, 1950; Ralph Hayes, The Coca-Cola Company to Hon. Harry J. Anslinger, Commissioner of Narcotics, May 18, 1950; Carroll E. Mealey, Deputy Commissioner to District Supervisor, NY, June 9, 1950; Albert J. Turner, Treasurer, Maywood Chemical Works to H.J. Anslinger, Commissioner of Narcotics, July 11, 1950; File 0480–9, Drugs—Beverages, 1947–1959; Box 63; 170–74–4; DEA; RG 170; NACP.

106. H.J. Anslinger, Commissioner of Narcotics to Ralph Hayes, June 20, 1950; Ralph Hayes to Mr. Albert Turner (Treasurer of the Maywood Com-

pany), Maywood Chemical Works, June 23, 1950; File 0480–9, Drugs—Beverages, 1947–1959; Box 63; 170–74–4; DEA; RG 170; NACP.

107. Nicholson, "Competitive Ideal," 152.

108. "Chronological Listing: Countries with Coca-Cola Bottling Operations and Year Introduced, 1906 through April, 1969"; Folder 5; Box 10; No.620-Coca-Cola Collection; Special Collections; RWL.

109. Walter P. McConaughy, Commercial Attaché to Secretary of States, December 30, 1943; File 78098; BEW; A1/Entry500B; FEA; RG 169; NACP.

110. Ibid.

111. "Population Data, Etc. Pertaining to Different Regions: Expansion Plan," circa 1937, undated; Folder 10; Box 5; No.10-Robert Woodruff Collection; RWL.

112. Memo, H.R. Horsey to Mr. R.W. Woodruff, President, The Coca-Cola Corporation, January 27, 1936; Folder 10; Box 5; No. 10-Robert Woodruff Collection; Special Collections; RWL. In an interesting example of how the "nationality" of a product affected its marketing, the report went on to say that "under the laws of Peru it is necessary that products sold there be labeled showing whether or not said product is national or foreign. In accordance with this law, we decided to permit the words 'INDUSTRIA PERUANA' to be placed on the skirt of the crown. The question of a proper customs declaration for concentrate is now being considered."

113. *Resources for Freedom*, vol. 1, 6.

3. RAW MATERIALISM

1. An earlier version of this chapter appeared as "Policing Development: Andean Drug Control and the Expansion of US Capitalism," *Social History of Alcohol and Drugs* 23, no. 2 (Spring 2009): 128–50.

2. At the end of the war, Peru and Bolivia were the main sites of coca cultivation. Unlike Peru and Bolivia, Colombia had only a minor domestic economy that was already being subject to government limitation and control, culminating in a policy of forbidding cultivation, distribution, and sale of coca leaves and payment of wages in coca with the passage of Decree No. 896, March 11, 1947.

3. "Legitimate needs" were defined by the conventions as being for either medical and scientific purposes or, reflecting the influence of the United States on establishing the parameters of the legitimate market, for use in the manufacture of a "nonnarcotic flavoring extract," i.e., for Coca-Cola.

4. Paul Gootenberg, "Secret Ingredients: The Politics of Coca in US-Peruvian Relations, 1915–65," *Journal of Latin American Studies* 36 (2004): 14.

5. UN, ECOSOC, CND, *Report to the Economic and Social Council on the First Session of the Commission on Narcotic Drugs Held at Lake Success, New York, from 27 November to 13 December 1946* (E/251), 27 January 1947, 11.

6. UN, *Report on the First Session of the Commission on Narcotic Drugs*; UN, ECOSOC, CND, Second Session, *Preparatory Work for a Conference to Consider the Possibility of Limiting and Controlling the Cultivation and Harvesting of the Coca Leaf* (E/CN.7/73), July 7, 1947, 5.

7. Before WWII coca leaf growing countries included Bolivia, Peru, Colombia, Ecuador, the Netherlands Indies (Java, Indonesia), Formosa (Taiwan), and Japan. Peru has always been the largest grower, followed by Bolivia (which was surpassed by Colombia only in the late 1970s and 1980s, where cultivation relocated as a result of the heavily militarized war on drugs). At the time of the UN commission, Peru and Bolivia were the most significant sites in South America, cultivation in Ecuador was considered "practically non-existent," and what was then only a negligible harvest in Colombia was already being reined in by the government (see *Report of the Commission of Enquiry*, 105; full cite in note 9). As for the rest of the world, with the end of WWII, the Supreme Allied Command assumed control over Japan and Japanese-occupied Formosa and Java, ensuring that whatever—if any—minimal production continued there was already firmly tied in to the drug control apparatus. While coca leaf was grown primarily in Peru and Bolivia, chewing was practiced in regions throughout the Andes and in some places in Brazil and Venezuela—but again, outside of Bolivia and Peru, consumption was considered relatively insignificant (at least to the eyes of international drug controllers).

8. The United States and other industrial powers had always been adamant that domestic policing of drugs was exclusively the terrain of their own national governments (which is partly why the drug control apparatus always focused on the supply side). For more details see William McAllister, *Drug Diplomacy in the Twentieth Century: An International History* (New York: Routledge, 2000).

9. UN, ECOSOC, *Report of the Commission of Enquiry on the Coca Leaf, May 1950*, Fifth Year, Twelfth Session, Special Supplement 1, Official Record (Lake Success, NY: UN, July 1950): 65, 68.

10. It seems that occasionally, when adequate supplies were not forthcoming from Peru, the United States also turned to Bolivia, which thus intermittently and on a much smaller scale had an export market (see for example UN, ECOSOC, CND, Third Session, *Limitation of the Production of Raw Materials* [/CN.7/110] 19 April 1948, 8) where in 1942 Bolivia exported 92 kg to the United States, in contrast with 343,290 kg to coca leaf chewers in Argentina).

11. Peru produced limited amounts of cocaine for domestic production. Peru also produced relatively minimal amounts of crude cocaine paste for export to European pharmaceutical houses, where it was refined into cocaine hydrochloride. The vast majority of this production was eliminated during WWII when the European market was cut off and the United States exerted economic pressures to limit production.

12. UN statistics for exports from Peru in 1946 showed 236,000 kg to the United States, 41,000 kg to France (perhaps tied to postwar allied operations), 635 kg to Switzerland, 514 kg to the United Kingdom, 7,000 kg to Argentina, and 11,000 kg to Bolivia. I have not found a similar breakdown for later years, but from various sources it appears that after this the United States (aside from the Andean regional market) was the exclusive importer (I know this to have been the case for the last twenty years, having seen the export records held at the offices of the national coca monopoly, ENACO, in Lima). UN, ECOSOC, CND, Second Session, *Coca Leaf: Request by the Government of Peru for a Field Survey* (E/CN.7/106), 30 July 1947, 57.

13. See chapter 2, and Gootenberg, "Secret Ingredients."

14. US Treasury Department, Bureau of Narcotics, *Traffic in Opium and Other Dangerous Drugs for the Year Ended December 31, 1942–1956* (Washington, DC: Government Printing Office, 1957).

15. US Treasury Department, Bureau of Narcotics, *Traffic in Opium and Other Dangerous Drugs for the Year Ended December 31, 1931*, 7.

16. *Report of the Commission of Enquiry*, 84.

17. UN, *Limitation of the Production of Raw Materials*, 13. In 1948 Bolivia reported to the United Nations that large landowners' estates only accounted for 17 percent of all coca grown, whereas small producers' lands accounted for the majority. For export, see *Report of the Commission of Enquiry*, 87. The "greater part of the coca leaf exported from Peru came from plantations operated either directly or indirectly by the exporters themselves. As regards Bolivia, one of the objects of the Bolivian Coca Producers' Corporation is to export the coca leaf produced by the members of the Corporation, which is composed mainly of large landowners."

18. *Report of the Commission of Enquiry*, 9.

19. *Report of the Commission of Enquiry*, 103.

20. Laura Gotkowitz, *A Revolution for Our Rights: Indigenous Struggles for Land and Justice in Bolivia, 1880–1952* (Durham, NC: Duke University Press, 2007).

21. Gotkowitz, *Revolution for Our Rights*, 235, 279.

22. Warwick Anderson, *Colonial Pathologies: American Tropical Medicine, Race, and Hygiene in the Philippines* (Durham, NC: Duke University Press, 2006), 1. See also Laura Briggs, *Reproducing Empire: Race, Sex, Science, and U.S. Imperialism in Puerto Rico* (Berkeley: University of California Press, 2002); and Mariola Espinosa, *Epidemic Invasions: Yellow Fever and the Limits of Cuban Independence, 1878–1930* (Chicago: University of Chicago Press, 2009).

23. Letter from M J Hartung, Vice President, Maywood Chemical Works to Mr. Stuart J. Fuller, Assistant Chief, Division of Far Eastern Affairs, Department of State, c/o American Consulate, Geneva, Switzerland, May 26, 1936; 12–19946–8070; LNA. Note that US corporations were also key mediators in Bolivia; in 1940 Maywood collected information for the US FBN on "Bolivian coca leaves," which was forwarded on to the League of Nations. See Letter from H J Anslinger, Commissioner of Narcotics to Mr. Herbert L. May, League of Nations, March 28, 1940; 12–10799–8070; LNA.

24. H.J. Anslinger to Mr. W. Edwin Clapham, Merck & Company, Inc., January 27, 1948. Re: Merck and Maywood's need for more coca leaves, see letter from W. Edwin Clapham, Narcotic Products Manager, Merck & Co., Inc. to H.J. Anslinger, January 22, 1948 and Maywood Chemical Works to Commissioner of Narcotics, July 20, 1948; File 0480–11, Drugs: Coca Leaves (1933–1953); 170–74–4; DEA; RG 170; NACP. Merck in fact proposed setting up plantations in Costa Rica or Guatemala to augment their supply, which Anslinger rejected as unnecessary and counter to the general interest in limiting production. He also mentioned previous government efforts to grow coca in Puerto Rico—discontinued for similar reasons.

25. Lehman makes the similar argument that the "political logic of pursuing a plan to which the United States was already ostensibly committed seemed self-evident." Kenneth D. Lehman, *Bolivia and the United States: A Limited Partnership* (Athens: University of Georgia Press, 1999), 117.

26. It is interesting to note that when the question of raw materials was first raised, Peru proposed the CND might include manufacturing countries in its inquiry—apparently to no avail. See the minutes of the UN, ECOSOC, *Social Affairs Committee of the Economic and Social Council, Summary Record of First Meeting* (E/AC.7/3), 8 March 1947, 4.

27. UN, *Request by the Government of Peru*, 46–47.

28. UN, *Request by the Government of Peru*, 48.

29. Letter from G.E. Yates (Director, Division of Narcotic Drugs) to Phillippe de Seynes (Department of Economic and Social Council), 14 February 1956. Narcotic Drugs, Advisory Services in the Field of Narcotics, Box RAG 2/109/021 Nov 55- Oct 56, UNANY.

30. UN, CND, *Report to the Economic and Social Council on the Second Session of the Commission, Held at Lake Success, New York, from 24 July to 8 August 1947* (E/575), 12 September 1947, 16.

31. H.J. Anslinger, Commissioner of Narcotics, to Howard Fonda, c/o American Embassy, Lima, Peru October 3, 1949. Howard Fonda to Harry Anslinger, October 5, 1949. Howard Fonda to Harry Anslinger, October 30, 1949; File, Fourth Session–UN, #4; 170–74–5; DEA; RG 170; NACP.

32. UN, *Report on the Second Session of the Commission*, 17.

33. UN, ECOSOC, CND, *Preparatory Work for an International Conference to Consider the Possibility of Limiting and Controlling the Cultivation and Harvesting of the Coca Leaf*, Second Session (E/CN.7/73) 7 July 1947, 5.

34. Letter from Eduardo Anze Matienzo, Delegacion de Bolivia ante la Organizacion de las Naciones Unidas, to Señor Dr. D. Tomás Manuel Elío, Ministro de Relaciones Exteriores y Culto, February 9, 1948; "Folder 4: Asunto Coca"; MRECB.

35. UN, *Request by the Government of Peru*, 58.

36. UN, ECOSOC, CND, Third Session, *Replies from Governments to the Questionnaire on the Limitation and the Control of the Cultivation and Harvesting of the Coca Leaf* (E/CN.7/110), 19 April 1948, 11.

37. UN, *Coca Leaf: Request by the Government of Peru*, 54.

38. "Para reprimir el tráfico ilícito de estupefacientes," *El Comercio*, Lima, April 27, 1949; "Comisión que efectuará un estudio integral del problema de la coca," *El Comercio*, Lima, September 10, 1949; "Se Efectuará un estudio a fondo de la hoja de coca," *El Diario*, La Paz, November 2, 1949. Marcial Rubio Correa, *Legislación Peruana Sobre Drogas: 1920–1993* (Lima: Centro de Información y Educación Para La Prevención del Abuso de Drogas, 1994), 32–36. Decreto Supremo March 26, 1949; Decreto-Ley 11005 March 28, 1949; Decreto Ley 11046 June 13, 1949; Decreto Supremo August 2, 1949.

39. "The White Goddess," *Time*, April 1949. Each decree in Peru was published in the main Lima daily newspaper, *El Comercio*, and generally appeared in the midst of sensational newspaper coverage recounting drug busts and successful police actions against alleged cocaine traffickers. For instance, this

orchestration and use of the media was apparent with the coverage of Decreto Ley 11005 of March 28. The full text of the decree was printed in the *El Comercio* a full month later, one day before the spectacular coverage of the capture of operatives in a cocaine trafficking ring—a bust that actually happened on April 13.

40. According to a contemporary "poll taken among the professional classes of Ecuador, Peru and Bolivia" there was considerable hostility towards US "imperialism." See Carleton Beals, "Ecuador, Peru and Bolivia," in *What the South Americans Think of Us*, ed. Carleton Beals et al. (New York: Robert M. McBride, 1945), 10–11. During the 1940s political parties such as the MNR in Bolivia and APRA in Peru publicly embraced anti-"Yankee," anti-imperialist party platforms.

41. "Forma cómo se efectuó la pesquisa que permitió detener a los componentes de una banda traficantes de cocaína y la incautación de cuatro plantas de producción y refinería de este alcaloide en Trujillo," *El Comercio*, Lima, April 30, 1949. Drug control was just one part of a broader strengthening of the coercive powers of the state. As just another example of this invocation of national prestige to justify increased police powers, in March 1949, Odría introduced the death penalty for murderers and "traitors" with Decreto Ley 10976. (It is worth pointing out that if determined, as alleged, that the drug traffickers had "attacked the national prestige," their actions might have thus constituted a capital crime.) He justified this legislation by suggesting that it was used "hoy por las naciones más civilizadas del mundo que aplican reitaradamente dicha pena como un instrumento inevitable para defender la supervivencia de la sociedad y del Estado." "El Junta Militar de Gobierno Establece la Pena de Muerte Para Los Asesinos y los Traidores de Patria," *El Comercio*, Lima, March 26, 1949.

42. Paul Gootenberg, *Andean Cocaine: The Making of a Global Drug* (Chapel Hill: University of North Carolina Press, 2008), 245.

43. While Bolivia did not manufacture cocaine—minimizing the opportunity for such spectacular drug busts—nevertheless, the policing functions of the state here too were increasingly modeled on US policing tactics and dependent on US military supplies and training. For example, the Bolivian Coronel de Carabineros Isaac Vincenti traveled to the United States for policing training: "en misión de estudios y perfeccionamiento policiarios," with the Washington Metropolitan police force and the FBI, and received the "Socio Honorario de la Asociación de Policía del Distrito." Letter from Bolivian Ambassador to Señor Dr. Javier Paz Campero, Ministro de Relaciones Exteriores y Culto, 7 January 1949; MRECB. Historian Kenneth Lehman has also described US involvement in Andean police and military training.

44. For a detailed overview of the case, including newspaper clippings about the cocaine bust from the *New York Times*, see *El Peru Y Colombia Ante La Corte Internacional de Justicia: Documentacion Pertinente Al Desarrollo Del Juicio Sentencia del 20 de Noviembre de 1950* (Lima: Ministerio de Relaciones Exteriores, 1951). Thanks are due to Dr. Uriel Garcia for making this publication available to me. Glenn J. Dorn has written about the FBN's pursuit of Haya de la Torre and how this became a delicate issue for the State Department when

Anslinger's proclivity to use publicity as a bulwark to policy caused an uproar in Peru over the appearance of the United States making impolitic interventions to ruin Haya's reputation. However, ultimately the US government did align itself with Odría, and as Dorn agrees, drug control and police collaboration became a critical site for performing this alliance. See Glenn J. Dorn, "'The American Reputation for Fair Play': Víctor Raúl Haya de la Torre and the Federal Bureau of Narcotics," *The Historian* 65, no. 5 (September 2003): 1083–101.

45. This political capital was also tied to the receipt of economic and materials support. Licit as well as illicit drugs were critical. In Bolivia a year later, the United States would help put down a political rebellion by the Movimiento Nacionalist Revolucionario (MNR) by providing military aid, which included, along with weapons technology, thousands of pounds of pharmaceutical stocks for the Bolivian police and military. "Detalle del Material Aquirido en los Estados Unidos de America y Despacho a Bolivia. Del 27 de Agosto al 12 de Octubre de 1949"; Files of the Embajada de Bolivia en Washington; MRECB.

46. Anslinger viewed the media as an outlet for influencing policy. Giving advice to the British representative before the UN CND on how to bring about legislative change in the face of political resistance, Anslinger explained: "In the United States, however the judiciary was not considered so sacrosanct. He had frequently explained to the judges the full meaning of this traffic and the need for rigorous punishment, otherwise the evil could grown unceasingly. The well-being of the country was affected. If his advice was not followed the press was notified and things took a turn for the better." For a transcript of this CND session, see UN, *Request by the Government of Peru*, 77.

47. For more information on the repression of trade unions and democracy in Peru and the installation of "authoritarian capitalism" during this era, see Jon V. Kofas, *Foreign Debt and Underdevelopment: U.S.-Peru Economic Relations, 1930–1970* (New York: University Press of America, 1996), 117–28.

48. Lehman, *Bolivia and the United States*, 138.

49. The newspaper account describes how Soberón: "Poseía licencia del Estado; pero toda su producción debía ser para el Estado . . . pero el excedente, terriblemente voluminoso, era extraído clandestinamente de Huánuco y servía para limentar los laboratorios clandestinos de refinación." Extracted from "Debido a las oportunas medidas dictadas por la Junta Militar de Gobierno, se efectúa una interesante investigación sobre la elaboración y el tráfico ilícito de drogas heroicas," *El Comercio*, April 28, 1949. A few days later another bust was reported; in this case the cocaine originated in the North, in Trujillo, and once again was manufactured by someone who had—but in this case, no longer—possessed a license for the legal production (see next footnote for citation).

50. "La Campaña Contra el Trafico Ilicito de Estupefacientes," *El Comercio*, April 29, 1949. For a recent study of the burgeoning illicit trade during this time period, see Gootenberg, *Andean Cocaine*.

51. Decreto Ley No. 11046, Rubio Correa, *Legislación Peruana*, 87

52. I believe this impact can be seen in what appears to have been the radical limitation of domestic cocaine production within a few years of these events—

which would support the argument that the Andes were being locked into the raw-material supply side of the international coca commodity circuit. The United Nations compiled lists of firms authorized to manufacture controlled substances and while in 1947, Peru reported eight such factories; by 1953 they were reporting none. See "List of Firms Authorized to Manufacture Drugs," UN E/NF.1947/1 and E/NF.1953/1.

53. "Llegada de la Comisión de las NU que estudiará el problema de la Coca," *El Comercio*, Lima, September 11, 1949, 3–4.

54. "Sobre el Problema de la Coca," *El Comercio*, Lima, September 13, 1949. The same questions were addressed in *La Cronica*, September 13, 1949.

55. *Report of the Commission of Enquiry*, 7–8.

56. "Investígase si la Coca es o no un Tóxico Para la Salud: Actuará la Comisión de la ONU libre de prejucios," *El Diario*, November 7, 1949.

57. For the broader historical context of these debates see Joseph Gagliano, *Coca Prohibition in Peru: The Historical Debates* (Tucson: University of Arizona Press, 1994).

58. Dr. Carlos Monge, "El Problema de la Coca en el Peru," *Anales de la Facultad de Medicina* 29, no. 4 (Lima, 1946): 311–15.

59. This interest translated into financial support from institutions such as the US National Institutes of Health, the US Public Health Service, and the US Air Force; see Marcos Cueto, "Andean Biology in Peru: Scientific Styles on the Periphery," *ISIS* 80 (1989): 648, 654.

60. "Conversando con el doctor Carlos Monge," *El Comercio*, Lima, 27 September 1949.

61. US Air Force interest in high-altitude studies had grown in part as a result of air campaigns during World War II, where all sides of the conflict used stimulants, like cocaine, to keep Air Force pilots alert on long flights. It was undoubtedly the significance of this research to the US military that ensured, as historian Marcos Cueto argues, "Peruvian high-altitude physiology played an unusually active role, compared to most other Latin American disciplines of the time, in the international scientific community." Cueto, "Andean Biology in Peru," 654.

62. "Invitado por importantes insituciones científicas viaga a los Estados Unidos el Dr. C. G. Gutiérrez-Noriega," *El Comercio*, Lima, 11 April, 1949.

63. Carlos Gutierrez-Noriega and Victor Wolfgang Von Hagen, "The Strange Case of the Coca Leaf," *Scientific Monthly* 70, no. 2 (February 1950): 83.

64. Gutierrez-Noriega and Von Hagen, "Strange Case," 87.

65. "El Problema de la Masticación de Hojas de Coca," *El Comercio*, Lima, 14 September 1949. Original in Spanish: "después de mucho 'chacchar' coca, se siente compensado de todas las frustraciones que ha tenido en su vida."

66. Decreto Ley No. 11046, Rubio Correa, *Legislación Peruana*, 87

67. *Report of the Commission of Enquiry*, 9.

68. *Report of the Commission of Enquiry*, 93.

69. *Report of the Commission of Enquiry*, 26.

70. Letter from Howard Fonda to Harry Anslinger, Lima, Peru, Friday 16 September, 1949; File 0660, Peru #3 1945–49; 170–74–12; DEA; RG 170; NACP.

71. *Report of the Commission of Enquiry*, 26.

72. "What the Doctor Ordered," *Time*, 60, cover, 38–44, August 18, 1952.

73. UN, Division of Social Activities, *Draft Report of Meeting of Consultant to Consider a Preliminary Programme for the Proposed Seminar on Social Problems of the Indian Population and Other Related Problems*, 1 September 1949; DAG 18/4.1.2.1 "Indian Affairs," UNANY.

74. *Report of the Commission of Enquiry*, 10.

75. UN, *Limitation of the Production of Raw Materials*, 14.

76. Gutierrez-Noriega and Von Hagen, "Strange Case," 85.

77. *Report of the Commission of Enquiry*, 10.

78. *Report of the Commission of Enquiry*, 53–54.

79. US corporations, followed by English and Canadian business, were the largest source of foreign investment in Peru and Bolivia at the time. Most US investment was in the oil and mining industries. See UN, ECOSOC, ECLA, *Economic and Legal Status of Foreign Investments in Selected Countries of Latin America: Foreign Investment in Peru* (E/CN.12/166/Add.11), 7 May 1951, and UN, ECOSOC, ECLA, *Investment in Bolivia* (E/CN.12/166/Add.10).

80. *Report of the Commission of Enquiry*, 58.

81. Letter from Ministro to Señor Presidente de la Junta Militar de Gobierno, February 6, 1952; Folder Asunto Coca; MRECB.

82. E/CN.7/SR.118 23 Feb 1951, "Commission on Narcotic Drugs, Fifth Session, Summary Record of the Hundred and Eighteenth Meeting, Held at Lake Success, NY, on Wednesday, 13 December 1950, at 10 a.m."

83. See Nicholas G. Barbella dn John V. Yates to Dr. Frederick J. Wampler, Chief of Field Party, ILAA, Memo, "September 1949, Progress Report on Coca Leaf Project"; File 0480–11, Drugs: Coca Leaves (1933–53); 170–74-4; DEA; RG 170; NACP; and Memo of Conversation, Re: Research Work into the Effects of Coca Leaf Chewing, Department of State, September 25, 1950; File 1230-1, 5th Session UN #3; 170–74-5; DEA; RG 170; NACP.

84. See, for example, Memo of Conversation Re: "Research Work into the Effects of Coca Leaf Chewing," September 25, 1950, Department of State; 170–74-5; File 1230-1, 5th Session UN #3; DEA; RG 170; NACP. Also see *Report of the Commission of Enquiry*, 22. The report mostly cites Gutiérrez-Noriega's work in this regard, and according to conversations with Marcos Cueto, much of this work was performed on prisoners.

85. L.W. Hughes, "Curse of Coca," *Inter-American* 5 (September 1946): 21, 42.

86. William H. Hodge, "Coca," *Natural History* 56 (February 1947): 86–93.

87. "Report of the United Nations Delegation at the Second Inter-American Congress of Indian Affairs," DAG 18/4.1.2.1, "Indian Affairs" Dr. Lozada, UN.

88. E/1666/Add.1, "Narcotic Drugs: Report on the Commission of Enquiry on the Coca Leaf," June 1, 1951, ECOSOC Thirteenth Session: 5

89. *Report of the Commission of Enquiry*, 93

90. "Report of the United Nations Mission of Technical Assistance to Bolivia," Comments, 13 October 1950; Assistance Technique—Bolivie—Memo II, SS-0544–0013; Department of Economic and Social Affairs; Department of Social Affairs Records, 1946–1960; UNANY.

91. Ralph Hayes to Mr. H.J. Anslinger, July 21, 1947; File 1230–1, Second Session UN; 170–74–4; DEA; RG 170; NACP.

92. H.J. Anslinger, Commissioner of Narcotics to Mr. Ralph Hayes, January 2, 1951; File 0480–11, Drugs: Coca Leaves (1933–53); 170–74–4; DEA; RG 170; NACP.

93. Ralph Hayes to Mr. M.J. Hartung, Maywood Chemical Works, November 10, 1950; File 1230–1, Fifth Session UN #3; 170–74–5; DEA; RG 170; NACP.

94. Airgram, Ambassador Tittman to Secretary of State, October 25, 1948; File 0480–11, Drugs: Coca Leaves (1933–1953); FBN 170–74–4; DEA; RG 170; NACP.

95. Dr. Carlos Monge, Presidente de la Comisión Peruana para el Estudio del Problema de la Coca to Señor Ministro del Trabajo y Asuntos Indígenas, General Dr. Armando Artola, January 16, 1951; and General Armando Artola, Ministro del Trabajo y Asuntos Indígenas to Dr. Hans Moliter, Merck Institute for Therapeutic Research, January 16, 1951; Folder Coca; CMM.

96. Hans Moliter, MD, Merck Institute for Therapeutic Research to Dr. Carlos Monge, Director, Instituto de Biologia Andina, February 28, 1951; Folder Coca; CMM.

97. Ralph Hayes to Hon. Harry J. Anslinger, April 8, 1952; File 0480–1, Drugs and Beverages, 1947–59; 170–74–4; DEA; RG 170; NACP.

4. THE ALCHEMY OF EMPIRE

1. H.T.N., Treasury Department to Miss Renfrew, July 22, 1941; File 0480–11, Drugs: Coca Leaves (1933–1953); 170–74–4; DEA; RG 170; NACP.

2. Roger Adams, "Man's Synthetic Future," Science 115, no. 2981 (Feb. 15, 1952): 162, 157.

3. H.J. Anslinger to Commander J.W. Macmillan, Director Human Resource Division, Office of Naval Research, October 13, 1950; File 0480–166, Drugs: Coca Chewing (1937–1963); 170–74–12; DEA; RG 170; NACP.

4. H.J. Anslinger to Dr. Robert Schwab, Massachusetts General Hospital, Electroencephalographic Laboratory, October 24, 1950; File 0480–166, Drugs: Coca Chewing (1937–1963); 170–74–12; DEA; RG 170; NACP.

5. Robert S. Schwab, MD to Commissioner Anslinger, October 10, 1950; File 0480–166, Drugs: Coca Chewing (1937–1963); 170–74–12; DEA; RG 170; NACP.

6. H.J. Anslinger to Dr. Robert Schwab, Massachusetts General Hospital, Electroencephalographic Laboratory, October 24, 1950; File 0480–166, Drugs: Coca Chewing (1937–1963); 170–74–12; DEA; RG 170; NACP.

7. UN, ECOSOC, Report of the Commission of Enquiry on the Coca Leaf, May 1950, Fifth Year, Twelfth Session, Special Supplement 1 (Lake Success, NY: UN, July 1950): 93.

8. UN, PCOB, Report to the Economic and Social Council on Statistics of Narcotics for 1950 and the Work of the Board in 1951, Nov. 1951 (E/OB/7), The Board, Geneva, 1951: 13.

9. Charles B. Dyar, Narcotics Control Officer, Office of the US High Commissioner for Germany, to Mr. H.J. Anslinger, Commissioner of Narcotics,

Treasury Department, January 2, 1951; File 0480–9, Drugs-Beverages 1947–59; Box 63; 170–74–4; DEA; RG 170; NACP.

10. H.J. Anslinger, Commissioner of Narcotics, Treasury Department, to Charles B. Dyar, Narcotics Control Officer, Office of the US High Commissioner for Germany, January 10, 1951; File 0480–9, Drugs-Beverages 1947–59; Box 63; 170–74–4; DEA; RG 170; NACP.

11. H.J. Anslinger, Commissioner of Narcotics to Mr. T.C. Green, Home Office, Whitehall, October 2, 1958; File 0480, Drugs-Beverages 1947–59; 170–74–4; DEA; RG 170; NACP.

12. Ralph Hayes to Commissioner Harry J. Anslinger, June 25, 1954 and H.J. Anslinger, Commissioner of Narcotics to Ralph Hayes, July 13, 1954; File 0480–11 #2, Drugs: Coca Leaves, 1954–1966; 170–74–4; DEA; RG 170; NACP.

13. Paul Gootenberg, "Secret Ingredients: The Politics of Coca in US-Peruvian Relations, 1915–65," *Journal of Latin American Studies* 36 (2004): 258. This article describes the regulatory shift as a "semantic change"; here I am trying to suggest its cultural, political, and economic ramifications.

14. For national and global statistics on the production and trade in cocaine across the time period, see UN Permanent Central Opium Board, *Report to the Economic and Social Council on Statistics of Narcotics for* 1946–onward . . . (E/OB).

15. UN, PCOB, Report to the Economic and Social Council on Statistics of Narcotics for 1954 and the Work of the Board in 1955, Nov. 1955 (E/OB/11), The Board, Geneva, 1955: 11.

16. It also made it easier for the Coca-Cola Company to claim (inaccurately) that their drink never contained cocaine, and to avoid the awkward discussion of the ongoing use of coca leaves in their famous product.

17. Robert S. Schwab, MD to Commissioner H.J. Anslinger, October 19, 1950; File 0480–11 #2, Drugs: Coca Leaves, 1954–1966; 170–74–4; DEA; RG 170; NACP.

18. J.W. Macmillan, Director Human Resource Division, Office of Naval Research, Department of the Navy to Mr. H.J. Anslinger, Commissioner of Narcotics, October 20, 1950; File 0480–166, Drugs: Coca Chewing (1937–1963); 170–74–12 DEA; RG 170; NACP.

19. H.J. Ansligner, Commissioner of Narcotics to Mr. Albert J. Turner, Maywood Chemical Works, October 30, 1951; File 0480–11, Drugs: Coca Leaves (1933–1953); 170–74–4; DEA; RG 170; NACP.

20. Yvan A. Reutsch, "From Cocaine to Ropivacaine: The History of Local Anesthetic Drugs," *Current Topics in Medicinal Chemistry* 1, no. 3 (August 2001): 175–82. It seemed to many that cocaine would be completely replaced by other drugs, but this never in fact happened. Yet, the promise was there as is captured in the headline: "New Analgesic Beats Cocaine" *Drug Trade News,* September 20, 1948.

21. William B. McAllister, *Drug Diplomacy in the Twentieth Century: An International History* (New York: Routledge, 2000), 164.

22. H. Halbach, "Coca Leaf, Public Health, and Narcotics Control," November 1, 1962; MHO/PA/216.62; WHO; DEA: 4.

23. US Senate, Committee on Appropriations, *Supplemental Federal Security Agency Appropriation Bill for 1949, Hearings before the Subcommittee of the Committee on Appropriations,* 80th Cong., 2d sess., May 10–12, 1948, 101.

24. "Drugs Stage a Recovery," *Business Week,* May 7, 1949, 81.

25. "Cure by Novocain," *Newsweek,* October 18, 1943. Such research was also conducted by other branches of the military; see for instance "Treatment for Flat Feet," *Science News Letter,* March 3, 1945.

26. "Pain-Killer Found Widely Effective," *New York Times* 34, no. 7, December 5, 1947.

27. "Anesthetic to Ease Arthritic Pain Found," *New York Times* 23, no. 3, September 12, 1947.

28. Dr. M.A. Vahcel, "The Role and Importance of the New Synthetic Antimalarial Drugs in the Prevention of Malaria," May 20, 1953; WHO/Mal/88; a60365; WHOA.

29. Vannevar Bush, *Science: The Endless Frontier: A Report to the President on a Program for Postwar Scientific Research* (Washington, DC: National Science Foundation, July 1945, reprinted 1960), 53–54.

30. Bush, *Science,* 53.

31. There is a longer colonial history to antimalarial research that is described in Charles Morrow Wilson, *Ambassadors in White: The Story of American Tropical Medicine* (New York: Kenikat Press, 1942) and Warwick Anderson, *Colonial Pathologies: American Tropical Medicine, Race, and Hygiene in the Philippines* (Durham, NC: Duke University Press, 2006).

32. Vahcel, "Role and Importance."

33. Vahcel, "Role and Importance."

34. Leonard A. Scheele, "Public Health and Foreign Policy," *Annals of the American Academy of Political and Social Science* 278, Search for National Security (November 1951): 62–64.

35. "U.S. Drug Makers: Overseas in a Big Way," *Business Week,* February 5, 1955, 94. About 26 percent of US drug exports went to Latin America, and of the companies in 1954 with $100 million or more in yearly sales, "few sell less than 25% of their output abroad. Some sell much more."

36. Marcos Cueto, "*Indigenismo* and Rural Medicine in Peru: The Indian Sanitary Brigade and Manuel Nuñez Butrón," *Bulletin of the History of Medicine* 65 (1991): 22. It is important to note that Cueto in this piece is actually writing about the convergence of a number of factors that actually made this particular initiative an exceptional example of collaboration and exchange rather than simply an imposition of Western scientific norms.

37. Ashish Nandy, "Introduction: Science as a Reason of State," in *Science, Hegemony, and Violence: A Requiem for Modernity,* ed. Ashish Nandy (Delhi: Oxford University Press, 1990), 1–3.

38. Shiv Visvanathan, *A Carnival of Science: Essays on Science, Technology, and Development* (Delhi: Oxford University Press, 1997), 22.

39. Stanley D. Tarbell and Ann Tracy Tarbell, *Roger Adams, 1889–1971: A Biographical Memoir* (Washington, DC: National Academy of Sciences, 1982), 3, 11, 13.

40. Adams, "Man's Synthetic Future," 163.

41. Adelaide Kerr, "Man-Made Morphine Substitutes Pose New Narcotics Problem," *Washington Post*, December 21, 1947, B8.

42. UN, ECOSOC, Third Committee, Social Humanitarian and Cultural Questions, 87th Meeting, 29 September 1948, Official Record, NY, 1948, 9–10, 14–15, 19–20.

43. UN, ECOSOC, Third Committee, Social Humanitarian and Cultural Questions, 88th Meeting, 30 September 1948, Official Record, NY, 1948, 23–24.

44. *Protocol Bringing Under International Control Drugs Outside the Scope of the Convention of 13 July 1931 for Limiting the Manufacture and Regulating the Distribution of Narcotic Drugs, as amended by the Protocol signed at Lake Success on 11 December 1946. Signed at Paris, on 19 November 1948*, UN Treaty Series, No. 688, 278–9.

45. WHO, "New Synthetic Drugs to be Examined by WHO Experts," Press Release No. 749, January 24, 1949; 463-3-1; WHOA.

46. Charles C. Fulton, "The Identification of Cocaine and Novocaine," *Pamphlets on Medical and Chemical Aspects of Dangerous Drugs* 16, nos. 255–92 (#283), Société de Nations, 178.8 A12, no.283, UN Library, Geneva.

47. Anslinger to Mr. E.L. Shamhart, Deputy Commissioner of Customs, August 6, 1945; File 0480–56, Novocaine (1933–1947); Box 133; 170–74–12; DEA; RG 170; NACP.

48. "Circular No. 51," G.W. Cunningham, Acting Commissioner, Bureau of Narcotics, August 20, 1952; File 0480, Drugs: General; 170–74–4; DEA; RG 170; NACP.

49. P.O. Wolff, Head, Unit of Habit-forming Drugs, WHO, to Dr. Eddy, October 25th, 1949; 463-2-1; WHOA.

50. Nathan B. Eddy, Medical Officer, USPS to Dr. P. Osvaldo Wolff, Office of the Director General, WHO, November 2, 1949; 463-2-7; WHOA.

51. "WHO: It's Achievements . . .," March 4, 1953; WHOA.

52. William H. Hodge, "Coca," *Natural History* 46 (February 1947): 86–93.

53. "WHO: It's Achievements . . .," March 4, 1953; WHOA.

54. On the racial politics in the history of cocaine regulation, see for example David F. Musto, *The American Disease: Origins of Narcotics Control* (New York: Oxford University Press, 1973), 6–8; and Michael M. Cohen, "Jim Crow's Drug War: Race, Coca-Cola and the Southern Origins of Drug Prohibition," *Southern Cultures* 12, no. 3 (Fall 2006): 55–79.

55. A.L. Tatum and M.H. Seevers, "Experimental Cocaine Addiction," *Journal of Pharmacology and Experimental Therapeutics* 36, no. 3 (July 1929): 401.

56. W.E. Dixon, "Cocaine Addiction," given as a talk at the Society for the Study of Inebriety, October 14, 1924, *Bound Volumes of Miscellaneous Pamphlets on Medical and Chemical Aspects of Dangerous Drugs* 12, nos. 131–60 (#138), Société de Nations, 178.8 A12, no. 138, UN Library, Geneva.

57. Tatum and Seevers, "Experimental Cocaine Addiction," 405.

58. US Senate, *Appropriation Bill for 1949*, 101–2.

59. US House, Subcommittee on Appropriations for Treasury and Post Office Departments, Committee on Appropriations, *Treasury Department Appropria-*

tions Bill for 1939, Hearings before the Subcommittee of the Committee on Appropriations, 75th Cong., 3d sess., December 1937, 376.

60. Nancy D. Campbell, *Discovering Addiction: The Science and Politics of Substance Abuse Research* (Ann Arbor: University of Michigan Press 2007), 30, 40.

61. US Senate, *Appropriation Bill for 1949,* 101.

62. See history of legislation as described in the *Narcotics Manufacturing Act of 1960,* Public Law 86–429, 86th Cong., 2d sess., April 22, 1960.

63. Campbell, *Discovering Addiction,* 119.

64. J.D. Reichard, "Addiction: Some Theoretical Considerations as to Its Nature, Cause, Prevention and Treatment," *American Journal of Psychiatry* 103 (1947): 721–28.

65. Campbell, *Discovering Addiction,* 81.

66. US Senate, *Appropriation Bill for 1949,* 113, 116.

67. Gertrude Samuels, "A Visit to Narco," *New York Times,* April 10, 1966.

68. US Senate, *Appropriation Bill for 1949,* 133.

69. John Welsh, "Lexington Narcotics Hospital: A Special Sort of Alma Mater," *Science,* New Series 182, no. 4116 (Dec. 7, 1973): 1005.

70. US Senate, *Appropriation Bill for 1949,* 136.

71. John T. Connor, "An Early Skirmish in the Global War Against Disease," 1958; pamphlet in RG 2; General Correspondence 1958; Series 200; RFA: 13.

72. Lawrence A. Clayton, *Peru and the United States: The Condor and the Eagle* (Athens: University of Georgia Press, 1999), 172.

73. Connor, "Early Skirmish," 7.

74. For more extensive discussions of development projects see Kenneth Lehman, *Bolivia and the United States;* and Jon Kofas, *Foreign Debt and Underdevelopment: U.S.-Peru Economic Relations, 1930–1970* (Lanham, MD: University Press of America, 1996).

75. See UN, ECOSOC, ECLA, *Economic and Legal Status of Foreign Investments in Selected Countries of Latin America: Foreign Investment in Peru,* 7 May 1951 (E/CN.12/166/Add.11) and *Investment in Bolivia* (E/CN.12/166/Add.10). Stephen Zunes has characterized Bolivia's relation to the United States as one of "extreme economic dependency." See Stephen Zunes, "The United States and Bolivia: The Taming of a Revolution, 1952–1957," *Latin American Perspectives* 28, no. 5 (September 2001): 34.

76. Lehman, *Bolivia and the United States,* 78.

77. John J. Bloomfield, "Plan Para Desarollo Un Programa de Salud Occupacional en Bolivia," *Salud Pública Boliviana* 2, no. 4 (March–May 1961): 41–48; PAHO.

78. Lehman, *Bolivia and the United States,* 27.

79. UN, *Report of the Commission of Enquiry,* 9.

80. See Joseph Gagliano, *Coca Prohibition in Peru: The Historical Debates* (Tucson: University of Arizona Press, 1994).

81. James Painter, *Bolivia and Coca: A Study in Dependency* (Boulder, CO: Lynne Rienner, 1994), 2.

82. UN, Division of Social Activities, *Draft Report of Meeting of Consultant to Consider a Preliminary Programme for the Proposed Seminar on Social*

Problems of the Indian Population and Other Related Problems, 1 September 1949; DAG 18/4.1.2.1 "Indian Affairs"; UNANY. This is discussed more extensively in the previous chapter.

83. Some 80 percent of "general taxes" revenue in the North and South Yungas, Bolivia's most densely populated region, was "derived from coca" and went toward agricultural development, road construction, and education. UN, ECOSOC, CND, Third Session, *Limitation of the Production of Raw Materials,* 19 April 1948, (E/CN.7/110), 14.

84. Carlos Gutiérrez-Noriega and Victor Wolfgang Von Hagen, "The Strange Case of the Coca Leaf," *Scientific Monthly* 70, no. 2 (February 1950): 85.

85. UN, *Report of the Commission of Enquiry,* 10.

86. United Nations, *Report of the United Nations Mission of Technical Assistance to Bolivia* (New York: UN Technical Assistance Administration, 1951), 106.

87. United Nations, "Raising Standards of Living in the Andes Mountains," *United Nations Review* 1, no. 19 (1954–1955): 19.

88. Enrique Sánchez de Lozada, *Bree ensayo sobre la realidad boliviana* (La Paz: Universo, 1940), 27, cited in Charles H. Weston, Jr. "An Ideology of Modernization: The Case of the Bolivian MNR," *Journal of Inter-American Studies* 10, no. 1 (January 1968): 96.

89. Allan R. Holmberg, "Vicos: A Peasant Hacienda Community in Peru," in *Economic Development and Social Change: The Modernization of Village Communities,* ed. George Dalton (New York: American Museum of Natural History, Natural History Press, 1971), 522.

90. UN, "Raising Standards," 19.

91. UN, *Report of the United Nations Mission of Technical Assistance to Bolivia* (New York: UN Technical Assistance Administration, 1951), 62, 64.

92. See chapter 2.

93. Holmberg, "Vicos," 531.

94. Allan R. Holmberg, "Experimental Intervention in the Field," in *Peasants, Power, and Applied Social Change: Vicos as a Model,* ed. Henry F. Dobyns et al. (London: Sage, 1971), 29.

95. Dobyns et al., *Peasants, Power,* "Introduction," 19.

96. Holmberg, "Vicos," 528.

97. See James F. Siekmeier, *Bolivian Revolution and the United States, 1952 to the Present* (University Park: Penn State University, 2011), especially chap. 2 for an overview.

98. Paul Doughty, "Human Relations: Affection, Rectitude, and Respect," in Dobyns et al., *Peasants, Power,* 96.

99. Holmberg, "Vicos," 544.

100. Holmberg, "Vicos," 547.

101. UN, *Report of the United Nations Mission,* 91–93.

102. Holmberg, "Vicos," 523.

103. James Le Fanu, *The Rise and Fall of Modern Medicine* (New York: Carroll & Graf, 2002), 215.

104. Verónica Montecinos and John Markoff, "From the Power of Economic Ideas to the Power of Economists," in *The Other Mirror: Grand Theory through*

the Lens of Latin America, ed. Miguel Angel Lentino and Fernando López-Alves (Princeton, NJ: Princeton University Press, 2001), 110.

5. THE CHEMICAL COLD WAR

1. US House, Committee on Appropriations, *Hearings before the Subcommittee on Appropriations, Treasury-Post Office Departments Appropriations for 1953,* 82nd Cong., 2d sess., 10, 11, 14–18, 21–25, 28 January 1952, 327. This echoed reports in the press. See, for instance, "Mau Mau Drug Use Seen," *New York Times,* May 12, 1953, 3; "House Committee Thinks Mau Mau Uses Narcotics," *Cleveland Call and Post,* May 23, 1953, 1C, 4C.

2. US House, Committee on Appropriations, *Hearings before the Subcommittee on Appropriations, Treasury-Post Office Departments Appropriations for 1954,* 83rd Cong., 1st sess., 10, 11, 13, 20, 25, 27, 30 March, 1, 2, 22–24 April 1953, 317.

3. US House, *Appropriations for 1954,* 317.

4. US consular officials in Nairobi doubted there were direct links between Kenyatta and the Mau Mau or Moscow; however, such highly charged accusations, much like the questionable accusations of the Mau Mau's link to drugs, provided leverage for discrediting the anticolonial struggle both in Kenya and elsewhere. The Consul General at Nairobi to the Department of State, no. 93, October 24, 1952, reprinted in *Foreign Relations of the United States, 1952–1954, Africa and South Asia* (Washington, DC: US Government Printing Office, 1979), 349–52.

5. J.A. Rogers, "Murder in Kenya!" *(Pittsburgh) Courier,* June 20, 1953, 18.

6. Ingrid Monson, *Freedom Sounds: Jazz, Civil Rights and Africa, 1950–1967* (Oxford: Oxford University Press, 2005), 134–35.

7. Odd Arne Westad, *The Global Cold War: Third World Interventions and the Making of Our Times* (New York: Cambridge University Press, 2007).

8. UN, ECOSOC, 569th Meeting, First Special Session, 24 March 1952, Official Record, NY, 1952, 2.

9. Ibid., 2. It is worth noting the vote on the US proposal to adjourn debate on the Soviet proposal was adopted with 12 votes to 3, with 2 abstentions, reflecting US influence in the council.

10. UN, ECOSOC, CND, *Report of the Seventh Session* (E/2219) 15 May 1952.

11. The CIA, for example, funded research at the USPHS Addiction Research Center on substances deemed potential useful as weapons of war, including lysergic acid diethylamide (LSD). This was only "one of fifteen penal and mental institutions utilized by the CIA in its super-secret drug development program during the 1950s." Martin A. Lee and Bruce Shlain, *Acid Dreams: The Complete Social History of LSD: The CIA, the Sixties and Beyond* (New York: Grove Press, 1992), 24.

12. UN, ESOSOC, 580th Meeting, Fourteenth Session, 25 May, 1952, Official Record, NY, 1952, 60.

13. US House, *Appropriations for 1954,* 301–2.

14. Albert E. Cowdrey, "'Germ Warfare' and Public Health in the Korean Conflict," *Journal of Medicine and Allied Sciences* 39 (1984): 154.

15. Ruth Rogaski, "Nature, Annihilation, and Modernity: China's Korean War Germ-Warfare Experience Reconsidered," *Journal of Asian Studies* 61, no. 2 (May 2002): 400.

16. US House, *Appropriations for 1954*, 300. An 1942 official report stated: "Wherever the Japanese Army goes, the drug traffic follows. In every territory conquered by the Japanese, a large part of the people become addicted to drugs."

17. UN, ECOSOC, CND, *Report to the Economic and Social Council on the Third Session of the Commission* (E/799), 28 May 1948, 22.

18. Cowdrey, "Germ Warfare," 155.

19. Cowdrey, "Germ Warfare," 153.

20. George W. Merck, "Official Report on Biological Warfare," *Bulletin of the Atomic Scientists* 2, nos. 7/8 (October 1, 1946): 17.

21. See Rogaski on these campaigns in China. For a sampling of some of the major contributions to the debate on whether the United States did in fact use biological warfare in Korea, along with Cowdrey, see Stephen Endicott, "Germ Warfare and "Plausible Denial": The Korean War, 1952–1953," *Modern China* 5, no. 1 (January 1979): 79–104; "Letters," *Journal of the American Medical Association*, 284, no. 5 (August 2, 2000): 561–62; Tom Buchanan, "The Courage of Galileo: Joseph Needham and the 'Germ Warfare' Allegations in the Korean War," *Journal of the Historical Association* 86 (October 2001): 503–22; Milton Leitenberg, "Resolution of the Korean War Biological Warfare Allegations," *Critical Reviews in Microbiology* 24, no. 3 (1998): 169–94.

22. "Germ Warfare in Korea?" *Science News Letter*, July 8, 1950, 22; "Defense Against BW," *Science News Letter*, August 21, 1954, 115.

23. "Secret Weapon—Opium," *New York Times*, January 2, 1953, 14. In a similar vein, the 2002 "National Youth Anti-Drug Campaign" run by the US Office of National Drug Control Policy put out a number of "I helped" terrorism Public Service Announcements featuring young people's confessions. "Where do terrorists get their money?" the ads asked. "If you buy drugs, some of it might come from you."

24. Alwyn St. Charles, *The Narcotics Menace* (Los Angeles: Borden, 1952), 20–21. His description also suggested that "doped-up" "Communist troops have plunged heedlessly into the bayonets of United Nations soldiers in wild (Banzai) charges," suggesting the widespread utility of invoking a drug frenzy as a disavowal of the political origins of conflict (24).

25. US House, *Appropriations for 1954*, 300.

26. William McAllister, *Drug Diplomacy in the Twentieth Century: An International History* (New York: Routledge, 2000), 185.

27. US Senate, Committee on Foreign Relations, *Hearing before a Subcommittee of the Committee on Foreign Relations, International Opium Protocol*, 83rd Cong., 2d sess., 17 July, 1954, 8.

28. "Protocol for Limiting and Regulating the Cultivation of the Poppy Plant, the Production of, International and Wholesale Trade in, and the Use of Opium," concluded at New York on 23 June 1953 (No. 456), *United Nations Treaty Series*, 56 (1963).

29. "Protocol," 5. The seven included Bulgaria, Greece, India, Iran, Turkey, USSR, and Yugoslavia.

30. "Protocol," 82.

31. "Protocol," 24; McAllister, *Drug Diplomacy*, 180–81; US Senate, *International Opium Protocol*, 26.

32. David R. Bewley-Taylor, *The United States and International Drug Control, 1909–1997* (New York: Pinter, 1999), 92–95.

33. US Senate, *International Opium Protocol*, 8. The Soviet Union was ready to participate in the drug control regime; it just challenged aspects that were being dictated by the United States. In fact, Anslinger testified, "We do not find any leakage from the Soviet orbit." In this, I argue, one can see a new imperial rivalry over the terms of global economic regulation.

34. Bewley-Taylor, *United States and International Drug Control*, 148–58.

35. Earle V. Simrell, "History of Legal and Medical Roles in Narcotic Abuse in the US," *Public Health Reports* 83, no. 7 (July 1968): 588.

36. Bewley-Taylor, *United States and International Drug Control*, 160.

37. McAllister, *Drug Diplomacy*, 185–211.

38. UN General Assembly, Fifteenth Session, 1960–61. Delegation from the US, *The United States in the United Nations—1960 A Turning Point*, Report to the Committee on Foreign Relations, US Senate by George D. Aiken [and] Wayne Morse, members of the Delegation of the US to the Fifteenth Session of the General Assembly of the United Nations (Washington, DC: US Government Printing Office, 1961), 10–11.

39. Harold Karan Jacobson, "The United Nations and Colonialism: A Tentative Appraisal," *International Organization* 16, no. 1 (Winter 1962): 40–41.

40. Rupert Emerson, "Colonialism, Political Development, and the UN," *International Organization* 19, no. 3, The United Nations: Accomplishments and Prospects (Summer 1965): 484; Edward T. Rowe, "The Emerging Anti-Colonial Consensus in the United Nations," *Journal of Conflict Resolution* 8, no. 3 (September 1964): 229.

41. Annette Baker Fox, "International Organization for Colonial Development," *World Politics* 3, no. 3 (1951): 343.

42. UN General Assembly, Seventh Session, Resolution 67 (VII), "The Right of Peoples and Nations to Self-Determination," December 20, 1952.

43. See Rowe, "Emerging Anti-Colonial Consensus," for an analysis of the powers' voting records at the United Nations during this time period. Rowe characterizes the United States as, along with New Zealand, having "the least pro-colonial records on an overall basis among the colonial powers." At this moment, the colonial powers responsible for non-self-governing territories included Australia, Belgium, Denmark, France, the Netherlands, New Zealand, the United Kingdom, and the United States. The trust territories, defined as temporary mandates on the road to self-government, were administered by Australia, Belgium, France, Italy, New Zealand, the United Kingdom, and the United States.

44. While the status of many shifted over the next two decades, in 1946 US non-self-governing territories included Puerto Rico, Alaska, the Panama Canal Zone, Hawaii, the US Virgin Islands, American Samoa, the Philippines, and Guam. The US Trust Territory of the Pacific Islands included what are now called the Federated States of Micronesia, the Northern Mariana Islands, the

Marshall Islands, and Palau. For an interesting discussion of US-trust territory politics, including the (exclusive) designation of the Pacific Island as a "strategic area" to provide greater control than ordinarily permitted under the UN Trusteeship system, see Harold Karan Jacobson, "Our 'Colonial' Problem in the Pacific," *Foreign Affairs* 39, no. 1 (October 1960): 56–66.

45. Henry Heller, *The Cold War and the New Imperialism: A Global History, 1945–2005* (New York: Monthly Review, 2006), 79. See also Fox, "International Organization," 342.

46. Jacobson, "United Nations and Colonialism," 40.

47. Mason Sears, *Memorandum by the United States Representative on the Trusteeship Council*, September 22, 1953, reprinted in *Foreign Relations of the United States, 1952–1954, United Nations Affairs* (Washington, DC: US Government Printing Office, 1979), 1165.

48. Delegation from the US, *United States in the United Nations*, 21.

49. Jacobson, "United Nations and Colonialism," 51.

50. Hollis W. Barber, "The United States vs. The United Nations," *International Organization* 27, no. 2 (Spring 1973): 146.

51. Barber, "United States," 146; Edward T. Rowe, "Financial Support for the United Nations: Evolution of Member Contributions, 1946–1969," *International Organization* 26, no. 4 (Autumn 1972): 655.

52. Barber, "United States," 148.

53. Emerson, "Colonialism," 484–85.

54. Edward McWhinney, "Introduction and Procedural History of the Declaration on the Granting of Independence to Colonial Countries and Peoples," accessed in November 2013 from the website of the United Nations Audiovisual Library of International Law, www.un.org/law/avl. For works on the non-aligned movement see Peter Willets, *The Non-Aligned Movement: The Origins of the Third World Alliance* (New York: Nichols, 1978); A.W. Singham, ed., *The Non-Aligned Movement in World Politics* (Westport, CT: Lawrence & Hill, 1978); F. Stephen Larrabee, "The Soviet Union and the Non-Aligned," *World Today* 32, no. 12 (December 1976): 467–75.

55. Emerson, "Colonialism," 495; United Nations, General Assembly, Fifteenth Session, Resolution 1514 (XV), "Declaration on the Granting of Independence to Colonial Countries and Peoples," December 14, 1960.

56. Seymour M. Finger, "A New Approach to Colonial Problems at the United Nations," *International Organization* 26, no. 1 (Winter 1972): 143–44; Barber, "United States," 151–52. Jacobson, "United Nations and Colonialism," describes the Latin American role in the General Assembly in a similar vein: "The Latin American states have generally been more sensitive to the Cold War implications of the UN's actions in this field and more responsive to US leadership" (44).

57. This effectively replaced the 1953 Protocol just one and a half years after it had received enough signatures to come into effect.

58. US House, Committee on Appropriations, *Hearings before a Subcommittee of the Committee on Appropriations, Treasury-Post Office Departments and Executive Office Appropriations for 1963*, 87th Cong., 2d sess., 22–25, 30, 31 February, 1, 2, 7, 8 March 1962, 283–84.

59. Anslinger's position was extreme and the State Department in fact supported the Single Convention. His use of anticommunist fear-mongering rhetoric was typical Anslinger fare, and was rooted in his effort to retain his and the FBN's authority at the helm of drug control, and a genuine reluctance to retreat at all from what he saw as regulatory advances (in this case the Single Convention's revision of the 1953 Protocol in allowing Chinese inclusion and extending the number of legal cultivators and exporters of opium). However, despite these changes, Anslinger did ultimately support the Single Convention. For a discussion of the State Department–Anslinger split and the enduring US influence on the final treaty, see Bewley-Taylor, *United States and International Drug Control,* 136–61.

60. US House, *Appropriations for 1963,* 285–86.

61. Quote in Bewley-Taylor, *United States and International Drug Control,* 80–81.

62. *Convention on Narcotic Drugs, 1961, Message from the President of the United States transmitting the Single Convention on Narcotic Drugs, 1961, open for signature at New York, March 30, 1961, to August 1, 1961, along with the final act of the United Nations conference at which the Convention was adopted* (Washington, DC: US Government Printing Office, 1967), iii, vi; see also McAllister, *Drug Diplomacy,* 217.

63. US Senate, *International Opium Protocol,* 17–18.

64. William O. Walker, *Opium and Foreign Policy: The Anglo-American Search for Order in Asia, 1912–1954* (Chapel Hill: University of North Carolina Press, 1991), 197.

65. US Senate, *International Opium Protocol,* 20. For more information on the embargo, see Shu Guang Zhang, *Economic Cold War: America's Embargo Against China and the Sino-Soviet Alliance, 1949–1963* (Stanford, CA: Stanford University Press, 2001).

66. In similar testimony before the House, the commissioner described Chinese efforts to sell opium as "perfectly ridiculous," while simultaneously confirming that "Unquestionably a lot of this has disappeared into the illicit traffic" (US House, *Appropriations for 1954,* 302). A number of historians have documented the fundamental inaccuracy and political expediency of Anslinger's allegations of Communist dope pushing. See, for example, Douglas Clark Kinder, "Bureaucratic Cold Warrior: Harry J. Anslinger and Illicit Narcotics Traffic," *Pacific Historical* Review 50, no. 2 (May, 1981): 169–91; Douglas Clark Kinder and William O. Walker III, "Stable Force in a Storm: Harry J. Anslinger and United States Narcotic Foreign Policy, 1930–1962," *Journal of American History* 72, no. 4 (March 1986): 908–27; McAllister, *Drug Diplomacy;* Jeremy Kuzmarov, *The Myth of the Addicted Army: Vietnam and the Modern War on Drugs* (Boston: University of Massachusetts Press, 2009), 38. For this ongoing tactic vis-à-vis US anticommunist foreign policy, see Alfred McCoy, *The Politics of Heroin in Southeast Asia* (New York: Harper and Row, 1972).

67. Stuart Hall et al., *Policing the Crisis: Mugging, the State, and Law and Order* (Hong Kong: Macmillan Press, 1982), vii–viii.

68. On Cold War cultural paranoia see Stephen J. Whitfield, *The Culture of the Cold War* (Baltimore: Johns Hopkins University Press, 1996); Richard M.

Fried, *The Russians Are Coming! The Russians Are Coming! Pageantry and Patriotism in Cold War America* (New York: Oxford University Press, 1998).

69. US Senate, *International Opium Protocol*, 45.

70. Ibid., 38, 50. The chairman concluded the hearing by reminding his audience "there are many weapons that the Communists use. . . . We can have Pearl Harbors again in many ways. This is one of them if we are not alert to the terrific impact of this opium menace" (51).

71. A number of scholars have described the long history of American ideological depictions of drug addiction as a foreign, imported contagious disease. See especially David F. Musto, *The American Disease: Origins of Narcotic Control* (New York: Oxford University Press, 1999), and chapter 1 in Daniel Weimer, *Seeing Drugs: Modernization, Counterinsurgency, and US Narcotics Control in the Third World, 1969–1976* (Kent, OH: Kent State University Press, 2011).

72. US House, *Appropriations for 1954*, 315–16.

73. "Article 1- No Title," *New York Times*, January 29, 1953, 3.

74. John H. Thompson, "Number of Vet Dope Users in Prisons Grows," *Daily Defender*, April 1, 1956, 24.

75. "Narcotics' Use by Korea Yanks Worries 'Brass'," *Chicago Daily Tribune*, February 9, 1953, B12.

76. US House, *Appropriations for 1954*, 299–300.

77. Richard H. Kuh, "A Prosecutor's Thoughts Concerning Addiction," *Journal of Law, Criminology, and Police Science* 52, no. 3 (September–October 1961): 322.

78. "Youth Forum Outlines Needs for Right Living," *Los Angeles Times*, November 20, 1952, B1.

79. Lois L. Higgins, "The Status of Narcotic Addiction in the United States," *American Biology Teacher* 16, no. 4 (April 1954): 94.

80. "Dope in Space Age Health Fair Topic," *Daily Defender* (Chicago), March 21, 1960, A20.

81. Frederic Sondern, Jr., "We Must Stop the Crime that Breeds Crime!" *Reader's Digest* 68 (June 1956): 21–26.

82. Jacquelyn Dowd Hall, "The Long Civil Rights Movement and the Political Uses of the Past," *Journal of American History* 91, no. 4 (March 2005): 1249 [emphasis in the original].

83. Joel Rosch, "Crime as an Issue in American Politics," in *The Politics of Crime and Criminal Justice*, eds. Erika Fairchild et al. (Beverly Hills, CA: Sage, 1985), 27. For good overviews of the connection between crime, race, and American society, see Loïc Wacqant, "From Slavery to Mass Incarceration," *New Left Review* 13 (January–February 2002): 41–60; Colin Dayan, *The Story of Cruel and Unusual* (Cambridge, MA: MIT Press, 2007); Michelle Alexander, *The New Jim Crow: Mass Incarceration in the Age of Colorblindness* (New York: New Press, 2009); Heather Ann Thompson, "Why Mass Incarceration Matters: Rethinking Crisis, Decline, and Transformation in Postwar American History," *Journal of American History* 97, no. 3 (December 2010): 703–34.

84. US House, Committee on Appropriations, *Hearings before a Subcommittee of the Committee on Appropriations, Treasury-Post Office Departments*

Appropriations for 1962, 87th Cong., 1st sess., 16, 28 February, 1, 2, 6–10, 13 March 1961, 267.

85. "Resume of Hearings Conducted on June 12, 13, 14 by Attorney General Nathaniel. L. Goldstein, at the State Office Building, New York City, Investigation Pursuant to Chapter 528 of the Laws of 1951"; Vol. I–IV, 46–59; Branch Registries; Archives and Records Services; Registry Section; S-0441–0511; United Nations Archives, NY [UNANY].

86. "Degradation in New York," *Newsweek* 37, June 25, 1951, 19–20. President Truman had dismissed General MacArthur in April 1951 over tactical disagreements in the Korean War.

87. "Narcotics: An Ever-Growing Problem," *Newsweek* 37, June 11, 1951. 26.

88. US House, Committee on Appropriations, "Control of Narcotics, Marihuana, and Barbiturates," 82nd Cong., 1st sess., 7, 14, and 17 April 1951, 40–41.

89. Harry J. Anslinger and William F. Tompkins, *The Traffic in Narcotics* (New York: Funk & Wagnalls, 1953), 166.

90. John C. McWilliams, *The Protectors: Harry J. Anslinger and the Federal Bureau of Narcotics, 1930–1962* (Newark: University of Delaware Press, 1990), 108. "Narcotics" was extended under the law to apply not simply to coca, opium, and their derivatives but also to barbiturates and marijuana. The Boggs Act did not distinguish between trafficking and possession, as Rep. Boggs explained: "It is not the intent of this legislation to affect a teen-ager or any such person who has possession of narcotics. But the gentleman also knows that if we try to make a distinction between possession and peddling, that we immediately open the law to all types of abuse." See Richard J. Bonnie and Charles H. Whitebread II, "The Forbidden Fruit and The Tree of Knowledge: An Inquiry Into the Legal History of American Marijuana Prohibition," *Virginia Law Review* 56, no. 6 (October 1970): 971–1203.

91. Alfred R. Lindesmith, "How to Stop the Dope Traffic," *The Nation* 182 (April 21, 1956): 337–39. These were the *only* crimes for which mandatory minimum sentences existed, apart from a federal statute decreeing twenty-five years for armed robbery of the mails. US House, Committee on Appropriations, *Hearings before a Subcommittee of the Committee on Appropriations, Treasury-Post Office Departments Appropriations for 1959*, 85th Cong., 2d sess., 22–24 January, 3 February 1958, 125.

92. US Treasury Department, *Traffic in Opium . . . Year Ended December 31, 1950*, 10.

93. "Control of Narcotics, Marihuana, and Barbiturates . . .," 82nd Cong., 1951, 69.

94. McWilliams, *Protectors,* 115.

95. Stanley Meisler, "Federal Narcotics Czar," *The Nation,* February 20, 1960.

96. In fact, according to a survey conducted by a committee convened by the president, "the size of the problem [was] considerably below that suggested by popular statements which have been made during recent years. The Committee feels that the problem has been somewhat exaggerated, though it does not wish

to deprecate its qualitative aspects. This is particularly true with respect to the numbers of juvenile addicts; while it is reassuring to find that the total number is considerably smaller than it had been thought to be, the fact that any young persons have become involved is clearly a matter of concern." "Revised Draft of Interim Report; Interdepartmental Committee on Narcotics," November 28, 1955; File 0120–40, Background Material; 170–73–1; DEA; RG 170; NACP.

97. "Degradation in New York," *Newsweek* 37, June 25, 1951, 19–20.

98. Mc Williams, *Protectors,* 10. In 1951, the government increased the FBN's appropriation by $650,000 to $2.5 million and in 1956 it was increased by another $530,000 to $3.7 million.

99. US House, Committee on Appropriations, *Hearings before a Subcommittee of the Committee on Appropriations, Treasury-Post Office Departments Appropriations for 1956,* 84th Cong., 1st sess., 31 January, 1–4, 7–9, 14, 16, 18, 23 March, 1955, 189.

100. US House, Committee on Appropriations, *Hearings before a Subcommittee of the Committee on Appropriations, Treasury-Post Office Departments Appropriations for 1958,* 85th Cong., 1st sess., 25, 28–31 January, 1, 4–6, 22 February 1957, 355.

101. US House, *Appropriations for 1963,* 294–95.

102. US House, *Appropriations for 1953,* 304.

103. US House, *Appropriations for 1958,* 368.

104. US House, *Appropriations for 1958,* 355.

105. US House, *Appropriations for 1954,* 309–10.

106. "Revised Draft of Interim Report . . .," November 28, 1955.

107. Alfred R. Lindesmith, "Dope: Congress Encourages the Traffic," *The Nation* 184 (March 16, 1957): 228–31.

108. US House, *Appropriations for 1959,* 104.

109. Mc Williams, *Protectors,* 115. There had been a general increase in the number of enforcement personnel assigned to narcotics squads at the state and municipal level as well. The FBN directed a special training program for local narcotics enforcement, which was part of a larger national effort to extend enforcement and coordinate policing at all levels, and the Interdepartmental Committee on Narcotics outlined a plan for the "coordination of enforcement activities in this field, including the exchange of reports and information with the Bureau of Narcotics and enforcement agencies of other States and municipalities." See "Revised Draft of Interim Report . . .," November 28, 1955.

110. Gene Sherman, "Police Meet Toughest Problem in Narcotics Traffic," *Los Angeles Times,* July 19, 1959, 1, 23.

111. "No 'Due Process' in 'Secret Indictments'," *Los Angeles Tribune,* October 2, 1958, 8, 10.

112. Mina Yang, "A Thin Blue Line Down Central Avenue: The LAPD and the Demise of a Musical Hub," *Black Music Research Journal* 22, no. 2 (Autumn 2002): 232.

113. Lindesmith, "Dope," 229; Alfred R. Lindesmith, "Our Immoral Drug Laws," *The Nation* 186, June 22, 1958, 558.

114. US House, *Appropriations for 1958,* 363–64.

115. Nathan B. Eddy and Harris Isbell, MD, "Addiction Liability and Narcotics Control," *Public Health Reports* 74, no. 9 (September 1959): 756–57 [emphasis added].

116. Eddy and Isbell, "Addiction Liability," 757, 759, 762.

117. See, for example, Charles O. Jackson, "The Amphetamine Democracy: Medicinal Abuse in the Popular Culture," *South Atlantic Quarterly* 74, no. 3 (1975): 308–23. For an interesting discussion of a drug panic attached to white middle-class women's consumption of valium in the late 1960s and early 1970s that unlike other drug panics did not result in punitive legal measures, see David L. Herzberg, "The Pill You Love Can Turn on You": Feminism, Tranquilizers, and the Valium Panic of the 1970s," *American Quarterly* 58, no. 1 (March 2006): 79–103.

118. US Senate, *International Opium Protocol,* 5.

119. US House, Committee on Appropriations, *Hearings before a Subcommittee of the Committee on Appropriations, Treasury-Post Office Departments Appropriations for 1961,* 86th Cong., 2d sess., 7, 25–29 January, 2–4 February, 1960, 164.

120. Kuh, "Prosecutor's Thoughts," 324–25.

121. "Legalized Addiction," *Newsweek* 49, January 7, 1957, 66; "Drug Addiction," *Science* 122, July 8, 1955, 67–68.

122. "Narcotic Dilemma," *Time* 66, October 3, 1955, 63–64.

123. "Letters," *The Nation* 182, June 2, 1956, inside cover.

124. These debates hark back to the aftermath of World War I, where potential socialist threats and growing hostility to behavior deemed deviant or subversive spilled over into disputes over whether maintaining addicts on drugs was a legitimate medical procedure, ultimately resolved in the negative by Supreme Court decisions in 1919 that led to the closing down of maintenance clinics, not to be opened again until the 1970s. H. Wayne Morgan, *Drugs in America: A Social History, 1800-1980* (New York: Syracuse University Press, 1981), 110–17; Musto, *American Disease,* 132–33.

125. Dan Wakefield, "Dope on the Downbeat," *The Nation* 185 (August 31, 1957): 92–93.

126. "Large Number of Dope Addicts Among Doctors," *Science News Letter,* March 23, 1957, 185. Similar sentiments are expressed toward "professional and business men who have families and business and social responsibilities" in Anslinger, *Traffic in Narcotics,* 210.

127. US House, *Appropriations for 1958,* 357.

128. US House, *Appropriations for 1958,* 367–68.

129. Winick, Charles, "Narcotics Addiction and Its Treatment," *Law and Contemporary Problems* 22, no. 1, Narcotics (Winter 1957): 15.

130. Harry Allen Feldman, "Jazz: A Place in Music Education?" *Music Educators Journal* 50, no. 6 (June–July 1964): 60.

131. Wakefield, "Dope on the Downbeat," 92–93.

132. Alan P. Merriam and Raymond W. Mack, "The Jazz Community," *Social Forces* 38 (1959–1960): 213–16.

133. Quoted in Yang, "Thin Blue Line," 218, 227.

134. Charles Mingus, *Beneath the Underdog,* 250, quoted in Robert K. McMichael, "'We Insist-Freedom Now!': Black Moral Authority, Jazz, and the

Changeable Shape of Whiteness," *American Music* 16, no. 4 (Winter 1998): 392.

135. Reflecting a different kind of response, in 1947 the American Federation of Musicians, a division of the American Federation of Labor, "adopted a resolution banning all members who are convicted of carrying or using narcotic drugs." This was likely an effort to target black musicians perhaps in response to the recent integration of the union. "Musicians' Union to Ban Narcotic Addicts; Petrillo to Be Reelected for Eighth Term," *New York Times,* June 13, 1947.

136. Wakefield, "Dope on the Downbeat," 92–93; George E. Pitts, "Narcotics Discussion Is Key Phase of Festival," *Pittsburgh Courier,* July 20, 1957, 19.

137. Wakefield, "Dope on the Downbeat," 92–93; "Jazz Group Plans Clinic Here," *New York Times,* September 6, 1957, 12.

138. Charles Winick, "The Use of Drugs by Jazz Musicians," *Social Problems* 7, no. 3 (Winter 1959–1960): 241, 251.

139. Charles Winick, "High the Moon: Jazz and Drugs," *Antioch Review* 21, 1 (Spring 1961): 53.

140. Winick, "Use of Drugs," 250.

141. Winick, "Narcotics Addiction," 19.

142. "Music, Newport Blues," *Time,* July 18, 1960.

143. Jesse H. Walker, "Theatricals," *New York Amsterdam News,* July 2, 1960, 17; John S., "2 Jazz Festivals Open in Newport," *New York Times,* July 1, 1960, 13; Stanley Robertson, "New Abbey Lincoln Album Hits Pay Dirt," *Los Angeles Sentinel,* August 17, 1961, C3.

144. Nat Hentoff, "Bringing Dignity to Jazz," in his *The Jazz Life* (Cambridge, MA: Da Capo Press, 1975), 105–12.

145. "Music, Newport Blues," *Time,* July 18, 1960; Thomasina Norford, "Rousing Jazz Revival at Newport," *New York Amsterdam News,* July 14, 1962, 16.

146. Langston Hughes, "Week By Week (2)," *Chicago Defender,* July 23, 1960, 10.

147. Hentoff, "Bringing Dignity," 110, 100.

148. Penny Von Eschen, *Satchmo Blows Up the World: Jazz Ambassadors Play the Cold War* (Cambridge, MA: Harvard University Press, 2004), 12.

149. Von Eschen, *Satchmo,* 21, 188.

150. Gene Lees, "Jazz Battles Communism," *Music Journal* (November–December 1962): 70–74, on 73.

151. Charles Siragusa, *The Trail of the Poppy: Behind the Mask of the Mafia* (Englewood Cliffs, NJ: Prentice-Hall, 1966), 49.

152. On US-Cuban relations see Louis A. Pérez, *Cuba and the United States: Ties of Singular Intimacy,* 3rd ed. (Athens: University of Georgia Press, 2003); Lars Shoultz, *That Infernal Little Cuban Republic* (Chapel Hill: University of North Carolina Press, 2009).

153. US House, Committee on Appropriations, *Hearings before a Subcommittee of the Committee on Appropriations, Treasury-Post Office Departments Appropriations for 1960,* 86th Cong., 1st sess., 26–30 January, 2–5, 10 February 1959, 128.

154. Siragusa, *Trail of the Poppy*, 56.

155. US House, *Appropriations for 1961*, 164.

156. Siragusa, *Trail of the Poppy*, 56.

157. "Peru: The White Goddess," *Time*, April 11, 1949, 44.

158. US House, *Appropriations for 1961,*164.

159. Siragusa to Secretary of State, Telegram, March 26, 1960; File 341.9; Box 551; State Department; 59–250–3–12–2; NACP.

160. Including officials from Ecuador, Peru, Bolivia, Venezuela, Mexico, Colombia, El Salvador, Honduras, and Nicaragua. Charles Siragusa, *Report of the United States Delegation to the Second Inter-American Meeting on the Illicit Traffic in Cocaine and Coca Leaves,"* January 4, 1962; Box 54, 2nd Inter-American Conference, Brazil, 1961; 174–74–4; NACP: 10.

161. Siragusa, *Report . . . to the Second Inter-American Meeting,* 15.

162. Charles Siragusa to Dr. Joao Amoroso Netto, Bureau de Policia Internacional, December 21, 1959; File 0345, 1st Inter-American Conference, Rio de Janeiro, Brazil, 1960; Box 54; 174–4–4; NACP.

163. G. E. Yates to Anslinger, December 7, 1959; File 1230–1, United Nations 15th Session Folder #1; Box 123; 170–74–5; NACP.

164. Anslinger to Elwyn F. Chase, March 9, 1960; File 0345, 1st Inter-American Conference, Rio de Janeiro, Brazil, 1960; Box 54; 174–4–4; NACP.

165. Charles Siragusa, *Report of the United States Delegation to the First Inter-American Meeting on the Illicit Traffic in Cocaine and Coca Leaves,"* April 14, 1960; Doc. 12/1/3; File 0345, 1st Inter-American Conference, Rio de Janeiro, Brazil, 1960; Box 54; 174–4–4; NACP.

166. Leland L. Johnson, "U.S. Business Interests in Cuba and the Rise of Castro," *World Politics* 17, no. 3 (April 1965): 440–59; Shoultz, *Infernal Little Cuban Republic,* 110, 117–19; Pérez, *Cuba and the United States,* 240–43.

167. See Alejandro De La Fuente, *A Nation For All: Race, Inequality and Politics in Cuba, 1900–2000* (Chapel Hill: University of North Carolina Press, 2000).

168. Jones, Leroi (Amiri Baraka), "Cuba Libre," in *Home: Social Essays,* ed. Leroi Jones (New York: William Morrow, 1966), 53.

169. Timothy B. Tyson, *Radio Free Dixie: Robert F. Williams and the Roots of Black Power* (Chapel Hill: University of North Carolina Press, 1999), 233. See also Brenda Gayle Plummer, "Castro in Harlem: A Cold War Watershed," in *Rethinking the Cold War: Essays on Its Dynamics, Meaning, and Morality,* ed. Allen Hunter (Philadelphia: Temple University Press, 1997), and Cynthia Young, *Soul Power: Cultural Radicalism and the Making of a U.S. Third World Left* (Durham, NC: Duke University Press, 2006).

170. Delegation from the US, *United States in the United Nations,* 6.

171. Tyson, *Radio Free Dixie,* 241.

172. Charles Siragusa, *Classified Report of the United States Delegation to the Second Meeting of the Inter-American Consultative Group on Narcotics Control,"* January 4, 1962.; Box 54, 2nd Inter-American Conference, Brazil, 1961; 170–74–4; NACP: 1–2.

173. Siragusa, *Classified Report,* 5.

174. US House, *Appropriations for 1963,* 276. In fact it has been shown that anti-Castro Cubans in the United States were deeply involved in the illicit drug

trade; see Peter Dale Scott and Jonathan Marshall, *Cocaine Politics: Drugs, Armies, and the CIA in Central America* (Berkeley: University of California Press, 1991).

175. US House, *Appropriations for 1964*, 483.

CONCLUSION

1. US, House, Subcommittee on Departments of Treasury and Post Office and Executive Office Appropriations, *Treasury-Post Office Departments and Executive Office Appropriations for 1964*, 88th Cong., 1st sess., 26–28 February, 4–8, 11–14 March 1963, 445–46.

2. US, Treasury Department, Bureau of Narcotics, *Traffic in Opium and Other Dangerous Drugs for the Year Ended December 31, 1950* (Washington, DC: US Government Printing Office, 1957), 9, 18.

3. W.E. Clapham, Product Coordinator, Narcotic Products, Merck & Co., Inc. to Members and the Secretariat of the UN CND, May 9, 1955; File 1230-1, United Nations Tenth Session #2; 170-74-5; DEA; RG 170; NACP.

4. Albert J. Turner to Commissioner Anslinger, May 22, 1958; File 1230-1, United Nations Thirteenth Session #2; 170-74-5; DEA; RG 170; NACP.

5. Ralph Hayes to Commissioner Harry J. Anslinger, May 5, 1955; File 0480-11, #2 Drugs: Coca Leaves (January 1954-66); 170-74-4; DEA; RG 170; NACP.

6. Anslinger to Mr. Rossow, November 24, 1962; File 0345, 3rd Inter-American Conference, Lima, Peru, 11–26 through 12-8-62; Box 54; 170-74-4; DEA; RG 170; NACP; Donald H. Francis to Edgard Velasco Arboleda, November 29, 1962; File 0345, 3rd Inter-American Conference, Lima, Peru, 11–26 through 12-8-62; Box 54; 170-74-4; DEA; RG 170; NACP.

7. Siragusa to Giordano, "Consultive Group on the Problems of the Coca Leaf," November 29, 1962; Box 54; 170-74-4; DEA; RG170; NACP.

8. The deep involvement of Coca-Cola executives in these negotiations has also been described by Paul Gootenberg in "Secret Ingredients: The Politics of Coca in US-Peruvian Relations, 1915–1965," *Journal of Latin American Studies* 36, no. 2 (May 2004): 261–62. Gootenberg argues Coca-Cola did not dominate US cocaine policy toward Peru, but rather was "a junior partner in evolving US drug policies" (265). Whatever their relative influence, I am more interested in pointing out the economic priorities that structured drug control toward the interests of US corporations, which were able through their very collaboration with drug control to limit scrutiny of their own direct involvement in marketing products that involved controlled substances, and in the process further entrench imperial inequities in the trade.

9. Miguel E. Bustamente, Secretary General, PASB to Miss Howell, Liaison Officer, WHO, March 29th, 1951; CC-4-1-AMRO; WHOA.

10. A. Drobney, Acting Chief, Health Promotion Branch, PASB to Dr. R.L. Coigney, Chief LOUN, Chief WHO Liaison Office, United Nations, October 7, 1960; A2/112/C/5; WHOA.

11. A.J. Lucas, M.D., Chief Section I, Division of Narcotic Drugs to Dr. Coigney, November 9, 1960; A2/112/C/5; WHOA.

12. "Preparations for the Implementation of the Single Convention of 1961"; *Single Convention on Narcotic Drugs;* A2/36/3; WHOA.

13. James W. Brown, Jr. MD to Director of Food and Drug Administration, July 29, 1969; Folder 521–521.95; 88-130-62-33-2; File 521.04, Cocaine; General Subject Files, 1938–1974; FDA; RG 88; NACP.

14. This information can be found on the Drug Enforcement Administration's Diversion Control Division's website: www.deadiversion.usdoj.gov/index. html.

15. United Nations, *Narcotic Drugs: Estimated World Requirements for 2012—Statistics for 2010* (New York: UN Office on Drugs and Crime, April 2012), 206–7. Peru is now a major manufacturer of cocaine once again (although not for export to the United States). The United States and Peru are the only national manufacturers of cocaine, and while UN statistics on the surface suggest Peru's manufacture is greater, since cocaine produced as a by-product in the process of making Coca-Cola is not included in the UN tally of cocaine yield, it seems that in fact the United States likely remains the largest producer worldwide manufacturer of cocaine.

16. United Nations, Economic and Social Council, *Report of the Commission of Enquiry on the Coca Leaf, May 1950,* Fifth Year, Twelfth Session, Special Supplement 1. Official Record (E/1666/Add.1) (Lake Success, New York: United Nations, July 1950), 82.

17. Economic and Social Council, United Nations, "Substantive Session of 2009," (E/2009/78), July 6–31, 2009, 4–5.

18. Global Commission on Drug Policy, *War on Drugs: Report of the Global Commission on Drug Policy* (June 2011), 8, accessed November 2, 2012, www. globalcommissionondrugs.org/wp-content/themes/gcdp_v1/pdf/Global_Commission_Report_English.pdf.

Works Cited

Abraham, Itty, and Willem van Schendel. "Introduction: The Making of Illicitness." In *Illicit Flows and Criminal Things: States, Borders, and the Other Side of Globalization,* edited by Willem van Schendel and Itty Abraham, 1–37. Bloomington: Indiana University Press, 2005.

Adams, Roger. "Man's Synthetic Future." *Science* 115, no. 2981 (February 15, 1952): 157–63.

Alexander, Michelle. *The New Jim Crow: Mass Incarceration in the Age of Colorblindness.* New York: New Press, 2009.

Anderson, Warwick. *Colonial Pathologies: American Tropical Medicine, Race, and Hygiene in the Philippines.* Durham, NC: Duke University Press, 2006.

Andrade, Victor. "Bolivia—Past and Future: Economic Diversification Necessary to Avoid Chaos." *Vital Speeches of the Day* 23, no. 2 (November 1, 1956): 62–65.

———. *My Missions for Revolutionary Bolivia, 1944–1962.* London: University of Pittsburgh Press, 1976.

Anslinger, Harry Jacob, and William F. Tompkins. *The Traffic in Narcotics.* New York: Arno Press, 1981, c1953.

Anslinger, Harry Jacob. *The Protectors: The Heroic of the Narcotics Agents, Citizens, and Officials in Their Unending, Unsung Battles Against Organized Crime in America and Abroad.* New York: Farrar, Straus, 1964.

Armstrong, O.K. "Lend-Lease in War and Peace." *Nation's Business,* August 1942, 25.

Aspiazu, René Bascopé. *La Veta Blanca: Coca y Cocaíne en Bolivia.* La Paz: Ediciones Aquí, 1982.

Associated Press. "Opium Put in Vaults of Treasury." *Deseret News,* March 8, 1940, 2.

———. "50 Armored Trains to Carry Federal Gold." *New York Times,* August 8, 1936, 1.

Bachrach, Fabian. "George W. Merck Dies at Age 63." *New York Times,* November 10, 1957, 86.

Barber, Hollis W. "The United States vs. the United Nations." *International Organization* 27, no. 2 (Spring 1973): 139–63.

Barron's. "Growth Stocks and the Investor." December 15, 1941, 13.

Baum, Dan. *Smoke and Mirrors: The War on Drugs and the Politics of Failure.* New York: Little, Brown, 1997.

Beals, Carleton. "Ecuador, Peru and Bolivia." In *What the South Americans Think of US,* edited by Carleton Beals, Bryce Oliver, Herschel Brickell, and Samuel Guy Inman, 7–88. New York: Robert M. McBride, 1945.

Benjamin, Jr., Ludy T., Anne M. Rogers, and Angela Rosenbaum. "Coca-Cola, Caffeine, and Mental Deficiency: Harry Hollingworth and the Chattanooga Trial of 1911." *Journal of the History of Behavioral Sciences* 27 (January 1991): 42–55.

Bewley-Taylor, David R. *The United States and International Drug Control, 1909–1997.* New York: Pinter, 2002.

Bidwell, Percy W. "Self-Containment and Hemisphere Defense." *Annals of the American Academy of Political and Social Science* 218, Public Policy in a World at War (November 1941): 175–85.

———. "Our Economic Warfare." *Foreign Affairs* 20, no. 3 (April 1942): 421–37.

Bloomfield, John J. "Plan Para Desarrollo Un Programa de Salud Occupacional en Bolivia." *Salud Pública Boliviana* 2, no. 4 (Mar–Mayo 1961): 41–48.

Boldó i Clement, Joan, ed. *La Coca Andina: Visión Indígena de una Planta Satanizada.* Coyoacán, Mexico: Instituto Indigenista Interamericano, 1986.

Bonnie, Richard J., and Charles H. Whitebread II. "The Forbidden Fruit and The Tree of Knowledge: An Inquiry Into the Legal History of American Marijuana Prohibition." *Virginia Law Review* 56, no. 6 (October 1970): 971–1203.

Briggs, Laura. *Reproducing Empire: Race, Sex, Science, and U.S. Imperialism in Puerto Rico.* Berkeley: University of California Press, 2002.

Bush, Vannevar. *Science: The Endless Frontier: A Report to the President on a Program for Postwar Scientific Research.* Washington, DC: National Science Foundation, July 1945, reprinted 1960.

Buchanan, Tom. "The Courage of Galileo: Joseph Needham and the 'Germ Warfare' Allegations in the Korean War." *Journal of the Historical Association* 86 (October 2001): 503–22.

Business Week. "Drugs Stage a Recovery." May 7, 1949, 81.

———. "U.S. Drug Makers: Overseas in a Big Way." February 5, 1955, 94.

Cabiesis, Fernando. *La Coca ¿Dilema Trágico?* Lima: Empresario Nacional de la Coca, 1992.

Campbell, Nancy D. *Discovering Addiction: The Science and Politics of Substance Abuse Research.* Ann Arbor: University of Michigan Press 2007.

Cardoso, Fernando Henrique, and Enzo Faletto, *Dependency and Development in Latin America.* Translated by Marjory Mattingly Murquidi. Berkeley: University of California Press, 1979.

Cassanelli, Lee V. "Qat: Changes in the Production and Consumption of a Quasi-Legal Commodity." In *The Social Life of Things: Commodities in Cultural Perspective,* edited by Arjun Appadurai, 236–60. New York: Cambridge University Press, 1986.

Chandler Jr., Alfred D. *Scale and Scope: The Dynamics of Industrial Capitalism.* Cambridge, MA: Belknap Press of Harvard University Press, 1990.

Chicago Daily Tribune. "Narcotics' Use by Korea Yanks Worries 'Brass'." February 9, 1953, B12.

Clayton, Lawrence A. *Peru and the United States: The Condor and the Eagle.* Athens: University of Georgia Press, 1999.

Cleveland Call and Post. "House Committee Thinks Mau Mau Uses Narcotics." May 23, 1953, 1C, 4C.

Cohen, Lizabeth. *A Consumer's Republic: The Politics of Mass Consumption in Postwar America.* New York: Vintage Books, 2004.

Cohen, Michael M. "Jim Crow's Drug War: Race, Coca-Cola and the Southern Origins of Drug Prohibition." *Southern Cultures* 12, no. 3 (Fall 2006): 55–79.

El Comercio. "El Junta Militar de Gobierno Establece la Pena de Muerte Para Los Asesinos y los Traidores de Patria." March 26, 1949.

———. "Invitado por importantes insituciones científicas viaga a los Estados Unidos el Dr. C.G. Gutiérrez Noriega." April 11, 1949.

———. "Para reprimir el tráfico ilícito de estupefacientes." April 27, 1949.

———. "Debido a las oportunas medidas dictadas por la Junta Militar de Gobierno. se efectúa una interesante investigación sobre la elaboración y el tráfico ilícito de drogas heroicas." April 28, 1949.

———. "La Campaña Contra el Trafico Ilicito de Estupefacientes." April 29, 1949.

———. "Formo cómo se efectuó la pesquisa que permitió detener a los componentes de una banda traficantes de cocaína y la incautación de cuatro plantas de producción y refinería de este alcaloide en Trujillo." April 30, 1949.

———. "Comisión que efectuará un estudio integral del problema de la coca." September 10, 1949.

———. "Llegada de la Comisión de las NU que estudiará el problema de la Coca." September 11, 1949, 3–4.

———. "Sobre el Problema de la Coca." Lima. September 13, 1949.

———. "El Problema de la Masticación de Hojas de Coca." September 14, 1949.

———. "Conversando con el doctor Carlos Monge." September 27, 1949.

Cooter, Roger, Mark Harrison, and Steve Sturdy, eds. *Medicine and Modern Warfare.* Atlanta: Rodopi, 1999.

Correa, Marcial Rubio. *Legislación Peruana Sobre Drogas: 1920–1993.* Lima: Centro de Información y Educación Para La Prevención del Abuso de Drogas, 1994.

Courtwright, David T. *Forces of Habit: Drugs and the Making of the Modern World.* Cambridge, MA: Harvard University Press, 2001.

Cowdrey, Albert E. "'Germ Warfare' and Public Health in the Korean Conflict." *Journal of Medicine and Allied Sciences* 39 (1984): 153–72.

Cueto, Marcos. "Andean Biology in Peru: Scientific Styles on the Periphery." *ISIS* 80 (1989): 640–58.

———. "*Indigenismo* and Rural Medicine in Peru: The Indian Sanitary Brigade and Manuel Nuñez Butrón." *Bulletin of the History of Medicine* 65 (1991): 22–41.

Daily Defender. "Dope in Space Age Health Fair Topic." March 21, 1960, A20.

Daniel, Howard. "Economic Warfare." *Australian Quarterly* 15, no. 3 (1943): 62–67.

Dayan, Colin. *The Story of Cruel and Unusual.* Cambridge, MA: MIT Press, 2007.

De Grazia, Victoria. *Irresistible Empire: America's Advance Through Twentieth-Century Europe.* Cambridge, MA: Harvard University Press, 2005.

De La Fuente, Alejandro. *A Nation For All: Race, Inequality and Politics in Cuba, 1900–2000.* Chapel Hill: University of North Carolina Press, 2000.

Delahanty, T.W. "Drugs." *Domestic Commerce* (January 1944): 17–18.

El Diario. "Se Efectuará un estudio a fondo de la hoja de coca." November 2, 1949.

———. "Investígase si la Coca es o no un Tóxico Para la Salud: Actuará la Comisión de la ONU libre de prejucios." November 7, 1949.

Dixon, W.E. "Cocaine Addiction." Given as a Talk at the Society for the Study of Inebriety. October 14, 1924. *Bound Volumes of Miscellaneous Pamphlets on Medical and Chemical Aspects of Dangerous Drugs,* Vol. 12, No. 131–160 #138, Société de Nations (178.8 A12), no. 138. Geneva: United Nations Library.

Dorn, Glenn J. "'The American Reputation for Fair Play': Víctor Raúl Haya de la Torre and the Federal Bureau of Narcotics." *The Historian* 65, no. 5 (September 2003): 1083–1101.

———. *Truman Administration and Bolivia: Making the World Safe for Liberal Constitutional Oligarchy.* State College: Pennsylvania State University, 2011.

Doughty, Paul. "Human Relations: Affection, Rectitude, and Respect." In *Peasants, Power, and Applied Social Change: Vicos as a Model,* edited by Henry F. Dobyns, Paul L. Doughty, and Harold D. Lasswell, 89–113. London: Sage, 1971.

Dowd Hall, Jacquelyn. "The Long Civil Rights Movement and the Political Uses of the Past." *Journal of American History* 91, no. 4 (March 2005): 1233–63.

Drug Trade News. "U.S. Industry to Get Technical Drug Data Dug Out of Germany: American Pharmaceutical Industry and Government Joined Forces to Organize Intelligence Teams." September 10, 1945.

———. "New Analgesic Beats Cocaine." September 20, 1948.

———. "Drug Industry Held Prepared for War Task." July 24, 1950.

———. "Key U.S. Agencies Move to Speed Up Mobilization Plans for the Drug Industry," December 25, 1950.

Eddy, Nathan B., and Harris Isbell, M. D. "Addiction Liability and Narcotics Control." *Public Health Reports* 74, no. 9 (September 1959): 755–63.

Emerson, Rupert. "Colonialism, Political Development, and the UN." *International Organization* 19, no. 3, The United Nations: Accomplishments and Prospects (Summer 1965): 484–503.

Endicott, Stephen. "Germ Warfare and 'Plausible Denial': The Korean War, 1952–1953." *Modern China* 5, no. 1 (January 1979): 79–104.

Enloe, M. D., and Cortez, F. "German Pharmacy Kaput!" *American Druggist,* June 1946.

Espinosa, Mariola. *Epidemic Invasions: Yellow Fever and the Limits of Cuban Independence, 1878–1930.* Chicago: University of Chicago Press, 2009.

Farley, James A. "Brand Names: A Basis for Unity, Our Greatest Hope of Expanding World Trade." *Vital Speeches of the Day* 18, no. 15 (May 15, 1952): 473.

Feldman, Harry Allen. "Jazz: A Place in Music Education?" *Music Educators Journal* 50, no. 6 (June–July 1964): 60, 62–64.

Finger, Seymour M. "A New Approach to Colonial Problems at the United Nations." *International Organization* 26, no. 1 (Winter 1972): 143–53.

Fortune. "Merck." 35, June 1947, 107–9.

Foucault, Michel. *Discipline and Punish: The Birth of the Prison.* New York: Vintage, 1995.

Fox, Annette Baker. "International Organization for Colonial Development." *World Politics* 3, no. 3 (April 1951): 340–68.

Frank, Andre Gunder. *Capitalism and Underdevelopment in Latin America: Historical Studies in Chile and Brazil.* New York: Penguin Books, 1971.

———. "The Wealth and Poverty of Nations: Even Heretics Remain Bound by Traditional Thought." *Economic and Political Weekly* 5, nos. 29/31, Special Number (July 1970): 1177–79, 1181–84.

Freese, Barbara, and Charles Medawar. *Drug Diplomacy: Decoding the Conduct of a Multinational Pharmaceutical Company and the Failure of a Western Remedy for the Third World.* London: Social Audit, 1982.

Fried, Richard M. *The Russians Are Coming! The Russians Are Coming! Pageantry and Patriotism in Cold War America.* New York: Oxford University Press, 1998.

Gaddis, John Lewis. *The United States and the Origins of the Cold War, 1940–1947.* New York: Columbia University Press, 1972.

Gagliano, Joseph. *Coca Prohibition in Peru: The Historical Debates.* Tucson: University of Arizona Press, 1994.

Galambos, Louis. *Values and Visions: A Merck Century.* Rahway, NJ: Merck, c1991.

Galluba, Luis. "Pharmacy and the War." *Vital Speeches of the Day* 1, no. 3 (November 15, 1944): 89–93.

Gereffi, Gary. *The Pharmaceutical Industry and Dependency in the Third World.* Princeton, NJ: Princeton University Press, 1983.

Global Commission on Drug Policy. *War on Drugs: Report of the Global Commission on Drug Policy* (June 2011). Accessed November 2, 2012. www.globalcommissionondrugs.org/wp-content/themes/gcdp_v1/pdf/Global_Commission_Report_English.pdf.

Gootenberg, Paul, ed. *Cocaine: Global Histories.* New York: Routledge, 1999.

———. "Secret Ingredients: The Politics of Coca in US-Peruvian Relations, 1915–65." *Journal of Latin American Studies* 36 (2004): 233–65.

———. *Andean Cocaine: The Making of a Global Drug.* Chapel Hill: University of North Carolina Press, 2008.

Gortler, Leon. "Merck in America: The First 70 Years from Fine Chemical to Pharmaceutical Giant." *Bulletin for the History of Chemistry* 25, no. 1 (2000): 1–9.

Gotkowitz, Laura. *A Revolution for Our Rights: Indigenous Struggles for Land and Justice in Bolivia, 1880–1952.* Durham, NC: Duke University Press, 2007.

Green, David. *The Containment of Latin America: A History of the Myths and Realities of the Good Neighbor Policy.* Chicago: Quadrangle Books, 1971.

Gutiérrez-Noriega, Carlos, and Victor Wolfgang Von Hagen. "The Strange Case of the Coca Leaf." *Scientific Monthly* 70, no. 2 (February 1950): 81–89.

Hall, Stuart, Chas Critcher, Tony Jefferson, John Clarke, and Brian Roberts. *Policing the Crisis: Mugging, the State, and Law and Order.* Hong Kong: Macmillan Press, 1982.

Headrick, Daniel R. "Botany, Chemistry, and Tropical Development." *Journal of World History* 7, no. 1 (Spring 1996): 1–20.

Heller, Henry. *The Cold War and the New Imperialism: A Global History, 1945–2005.* New York: Monthly Review Press, 2006.

Hentoff, Nat. *The Jazz Life.* Cambridge, MA: Da Capo Press, 1975.

Herzberg, David L. "The Pill You Love Can Turn on You": Feminism, Tranquilizers, and the Valium Panic of the 1970s." *American Quarterly* 58, no. 1 (March 2006): 79–103.

Higgins, Lois. "The Status of Narcotic Addiction in the United States." *American Biology Teacher* 16, no. 4 (April 1954): 94–98.

Hillman, John. "Bolivia and British Tin Policy, 1939–1945." *Journal of Latin American Studies* 22, no. 2 (May 1990): 289–315.

Hodge, William H. "Coca." *Natural History* (February 1947): 86–93.

Holland, Emmett James. "A Historical Study of Bolivian Foreign Relations 1935–1946." PhD diss., American University, 1967.

Holmberg, Allen R. "Vicos: A Peasant Hacienda Community in Peru." In *Economic Development and Social Change: The Modernization of Village Communities,* edited by George Dalton, 515–55. New York: American Museum of Natural History, Natural History Press, 1971.

———. "Experimental Intervention in the Field." In *Peasants, Power, and Applied Social Change: Vicos as a Model,* edited by Henry F. Dobyns, Paul L. Doughty, and Harold D. Lasswell, 21–32. London: Sage, 1971.

Huggins, Martha H. *Political Policing: The United States and Latin America.* Durham, NC: Duke University Press, 1998.

Hughes, L.W. "Curse of Coca." *Inter-American* 5 (September 1946): 18–22, 42.

Hughes, Langston. "Week By Week (2)." *Chicago Defender,* July 23, 1960, 10.

Hurst, James Willard. *A Legal History of Money in the United States, 1774–1970.* Lincoln: University of Nebraska Press, 1973.

Jackson, Charles O. "The Amphetamine Democracy: Medicinal Abuse in the Popular Culture." *South Atlantic Quarterly* 74, no. 3 (1975): 308–23.

Jacobson, Harold Karan. "Our 'Colonial' Problem in the Pacific." *Foreign Affairs* 39, no. 1 (October 1960): 56–66.

————. "The United Nations and Colonialism: A Tentative Appraisal." *International Organization* 16, no. 1 (Winter 1962): 37–56.

Johnson, Leland L. "U.S. Business Interests in Cuba and the Rise of Castro." *World Politics* 17, no. 3 (April 1965): 440–59.

Jones, Leroi (Amiri Baraka). "Cuba Libre." In *Home: Social Essays*, edited by Leroi Jones, 11–62. New York: William Morrow, 1966.

Kahn, Jr., E.J. *The Big Drink: The Story of Coca-Cola*. New York: Random House, 1960.

Karch, Steven B. *A Brief History of Cocaine*. New York: CRC Press, 1998.

Kerr, Adelaide. "Man-Made Morphine Substitutes Pose New Narcotics Problem." *Washington Post* (December 21, 1947): B8.

Kinder, Douglas Clark. "Bureaucratic Cold Warrior: Harry J. Anslinger and Illicit Narcotics Traffic." *Pacific Historical Review* 50, no. 2 (May, 1981): 169–91.

Kinder, Douglas Clark, and William O. Walker III. "Stable Force in a Storm: Harry J. Anslinger and United States Narcotic Foreign Policy, 1930–1962." *Journal of American History* 72, no. 4 (March 1986): 908–27.

Kofas, Jon. *Foreign Debt and Underdevelopment: U.S.-Peru Economic Relations, 1930–1970*. New York: University Press of America, 1996.

Kramer, Paul A. "Power and Connection: Imperial Histories of the United States and the World." *American Historical Review* 116, no. 5 (December 2011): 1348–91.

Kuh, Richard H. "A Prosecutor's Thoughts Concerning Addiction." *Journal of Law, Criminology, and Police Science* 52, no. 3 (September–October 1961): 321–27.

Kuzmarov, Jeremy. *The Myth of the Addicted Army: Vietnam and the Modern War on Drugs*. Boston: University of Massachusetts Press, 2009.

Larrabee, F. Stephen. "The Soviet Union and the Non-Aligned." *World Today* 32, no. 12 (December 1976): 467–75.

Lauderbaugh, George M. "Bolivarian Nations: Securing the Northern Frontier." In *Latin America During World War II*, edited by Thomas M. Leonard and John F. Bratzel, 109–25. New York: Rowman & Littlefield, 2007.

Le Fanu, James. *The Rise and Fall of Modern Medicine*. New York: Carroll & Graf, 2002.

Lee, Martin A., and Bruce Schlain. *Acid Dreams: The Complete Social History of LSD: The CIA, the Sixties and Beyond*. New York: Grove Press, 1992.

Lees, Gene. "Jazz Battles Communism." *Music Journal* (November–December 1962): 70–74.

Leffler, Melvin P., and David S. Painter. *Origins of the Cold War: An International History*. New York: Routledge, 1994.

Lehman, Kenneth. *Bolivia and the United States: A Limited Partnership*. Athens: University of Georgia Press, 1999.

Leitenberg, Milton. "Resolution of the Korean War Biological Warfare Allegations." *Critical Reviews in Microbiology* 24, no. 3 (1998): 169–94.

Léons, Madeleine Barbara, and Harry Sanabria. *Coca, Cocaine, and the Bolivian Reality*. New York: State University of New York Press, 1977.

Lindesmith, Alfred R. "How to Stop the Dope Traffic." *The Nation* 182 (April 21, 1956): 337–39.

———. "Letters." *The Nation* 182 (June 2, 1956): 92–93.

———. "Dope: Congress Encourages the Traffic." *The Nation* 184 (March 16, 1957): 228–31.

———. "Our Immoral Drug Laws." *The Nation* 186 (June 22, 1958): 558–62.

Lipsitz, George. *Rainbow at Midnight: Labor and Culture in the 1940s.* Chicago: University of Illinois Press, 1994.

Los Angeles Times. "Youth Forum Outlines Needs for Right Living." November 20, 1952, B1.

Los Angeles Tribune. "No 'Due Process' in 'Secret Indictments'." October 2, 1958, 8, 10.

Louis, J.C. and Harvey Z. Yazijian. *The Cola Wars.* New York: Everest House, 1980.

Mahoney, Tom. *The Merchants of Life: An Account of the American Pharmaceutical Industry.* New York: Harper & Brothers, 1959.

Marez, Curtiz. *Drug Wars: The Political Economy of Narcotics.* Minneapolis: University of Minnesota Press, 2004.

Marshall, Jonathan. *To Have and Have Not: Southeast Asian Raw Materials and the Origins of the Pacific War.* Berkeley: University of California Press, 1995.

May, Elaine Tyler. *Homeward Bound: American Families in the Cold War Era.* New York: Basic Books, 1999.

McAllister, William. *Drug Diplomacy in the Twentieth Century: An International History.* New York: Routledge, 2000.

McCormick, Thomas. "'Every System Needs a Center Sometimes': An Essay on Hegemony and Modern American Foreign Policy." In *Redefining the Past: Essays in Diplomatic History in Honor of William Appleman Williams,* edited by Lloyd C. Gardner, 195–220. Corvallis: Oregon State University Press, 1986.

McCoy, Alfred. *The Politics of Heroin in Southeast Asia.* New York: Harper and Row, 1972.

McMichael, Robert K. "'We Insist-Freedom Now!': Black Moral Authority, Jazz, and the Changeable Shape of Whiteness." *American Music* 16, no. 4 (Winter 1998): 375–416.

McNutt, Paul V. "How Do We Stand on Medical Drugs?" *Domestic Commerce* 27 (April 10, 1941): 333–36.

McWhinney, Edward. "Introduction and Procedural History of the Declaration on the Granting of Independence to Colonial Countries and Peoples." Accessed in November 2013 from the website of the United Nations Audiovisual Library of International Law, www.un.org/law/avl.

McWilliams, John C. "Unsung Partner against Crime: Harry J. Anslinger and the Federal Bureau of Narcotics, 1930–1962." *Pennsylvania Magazine of History and Biography* 113, no. 2 (April 1989): 207–36.

———. *The Protectors: Harry J. Anslinger and the Bureau of Narcotics, 1930–1962.* Newark: University of Delaware Press, 1990.

Meisler, Stanley. "Federal Narcotics Czar." *The Nation,* February 20, 1960.

Merck, George W. "Official Report on Biological Warfare." *Bulletin of the Atomic Scientists* 2, nos. 7/8 (October 1, 1946): 16–18.

Merriam, Alan P., and Raymond W. Mack. "The Jazz Community." *Social Forces* 38 (1959–1960): 211–22.

Monge, Dr. Carlos. "El Problema de la Coca en el Peru." *Anales de la Facultad de Medicina* 29, no. 4 (Lima, 1946): 311–15.

Monson, Ingrid. *Freedom Sounds: Jazz, Civil Rights and Africa, 1950–1967.* New York: Oxford University Press, 2005.

Montecinos, Verónica, and John Markoff. "From the Power of Economic Ideas to the Power of Economists." In *The Other Mirror: Grand Theory through the Lens of Latin America,* edited by Miguel Angel Lentino and Fernando López-Alves, 105–50. Princeton, NJ: Princeton University Press, 2001.

Morales, Edmundo. *Cocaine: White Gold Rush in Peru.* Tucson: University of Arizona Press, 1996.

Morgan, H. Wayne. *Drugs in America: A Social History, 1800-1980.* Syracuse, NY: Syracuse University Press, 1981.

Musto, David F. *The American Disease: Origins of Narcotic Control.* New York: Oxford University Press, 1999.

Nandy, Ashish. "Introduction: Science as a Reason of State." In *Science, Hegemony, and Violence: A Requiem for Modernity,* edited by Ashish Nandy, 1–23. Delhi: Oxford University Press, 1990.

Neushul, Peter. "Science, Government, and the Mass Production of Penicillin." *Journal of the History of Medicine and Allied Sciences* 48 (October 1943): 3711–95.

New York Times. "Musicians' Union to Ban Narcotic Addicts; Petrillo to Be Reelected for Eighth Term." June 13, 1947.

———. "Anesthetic to Ease Arthritic Pain Found." 23, no. 3, September 12, 1947.

———. "Pain-Killer Found Widely Effective." 34, no. 7, December 5, 1947.

———. "Cuba Enforces Vaccinations." March 24, 1949, 10.

———. "Navy to Fly Vaccine to Cuba." March 29, 1949, 22.

———. "Secret Weapon—Opium." January 2, 1953, 14.

———. "Mau Mau Drug Use Seen." May 12, 1953, 3.

Newsweek. "Cure by Novocain," October 18, 1943

———. "Narcotics: An Ever-Growing Problem." 37, June 11, 1951. 26.

———. "Degradation in New York." 37, June 25, 1951, 19–20.

———. "Legalized Addiction." 49, January 7, 1957, 66.

Nicholson, H.B. "The Competitive Ideal: The Economic Route to Friendship." *Vital Speeches of the Day* 19, no. 5 (December 15, 1952): 152–54.

Nixon, Richard. "Special Message to the Congress on Control of Narcotics and Dangerous Drugs." July 14, 1969. Online by Gerhard Peters and John T. Woolley, *The American Presidency Project.* www.presidency.ucsb.edu/ws/?pid = 2126.

———. "Telephone Remarks to Students and Educators Attending a Drug Education Seminar in Monroe, Louisiana." October 4, 1971. Online by Gerhard Peters and John T. Woolley, *The American Presidency Project.* www.presidency.ucsb.edu/ws/?pid = 3179.

Norford, Thomasina. "Rousing Jazz Revival at Newport." *New York Amsterdam News,* July 14, 1962, 16.

Pacini, Deborah, and Christine Franquemont, eds. "Coca and Cocaine: Effects on People and Policy in Latin America." *Cultural Survival Report* 23. Peterborough, NH: Transcript Printing, 1991.

Painter, James. *Bolivia and Coca: A Study in Dependency.* Boulder, CO: Lynne Rienner, 1994.

Paterson, Thomas G., and Robert J. McMahon, eds. *The Origins of the Cold War.* Boston: Houghton Mifflin, 1999.

Paul, Joseph. "Theft of Drugs from Treasury Is Revealed." *Washington Post,* May 24, 1952, 1–2.

Pérez, Louis A. *Cuba and the United States: Ties of Singular Intimacy,* 3rd ed. Athens: University of Georgia Press, 2003.

Peru. *El Peru Y Colombia Ante La Corte Internacional de Justicia: Documentacion Pertinente Al Desarrollo Del Juicio Sentencia del 20 de Noviembre de 1950.* Lima: Ministerio de Relaciones Exteriores, 1951.

Pitts, George E. "Narcotics Discussion Is Key Phase of Festival." *Pittsburgh Courier,* July 20, 1957, 19.

Plummer, Brenda Gayle. "Castro in Harlem: A Cold War Watershed." In *Rethinking the Cold War: Essays on Its Dynamics, Meaning, and Morality,* edited by Allen Hunter, 133–56. Philadelphia: Temple University Press, 1997.

Pendergrast, Mark. *For God, Country and Coca-Cola: The Definitive History of the Great American Soft Drink and the Company that Makes It.* New York: Basic Books, 2000.

Provine, Doris Marie. *Unequal Under Law: Race in the War on Drugs.* Chicago: University of Chicago Press, 2007.

Reichard, J.D. "Addiction: Some Theoretical Considerations as to Its Nature, Cause, Prevention and Treatment." *American Journal of Psychiatry* 103 (1947): 721–28.

Reiss, Suzanna. "Beyond Supply and Demand: Obama's Drug Wars in Latin America." *NACLA Report on the Americas* (January/February 2010): 27–31.

Reutsch, Yvan A. "From Cocaine to Ropivacaine: The History of Local Anesthetic Drugs." *Current Topics in Medicinal Chemistry* 1, no. 3 (August 2001): 175–82.

Rivera Cusicanqui, Silvia. *Las Fronteras de la Coca: Epistemologías Colonialies y Circuitos Alternativos de la Hoja de Coca.* La Paz: Instituto de Investigaciones Sociológicas "Mauricio Lefebvre," Universidad San Andrés y Ediciones Ayuwiri, 2003.

Robertson, Stanley. "New Abbey Lincoln Album Hits Pay Dirt." *Los Angeles Sentinel,* August 17, 1961, C3.

Rogaski, Ruth. "Nature, Annihilation, and Modernity: China's Korean War Germ-Warfare Experience Reconsidered." *Journal of Asian Studies* 61, no. 2 (May 2002): 381–415.

Rogers, J.A. "Murder in Kenya!" *(Pittsburgh) Courier,* June 20, 1953, 18.

Rosch, Joel. "Crime as an Issue in American Politics." In *The Politics of Crime and Criminal Justice,* edited by Erika Fairchild and Vincent J. Webb, 19–34. Beverly Hills, CA: Sage, 1985.

Rout, Leslie B., and John F. Bratzel. *The Shadow War: German Espionage and United States Counterespionage in Latin America during World War II*. Frederick, MD: University Publications of America, 1986.

Rostow, Walt. *The Stages of Economic Growth*. New York: Cambridge University Press, 1960.

Rowe, Edward T. "The Emerging Anti-Colonial Consensus in the United Nations." *Journal of Conflict Resolution* 8, no. 3 (September, 1964): 209–30.

———. "Financial Support for the United Nations: Evolution of Member Contributions, 1946–1969." *International Organization* 26, no. 4 (Autumn 1972): 619–57.

S., John. "2 Jazz Festivals Open in Newport." *New York Times*, July 1, 1960, 13.

Samuels, Gertrude. "A Visit to Narco." *New York Times*, April 10, 1966.

Sánchez de Lozada, Enrique. *Bree Ensayo sobre la Realidad Boliviana*. La Paz: Universo, 1940.

Scheele, Leonard A. "Public Health and Foreign Policy." *Annals of the American Academy of Political and Social Science* 278, The Search for National Security (November 1951): 62–72.

Schwartztrauber, Evelyn. "New Markets from New Drug Products." *Domestic Commerce* (April 1944): 13–17.

Science. "Drug Addiction." *Science* 122, July 8, 1955, 67–68.

Science News Letter. "Treatment for Flat Feet." March 3, 1945.

———. "Morphine Substitute." August 16, 1947, 98.

———. "Germ Warfare in Korea?" July 8, 1950, 22.

———. "Defense Against BW." August 21, 1954, 115.

———. "Large Number of Dope Addicts among Doctors." March 23, 1957.

Scott, Peter Dale, and Jonathan Marshall, *Cocaine Politics: Drugs, Armies, and the CIA in Central America*. Berkeley: University of California Press, 1991.

Sears, Mason. *Memorandum by the United States Representative on the Trusteeship Council*, September 22, 1953. Reprinted in *Foreign Relations of the United States, 1952–1954* (Washington, DC: US Government Printing Office, 1979), 1165.

Sherman, Gene. "Police Meet Toughest Problem in Narcotics Traffic." *Los Angeles Times*, July 19, 1959, 1, 23.

Shoultz, Lars. *That Infernal Little Cuban Republic*. Chapel Hill: University of North Carolina Press, 2009.

Siekmeier, James F. "Trailblazer Diplomat: Bolivian Ambassador Victor Andrade Uzquiano's Efforts to Influence U.S. Policy, 1944–1962." *Diplomatic History* 28, no. 3 (June 2004): 385–406.

Siekmeier, James F. *Bolivian Revolution and the United States, 1952 to the Present*. University Park: Penn State University, 2011.

Silverman, Milton, Mia Lydecker, and Philip Lee. *Bad Medicine: The Prescription Drug Industry in the Third World*. Stanford, CA: Stanford University Press, 1992.

Simrell, Earle V. "History of Legal and Medical Roles in Narcotic Abuse in the U.S." *Public Health Reports* 83, no. 7 (July 1968): 587–93.

Singham, A.W., ed. *The Non-Aligned Movement in World Politics*. Westport, CT: Lawrence & Hill, 1978.

Siragusa, Charles. *The Trail of the Poppy: Behind the Mask of the Mafia.* Engle-wood Cliffs, NJ: Prentice-Hall, 1966.

Sondern, Jr., Frederic. "We Must Stop the Crime that Breeds Crime!" *Reader's Digest* 68 (June 1956): 21–26.

Spillane, Joseph F. *Cocaine: From Medical Marvel to Modern Menace in the United States, 1884–1920.* Baltimore: Johns Hopkins University Press, 2000.

St. Charles, Alwyn. *The Narcotics Menace.* Los Angeles: Borden, 1952.

Stevens, Donald G. "Organizing for Economic Defense: Henry Wallace and the Board of Economic Warfare's Foreign Policy Initiatives, 1942." *Presidential Studies Quarterly* 26, no. 4 (October 1, 1996): 1126–39.

Tarbell, Stanley D., and Ann Tracy Tarbell, *Roger Adams, 1889–1971: A Bio-graphical Memoir.* Washington, DC: National Academy of Sciences, 1982.

Tatum, A.L., and M.H. Seevers. "Experimental Cocaine Addiction." *Journal of Pharmacology and Experimental Therapeutics* 36, no. 3 (July 1929): 401–10.

Taylor, Arnold H. *American Diplomacy and the Narcotics Traffic, 1900–1939: A Study in International Humanitarian Reform.* Durham, NC: Duke University Press, 1969.

Taylor, Graham D. "The Axis Replacement Program: Economic Warfare and the Chemical Industry in Latin America, 1942–44." *Diplomatic History* 8, no. 2 (April 1, 1984): 145–64.

Temin, Peter. "Technology, Regulation, and Market Structure in the Modern Pharmaceutical Industry." *Bell Journal of Economics,* 10, no. 2 (Autumn 1979): 429–46.

Thompson, Heather Ann. "Why Mass Incarceration Matters: Rethinking Crisis, Decline, and Transformation in Postwar American History." *Journal of American History* 97, no. 3 (December 2010): 703–34.

Thompson, John H., "Number of Vet Dope Users in Prisons Grows." *Daily Defender.* April 1, 1956, 24.

Time. "Peru: The White Goddess." April 1949.

———. "Coca-Cola: World and Friend." May 15, 1950, 28–32.

———. "What the Doctor Ordered." August 18, 1952, cover, 38–44.

———. "Narcotic Dilemma." October 3, 1955, 63–4.

———. "Music, Newport Blues." July 18, 1960.

Tyson, Timothy B. *Radio Free Dixie: Robert F. Williams and the Roots of Black Power.* Chapel Hill: University of North Carolina Press, 1999.

United Nations. "Report on the 1st Session of the Commission on Narcotic Drugs, Economic and Social Council." (E/251) 27 November–13 December 1946, 27 January 1947.

———. *Protocol Bringing Under International Control Drugs Outside the Scope of the Convention of 13 July 1931 for Limiting the Manufacture and Regulating the Distribution of Narcotic Drugs, as amended by the Protocol signed at Lake Success on 11 December 1946. Signed at Paris, on 19 November 1948* (No. 688). United Nations Treaty Series, 1 December 1949.

———. *Report of the United Nations Mission of Technical Assistance to Bolivia.* New York: UN Technical Assistance Administration, 1951.

———. "Raising Standards of Living in the Andes Mountains." *United Nations Review* 1, no. 19 (1954–1955): 19–24.

————. *Protocol For Limiting and Regulating the Cultivation of the Poppy Plant, the Production of, International and Wholesale Trade in, and the Use of Opium,* Concluded at New York on 23 June 1953 (No. 456). United Nations Treaty Series, 56 (1963).

————. *Narcotic Drugs: Estimated World Requirements for 2012—Statistics for 2010.* New York: United Nations Office on Drugs and Crime, April 2012.

United Nations, Economic and Social Council. *Report of the Commission of Enquiry on the Coca Leaf, May 1950.* Fifth Year, Twelfth Session, Special Supplement No. 1. Official Record (E/1666/Add.1) Lake Success, NY: United Nations, July 1950.

————. *Social Affairs Committee of the Economic and Social Council, Summary Record of First Meeting* (E/AC.7/3) 8 March 1947.

————. *Summary Record of the Hundred and Eighteenth Meeting.* Fifth Session (E/CN.7/SR.118 23) New York: United Nations, February 1951.

————. 569th Meeting, First Special Session, 24 March 1952, Official Record, New York, 1952.

————. 580th Meeting, Fourteenth Session, 25 May, 1952, Official Record, New York, 1952.

————. "Substantive Session of 2009" (E/2009/78) July 6–31, 2009.

————. Commission on Narcotic Drugs. *Report to the Economic and Social Council on the First Session of the Commission on Narcotic Drugs Held at Lake Success, New York, from 27 November to 13 December 1946* (E/251) 27 January 1947.

————. Commission on Narcotic Drugs. *Preparatory Work for an International Conference to Consider the Possibility of Limiting and Controlling the Cultivation and Harvesting of the Coca Leaf.* Second Session (E/CN.7/73) 7 July 1947.

————. Commission on Narcotic Drugs. *Coca Leaf: Request by the Government of Peru for a Field Survey.* Second Session (E/CN.7/106) 30 July 1947.

————. Commission on Narcotic Drugs. *Report to the Economic and Social Council on the Second Session of the Commission, Held at Lake Success, New York, from 24 July to 8 August 1947* (E/575) 12 September 1947.

————. Commission on Narcotic Drugs. *Replies from Governments to the Questionnaire on the Limitation and the Control of the Cultivation and Harvesting of the Coca Leaf.* Third Session (E/CN.7/110) 19 April 1948.

————. Commission on Narcotic Drugs. *Limitation of the Production of Raw Materials,* Third Session (E/CN.7/110) 19 April 1948.

————. Commission on Narcotic Drugs. *Report to the Economic and Social Council on the Third Session of the Commission* (E/799) 28 May 1948.

————. Commission on Narcotic Drugs. *Report of the Seventh Session* (E/2219) 15 May 1952.

————. Economic Commission for Latin America. *Economic and Legal Status of Foreign Investments in Selected Countries of Latin America: Investment in Bolivia* (E/CN.12/166/Add.10) 7 May 1951.

————. Economic Commission for Latin America. *Economic and Legal Status of Foreign Investments in Selected Countries of Latin America: Foreign Investment in Peru* (E/CN.12/166/Add.11) 7 May 1951.

United Nations, Permanent Central Opium Board. *Report to the Economic and Social Council on Statistics of Narcotics for 1950 and the Work of the Board in 1951.* (E/OB/7) November 1951.

United States. *Convention on Narcotic Drugs, 1961. Message from the President of the United States transmitting the Single Convention on Narcotic Drugs, 1961, open for signature at New York, March 30, 1961, to August 1, 1961, along with the final act of the United Nations conference at which the Convention was adopted* (Washington, DC: US General Printing Office, 1967).

United States, Delegation from the United States. *The United States in the United Nations—1960 A Turning Point,* Report to the Committee on Foreign Relations, United States Senate by George D. Aiken [and] Wayne Morse, members of the Delegation of the United States to the 15th session of the General Assembly of the United Nations (Washington, DC: US Government Printing Office, 1961).

United States, Department of Commerce, Office of International Trade. "Overseas Sales of United States Drug Products." *World Trade in Commodities* 7, part 3, no. 19. Washington, DC: US Government Printing Office, January 1949.

———. "Cultivating Health Products Manufacturing Opportunity—Abroad." *World Trade in Commodities* 7, part 3, no. 76. Washington, DC: US Government Printing Office, November 1949.

United States, Department of State. *Foreign Relations of the United States, 1952–1954, United Nations Affairs.* Washington, DC: US Government Printing Office, 1979.

———. *Foreign Relations of the United States, 1952–1954, Africa and South Asia.* Washington, DC: US Government Printing Office, 1979.

United States. House. *Act to Create in the Treasury Department a Bureau of Narcotics,* Public Law 71–357, 71st Cong., 2d sess., June 14, 1930.

United States. House. Subcommittee on Appropriations for Treasury and Post Office Departments, Committee on Appropriations. *Treasury Department Appropriations Bill for 1939, Hearings before the Subcommittee of the Committee on Appropriations,* 75th Cong., 3d sess., December 1937.

———. *Treasury Department Appropriations Bill for 1941, Hearings before the Subcommittee on Appropriations for Treasury and Post Office Departments,* 76th Cong., 3d sess., 11–16, 18–19 December 1939, 4, 12 January 1940.

———. *Treasury Department Appropriations Bill for 1943, Hearings before the Subcommittee of the Committee on Appropriations House of Representatives,* 77th Cong., 2d sess., 6, 15–18 December 1941, 7–8 January 1942.

———. *Treasury Department Appropriations Bill for 1945, Hearings before the Subcommittee of the Committee on Appropriations House of Representatives,* 78th Cong., 2d sess., 29–30 November, 1–4, 6–9 December 1943.

———. *Treasury Department Appropriations Bill for 1944, Hearings before the Subcommittee on Appropriations for Treasury and Post Office Departments,* 78th Cong., 1st sess., 10–12, 14–16 December 1943, 8, 18 January 1944.

———. *Treasury Department Appropriations Bill for 1946, Hearings before the Subcommittee of the Committee on Appropriations House of Representatives,* 79th Cong., 1st sess., 17 January 1945.

————. *Treasury Department Appropriations Bill for 1947, Hearings before the Subcommittee of the Committee on Appropriations House of Representatives,* 79th Cong., 2d sess., 12 November 1945.

————. *Hearings before the Subcommittee on Appropriations for Treasury and Post Office Departments, Treasury Department Appropriations Bill for 1950,* 81st Cong., 1st sess., 26–28 January, 1–4, 9 February 1949.

————. *Hearings before the Subcommittee on Appropriations for Treasury and Post Office Departments, Treasury Department Appropriations Bill for 1952,* 82nd Cong., 1st sess., 8, 9, 14–16, 19, 20 February 1951.

————. *Hearings before the Subcommittee on Appropriations, Treasury-Post Office Departments Appropriations for 1953,* 82nd Cong., 2d sess., 10, 11, 14–18, 21–25, 28 January 1952.

————. *Hearings before the Subcommittee on Appropriations, Treasury-Post Office Departments Appropriations for 1954,* 83rd Cong., 1st sess., 10, 11, 13, 20, 25, 27, 30 March, 1, 2, 22–24 April 1953.

————. *Hearings before a Subcommittee of the Committee on Appropriations, Treasury-Post Office Departments Appropriations for 1956,* 84th Cong., 1st sess., 31 January, 1–4, 7–9, 14, 16, 18, 23 March 1955.

————. *Hearings before a Subcommittee of the Committee on Appropriations, Treasury-Post Office Departments Appropriations for 1958,* 85th Cong., 1st sess., 25, 28–31 January, 1, 4–6, 22 February 1957.

————. *Hearings before a Subcommittee of the Committee on Appropriations, Treasury-Post Office Departments Appropriations for 1959,* 85th Cong., 2d sess., 22–24 January, 3 February 1958.

————. *Hearings before a Subcommittee of the Committee on Appropriations, Treasury-Post Office Departments Appropriations for 1960,* 86th Cong., 1st sess., 26–30 January, 2–5, 10 February 1959.

————. *Hearings before a Subcommittee of the Committee on Appropriations, Treasury-Post Office Departments Appropriations for 1961,* 86th Cong., 2d sess., 7, 25–29 January, 2–4 February 1960.

————. *Hearings before a Subcommittee of the Committee on Appropriations, Treasury-Post Office Departments Appropriations for 1962,* 87th Cong., 1st sess., 16, 28 February, 1, 2, 6–10, 13 March 1961.

————. *Hearings before a Subcommittee of the Committee on Appropriations, Treasury-Post Office Departments and Executive Office Appropriations for 1963.* 87th Cong., 2d sess., 22–25, 30, 31 February, 1, 2, 7, 8 March 1962.

————. *Hearings before a Subcommittee of the Committee on Appropriations, Treasury-Post Office Departments and Executive Appropriations for 1964,* 88th Cong., 1st sess., 26–28 February, 4–8, 11–14 March 1963.

————. "Control of Narcotics, Marihuana, and Barbiturates." *Hearings before a Subcommittee of the Committee on Ways and Means,* 82nd Cong., 1st sess., 7, 14, and 17 April 1951.

United States, Joint Army and Navy Munitions Board. *The Strategic and Critical Materials.* Washington, DC: Army and Navy Munitions Board, 1940.

United States Military Academy, Department of Social Sciences. *Raw Materials in War and Peace.* West Point, NY: USMA AG Printing Office, 1947.

United States, Office of Defense Mobilization. *The Story of Defense Mobilization: How the United States Is Building Its Might in Order to Avert a Third World War.* Washington, DC: US Government Printing Office, 1951.

United States, President's Materials Policy Commission. *Resources for Freedom: A Report to the President by the President's Materials Policy Commission.* Washington, DC: US Government Printing Office, 1952.

United States. Senate. Committee on Appropriations. *Supplemental Federal Security Agency Appropriation Bill for 1949, Hearings before the Subcommittee of the Committee on Appropriations,* 80th Cong., 2d sess., May 10–12, 1948.

———. Committee on Foreign Relations, *Hearing before a Subcommittee of the Committee on Foreign Relations, International Opium Protocol,* 83rd Cong., 2d sess., 17 July 1954.

———. Committee on Military Affairs, *Strategic and Critical Materials and Minerals, Hearings before the Subcommittee of the Committee on Military Affairs,* 77th Cong., 1st sess., May–July 1941.

United States, Treasury Department, Bureau of Narcotics. *Traffic In Opium and Other Dangerous Drugs.* Washington, DC: US Government Printing Office, 1927–1956.

Visvanathan, Shiv. *A Carnival of Science: Essays on Science, Technology, and Development.* Delhi: Oxford University Press, 1997.

Von Eschen, Penny. *Satchmo Blows Up the World: Jazz Ambassadors Play the Cold War.* Cambridge, MA: Harvard University Press, 2004.

Wacqant, Loïc. "From Slavery to Mass Incarceration." *New Left Review* 13 (January–February 2002): 41–60.

Wadden Jr., Thomas. "We Put the Heat on Washington Dope Peddlers." *Saturday Evening Post,* October 3, 1953.

Wakefield, Dan. "Dope on the Downbeat." *The Nation* 185 (August 31, 1957): 92–93.

Walker III, William O. *Drug Control in the Americas.* Albuquerque: University of New Mexico Press, 1981.

———. *Opium and Foreign Policy: The Anglo-American Search for Order in Asia, 1912–1954.* Chapel Hill: University of North Carolina Press, 1991.

Walker, Jesse H. "Theatricals." *New York Amsterdam News,* July 2, 1960, 17.

Wallerstein, Immanuel. *World-Systems Analysis: An Introduction.* Durham, NC: Duke University Press, 2004.

Washington Post. "Ample Opium, Other Drugs Stored, McNutt Declares." December 10, 1941.

Watters, Pat. *Coca-Cola: An Illustrated History.* New York: Doubleday, 1978.

Weimer, Daniel. *Seeing Drugs: Modernization, Counterinsurgency, and U.S. Narcotics Control in the Third World, 1969–1976.* Kent, OH: Kent State University Press, 2011.

Welsh, John. "Lexington Narcotics Hospital: A Special Sort of Alma Mater." *Science,* New Series 182, no. 4116 (December 7, 1973): 1004–5 and 1007–8.

Westad, Odd Arne. *The Global Cold War: Third World Interventions and the Making of Our Modern Times.* New York: Cambridge University Press, 2007.

Weston, Charles H. Jr. "An Ideology of Modernization: The Case of the Bolivian MNR." *Journal of Inter-American Studies* 10, no. 1 (January 1968): 85–101.

Whitehead, Laurence. "Bolivia." In *Latin America between the Second World War and the Cold War,* edited by Leslie Bethel and Ian Roxborough, 120–46. Cambridge: Cambridge University Press, 1992

Whitfield, Stephen J. *The Culture of the Cold War.* Baltimore: Johns Hopkins University Press, 1996.

Whorthen, Dennis B. *Pharmacy in World War II.* New York: Haworth Press, 2004

Willets, Peter. *The Non-Aligned Movement: The Origins of the Third World Alliance.* New York: Nichols, 1978.

Williams, Martin. "Foreign Economic Administration Activities in the Chemicals Field." *Chemical and Engineering News* 23, no. 24 (December 25, 1945): 2322–27.

Wilson, Charles Morrow. *Ambassadors in White: The Story of American Tropical Medicine.* New York: Kenikat Press, 1942.

———. "New Crops for the New World." *Nation's Business,* August 1943, 96.

Winick, Charles. "Narcotics Addiction and Its Treatment." *Law and Contemporary Problems* 22, no. 1, Narcotics (Winter 1957): 9–33.

———. "The Use of Drugs by Jazz Musicians." *Social Problems* 7, no. 3 (Winter 1959–60): 240–53.

———. "High the Moon: Jazz and Drugs." *Antioch Review* 21, no. 1 (Spring 1961): 53–68.

Wood, Julius B. "War Remakes South America." *Nation's Business,* April 1945: 23–24.

Wood, Walter. "Quinine Supply Sufficient for Bare Needs." *Washington Post,* November 10, 1943, 9.

Woodward, E.F. "Botanical Drugs: A Brief Review of the Industry with Comments on Recent Developments." *Economic Botany* 1, no. 4 (October–December 1947): 402–11.

Yang, Mina. "A Thin Blue Line Down Central Avenue: The LAPD and the Demise of a Musical Hub." *Black Music Research Journal* 22, no. 2 (Autumn 2002): 217–39.

Young, Cynthia. *Soul Power: Cultural Radicalism and the Making of a U.S. Third World Left.* Durham, NC: Duke University Press, 2006.

Zhang, Shu Guang. *Economic Cold War: America's Embargo Against China and the Sino-Soviet Alliance, 1949–1963.* Port Chester, NY: Stanford University Press, 2001.

Zunes, Stephen. "The United States and Bolivia: The Taming of a Revolution, 1952–1957." *Latin American Perspectives* 28, no. 5 (September 2001): 33–49.

Index

AMERICAN CROSSROADS

Edited by Earl Lewis, George Lipsitz, George Sánchez, Dana Takagi, Laura Briggs, and Nikhil Pal Singh